IT'S BETTER TO
BE FEARED

IT'S BETTER TO BE FEARED

The New England Patriots Dynasty and the Pursuit of Greatness

SETH WICKERSHAM

LIVERIGHT PUBLISHING CORPORATION

A DIVISION OF W. W. NORTON & COMPANY

Independent Publishers Since 1923

For information about permission to reproduce selections from this book,
write to Permissions, Liveright Publishing Corporation,
a division of W. W. Norton & Company, Inc.,
500 Fifth Avenue, New York, NY 10110

For information about special discounts for bulk purchases, please contact
W. W. Norton Special Sales at specialsales@wwnorton.com or 800-233-4830

Manufacturing by Lakeside Book Company
Book design by Lovedog Studio
Production manager: Anna Oler

ISBN 978-1-63149-823-7

Liveright Publishing Corporation
500 Fifth Avenue, New York, N.Y. 10110
www.wwnorton.com

W. W. Norton & Company Ltd.
15 Carlisle Street, London W1D 3BS

2 3 4 5 6 7 8 9 0

For Alison, Maddie, and Grant—
whom I respect, whom I admire, whom I love

C ONTENTS

PART III: FEARED AGAIN *(2015–2020)*

*More than rich, more than famous,
more than happy, I wanted to be great.*

—*Bruce Springsteen*

Few men try for best ever . . .

—*Richard Ben Cramer*

PROLOGUE

HOURS BEFORE HIS FINAL PLAYOFF GAME WITH THE only team he had ever known, the quarterback posted a video on social media. Not just any video: a hype video, with a hint of trash talk. That was rare for him—prior to a game, at least. After a win, he would hold his phone above his head, peering down on his face, and smile and talk about the game, often concluding the recording with his almost trademarked battle cry: "Let's goooo!" Tom Brady usually let his actions speak for him—"Well done is better than well said," his dad taught him—but on this day, January 4, 2020, he felt it necessary to make what in the National Football League amounted to a declaration of war. At 11:10 a.m., hours before the New England Patriots were due to play the Tennessee Titans at Gillette Stadium in Foxborough, Massachusetts, the 55-second video went up on Instagram and Twitter. It was not self-shot. It was professionally produced, choreographed, soundtracked, considered, and calculated. It began with a shot of a lion's eye—"The lion is king of the jungle," the narrator said—and continued into a visual tour of the quarterback's mind, depicting him running out of a tunnel before a game, all business, a seriousness on his iconic face that was a stark contrast to the joy of his early years, during his rise, when football as a member of the Patriots was fun. The narrator explained that the lion lies down under a tree, not wanting to move, and other animals—hyenas, interspersed with shots of Titans players—move in, "barking at him, laughing at him, closer and closer, until one day, the lion gets up and tears the shit out of everybody." A shot of the quarterback flashed, screaming after a big play, followed by a cut to the lion's face. "It's too late to be scared. It's time to kill."

Almost 13 million people watched the video—including Mike Vrabel, a former teammate and good buddy of Brady's, now the Titans' head coach. Vrabel saw it as free inspiration for his team. This was something Tom Brady had never done, in almost two decades of brilliance: he had never made it easier for the opponent. When the video appeared, it was not only too late to be scared, it was too late for a lot of things. Before the game, Vrabel walked from the locker room to the field where he had helped build the Patriots dynasty and told one of the quarterback's friends:

"We're gonna knock Brady's dick off."

KICKOFF NEARED. Members of Tom Brady's family took their seats in his suite at the northwest corner of the stadium. There was a palpable sense of finality in the air. The suite had become a refuge in the previous couple of years, a place to which the most accomplished quarterback in NFL history could escape for a quiet break from work, or even for a massage from his controversial trainer. It felt like a small home. When you entered, you saw on the wall the logo for TB12, Brady's lifestyle business that had caused all kinds of trouble within the team. There were framed photographs of his wife, retired supermodel Gisele Bündchen, and his three young children: Jack, Benny, and Vivian. Over the years, CEOs, actors, and other luminaries had watched games here.

Brady was 42 years old and in his 20th year in the NFL. He was a transcendent figure—not only an incomparable athlete, but a celebrity and member of the global elite. He had entered adulthood with the entire country watching him achieve greatness early, but now he was truly an unprecedented force. No football player, no quarterback—no American professional athlete—had ever been so good at this stage of life. He had won three Super Bowls in the first half of his career and three in the second half. He had been named Super Bowl MVP four times. Tonight's game, under a dark mist, would be the 41st playoff contest of his career, more than 21 NFL franchises had played in across the entire Super Bowl era—which began in 1967, ten years before he was born. Brady had played more than two extra seasons of football in the postseason. He had won nearly three-quarters of those games, against the best teams and quarterbacks in the league, under the intense pressure not only of the playoffs, but, after the opening successes of the Patriots dynasty, of being the favorite with more to lose than his opponents.

For this game, the box was limited to family and close friends. Within ten days, it would be cleaned out.

The suite's window was open, allowing the unseasonably warm and wet air in, enabling the Brady family to feel the crowd's energy. Normally, Bündchen and the kids liked to scream along with the fans. She had been married to Brady for 11 years, and she had witnessed him win and lose Super Bowls, be named the league's most valuable player, miss a year due to injury, and sit out a month due to a cheating suspension. She was a fiercely driven professional, the world's best at her job before she walked away, whose husband's ambition first matched, then seemed to eclipse her own. Football, she once said with a laugh, was her husband's "main love." It wasn't a joke. When they met in 2006, Brady had told her he wanted to play ten more years and walk away at age 40. As 40 neared, he moved the endpoint to 45. He both loved the game and seemed terrified of what shape life might take without it.

Brady's contract would expire in two months, and his future had been the subject of unending speculation all year. He knew this was his last season in New England, but had yet to officially and publicly decide. His wife seemed ready to go. Their mansion in Brookline had hit the market the previous August, 48 hours after contract negotiations between Brady and the Patriots ended in an impasse for the third straight year. The quarterback wanted a two-year contract that would take him to age 45. The Patriots refused. No—Bill Belichick, the head coach who had first given Brady his chance and whose legacy was bound up with his quarterback's, refused it. Robert Kraft, the team's owner and league power broker who for years had served as a middleman and mediator for his two most valuable and cherished employees, was all for it—anything to keep the band together. But he felt he couldn't pull rank, not now. Brady considered walking out of training camp, but he returned, as he always did, and worked hard, as he always does. He signed a deal spun to the public as an extension but which was, in reality, a one-year contract, with an out for Brady at season's end.

Brady made it clear that he had been put in his place. A legend who had once starred in a cheeky comedy sketch in which he yelled, "I'm the fucking quarterback!" now referred to himself as "an employee." During training camp, a reporter noticed a sequence where a receiver lined up in the wrong spot, a mistake the perfectionist quarterback would normally correct. Belichick ran a tough program—fiercely focused on the bottom line, largely emotionless in the pursuit of victory, known as the Patriot Way—and couldn't have asked for a better steward and exemplar for two decades than Brady. Now things had changed. Brady stared at the coaches, waiting for them to jump in and fix the receiver's mistake. The message was unmissable: after a career of assuming responsibility for the entire offense, Brady would take a step back.

It did not lead him to more happiness. During the regular season— the Patriots' strong 12–4 record belied what was a strange slog for the quarterback and much of the rest of the team—he asked a friend, "Why am I doing this?"

In December, Bündchen had started to clean out the Brookline mansion, preparing for life elsewhere. As the Patriots and Titans took the field, something big felt like it was coming to an end. Nobody knew better than the New England Patriots how essential it is in the NFL to peak at the right time in a season and postseason. A sold-out crowd of over 65,000 showed up in the light rain, but the Patriots had been so good for so long that even fans had become numb. At 8:15 p.m., Bündchen sat in the front row of the suite, separated from seven-year-old Vivian by a bowl of yellow popcorn, and watched her husband play for the New England Patriots for the last time.

BELICHICK WAS FURIOUS as one of his own tricks was used against him. There was 6:39 left in the game and New England trailed, 14–13. The Titans were facing a fourth down at midfield. Vrabel sent out the punt team. But then something weird happened: Tennessee didn't line up to punt. The Titans players stood on their assigned positions, unrushed and unbothered, body language more commonly seen during a long timeout in an unimportant and already decided game. But the game clock was running. When the 40-second play clock expired, the officials penalized the Titans five yards for delay of game.

Once again, the Titans lined up to punt. Once again, they didn't punt. The clock ran, dripping down to 5:29. Tennessee then incurred an intentional false start penalty and backed up five *more* yards. What was going on? It was bizarre. The clock kept moving.

"That's fucking bullshit!" Belichick screamed at the referees.

Belichick knew better. He was the greatest coach in modern NFL history for many reasons—variously admirable, dark, and mythic—but one was his unmatched mastery of the details of the game that others missed. Three months earlier, in the fourth quarter of a 33–0 humiliation of the New York Jets, Belichick had instructed his players to take two consecutive penalties on fourth down, exploiting a loophole in the rule book that allowed the game clock to run after multiple dead-ball fouls. Cameras panned to Belichick on the sidelines, arms folded and a muted smirk on his face, as he tormented a team he pathologically hated. The loophole— Rule 4, Section 3, Article 2—was Belichick reduced to his essence. Over two decades, he had created an expansive vision of coaching and control, winning consistently in the free-agency era of football, in which NFL rules and structure collude to quickly turn great teams into mediocre ones. He was an unusual and ruthless man, a brainy introvert in a profession of glorified gym teachers. Belichick had spent his entire adult life in the NFL, winning two Super Bowls as the defensive coordinator for the New York Giants and six as the Patriots' head coach. His fishing boat, docked off the coast of Nantucket Island, had an ever-evolving name. It was currently called *VIII Rings*.

Most people paid more attention to Belichick's smirk against the Jets than to what he had done. Vrabel, though, studied the rule as a way to learn from his mentor and model, in case newly gained knowledge met opportunity. Now it was Vrabel who stood calmly on the sidelines, arms folded, watching his preparation play out at a critical moment. Belichick cussed and roared, powerless to stop the clock. In the NFL offices, Walt Anderson, the head of officiating, was laughing. "It was like, touché!" he recalled. With 4:51 left, the Titans finally punted—after draining almost two minutes from the game clock.

Still, though: New England took over at its 11-yard line, and the crowd rose in Pavlovian anticipation. Tom Brady had the ball, with most of the field to go, trailing by a point—the kind of critical situation in which he had excelled so often that it was easy to take for granted. He had pulled off 58 game-winning drives in the fourth quarter or overtime, including six in Super Bowls. He was close to automatic, and he started the drive as expected, with two completions. New England was rolling. On second and four, Brady took a three-step drop and threw toward the sideline to receiver Julian Edelman, one of many players who came to embody the Patriots ethos, plucked out of nowhere and now a superstar. He was a 5-foot-10 quarterback at Kent State who had converted to receiver in New England and ended up becoming a Super Bowl MVP. Edelman broke to the sideline a few yards beyond the first-down marker, the type of route he and Brady had practiced and executed thousands of times. Edelman and the crowd seemed to see an inevitable big play developing, and he turned upfield as the ball arrived softly and on time, hitting him in the chest.

It bounced off his numbers and fell to the ground.

Time seemed to stop, as if the deterministic laws of physics had been broken. It was not just a drop; it was as though, after two decades of radiance, the supernova that was Tom Brady and Bill Belichick's New England Patriots finally had flared out. A few minutes later, Brady's desperation pass with 11 seconds left was intercepted by another former teammate, Logan Ryan, and returned nine yards for a touchdown. New England lost, 20–13. Brady walked off the field, surrounded by a mass of security personnel and cameramen that grew so thick that it became impossible to distinguish one type from the other, then jogged inside as men and women wearing his jersey cheered him and held signs begging him to stay.

Near another tunnel in the bowels of the stadium, Vrabel high-fived his players and yelled as they entered the locker room.

"They wanted hyenas! They fucking got hyenas!"

BELICHICK STOOD AT a podium, in a state of morbid shock. He had once described a season-ending loss as "a crash landing," and now he was tasked with explaining something he had yet to process. He said little, expressing pride in his team and complimenting the opponent.

Dead air hung between reporters' questions; nobody tolerated awkward silences like Belichick. His breath—heavy through his nose and into a microphone—was the loudest sound in the room. One reporter asked if Belichick expected Brady would be back in 2020.

"Yeah, we just finished this game," Belichick said. "So we're focused on this game, okay?"

The coach glared, narrowing his eyes.

"I mean, really?" he said.

Someone asked Belichick to address the fans that had supported him through "thick and thin."

"I wouldn't say it's been all that thin around here, personally. Maybe you feel differently."

A few minutes later, Belichick exited through the side door. Brady was due to speak next. He usually took his time after games, win or lose, styling his hair and buttoning up his suit until it was just right. But Brady appeared pieced together in a navy shirt and a stocking hat, as if he hadn't even showered. He often looked ill after a season-ending loss and took an inordinate amount of pride in his ability to stifle his raw and honest feelings. This time was different. He was disappointed but unhurried, relieved, almost liberated.

"Who knows what the future holds?" he said. "We'll leave it at that."

Brady chatted with a few more reporters, gave a Patriots executive a goodbye slap of a handshake, and soon after emerged from a black curtain behind which only family and friends were allowed. Bündchen at his side, Brady walked quickly, carrying his exhausted daughter like a father after a long day at an amusement park, past Patriots staffers and security, past people who held their phones for a shot of a legend on his way out, before turning toward the parking lot and fading into the foggy darkness.

I LEFT THE STADIUM sometime after midnight and drove north on Route 1, thinking about Tom Brady and Bill Belichick and what had been gained and lost over the past two decades. I had covered all aspects of their careers as a writer at ESPN. I had visited Brady's home and had late-night conversations with Belichick. I knew their friends and enemies. My writing at times had flattered them and at other times had angered them. They are two American originals, two very different men with very different personalities who had entered the world of professional football at different times and thrived in it together more successfully and for longer than anyone else in the history of the sport. They both arrived in New England in 2000, broken and scarred by the fragility of their dreams and driven in a way few can understand, much less articulate, their status in a game comprising mostly random and barbaric events absolutely central to their identities, crowding out almost everything else. From the start, they were extremists within an extreme profession.

There have been many books and documentaries that tried to capture what it's like to work inside an NFL team facility. But you can't understand it unless you live it, and if you live it, you spend the rest of your life trying to come to terms with the parts of you it formed and the parts it corrupted. Professional football is sometimes compared to war, including by the players themselves, but it's not, even if the stakes for some—including at least one player who spent time on the Patriots, Junior Seau—may well be life and death. But short of the military, it's hard to think of another profession where contingency reigns, where one's legacy and fate can be decided in an instant by events beyond one's control. You struggle side by side with other men also struggling—against the opponent, against themselves, against the cruelty of an oblong ball that seemingly never bounces your way—with no knowledge beyond the assignment at hand, or what today's decisions will mean about the ease or difficulty of tomorrow. At risk is not just glory and health, but huge sums of money. Player contracts are often not guaranteed. Franchises are both family businesses and sprawling enterprises—"billion-dollar lemonade stands," as a longtime front office executive once put it to me. No other American sport has more executives, coaches, support staff, and players on each roster. No other American sport so easily fills such vast stadiums and is under such intense media scrutiny. But at its heart, the NFL is a lonely game. You are alone with your thoughts, pain, regrets, joy, anguish, and ambition. It doesn't matter whether you're a coach, player, or owner. You are part of a team in name only.

The New England Patriots were a subculture within a spectacularly unhealthy world. They were defined by many of the things that defined America during the first two decades of the current century: an embrace of overwork; a refinement of craft to a previously unseen level; empiricism and a love of data, along with the creation and marketing of pseudoscience; tribalism and both its cohesive and splintering features; the pursuit of agelessness; an erosion of ethics; and, finally, a zero-sum ethos toward victory. What made them distinct was their sheer endurance. As everything in the world seemed to speed up and fracture, the team's excellence remained a hard fact of life. The New England Patriots of Tom Brady, Bill Belichick, and Robert Kraft embodied a pitilessness and selfishness and ambition that any maniacally driven person possesses, but which they had in greater measures. By January of 2020, the three of them had become denizens of a football world they could not live without. They blew past all the off-ramps and pushed every norm and boundary and rule until they had helped create a new football world altogether.

This book was sold with a trigger written into its contract: the moment Tom Brady left the Patriots or Bill Belichick retired or even joined another team, the clock would start. So, from the beginning, this book has been about the end of something, about understanding the Patriots' greatness and the larger idea of greatness itself—what they traded for it, what they received in return, and what ultimately they sought but did not find.

If this book was born at the end, the loss to the Tennessee Titans was technically not that moment. It would come two months later, on a March evening amid the onset of a global pandemic, when Brady's contract officially expired. Within days, he signed with the Tampa Bay Buccaneers. The implications were clear for both the quarterback and his former coach: whichever had more success without the other would begin to control how the Patriots dynasty would be judged by fans and by history. The end of New England's dominance wasn't really an end at all. It was the beginning of the great sorting out of what had happened— of what we all had witnessed over two decades, as we grew up or raised kids or grew old with the Patriots winning in the background. That collective process of understanding can start, at least, with the confident knowledge that we will never see anything like it again.

PART I

NINE POINTS

2001–2006

1

ONE OF A KIND

NOBODY SAW GREATNESS WALKING ONTO THE FIELD. Nothing about the quarterback projected an aura of anything other than ordinariness. The quarterback had a generic name—Tom Brady—and wore a classic quarterback number: 12. His body seemed both lanky and soft, the frame of a thin man who had been ordered to gain weight and had done so by banging weights and eating junk food. A helmet and shoulder pads somehow made him look less imposing, exposing his build rather than amplifying it. He was 24 years old on October 14, 2001, and his team, the New England Patriots, trailed the San Diego Chargers, 26–19, with a little more than two minutes left. He was in the huddle. It was the type of moment that defined quarterback careers and that he used to define himself. If he failed, he might not get another chance. No—wouldn't *deserve* another chance, as if he would have committed a mortal sin punishable by lifetime banishment.

Two head coaches stood on opposing sidelines, both in their late 40s, both defensive-minded, both with fates tied to the young quarterback. One of them was Bill Belichick, 49 years old, in his second season in New England, author of one winning season in a total of six years as a head coach of the Cleveland Browns and then the Patriots. The other was Mike Riley, 48 years old, in his second season with San Diego. Belichick was invested in Tom Brady. He had drafted him and liked his leadership and decision-making, but he was only playing Brady because the team's starting quarterback had nearly died in an on-field collision three Sundays prior. Riley was even more invested in Brady, even if the quarterback was on the other team. He knew more about what Tom Brady was capable of than anyone. He had known Brady personally for eight years, and from the start, saw something special in him—not that he would be a legend, exactly, but enough to perceive that he possessed qualities exclusive to the most gifted in his profession. He didn't know what Tom Brady would become; nobody did. But Riley understood that, in that moment, with the game on the line and Tom Brady at the line of scrimmage, he was in trouble.

"WHAT DO YOU THINK makes a good ballplayer?" the television reporter asked the six-year-old boy.

"Umm," the boy replied, mind whirring.

He was standing to the side of a baseball field, on a sunny day in the early 1980s. He wore a blue baseball hat too big for his head, with a white *R* on it, for the Royals, his first team. He was tan and cherubic, with soft green eyes. He stared off, thinking hard. Seconds passed. He shrugged and broke into a goofy grin, a smile that wouldn't change much over the years.

"I don't know."

His name was Thomas Edward Brady Jr. Everyone called him Tommy. He had three older sisters, all of whom played sports. He was a quiet and shy kid with a temper that stunned and even embarrassed his parents, Tom Sr. and Galynn. Tom Sr. was a member of the California Golf Club in San Francisco, and on Sunday mornings, he would bring Tommy to play, as early as 6:30 a.m., squeezing in a quick round before Mass. When Tommy missed a shot, he took it out on his club, sometimes throwing it across the fairway. His father would warn him and try to discipline him, and even pulled him off the course at one point. Tommy promised not to do it again. But he always did it again, as if driven by biological imperative, a competitive rage in "every fiber of his body," his dad later said. There was nothing anyone could do to change him.

Such stories became lore only in retrospect, told by Brady's parents to make sense of what came to be. Nobody knew the exact mix of ability, confidence, anger, ruthlessness, and belief it took to create a great quarterback—even the parents of the greatest of all time. "He didn't get it from his mother," Tom Sr. once told me, "and he didn't get it from me."

They would retrace paths of their own lives, looking for clues. They met in 1968, when Tom Brady knocked on Galynn Johnson's apartment in San Francisco. He was a door-to-door insurance salesman. He had been born in Haight-Ashbury in 1944—"before it was Haight-Ashbury," he said—a second-generation Californian in a Catholic family. The family belonged to San Francisco's Olympic Club, and by age eight, Tom played basketball and boxed and wrestled. When he was 14, he left for Maryknoll Seminary outside of Chicago, where he spent seven years. He considered becoming a priest, but one day, his bunkmate got in trouble for listening to a baseball game on a transistor radio. The harsh rules— to say nothing about celibacy—led him to skip the church and try the military. As a student at the University of San Francisco, he joined the Marines. He was set to go to Vietnam, but tore up one of his knees in training and was discharged as a lance corporal. Tom Sr. was always chatty and charming, able to make small talk with anyone, and so he took the job in insurance sales.

Galynn Johnson was a flight attendant for Trans World Airlines. She had just moved to San Francisco from Browerville, Minnesota. She had grown up on a farm, surrounded by her extended family—she could never recall her parents having friends over for dinner, just her aunts and uncles. She itched to see the rest of the country, and so, after a short time working at a Minneapolis advertising agency, Galynn got a job in San Francisco, working for TWA. Galynn opened the door and ended up inviting Tom in. They didn't talk insurance. They talked about their lives and families, and he asked her out on a date for the following Friday. Six months later, they were married, and they moved 15 miles south to San Mateo, eventually buying a four-bedroom, two-story house on Portola Drive, a few blocks away from El Camino Real, the major artery of the peninsula.

Their marriage was built on a spark that never waned; they were two people who always seemed happiest together—and competing against each other. I once met them for dinner at a steak and seafood restaurant in San Mateo. I arrived first, then Tom Sr. appeared. He was alone. When he told the host that Tom Brady was here for his reservation, her face sank a bit. It wasn't *that* Tom Brady. "Happens all the time," Tom Sr. said. We were deep in conversation, but when Galynn arrived, he cut himself off and rose from the table to greet her with a kiss and to ask her about her day. Though the Brady family is a family of kissers—Tom Jr. would kiss his dad on the cheek in the locker room after games, in full view of his teammates—it was clear that, after more than four decades of marriage at the time, Tom Sr. still treated Galynn with the grace and joy that he did as a young man, when he showed up at the airport to meet her parents for the first time, holding a bouquet of flowers. That is not to suggest that their relationship is all sweetness. "She and I will compete driving home," Tom Sr. said. "We competed last night playing cards. She wins for the first time in seven or eight years and she's taunting me. Can you believe that, after 43 years? She's taunting me."

You believed it if you grew up in that household. The Bradys always begin to explain their son by pointing to his three older sisters. All of them—Maureen, Julie, and Nancy—were intense competitors, in softball, soccer, and school. Maureen pitched 14 perfect games in high school before going on to an All-American career at Fresno State. Julie was a scholarship soccer player at St. Mary's. Nancy was a star on her high school debate team and earned a softball scholarship at the University of California, Berkeley. They refused to lose at anything; years later, their younger brother posted a video on social media of a family dodgeball game—one with a proviso that aiming at the face was legal.

The sisters were excited to have a little brother when he arrived on August 3, 1977. To the girls, he became an object of attention and affection, a toy to dress up. To Tom Sr., he was the man in the house, even as a boy. By the time Tommy was four, his father was entering them in father-son golf tournaments. On one particular Sunday, Tommy wanted two things: a milkshake and to be the only one to hit the ball. It was an alternate-shot tournament. On the 13th hole, Tom Sr. sank a long putt and his son started to cry, because he wasn't getting a chance to hit. On the next hole, Tom tapped the ball within two inches of the cup. He let his son finish. Tommy whacked it with all his strength and it sailed about 60 feet, his putter ripping a divot out of the green. They finished last—but Tommy got a milkshake.

Tom Sr. left early each morning and traveled the region, trying to build his insurance business. He returned home by 6 p.m., when his son would inevitably ask him to turn around and go back out. "I'd be like,

'Dad, I had baseball practice and didn't hit the ball well—can we go to the batting cages tonight?' 'Yep, let's do it,'" Brady recalled. "Or, 'Can we go up the field and you hit me ground balls?' 'Yep, no problem.' Or, 'Can we go to the gym and work on—during basketball season—shooting the ball?' 'Yep, no problem.'" Brady never forgot the image of his father entering home tired and then leaving, often still in his work clothes, to help his son. "Being available to me was the greatest gift I could ever receive from my dad. He never said no to me."

Tom Sr. did well enough financially to buy season tickets to San Francisco 49ers games, ten rows from the top of Candlestick Park in the south end zone. Though Tommy was too young to remember it—he remembers crying because he wanted a foam finger that read "49ERS ARE NO. 1"— the family was in the stands on January 10, 1982, when Joe Montana threw to Dwight Clark in the back of the end zone in a play soon dubbed as The Catch, beating the Dallas Cowboys in the NFC Championship Game. The 49er games became the centerpiece of the family's weekend. Tom Sr. and Tommy would play golf early on Sunday mornings, then go to Mass, then tailgate before the game—Tommy sometimes in a scarlet Montana jersey, throwing passes in the dirt parking lot—then tailgate after the game, then huddle around the TV at night to watch highlights. Monday morning was spent devouring the sports page, analyzing the box scores and statistical leaders. When *Sports Illustrated* arrived on Thursdays, Tommy always leafed through it, looking for a 49ers story.

Tommy was a sweet and accommodating child, with a touch of body fat that he didn't shed until high school. He was always at a field of some sort; when he wasn't playing himself, he was watching his sisters compete, riding his bike and munching on a bacon cheeseburger. Tom Sr. coached his daughters' softball teams, and coached Tommy's basketball and baseball teams. He had one rule: every child would play in each game, which made him unpopular with some of the more intense parents. Galynn was the team mom, bringing pizza after every game. Tommy was so proud to be a member of his first baseball team and so excited to play that he wore his uniform from morning till night on game day. He showed promise, from the start. "I think he would have been a great baseball player," Galynn later said. "He was a catcher with a wonderful swing."

"I'm not as convinced," Tom Sr. replied. "He could leg a triple into a single better than anybody."

Tommy was secure in his skills as a young athlete, but he contended with a palpable fear of being left behind. What if nobody saw what he saw in himself? It stirred something in him that never stopped. He taught himself to love—to be addicted to—the feeling of improvement. He always remembers how rewarding it felt to drive home with his dad after batting practice or hitting balls at the driving range, content in the knowledge that he was a little bit better, even if he was the only one who noticed.

Tom Sr. tried to be the disciplinarian toward his son, because Galynn couldn't quite bring herself to do it. She adored her boy too much. She cut his hair. She drove him at dawn on his paper route; he flung newspapers from the passenger seat, one of the first signs of the power and potency of his right arm. She made his lunch each morning and delivered it to school. And she excused her son's competitive rage—she even loved it, on some level. Tommy would be so angry at losing at a video game that he would throw the controller. He broke a television on one occasion and put a hole in the wall on another after throwing a remote. His sisters wondered what was wrong with him. Galynn knew that if her husband saw the wreckage, he would have, as he later put it, with understatement, "taken strong measures." So, she covered for her boy by covering up the hole, hanging a photo over it. "My mom spoiled all of us," Brady later said. "But as the baby, and then as the only boy, it was the best for me."

He was also his father's best friend. Tom Sr. taught his son how to scrub the grooves on his golf clubs. Tommy took obsessive pride in it, wanting every detail precise and correct. "There was a reflection of myself in that," Tom Sr. later said. Father and son would make bets on the golf course. Tom Sr. would bet money, but his son didn't have any, so he would pay off the bet by washing his father's car. "I washed a lot of cars growing up," Brady recalled. It was time that the father treasured, and that the son both loved then and appreciated more later in life, when he became a father himself. One day, when Tommy was 13, Tom Sr. told him, "There's nobody I love playing golf with more than you."

By the time Tommy was due to be a freshman at Junipero Serra High, an all-boys school nestled in the San Mateo hills, sports had overrun the family. Tom Sr. and Galynn drove their Volkswagen van to 315 games one year, not counting practices. In summer, Tommy would go and watch the San Francisco Giants play at Candlestick Park for free with a friend whose father worked the games as a police officer. He sat in the sunbaked bleachers and shagged home run balls. At home, he would play street football with the neighborhood kids. His favorite play was called "secret weapon," in which his receiver, his buddy David Aguirre, would run to the fire hydrant on Portola Drive, then break in on a post route. Tommy was a good student who enjoyed math and statistics, though he would later joke that in a school that prided itself on athletics, his grades often coincidentally rose with his batting average. He was competitive in all arenas, including trivia club, but nothing made him feel more alive than sports. And nothing fascinated him more than football, even though he had yet to play it. He was always curious about how Joe Montana made something complicated look so effortless, how he danced in the pocket, how he was always in control, how he always seemed to find the open receiver and hit him in stride, not with an overpowering arm, not like John Elway or Dan Marino or Joe Namath—not something gifted from above—but with deadly precision that, when viewed in totality, completion after completion, was its own unstoppable force. Tommy always felt secure in his arm, his potential with a ball in his hand. When he threw a perfect pass, even on Portola Drive, time would almost slow and he could watch it in flight: a tight spiral hissing in the air, the ball's nose rising and falling in a delicate flight pattern. It was beautiful. An addictive surge of feeling—of satisfaction, of joy—would shoot through him; as the years went on, he likened it to a mild climax.

In 1991, at age 14, Tommy decided to try out for football. He made Serra High's freshman team. Before his first practice, he watched other players assemble their pants, slipping the pads into the thigh and knee slots, because he had no idea how it worked. Nothing about him indicated a future in the sport, much less future excellence. That year, he was a backup quarterback on a winless team. His only playing time came as a linebacker, and in one game, his coach yelled from the sideline, "Brady, you look like you're running in slow motion!" But he loved practice, even tackling drills—*especially* tackling drills. Something about football seemed natural to him, a language he inherently spoke. He decided he was going to be a starting quarterback.

THERE'S A VIDEO OF John Elway in the early 1980s that became seared in Tom Brady's mind, and not just because Elway was wearing tight red-and-white-striped shorts that looked as though Daisy Dukes came in a candy cane pattern. It was an instructional video from Elway's Stanford years, and a man named Tom Martinez liked to show it to quarterbacks. Martinez was the head coach at the College of San Mateo and an expert on throwing mechanics, and Elway was the most mechanically sound quarterback Martinez had ever seen. His shoulder and torso torqued violently with every throw, allowing him to pass across the field or from inconceivable angles with more power than seemed possible without more of a windup.

As a preteen, Tom Brady attended the camp Martinez ran for high school quarterbacks and watched the video for the first time. It opened the mind of a young man only beginning to realize the steep learning curve and beauty of his chosen craft. He started thinking about throwing at all hours. Tom Sr. fed his son's obsession. He hired Martinez as a personal tutor, and like all great teachers, Martinez became a lifetime friend and counselor who helped Brady by empowering him. "He was a really quick learner," Martinez later said of Brady. "He worked on it. He worked on it every day." After Brady's first career NFL victory in 2001, 44–13 over the Colts, he sent Martinez the game ball, signed *The First of Many*. At the start of Brady's sophomore year, after a summer spent with Martinez, he was named the starting quarterback on the junior varsity. The quarterback who had played ahead of him as a freshman, Kevin Krystofiak, quit football to focus on basketball, having absorbed sufficient punishment on the winless team. On the night before Brady's first career start—for the first time his father could remember then or since—he panicked.

"I forgot how to throw," Tommy said.

"What do you mean?" Tom Sr. said. He knew when his son seemed anxious. He would be on edge, reserved. He would get canker sores. But this was different.

"Of course you know how to throw," Tom Sr. said.

"No, Dad, I've lost it. I just don't know how to throw a football."

"Get in the car," Tom Sr. said. "Let's go see Tom."

They drove to Martinez's office. He was in a staff meeting. Ten minutes later, Martinez walked Brady outside. They stood on a track, ten yards apart.

"Just throw," Martinez said.

Brady did so, for three straight minutes. Doubt started to seep away. No magic, no whispering, just doing what came naturally until it felt natural again, an approach Martinez would demand of Brady after he was a pro, after he was a champion—even when Martinez was bound to a wheelchair, in awful health due to kidney failure, complications of which would claim his life—barking instructions for more than an hour one day, until he felt that Brady had gained just a little more confidence. The day after Martinez met with 15-year-old Tommy, Serra trailed Mission San Jose's junior varsity by five points late in the fourth quarter. Brady entered the huddle and uttered a version of what he later would say when the Patriots trailed in Super Bowls. "C'mon, let's get this thing going!" The parents sparsely filling the rickety bleachers started to cheer. Brady drove Serra down the field and hit one of his best friends, John Kirby, on a curl route—a beautiful pass, low and inside, nestled between a linebacker and safety. A "pro throw," Kirby recalled. It would have been the winning score, but Serra's defense blew the lead.

Still, something mysterious fastened itself inside Tom Brady. He could play. Not just that, he could *deliver*. He had watched his heroes—Joe Montana and Steve Young and John Elway and Michael Jordan and Wayne Gretzky—and asked himself how they did it, how they always played their best when it mattered most. Brady had just done it—and a few weeks after the loss to Mission San Jose, Brady led Serra on another late drive, and this time, won on a last-second field goal. He ran onto the field, both arms in the air, an image that wouldn't change much over the coming decades. I once had a long discussion with Brady about two-minute drills, interested to learn how his mind worked during them, and he started off with a simple premise: "You have to have confidence, and it comes one way: doing a two-minute drill before and succeeding."

Brady had pulled off one of the defining acts for a quarterback in those precious, embryonic moments, and belief was forged rather than lost.

MIKE RILEY KNEW IT right away. This Brady kid, he was—in coach parlance—*special.*

It was 1993. Riley was in his first year as offensive coordinator and quarterbacks coach at the University of Southern California, and he recognized a little of himself in Brady. Riley, the son of an Oregon State coach, had been a quarterback at Corvallis High. He was thin and overlooked and called "Frog" by kids at school—until he threw a ball, and his entire identity changed. As a senior in 1971, Riley led Corvallis High to state championships in football and baseball. He was offered scholarships to most of the schools in the Pacific-8 as a quarterback, but he wanted to test himself on a bigger stage. He sent a tape of his highlights to the University of Alabama, hoping to catch the eye of legendary coach Paul "Bear" Bryant, who had coached Joe Namath. When Riley arrived in Tuscaloosa, he learned the limits of his own talent: Bryant moved him to defensive back. Few things scar a young man who identifies as a quarterback more than being told he is no longer one. Riley knew that being a great quarterback required more than a great arm. You needed an innate command of self and skill amid chaos, a quality invisible to most and barely discernible to trained eyes. He spent the rest of his life trying to identify it, trusting his own eyes and experience rather than statistics.

One day in the fall of Brady's junior year, Riley visited Serra High and watched him throw. He always looked first at a quarterback's motion. Was it easy? Was it clean? Was it consistently over the top, or situational, taking different angles as necessary or due to sloppiness? How did the ball come out of a quarterback's hand? Brady had a smooth arm—"a loose arm," Riley later said. The 16-year-old threw a tight spiral, most of the time. His feet were heavy, but Riley didn't care; in fact, he saw it as a virtue. Brady couldn't escape the pocket. He couldn't outrun anybody. So, rather than allowing his eyes to drop to the pass rush closing in on him—the telltale sign of fear in a quarterback—he would keep his vision fixed downfield, willing to hold the ball until the last possible second, allowing his receivers to get open. His mechanics didn't crumble under pressure; if anything, they sharpened. His teammates, most of whom were not exceptionally talented, responded well to him. Brady and Kirby had developed their own sign language. When Brady tugged slightly on his face mask, Kirby ran deep. And Riley noted not just that Brady loved the game, but *how*: on Sundays, he hosted film sessions with Kirby, dissecting plays as Galynn served sandwiches. Brady was handsome and disarmingly polite, yet he possessed this astounding drive that, no matter how many times the high school junior was described as "competitive," didn't do it justice.

Riley believed Brady was a natural. Best of all, no one else was looking at him—at least not yet. Riley recruited Brady by recruiting the Brady family. He liked Tommy and his parents, and they liked *him*, especially Tom Sr., who, even after all of the success of the Brady daughters, was pleasantly surprised to see major schools recruiting his son. Tommy had told his parents that he would be a Division I quarterback, and they had nodded along, hiding their skepticism. It wasn't their role to end their son's dream, Tom Sr. later said, it was their role to support him, and that support was going to involve some work. Serra head coach Tom MacKenzie told Tom Sr. that his son had a "Division I arm," but that his lower body was "not close to Division I," and he implored Brady to improve his quickness and agility.

"He can't wait until his senior season to become a Division I candidate," MacKenzie told Tom Sr.

Brady had fully committed to football, even though most at Serra viewed him primarily as a baseball player. Weirdly, football hurt Brady's body less than baseball. His knees killed him after catching a game; after football, he was sore, but it felt manageable. He started to work out before school, waking up at 6 a.m. for agility drills and to run up hills. MacKenzie put his players through a footwork exercise called the five-dot drill. On a square mat marked with five white dots, the players quickly shifted their feet from one position to another, like in hopscotch. Brady was awful. But he spray-painted the five dots on his garage floor so that he could practice it before and after he did it at school. He improved, but still was slower than the other players.

The one area where he excelled was throwing the ball, and if something went wrong—if guys dropped passes, or if he missed a read or, God forbid, a throw—he couldn't handle it, just as he couldn't handle a missed putt as a child. Later, in his own words, he was a "whiner," quick to blame everyone and everything except himself. He sometimes committed the quarterbacking sin of holding the ball too long, neglecting the easy pass in favor of the deep throw—"You have a love affair with your arm," MacKenzie would tell him—but most of all, he suffered from the impatience of the gifted. During one windy day, Brady was leading a seven-on-seven passing drill and his receivers were dropping balls, struggling to judge them in the swirling air. Brady dialed up more power to cut through the wind. It didn't work; his receivers simply weren't good enough to adjust. After practice, Brady was fuming, complaining to MacKenzie, when the coach cut him off.

"You need to be more patient," MacKenzie said.

It wasn't what Brady wanted to hear. Few people ever did anything great by being patient. How was this *his* fault?

MacKenzie took a deep breath. "Look around at everybody else on this field. You know what? There's a very good chance that in ten years from now, everybody else on this field will no longer be playing. You're still going to be playing. You need to understand that you are one of a kind."

Nobody had ever spoken to Brady in those terms before, in the language of potential and promise extending perhaps even beyond a college career. MacKenzie saw in Brady what Brady saw in himself—that he could do *this*, play football, professionally. Riley saw it, too. He compared Brady to Rob Johnson, whom Riley coached in 1993 and 1994 at USC: tall and skinny, elusive in the pocket but not a runner, deadly accurate with the ball. Riley also saw rare charisma and leadership in Brady, much tougher skills to teach than footwork. Even in high school, when in conversation, Brady held eye contact so intensely that it almost muted surrounding noise. He knew how to make people feel special. He was popular with both guys and girls. He had fun off the field, but not too much. He'd tried chew once, but ended up throwing up on the side of the road. After trying weed, he felt guilty that he'd let his dad down.

Nobody but Riley saw Brady play in person during Brady's senior year in 1994. Reliant more on the pass than the run with Brady at the helm,

Serra High finished 5–5. One of the losses, to Sacred Heart Cathedral, was especially crushing. Tommy's uncle and Tom Sr.'s brother, Chris Brady, was the principal at Sacred Heart. The family had bet on the game: whichever side won would host Thanksgiving. With 15 seconds left, Serra was at the Sacred Heart seven-yard line, with the game on the line. But Tommy forced a pass into the end zone. It was intercepted and returned 101 yards for a touchdown. When the Bradys arrived for Thanksgiving, Chris had hung posters of the score and blown-up photos of a dejected Tommy at the end of the game.

MacKenzie cared about his players, but wasn't focused on helping them get on the radar of college programs. The Bradys had to do that themselves. With the help of a local video editor, Tom Sr. started to assemble a tape of his son's highlights. Brady had two cameras on him every game of his senior year: a professional MacKenzie had hired, and Tom Sr. in the stands with his handheld, keeping passing statistics between plays. The resulting highlight video began with a shot of Brady being introduced by the stadium announcer before a game: "At quarterback, a 6-foot-3, 205-pound junior from San Mateo, number 12, Tom Brady!" MacKenzie stood next to Brady at the Serra football field. The camera was unsteady and off-center. "He is a big, strong, durable athlete with an excellent work ethic, especially in the off-season," MacKenzie said. Brady shifted a few times and smiled faintly at MacKenzie's compliments, as though embarrassed.

Tom Sr. and Tommy sat down with a book listing every Division I and Division II school and asked each other, Should we send a tape to this place? At one point, Tommy said, "Dad, you think we should send one to Michigan?"

"Sure, yeah," Tom Sr. replied.

They cast a wide net, mailing copies of Tommy's tape to 55 schools. Fifty-two replied. Only three—all of them schools that ran option offenses and needed running quarterbacks—dismissed him out of hand. The Michigan Wolverines were late to the game, but caught up fast. Brady's tape had been passed around the office and landed on the desk of defensive backs coach Bill Harris, who shared it with Kit Cartwright, the quarterbacks coach. Both men liked what they saw, and Harris, whose recruiting area included the West Coast, flew to San Mateo to meet Brady. When Harris arrived, he asked MacKenzie for more film of Brady—specifically, of Brady at his worst. He wanted to see how Brady rebounded when the game wasn't going his way. Harris found that he loved Brady's decision-making, even if the pass wasn't complete. In January 1995, Brady flew to Ann Arbor for an official visit. Head coach Gary Moeller sold Michigan hard, and later flew to San Mateo to try to seal the deal. Michigan's history and lore, the cool winged helmet design, the chance to compete with the best quarterbacks in the country—all of it appealed to Brady's ego and drive.

Later on, there was a story that Tom Brady told about himself: "I wasn't really a highly recruited athlete." He believed it to the bottom of his soul, even as an adult—especially as an adult—and it became as central to his own narrative as his championships. He saw himself as a product of hard work and self-belief, an underdog who had to navigate massive, ever-shifting obstacles. While he didn't have dozens of schools chasing him, midway through his senior year, he had five elite football programs—USC, UCLA, Cal Berkeley, Illinois, and Michigan—circling him, along with baseball's Montreal Expos. When his high school counselor asked him where he was applying to college, Brady replied, "I don't need to apply. I'm going to play college football." His talent was evident, as was his need to collect scars. The latter was as essential to his rise as his wondrous right arm.

As HAPPENS WITH many athletes, options narrowed as Signing Day neared. UCLA dropped Brady after Cade McNown, a star quarterback out of Oregon who would become an All-American and first-round NFL draft pick, chose the Bruins. Brady didn't want to play in Champaign, Illinois—too dreary. Cal was appealing, but something about it was too easy, as if playing locally wouldn't maximize Brady's potential or help him grow up. The choice was between USC and Michigan—and it turned out not to be a choice at all.

One winter weekend, Riley flew north to see the Bradys and arrived at their house, a place he had been many times before, including just a few weeks earlier. Riley was friendly, but looked ashen. He had bad news. A few days earlier, head coach John Robinson had told Riley that the

Trojans had landed a commitment from a quarterback out of the Chicago suburbs named Quincy Woods. "We don't have room for Brady," Robinson said.

Riley almost "fell over," he recalled. He thought it was a mistake—Woods would leave the team after four seasons—and worse, he had to deliver the news and "felt a responsibility to make sure the Bradys understood face to face." And so, Riley flew to San Francisco and, in the home he'd had so many warm conversations in, told the family that USC, after a year and a half of dialogue, wouldn't be offering Brady a scholarship after all.

The Bradys took the news with grace—they knew it wasn't Riley's call—but it hurt. Brady now had two options: Cal or Michigan. Cal was offering him a chance to play sooner than he would at Michigan, but Tommy's mind and heart were set on Ann Arbor. He would write in his senior yearbook, "If you want to play with the big boys, you gotta learn how to play in the tall grass."

One late-winter day, Harris called Brady to see how he was leaning.

"I want to be a Michigan man," Brady said.

Every life is made at the expense of roads not taken and choices not made, and in the coming years, Tom Brady Sr. wondered whether Tom Brady would have become a legend if he had attended Cal. Probably not, he concluded. His son likely would have had a fine college career and gone on to the world of finance, grinding away at a desk. At the time, though, Tommy's decision wounded his dad. Tom Sr. had been as invested in his son's sports career as his son was—many son's dreams being created out of the ashes of the father's—and it winnowed his world beyond the normal pain of an empty nest. Before Tommy left, Tom Sr. told him that their relationship was about to change.

"Dad, I know," Brady said. "It has to."

Riley, though, was relieved when he heard that Brady had passed on Cal. It spared him the torture of facing Brady in the Pacific-10. And it seemed to spare him an inevitable loss to the young man he had spotted first.

2

YOU WANT
TO LEAVE?
GO 'HEAD!

T OM BRADY'S WHITE T-SHIRT READ QB1. IT WAS FEB-
ruary 2000, and Mike Riley was walking through the NFL's
annual scouting combine in Indianapolis when he saw a familiar face. Riley was now the head coach of the San Diego Chargers; like all
players at the combine, Brady was an anonymous prospect going through
football's version of boot camp, having been given a T-shirt and gray jumpsuit, identified not by name but by number, as if he were a product coming
off an assembly line. The 2000 quarterback class was not considered special. Marshall University's Chad Pennington, a finalist for a Rhodes scholarship, was considered the best of the group. Brady had told his parents
that he was going to be "one of 32" starting quarterbacks in the NFL, but
most teams saw him as a backup, if anything. Scouts liked his leadership,
accuracy, and 20–5 record as a starter at Michigan. They did not like his
slight build, stunning lack of quickness—his time in the 40-yard dash and
vertical jump were the worst of 576 quarterbacks that ESPN draft guru
Mel Kiper Jr. had recorded in 30 years to that point—and the fact that, as a
senior, he had split time for half the season with Drew Henson, a star baseball and football prospect whom many scouts considered the next John
Elway. "A little bit of a red flag," Bill Belichick later said.

Brady was eager to dispel all doubts at the combine—until he learned,
like every prospect does, that the combine has very little to do with
football. He posed for scouts shirtless, wearing only shorts, facing the
camera and then from the side, as in a mug shot. The photo of his unim-
pressive build—if one could call it a build—would become legendary

and serve as motivation for Brady to transform himself into something closer to statuesque. Years later, when Brady first graced the cover of *Men's Health*, Tom Sr. deadpanned that his son was the magazine's first cover boy to wear a shirt. Brady threw well at the combine, although neither his arm strength nor his accuracy jumped out. During the written psychological test, which often reveals more about those asking the questions than those answering them, Brady was asked if he used to kick cats and if he liked *Alice in Wonderland.*

"No, I wasn't a cat kicker," Brady replied.

"So, did you pass?" a reporter later asked him.

"I hope so. I see myself as pretty normal."

Riley still saw Brady as exceptional, five years later. He had followed Brady's career from the West Coast. In 1997, after four stellar years running USC's offense, Riley was hired by Oregon State as its head coach, then jumped to the Chargers, an organization in a tailspin since it picked Washington State quarterback Ryan Leaf in 1998. Brady had watched Leaf up close in the Rose Bowl that year, when Brady was a backup and Leaf was a superstar who nearly pulled off an upset of the undefeated Michigan Wolverines. But after two years in the NFL, the former second-overall draft pick was a toxic mix of incompetence and entitlement. The Chargers wanted to draft a developmental quarterback in the mid-to-late rounds. Riley thought he might finally get his man.

When Riley saw Brady at the combine, the two men picked up right where they left off, both occupying familiar roles: Riley the believer, Brady desperate to be believed in.

"I missed you once," Riley told Brady. "I won't miss on you again."

A few weeks later, at the Chargers' facility—the practice fields were nestled against a bluff, and rumor had it that opposing teams, especially Al Davis's Raiders, would secretly videotape practices from above—everyone was drafting and coaching for their jobs. Bobby Beathard, the general manager, was a future Hall of Fame executive who had won Super Bowls with the Washington Redskins in the 1980s, but was now humbled by the Leaf debacle. Beathard gave the coaching staff a list of ten mid-to-late-round quarterbacks to evaluate. Brady was one of them. Beathard knew that Riley wanted Brady. Riley, though, wanted his scouting report to be scouted. He worried that he loved Brady so much—as a person, as a quarterback, as a vessel of redemption—that bias had crept into his analysis. He sent quarterbacks coach Mike Johnson to Ann Arbor to research Brady.

"Talk to everyone," Riley told him.

JOHNSON FLEW TO Detroit and drove the half hour to Ann Arbor, winding his way through streets lined with frat houses and apartments whose yards were littered with beer bottles and bicycles before arriving at Michigan Stadium, a redbrick temple rising out of the flat land. He attended Michigan's pro day, where scouts ran prospects from the school through a series of mostly perfunctory tests that teams somehow considered predictive and therefore valuable. Brady weighed in at 195 pounds and was "slow as shit," the quarterback later said, in his speed tests. But then Johnson made the rounds of the football building, visiting assistant coaches and strength coaches and even secretaries, trying to bridge the gap between the quarterback Riley loved and the afterthought Johnson had just witnessed up close.

Brady had committed to Michigan as part of what would be seen, in retrospect, as one of the greatest recruiting classes in college football history, with a Heisman Trophy winner in defensive back Charles Woodson and five future NFL players in addition to Woodson and Brady. But before Brady set foot on campus, most of the coaches who had championed him were gone. Michigan had recruited Brady to be the fourth or fifth quarterback on the depth chart; when he arrived, he was seventh. He tried not to get discouraged, and on his first day of practice, after watching the other quarterbacks throw, Brady thought, *Man, I'm better than these guys!* He wasn't, but he didn't care. His self-belief was already in place.

Michigan was an adjustment for the California kid. His roommate, Pat Kratus, gave him a winter jacket, the first of his life. Brady would crank up the heat so high in his apartment that friends didn't want to visit. "When it's ten degrees in the middle of January, I'm like, 'Fuck this,'" Brady later said. But he fell in love with college life. Michigan was a fun place to be a football player. Bouncers at the bars—like Rick's, a legendary underground club just off campus that "was like a dungeon,"

Brady later said—waved you in. Although he would later dismiss his general studies degree as "majoring in football," Brady earned a 3.3 grade point average and made academic all–Big Ten. His parents would fly out for almost all of the games—Tommy joked that they graduated from the University of Northwest Airlines—even though he redshirted as a freshman. He took his parents to Angelo's, a diner just off campus with a line that often curled around the block. Inside were photos of famous Michigan athletes. Tommy told them that, one day, he was going to be a household name, with his photo on the wall. That would happen, but at the time, it was a boyish dream that was at severe odds with his reality.

All athletes, especially great ones—especially those with impossible expectations for themselves—swing between extreme confidence and extreme insecurity in a way unfathomable to fans. By 1996, sitting with his dad in the car after another game for which his parents had flown out to watch him warm up, Brady felt he was out of options. He was now third-string, but the two young men above him were not going anywhere soon. Backup Brian Griese, the son of Hall of Fame quarterback Bob Griese, was two years ahead of Brady. Starter Scott Dreisbach was only a year ahead.

"Dad, I don't know if I'm ever going to get to play here. I mean, I don't think I'll ever get my chance."

"You're probably right," Tom Sr. replied. "You probably won't."

With ten minutes left against UCLA in the fourth game of the 1996 season and Michigan leading, 35–3, Tom Brady ran onto the field for the first time. It was blustery and cloudy—Big Ten weather. Keith Jackson was calling the national broadcast on ABC. Brady's parents were in the stands. It was everything Brady had imagined. All the long hours, all the slights, real and imagined, that had led him to this moment "seemed to pay off," he later said. On third down, the coaches called his first pass, a little toss over the middle just past the sticks, his favorite play. Brady dropped back, tried to look off the safety, just as he had been coached, and threw short and sharp to his receiver, who was cutting from the middle of the field toward the sideline . . . and the pass was intercepted by a UCLA linebacker and returned for a touchdown. Brady stood in the end zone, his hands on his hips and head tilted back, wondering if he had blown his only chance.

As the 1996 season ended and early preparations for 1997 began, Brady felt the world was conspiring to keep him off the field. He suffered an emergency bout of acute appendicitis that caused him to lose 20 pounds and left him devouring 18-inch meatball subs from Subway to try to gain it back. Kit Cartwright, the quarterback coach who had recruited Brady, took a job as passing game coordinator at Indiana University, leaving Brady entirely bereft of champions. Brady was becoming the worst version of himself, whining and pouting. He needed a plan— needed someone who could do for his mind what Tom Martinez had once done for his arm. The person he found ended up changing his life, as Martinez had.

Many years later, in 2007, when Brady's legend was already secure but still not close to finished, and when his future wife was many magnitudes more famous than any athlete except Michael Jordan, there was a celebration of the tenth anniversary of Michigan's 1997 national championship team at an Ann Arbor steakhouse. Among those players and coaches who attended was a thin man named Greg Harden, who worked in the athletic department as a counselor. Harden is friendly, but direct, with a hard face around soft eyes, and he stopped at Brady's table to catch up. Brady looked up. He smiled. He turned to his wife, to introduce her, but before he could say anything, her eyes widened and warmed.

"Oh," she said. "I know who this is."

As a freshman, Brady had been assigned to Harden, just in case he ever needed an ear. Harden had graduated from Michigan with honors at age 28 and worked in a local rehab center. Bo Schembechler, Michigan's legendary football coach, hired him in 1986 to work with athletes. Harden's title was director of counseling, and he mentored the likes of Jalen Rose of the Fab Five and Desmond Howard, who had won the Heisman Trophy and, in January of 1997, been named Super Bowl MVP as a kick returner for the Green Bay Packers—in that game, they beat the New England Patriots, led by Bill Parcells, assistant head coach Bill Belichick, and quarterback Drew Bledsoe. Harden had a phrase in his office, unmissable to all who entered: "Control the controllables."

Harden always tried to be present at practice, in the weight room, and in meetings, so players would feel comfortable visiting him. He hadn't talked much to Brady. He had found Brady "pleasant," albeit too skinny and pretty to be a Big Ten quarterback. But he could tell something was wrong. He seemed discouraged, out of his element.

"Hey, if you ever wanna talk," Harden told him one day, "I'm available to you."

A few weeks later, Brady entered Harden's office. If Brady wasn't depressed, Harden thought, he was close.

"I need help," Brady said.

He took a seat in Harden's office. Harden had a routine with new clients: let them whine for a bit, and then he would develop a plan of action. Brady whined, all right, but when he said, "I'm never going to get my chance. They're giving me only three reps," Harden seized on the comment.

"Three reps?" Harden replied. "Three reps is a heck of a lot better than zero reps. I want you to do the best you can with those three reps they give you, Tommy. If you do anything less, then shame on you. Now, go out and do those three reps well."

Brady was quiet.

"Tom, whether you play or never play—and there's a possibility you never play"—Harden paused, letting the words hang for maximum effect—"but you certainly won't play if you don't change your mind and attitude. I'm not in a position to get you a starting job. If nobody else believes in your ass, you've gotta believe."

Fuck, Brady thought. *More of that.*

"Let's go," he replied.

Brady began visiting Harden weekly, trying to get his mind right. Sometimes, Harden listened and was spare with words; at other times, he yelled at Brady, trying to break his funk. At one point, Harden told him, "You say you're the guy. I see no evidence of that. If you're the guy, show me. Show everybody."

Harden had a way of turning negatives into positives, which "jumpstarted my own competitiveness," Brady later said.

Brady's mindset improved, but his situation did not. He saw himself buried on the depth chart and looked for an escape hatch back home to

Cal. Brady met with head coach Lloyd Carr, who had been hired after Brady committed to Michigan, to tell him he was considering a transfer. Brady explained that where he was and where he wanted to be were two different places.

"You have the potential to be a very good player," Carr replied. "You need to go out there and compete and worry about the things you can control, and not worry about the things you can't." Carr reminded Brady that he had chosen Michigan for a reason. He could have gone to Cal and played earlier; he chose Michigan to test his own limits and to compete with the best.

Brady told Carr he would think over it that night. At a staff meeting, Carr thought Brady's mind was made up.

"Tom's going to leave."

That night, Brady spoke to Harden. Brady reiterated what both men knew: he was considering a transfer; Michigan wasn't the place for him. Maybe Brady expected Harden to react differently than Carr, with more empathy, or even more tough love. But Harden wasn't angry, or even sad. He thought the entire episode was funny.

"Who gives a fuck if you leave?" Harden said. "You ain't done shit anyway. You want to leave? Go 'head."

Brady had no response. Harden was right. Carr later would be cast as a foil of sorts, the primary example of a failure to recognize untapped greatness. But Carr didn't miss the real Tom Brady, because the real Tom Brady had yet to be formed. Brady didn't want to be remembered as a player who couldn't cut it, and the next day, he surprised Carr by telling him he was staying—and added a shot across the bow: "Coach, I'm not going to leave, and I'm going to prove to you that I'm the best quarterback."

By the fall of 1997, Brady had taken his three reps and methodically turned them into more. He had leapfrogged Dreisbach and was dead-locked in a fierce battle for the starting job with Griese, whom Brady first viewed as an obstacle, then as a template. Brady had never seen anyone grind harder than Griese—"a man on a mission," Brady said— which was all the more impressive given that he came from football roy-alty. Like Brady, Griese was not athletically gifted, but could identify the open receiver and throw the ball accurately. "Nobody worked harder than Brian Griese," Brady recalled. Griese won the job. More specifically, Brady and Griese tied, and Carr always gave the tie to the upperclassman. Brady was the backup on the 1997 co–national championship team, and by the end of his first three years at Michigan, he had thrown a grand total of 20 passes, none for touchdowns. Entering his fourth year, his junior year, he was in line to be the starting quarterback after Griese's graduation. But now he had a new problem.

DREW HENSON WAS designed to be Tom Brady's own personal hell, a local Michigan superstar and archetype of everything that a quarterback should be. He was a 6-foot-4, 210-pound, three-sport superstar out of Brighton High. He had hit a high school record 70 home runs and had such command of the football that every pass followed a predestined arc. As a high school senior, Henson had been the subject of a fawning spread in *Sports Illustrated*. The New York Yankees had already paid him $2 million to play baseball during the summer. Carr was heavily involved in recruiting Henson, leaving the Brady family to believe that he had guaranteed Henson playing time, a charge Carr always denied. But it was clear that Carr was invested in Henson in a way that he was not with Brady. When Carr announced Brady as the starter in 1998, he added a caveat that Henson—"the most talented quarterback I've been around"—would play, too.

If the entire situation seemed ridiculous, Brady never complained to his parents. Once he had decided to stay at Michigan, "he owned it," his father later said. "And it was for him to work his way out of it." So, he worked: training before and after class, pathologically driven to play and to prove himself. He practiced a footwork drill in which he dragged his plant foot on throws so intensely that he ripped the nail off of his big toe. One bad rep, one awful practice—God forbid, one bad game—might cost him his career. Fear became hardwired into him and never went away. "Deep scars," Brady said. He was processing so much anger—and, with Harden's help, trying to channel it into something useful—that his parents learned to avoid bringing up his central purpose in his young life. "We wouldn't talk about football with him on the phone," Tom Sr. said. "He didn't know if football was worth it for him."

Before his first career start, on September 5, 1998, at Notre Dame, Brady was nervous. He had detoured to Notre Dame Stadium over the summer on the way home from a wedding, hoping to take in its lore and atmosphere so that, when Michigan's September game there came around, he wouldn't be overwhelmed. He snuck in through an open gate and walked around, imagining the fall. Down below was the field where Joe Montana first began authoring his legend. To the north was the mural known as Touchdown Jesus. He returned to the gate. There was a problem: it was closed. He tried to open it; it was locked. He looked around. There was no obvious escape. This wasn't good. He imagined the headlines: Michigan's quarterback getting popped for trespassing at Notre Dame. He ended up using a small ladder to hop a fence.

But if the point of the trip was to erase nerves, it failed. On September 4, with kickoff a day away, Brady felt tight. He visited Harden. As Brady tried to sort through his anxiety, Harden cut him off.

"Let's assume that I came from another planet," Harden said. "Could you explain football to me?"

"Yeah," Brady said.

"What's the game?" Harden said.

Brady explained football in the most basic terms, of having a certain number of downs to outscore the opponent.

"How many downs?"

"Four."

"What's the field? Can you draw the field?"

Brady got up and stood at a whiteboard, sketching the dimensions of a field.

"Ten-yard increments?" Harden said.

"Yeah."

"Is it like that at every stadium?"

"Yeah."

"See where I'm going?"

"I got it," Brady said.

IT WAS A SIMPLE GAME, the same one Brady had played well enough to land at Michigan. But he felt as though he was on a clock, as if his job inevitably would be yanked away. Under Brady, the defending-champion Wolverines dropped their first two games in 1998, including at Notre Dame, but rebounded to finish 10–3, capping the year with a blowout of Arkansas in the Citrus Bowl. He completed 61.9 percent of his passes, with 14 touchdown passes and 10 interceptions. It all left Carr to wonder if the team could do better. Brady knew. Harden knew, too. He would watch Brady closely during games, and he noticed that the quarterback had a habit of desperately looking to the sideline, not for the next play call, but for approval from the coaches that never came.

"Why are you doing that?" Harden said. "You the starting quarter-back or not? They chose you. You got chosen because you're the best of the bunch."

"You're absolutely right," Brady said, badly needing to be convinced.

Harden told Brady to study confident leaders. Brady looked first to Montana, watching tape of him, noticing how he always seemed relaxed, regardless of situation or circumstance. But more than that, Brady started to study everything football, from the assignments for every offensive player on each snap to the nuances of defenses. That was the thing about Brady: if you told him to do something to help him improve, he did it. "Coachable," Harden later said. Carr admired Brady's drive—he would later remark that nobody relished football's inherent struggle more—but like most football coaches, most not named Bill Belichick, he was seduced by the irresistible promise of physical talent. Five days before the season opener against Notre Dame in 1999, Carr was asked who would start at quarterback.

"What time is the game?" Carr asked.

"Three-thirty," a reporter replied.

"Three-thirty. You'll see then."

Carr had devised a plan: Brady would start and play the first quarter, then Henson would come in during the second quarter. Carr would decide at halftime who would finish the game. The football world loves quarterback controversies, and despite the wishes of quarterbacks coach Stan Parrish, who believed that Brady should start, Carr was inviting Michigan fans and the public to watch one play out. Brady had spent years training himself to thrive without much margin for error. At a point in his career when, as an upperclassman and returning starter, the margins should have been expanding, they were smaller than ever.

Carr's whole act offended some players, who saw him as needlessly stringing along not just the better quarterback but an unquestioned team leader. Before the season opener, for the first time since high school, Brady received a piece of recognition: his teammates voted him a team captain. All of his largely invisible work had finally been noticed, and it was an honor that stayed with him through the decades, even as supposedly greater awards piled up. In 2013, on a preseason trip to play the Detroit Lions, Brady visited Ann Arbor and addressed the team in the same auditorium where he had once sat, telling the only story he ever told. "I didn't have an easy experience," he recounted for the room. "I didn't come in as a top-rated recruit. I didn't come with the opportunity to play right away. I had to earn it." He paced back and forth, never breaking eye contact with the young men in front of him. "You know what the greatest honor I've ever received as a player is?" It was being voted team captain. "That, to this day, is the single greatest achievement I've ever had as a football player, because the men in this room chose me to lead their team." His eyes brimmed, and he stopped pacing, fighting through feelings that most would have believed were long past—after all the Super Bowls and MVP awards—but in truth remained close to, if not at, the surface.

THERE ARE DIFFERENT KINDS of boos in sports, and Tom Brady has experienced them all. One is from a home crowd toward the opposing team. Tom Brady loved those. Another is from a home crowd toward its own team, kicking it in the ass to play better. Brady felt those were always deserved. But, as a fifth-year senior in 1999, Brady encountered the rarest of boos: from a home crowd, directed at nobody other than him. In the first game, against Notre Dame, Brady started, then sat. When Henson jogged onto the field in the second quarter, the crowd cheered. Wearing a headset, Brady stared down for a moment, perhaps the only sign of anger he allowed himself. But when Brady was inserted back into the lineup in the third quarter, some of the crowd booed, a scattered but unmistakable sound.

But Brady pulled off what he had been known for in high school and what would become his trademark at Michigan and beyond: he led his team to a comeback. After a last-minute 26–22 victory, the press asked him about the boos. "I think we're way beyond that," Brady said. But was he? Could he ever be? Looking back, Brady harbored no ill will toward Carr. He tried to be grateful to the coach for delivering what would be the ordering principle of his life: no snap could be taken for granted. It was a foundational concept in the NFL—and of Bill Belichick's Patriots above all. Brady later realized he was soft when he arrived at Michigan, and that it was there that "I really learned to compete. I really learned to grow up." And he *really* learned football. He would help offensive coordinator Mike DeBord develop the game plan on his off days, knowing that no matter how complimentary the coaches were—"Not every player could be a coach," DeBord later said. "He could. He can process a lot of football quickly"—Carr refused to guarantee that Brady would finish the next game.

By now, even Harden, for all his tough love, was openly rooting for Brady. They met Friday afternoons before Saturday games, and Brady would let down his guard. He would vent, rage, recover, and plot a path forward. He was stuck in a cruel psychological loop: he fretted that he would play tentatively, scared of losing his job, but also worried that Carr would bench him for playing tentatively *and* scared. Brady couldn't allow it to become a self-fulfilling prophecy, so Harden had to shock him out of his spiral.

"This is your team!" he yelled. "Start acting like it!"

The rotation with Henson continued through the next six games. Against unbeaten Michigan State, Henson started the second half, threw an interception, and was benched with Michigan trailing, 27–10. Brady led the team to three touchdowns on three straight possessions in a 34–31 loss. He hoped Carr would end the rotation, but he didn't, believing that the next game would be the one where Henson would unlock his potential. But then Michigan lost to Illinois. Brady was completing 65 percent of his passes, ten percentage points higher than Henson. It was absurd. Carr defended the rotation—Michigan had won most of the time with it—but the staff noticed that Brady, the skinny California kid, was physically tougher than Henson. Brady never flinched in the pocket. Carr called Brady into the office to tell him that the rotation was over.

With five games left in his fifth year, Tom Brady could finally to look to the sideline not for approval, not to see if Henson was putting on his helmet, but to learn the next play call.

CARR LATER SAID that Bobby Grier of the New England Patriots was the only scout from an NFL team to call him about Brady. But that wasn't exactly true. Mike Johnson, the Chargers' quarterback coach, spent hours with Carr and quarterbacks coach Stan Parrish. Everyone said the same thing: Carr had put Brady in a tough spot, and he could have torn the team apart, but instead he handled it with maturity and grace. Johnson watched Brady's final two games, against Ohio State and then against Alabama in the Orange Bowl, both ending up as variations on the same theme: Michigan trailed until Brady single-handedly turned the momentum, one of the hardest and most essential tasks a quarterback faces. Against Ohio State, Brent Musburger began the telecast by calling Brady college football's "man of the year" and ended it by calling him the "comeback kid" after he threw two touchdown passes in the second half to rally Michigan to a 24–17 win. Against Alabama, Brady rallied Michigan twice from 14 points down and won in overtime, 35–34. Brady wasn't always perfect, but in critical moments, he had a sort of ruthless efficiency, a knack for throwing to the open receiver—or throwing open a receiver—to the point that a win felt inevitable. Five of Michigan's ten victories in 1999 were Brady-led comebacks. Johnson loved what he saw, especially from a projected late-round pick. "Every time he played in a big game, he played big," Johnson recalled.

Johnson interviewed one of the secretaries in the football office, and she raved about Brady's kindness. He met with strength coaches and trainers, who painted a portrait of a leader in the weight room. He even met with one of Brady's professors. Finally, Johnson sat down with Brady himself. They had met years earlier, in the USC locker room, when Tommy and his father were on his official visit to Mike Riley's Trojans before the offer evaporated. After the Bradys left, Riley told Johnson, "I really like this quarterback from San Mateo." The teenager Johnson met in 1994 was now an impressive young man who "had the ability to make you believe," Johnson later said.

Johnson returned to San Diego and typed up a two-page report on Brady. In draft meetings with Bobby Beathard and the scouts, Johnson presented and testified on Brady's behalf, to a room of closed minds.

"Mike," Beathard said, "you've done a lot of research on him and all you've talked about are the intangibles. But we don't *know* if he's going to be that good."

It was that line of thinking that later haunted NFL evaluators, proof that Beathard had learned nothing from the Leaf disaster. Here was a tall, accurate, smart, winning quarterback, available in the middle rounds—virtually free—and Beathard refused to budge. Johnson knew that he held limited sway, but he was still taken aback. Why didn't Beathard see what the coaches saw?

"His intangibles are off the charts," Johnson argued.

"They don't lie," Riley added. "And no matter what, he did throw for [369] yards against Alabama in the Orange Bowl."

THERE'S AN UNWRITTEN RULE among NFL general managers: you give the coach his quarterback. The rest of the roster is yours, but with the most important position, the coach gets to choose. And so, on April 16, 2000, early in the sixth round of the draft, Riley took it as a good sign when Beathard stopped by his office. The first of the Chargers' three sixth-round picks, number 184 overall, was coming up in the next hour.

"Who do you want to draft?" Beathard asked.

"Tom Brady," Riley replied.

"Okay," Beathard said.

Finally. Riley had closed the deal.

FIVE-HUNDRED-SOME MILES up the coast, the Bradys were on Portola Drive, huddled around the television. Brady had hoped to go in the second round, but expected to go in the third. Those rounds had come and gone. Brady was running out of ways to distract himself. He had attended a San Francisco Giants game the first day of the draft, coming home to word that Chad Pennington had gone to the New York Jets with the 18th pick. In the third round, Giovanni Carmazzi of Hofstra went to the 49ers and Chris Redman of Louisville went to the Baltimore Ravens. The Carmazzi pick hurt. Brady had thrown for the 49ers when the team held a workout for San Francisco–area prospects and thought he had made a good impression, especially in front of team president Bill Walsh, nicknamed "The Genius," a three-time Super Bowl champion who had revolutionized offensive football and was instrumental in the drafting of four future Hall of Famers. Of all the talent evaluators in the league, Walsh should have been able to recognize Brady's subtle gifts. Instead, he gravitated toward Carmazzi, who would never play a down in the NFL. Nobody—not even undisputed legends, not even the man who had drafted and coached Joe Montana, to whom Brady would be compared perhaps more frequently than anyone else, and who traded for Steve Young—hit on every quarterback. Or came close, for that matter.

Brady was in the living room with his family when the Pittsburgh Steelers picked quarterback Tee Martin out of Tennessee in the fifth round. Brady wanted to be alone; he went up to his room. Marc Bulger out of West Virginia, a quarterback similar to Brady—natural arm, great production, underwhelming build—was the second pick of the sixth round, by the New Orleans Saints. Brady looked at the upcoming picks and realized none of the teams, from the Seattle Seahawks to the Arizona Cardinals to the Chicago Bears, had shown interest in him. He was getting anxious.

Pick numbers 183 and 184 were daggers. At 183, the Cleveland Browns chose quarterback Spergon Wynn out of Southwest Texas State. Of all the quarterbacks to go ahead of Brady, Wynn got under Tom Sr.'s skin the most. He had completed only 47 percent of his passes against second-rate competition, compared to Brady's 62 percent on college football's biggest stages. "Forty-seven percent," Tom Sr. often said in disgust.

At 184, though, the Chargers seemed like a lifeline. But, before the pick, Beathard rewatched 20 minutes of Brady's film. He decided that two quarterbacks, Florida A&M's Ja'Juan Seider and Stanford's Todd Husak, were good enough that the team could hold off on selecting one. He walked down to Riley's office.

"We made a different decision," Beathard said.

That decision was a linebacker from Virginia named Shannon Taylor, who would start all of two games in a four-year career. Riley knew another chance had slipped away. He would later suggest that a piece of him died in that moment.

"I DON'T UNDERSTAND THIS," Brady said to his family. "I do not understand this."

Nobody knew what to say. Brady needed to do something other than watch his dream disintegrate in slow motion on live television. He picked up a baseball bat and left the house. Tom Sr. and Galynn were concerned for the cars in the neighborhood.

Tom Sr. had envisioned this moment, had even rehearsed a speech for it. Years earlier, he had been at a hotel pool with other parents at a softball tournament. One of the dads said, "You know, Tom, some of these kids will never progress beyond this. Some kids peak out at 12, some kids peak out at 14, some kids don't make it on the varsity high school team, some kids peak out in college. Sooner or later, all of the kids are going to peak out." It struck Tom Sr. as profound. "I had always thought kids kept *progressing*," he later said. He came up with a version of the necessary talk with his son, not knowing when he would deliver it: *People's careers come to an end at various times. Some come to an end in sixth grade, some come to an end after nine years in the pros. But they're all going to come to an end. So, the end of an athletic career isn't the end of the world . . .*

The phone rang.

Tom Sr. answered. His son was still outside, circling the block. Berj Najarian, Bill Belichick's assistant, was on the line and asking for Tom Brady.

Belichick was running his first draft in five years, since his final one as the head coach of the Browns in 1995. The Patriots had three quarterbacks on the roster, including Drew Bledsoe, their franchise. Belichick sat at the center of a long table in the Patriots' draft room, in a brown suit, binders and bulky laptops and highlighters scattered around. In the fifth round, everyone in the room looked at the team's draft board.

Brady was one of the names on the left, in the ranking of the best available players according to the Patriots' consensus. Belichick told Robert Kraft, "Wow, Brady's still on the board." Belichick had been worried about the Henson situation at Michigan, but he liked Brady's demeanor and leadership, liked that, as a senior, his touchdown passes had gone up and interceptions had gone down, liked his performance in the Orange Bowl, and most of all, loved his record as a starter. One day, Belichick stopped by the weight room to chat with fullback Chris Floyd, who had overlapped with Brady at Michigan. Floyd told Belichick that, even as a sophomore, Brady would help older players understand the playbook, himself included. Belichick had watched other teams, especially the Green Bay Packers in the 1990s, stockpile and develop quarterbacks as insurance and currency. Scott Pioli, the Patriots' top personnel guy, and Dick Rehbein, the team's quarterbacks coach, who had flown to Ann Arbor to scout Brady, saw him as a low-risk choice with high upside. Belichick was sold. He made the pick, number 199 overall. It was Belichick's 48th birthday.

On the phone, Tom Sr. tried to stall. "Uhh, he's in the shower," he said.

"Well, Coach Belichick would like to talk to him," Najarian said.

Just then, Brady reentered and traded the bat for the phone. Everyone stood around him, smiling, and his father prepared to pop a bottle of champagne. "We just wanted to let you know you've been drafted by the New England Patriots," Najarian said.

"You won't regret this," Brady said.

3

DREW'S OUT, YOU'RE IN

W HERE DID THE NEW ENGLAND PATRIOTS PLAY, anyway? Tom Brady had no idea. The team was the only franchise named for a region, not a state or city. The team was also mostly irrelevant. It had been in the Super Bowl twice, after the 1985 and 1996 seasons, losing both times. Drew Bledsoe was its only superstar player. After the draft, Brady flew to Providence, then drove the half hour to Foxborough, a strip of hardcore blue-collar Massachusetts south of Boston. Foxboro Stadium, rising from the nothingness of Route 1, mostly unpaved on both shoulders in that stretch, looked like a high school field. It was nothing like Michigan Stadium, but it was Brady's new home. At first, he was disoriented. For most of his life, the ocean was due west; now it was east. But in one of the first team meetings, after the 2000 draft, Brady knew he'd landed in a good spot. Belichick, in his first year as head coach, told the players that he valued competition above all. There was no entitlement. The remarks scared some players and pissed off others, but it was a language Brady spoke, too. He knew how to compete. He'd had no choice.

Brady lived with other Patriots rookies at a motel called the End Zone Motor Inn, a temporary home for many players who were temporary themselves. But at the start of training camp, he wanted to buy a condo that Ty Law, the Patriots' star cornerback, had put up for sale. Brady called his agent, Don Yee, conveying the message that he wanted to lock in a good interest rate.

"I think you should make the team first," Yee said.

"Don't worry about that," Brady replied. "I'm going to make the team. I ain't worried about that."

For Brady, uncertainty prompted a strange reflex. Every time he was doubted, or he doubted himself, whether he admitted it or not, he upped the stakes, to prove others wrong and to prove himself to himself. First in high school, vowing to play college ball. Then at Michigan, promising his folks that his name would be on the wall among the other legends at Angelo's. In Foxborough, he made the team after training camp—barely. Despite already rostering three quarterbacks, Belichick wanted to keep Brady—he saw promise in him, even if he was skinny and slow—and took the rare step of keeping four quarterbacks on the team. Brady had reached the first in a series of dreams: he was an NFL quarterback. And in August of 2000, he signed a three-year contract. His rookie salary was $193,000. Tom Sr. immediately busted Tommy's chops over it, reminding his son that he still outearned him.

Brady bought 9 Cherrywood Lane in Franklin, Massachusetts, from Law. The condo was 15 minutes west of the stadium. He invited two other Patriots—defensive lineman David Nugent, who was a fellow sixth-round pick in 2000, and tight end Chris Eitzmann, an undrafted tight end out of Harvard—to be his roommates. It became a frat house and a football laboratory, and the site of the final year of Brady's life when he would be anonymous and overlooked. They played serious games of Tecmo Bowl on a Nintendo Entertainment System that Brady purchased from a pawnshop. Losers were forced to streak naked through the condo park, which Brady dutifully did one cold night. His roommates saw Brady's rage, something he never outgrew. He once stomped the floor so hard that the game cartridge popped out of the console. He threw the controller at the wall, the second known home that he dented during video game meltdowns. Their collective diet consisted of pizza, soda, beer, and hot wings. Their grooming consisted of Brady shaving Nugent's back and Nugent cutting Brady's hair. Their wardrobe centered around a shirt they liked from Men's Wearhouse, bought in every available color.

Brady pushed both men to be better players, though still with a fraction of the intensity with which he pushed himself. Brady was at the stadium by 6 a.m. most mornings to lift weights, an hour earlier than most players. He watched film, studied, practiced, threw extra passes, went home around 7 p.m.—his roommates often saw him carrying his dinner downstairs to the TV room to watch more film and sometimes do shirtless yoga, which Nugent once photographed and shared with teammates at the stadium—and then returned to the office at 9:30 at night for more work. It was peaceful, being in a mostly empty and dark facility, pursuing his dream in anonymity, at the beginning of something only he felt was special.

Brady's work ethic was so impressive that it became a security issue. The stadium guards weren't supposed to allow players into the office so late at night. One guard asked Pioli for advice, and Pioli didn't believe a player was in the facility at that hour. For two straight weeks, Pioli stopped by to see if Brady was actually working. Brady was not only working, he was doing so quietly, watching film away from the coaches' offices, choosing the visitors' locker room instead, not wanting to show off or be noticed. One Friday night, Pioli saw the bubble lights on at the team's indoor practice facility, and Brady's yellow Jeep parked outside. He entered to see Brady alone, with a boom box playing and a pile of footballs before him. Brady wore elastic bands around his ankles and dropped back and threw to nets scattered on the field, trying to improve his footwork and quickness. Pioli was floored. Brady was embarrassed to be spotted in the facility on a Friday night in the off-season. "Babe," he told Pioli—like his father, Brady called everyone "babe"—"please don't tell anyone you saw me here."

One evening, Brady was working late and holding a pizza, when he saw the team's owner.

"Hey, Mr. Kraft," Brady said.

"Hey . . . Kyle," Kraft said.

No—this was Tom. There was, in fact, a Kyle Brady in the league at the time, playing tight end for the Jacksonville Jaguars. But whatever. He wasn't about to correct the owner.

"You're the quarterback," Kraft said. "I've seen you play. You're doing a good job."

"I just wanted to tell you, it's one of the best decisions you ever made, picking me."

IF YOU WANTED TO KNOW how powerful Drew Bledsoe was, all you had to do was notice the bathroom breaks during quarterback meetings. Dick Rehbein, the position coach, would be trying to make an important point, but if Bledsoe had to hit the head, the room paused until he returned. Brady had never seen anything like that, and if he ever became the starter—no, *when* he became the starter, he always said—he wouldn't be the type of quarterback around whom the room revolved.

An astute observer of situation and context, Brady sensed a quiet divide between how the coaches felt about Bledsoe and how Robert Kraft did. Kraft, like most NFL team owners and their franchise quarterbacks, spoke of Bledsoe in language usually reserved for family members. "Like a son," he'd say. He would later deploy the same term for Brady. Who could blame him? Bledsoe had been drafted with the first-overall pick in 1993 after a stellar college career at Washington State University, a quarterback out of central casting, like a version of Drew Henson who realized his innate talent. He was tall and strong and handsome and charismatic, leading the Patriots to the Super Bowl in his fourth year and playing himself in *Jerry Maguire*. Brady watched Bledsoe injure his thumb in a late-season loss to the Buffalo Bills in 2000 and play the rest of the year—"Nobody I've seen that's ever been tougher than him," Brady said.

Like everyone else, Bledsoe underestimated Brady's drive, viewing him as a nice guy but a non-threat. He hosted Brady for dinner every few weeks. Bledsoe joked that his wife, Maura, liked having Brady over because she thought he was cute. But Brady, for his part, saw Bledsoe's weaknesses, and how they mirrored his own strengths: in consecutive games in 2000, against the Minnesota Vikings and Miami Dolphins, Bledsoe had a chance to pull out a last-second win, and both times he whiffed. Coaching the Browns, and later, as defensive coordinator for the Jets, Belichick had success against Bledsoe, knowing that he would hold the ball too long, looking for the big play downfield rather than the easy one in front of him, and that he struggled to throw accurately to his left. Privately, Belichick had reservations about Bledsoe's future, many of which would be detailed that autumn in a Peter King article for *Sports Illustrated* titled "What Price Mediocrity?" Bledsoe took his job for granted, and it was an affront to the central tenet of Belichick's ethos. He had learned from his Browns days that few players were truly transcendent, like Lawrence Taylor. And he had been on New York Giants teams that had won championships without a superstar quarterback. During one team meeting in 2000, Belichick showed footage of Bledsoe patting the ball endlessly in the pocket, unable to make a decision, and told the quarterback to "stop jerking off the ball."

Brady, sensing an opening, told family and close friends that he was going to unseat Bledsoe. "You watch," he said.

The coaches watched, and not all were impressed. After practice, there were extended workouts for young players called "opportunity periods." Secondary coach Eric Mangini ran the defense, special-teams coach Brad Seely ran the offense, and they'd bet a dollar on who would win. Mangini fleeced Seely, "not because my guys were doing such a great job covering, but because Tom was throwing the ball in the dirt," he later joked. But even then, Brady stood out. An assistant often ran onto the field to tell him that quarterback meetings were about to begin, and Brady would reply, "One more throw!" If it wasn't perfect, he couldn't leave.

Kraft needed Bledsoe, regardless of Belichick's doubts. He was building a new, modern stadium adjacent to the old, decrepit one, and it was slated to open in 2002. The Patriots had some good players, from Tedy Bruschi to Willie McGinest to Ty Law to kicker Adam Vinatieri—whom Belichick believed was the team's best player—but Bledsoe was the only one famous enough to drive suite sales. In March of 2001, Kraft signed Bledsoe to a 10-year, $103 million contract, a record deal that left Belichick underwhelmed. Kraft boasted that he and Bledsoe had negotiated it by themselves and told reporters that he viewed the quarterback alongside Larry Bird, Bill Russell, Ted Williams, and Bobby Orr in the pantheon of Boston sports legends. It was "an opportunity to sign one of the great Patriots for the rest of his career," and he couldn't say no.

Brady was unfazed and continued to tell teammates, and even offensive coordinator Charlie Weis, that he was going to unseat Bledsoe. Back in June of 2000, not so long after being drafted, Brady was alone in the quarterback room and peeked in Rehbein's notebook, searching for the coach's assessment of him. *Everything he does is slow*, it read. *He needs to do everything quicker.* It was an evaluation of Brady's career to that point, going back to high school. Belichick later said that, based on what the team saw of Brady as a rookie, he shouldn't have been drafted before the sixth round. Brady, though, worked on his speed daily. He saw action in one game as a rookie, picking up garbage time in a November blowout loss to the Detroit Lions, and hit one of three passes for six yards. New England finished 5–11, and the pressure was building on Belichick. By training camp in 2001, Brady recalled, "I was outrunning guys—kind of. I felt more mobile. And I was able to get the ball away in a hurry." Ahead of his second season, Brady shot up to second string. Belichick thought Brady actually outperformed Bledsoe in training camp in 2001, but was wary of playing an inexperienced quarterback. The Patriots lost the season opener to the Cincinnati Bengals. Entering the second game of the season, against the New York Jets—delayed a week after the September 11 attacks—the coaching staff was worried they would be fired at the end of the year. And they were losing patience with Bledsoe, who made a pair of crucial mistakes in the red zone against the Jets, taking a delay-of-game penalty on fourth and goal on one drive and throwing an end-zone interception on another.

And then, on third and ten, with just more than five minutes remaining, Bledsoe fled right out of a crumbling pocket, a routine breakdown that ended up changing American sports. As Bledsoe slanted upfield and toward the sideline, nearing the first-down marker, he saw Jets linebacker Mo Lewis closing fast. Bledsoe faced a decision: go out of bounds or try for the first down. He tried for the first down. But Jets defensive end Shaun Ellis was at his ankles, thwarting his momentum, leaving him standing straight up, an easy target. Lewis leveled Bledsoe high and hard and stood over the quarterback as he lay in a daze. "He got massacred," Brady later said. Bledsoe picked himself up off the ground and went out for one more drive, which ended in a Patriots fumble. When he came to the sideline, he asked Brady, "How do I call the two-minute plays?"

"Drew, are you sure you're all right?" Brady said.

Bledsoe was trying to find his bearings. He asked Brady about the audible system. "How we do call the check-with-me's?" He couldn't remember anything.

"We gotta get him out of the game," Brady told Damon Huard, the third-string quarterback.

"Drew's out, and you're in," Belichick said to Brady.

Trailing 10–3, Brady moved the Patriots into Jets territory before throwing four straight incomplete passes in desperation as the clock ticked down. Brady was livid after the game; he fully expected himself to pull out a win in that situation. Bledsoe was entering the locker room for the team prayer when one of the Patriots doctors grabbed him and said, "Why don't you come with me?" Bledsoe had his pulse taken. His heart rate was accelerating, the opposite of what typically happens after a concussion. His pain had increased. Something was seriously wrong. The Patriots put Bledsoe in an ambulance and it headed for Massachusetts General Hospital. Bledsoe's younger brother, Adam, rode along with him. In the middle of a conversation, Bledsoe passed out. Adam was worried he had died. "I don't care what you do to get us there!" Adam yelled at the driver. Bledsoe woke up hours later with a tube in his chest, hooked up to a machine that pumped blood out of his body, cleaned it, and cycled it back in. He had torn a blood vessel in his chest and was bleeding internally, at the rate of one liter of blood per hour. If Bledsoe had fallen asleep at home, he might not have woken up.

Word spread the next morning that Bledsoe would be out indefinitely. It wasn't how Brady envisioned getting his shot, but this was his chance. Belichick spoke at a team meeting, and then Brady asked if he could take the floor. "Coach, if you don't mind, I'd like to talk to the team."

No, Tom, a few of his friends on the team thought, cringing. *Not a college pep talk.*

"I know I'm not the quarterback you want leading the team this year," Brady said, "but I'm going to do everything in my power to help us win games."

It wasn't the greatest speech in sports history. But something funny happened: the Patriots blew out the Indianapolis Colts in Brady's first start.

TWO WEEKS LATER, Brady was in his third start, against Mike Riley's San Diego Chargers, entering the huddle with his first fan's team up seven. On third and ten with 1:24 left, Brady lined up in the shotgun. A rusher closed in from his back side and reached around Brady, swiping at the ball and hitting the quarterback's elbow. Brady drifted up the pocket and away from him, eyes focused downfield, and lofted a pass over the middle to receiver Troy Brown, fitting it between three defenders for 16 yards. It was a first down, and it was the first glimpse of an essential quality for quarterbacks: magic. Brady could not only deliver in clutch situations, but he had that sixth sense that told him when and how to dance away from the rush. It was a quality Joe Montana had, and that Drew Bledsoe did not.

With 40 seconds left, Brady faked a run left and rolled right. Tight end Jermaine Wiggins had slipped free, and Brady dropped a pass over two defensive backs for a game-tying touchdown.

The Chargers went three and out to start overtime. Brady took over. On first down, the Chargers crowded the line of scrimmage, showing a blitz up the middle. Charlie Weis had anticipated this particular blitz. On each snap, Brady had two plays to choose from, then a separate set of audibles. Weis spent all week preparing Brady to recognize this look and to exploit it by checking to a deep throw. From the sideline, Weis saw the Chargers preparing that specific blitz and thought there was "no chance in hell" that Brady would recognize it, in his third game, after already playing 60 minutes of football that day. But Brady saw it. He switched to a protection scheme called "81 Max" and, with three Chargers in his face, threw down the sideline to receiver David Patten, who likely would have caught the ball had he not been interfered with by cornerback Alex Molden. It was a 37-yard penalty.

Riley was dispirited and out of answers against a force only he had seen coming. Two plays later, on third and five, the Chargers again blitzed Brady and again reached him, sandwiching him in the pocket, low from behind and high from the front. But before he was brought down, he managed to send a perfect pass to running back Kevin Faulk, who had flared out of the backfield. Faulk ran for nine yards and a first down, putting the Patriots in field goal range. Adam Vinatieri eventually kicked the game-winning field goal from 44 yards. It was not only a Patriots win; it was a Brady win. He had hit 33 of 54 passes for 364 yards and two touchdowns. Riley walked off the field in what would be his last season as an NFL head coach, wondering what might have been, how his life—many lives—would have gone if he could have collected his prize. The Patriots, though: they had a feeling they had won the lottery. After the game, Belichick told the press, "I can't say enough about Tom Brady." That night, Weis told his wife, Maura, "We got something special here." Years later, as a former coach and occasional corporate speaker, Eric Mangini showed video of three plays from the Chargers game—a defensive stop on third and one, a long punt return by Troy Brown, and the Brady touchdown pass—and referred to them as "the start of our avalanche."

Brady stood in front of the Boston press after the win, much of which had written off the season when Bledsoe got hurt, and said with a goofy grin:

"Never a doubt, huh? Never a doubt."

A FEW WEEKS LATER, I found myself northbound on I-95, from New York to Foxborough, to write about Tom Brady and Bill Belichick. Drew Bledsoe was inching closer to being fully recovered from his injury, but the Patriots were winning more often than not without him. After defeating the Chargers, New England beat the Colts for the second time in four weeks, on the strength of three one-play drives that resulted in touchdowns. "I can't remember a game like that," Weis would recall. Brady had mostly played well for a virtual rookie, although he had two horrible outings, one in the blowout loss to the Dolphins—after which Belichick dug a hole and buried the game ball on the Patriots' practice field, with Brady then stomping on the dirt—and another in a bad loss at Denver, when he threw a dreadful four interceptions in the second half.

A collision was coming: Bledsoe expected his job back, and Brady had no intention of returning it.

Brady had called me from a Massachusetts area code—508—and told me to meet him near the team store at the stadium. It was dark and cold. I parked in front of what seemed to be the main entrance. The headlights of a yellow Jeep emerged in the night, and I saw a smiling face behind the wheel and under a baseball hat, a hand waving. He spoke like an adult, but looked like a college student: gray hoodie and a backpack heavy with beer cans. A few days earlier, Michigan had lost as time expired to Michigan State. He now owed all of his Spartan teammates the payout from a lost bet. We walked inside the stadium, through the team store, and pulled up at a small table near a big glass window. He seemed surprised and grateful that someone would travel to interview him in person rather than by phone.

"You drove all the way up from New York just for this?" he said.

Brady and I had graduated high school and college the same year. We were both getting our career breaks at the same time. It was a slight bond. He asked what it was like to be in New York City on 9/11. But he soon moved on to football—he always moved on to football—and said something unforgettable:

"Football's always come very easy to me."

It was not the remark of a typical sixth-round pick. It was the remark of a gifted athlete—or, more precisely, of an athlete confident in his gifts. Over dinner one night at Abe & Louie's steakhouse in the Back Bay, he had told teammates that Bledsoe was not "getting his fucking job back," startling some who witnessed it. Brady was cocky as hell, but he had a way of making cockiness endearing. He knew how thin the line was for him, between wearing a helmet or a headset, and he simply refused to fail.

DREW BLEDSOE BELIEVED that Tom Brady was talented, in a supporting-actor way. Yet, after his injury, it was Bledsoe's job to serve as a resource and a support system for Brady, and he did so almost from the moment he woke up in the hospital. Against the Atlanta Falcons, in Brady's sixth career start, Bledsoe advised the rookie to target a cornerback named Ray Buchanan with both deep routes and comebacks, and

Brady burned Buchanan five times. Brady and Bledsoe pranked each other, a war that had begun in 2000, when Brady locked Bledsoe's shoulder pads in his car and swiped the keys. Bledsoe responded by stacking the vents of Brady's car with confetti and glitter, and then turning the air conditioning to full blast. Bledsoe had also sprinkled permanent powdered dye into Brady's practice socks, leaving his feet purple for three weeks.

But Bledsoe wanted his job back, the only job he had ever known: starting quarterback for the New England Patriots. Brady was young, but he understood the position he was in: if he returned to the bench now, he might never see the field again. That's how he had conditioned himself, how he had been conditioned at Michigan.

A few weeks later, before the 5–4 Patriots hosted the St. Louis Rams, who were then the class of the NFL, Patriots doctors cleared Bledsoe to play. He and Brady split practice snaps that week. New England lost, 24–17, but scored only 10 points on offense; one of the Patriots' touchdowns was a defensive score. Belichick believed he had coached poorly, not only by failing to design a defense to slow the Rams attack, but also by splitting reps between the quarterbacks, leaving Brady out of rhythm. The team was at a critical juncture, both in the season and in Bill Belichick's career. The Patriots were 5–5 with six games left. Belichick couldn't afford a second-straight losing season. The city of Boston was split—Bledsoe or Brady?—and television crews were polling fans at local pubs. Belichick, though, felt it was an easy call. Despite Brady's rough moments, he did what the coaches asked him to do. He was 5–3 as a starter. Three of the wins were blowouts. His completion rate, 64 percent, was higher than Bledsoe had reached in his entire career.

Belichick pulled Bledsoe aside, with the lack of affect he was already known for within the league, and for which he would become famous during the Patriots' rise. "Hey," he said, "we decided to go with Tom."

Bledsoe was furious. He thought Belichick had lied to him by promising him a chance to compete. Bledsoe barely masked his contempt when approached by reporters at his locker, deflecting questions before saying, "I look forward for the chance to compete for *my* job." It was the exact kind of entitlement that Belichick despised. That night, Bledsoe's wife suggested that they leave town for good. Bledsoe complained directly to Kraft, who felt the decision was unfair on a "human basis," given that Bledsoe had nearly died playing for a franchise that he had carried for almost a decade. Kraft knew he could pull rank, but although "emotionally it was very difficult," he decided to trust his coach.

Patriots staff thought Belichick had not only made the right call, but had also shown leadership growth in how he handled it. In Cleveland, when Belichick cut beloved quarterback Bernie Kosar during the 1993 season, he was brutally honest to the press, saying that the decision came down to "the diminishing of his physical skills." It caused an uproar and cast Belichick as cruel, kicking a local icon at his lowest point. He was determined not to repeat mistakes, and so with Bledsoe, Belichick refrained from publicly criticizing the quarterback's skill set, framing the decision not as a referendum on the franchise's most famous player, but rather as what was best for the team. "T-E-A-M as in team," he told reporters.

A controversial decision became less so within days. Brady rebounded from the Rams loss with the best game of his young career the next week, against the New Orleans Saints, needing only 19 completions to throw four touchdowns in the rain, a performance that Belichick would remember decades later as a "turning point in that season and ultimately in the evolution of Tom's great career." The Patriots won their final six regular-season games, finishing 11–5 and earning a first-round bye in the playoffs. Late in the regular season, I stood with Belichick in a hallway at the stadium. We were discussing Brady, and what made him unique, and Belichick started to do a little three-step drop, holding an invisible ball to his chest. "I'll get mad at him and say, 'Why did you do that?'" He paused. "And he'll say, 'Well, I saw the corner here. I saw the linebacker there. It looked like the receiver slipped a bit on his cut, and I didn't want to throw it to him. I had a guy in my face, so I came back late and tried to throw it in the flat. I should have thrown it away.'"

But then, Belichick said, "I go and look at the tape, and I see all that's happening, just as he sees it."

What seemed like a simple exercise in explaining the game to a novice was in retrospect a significant revelation. Until 2001, Brady's opponent was not the other team, but conventional wisdom. Lloyd Carr, Bobby Beathard, every other NFL team—none could see Brady's talent because they couldn't see past what they had been told to believe about what makes a great quarterback. Brady could overcome a lot, but that was too much. That is, until he found Bill Belichick, who had prepared for this moment his entire life, who not only had spent his career to that point opposed to lazy football thinking, but had been a victim of it himself.

4

I WON'T
SCREW UP
AGAIN

O N THE THIRD FLOOR OF A BUILDING AT THE UNITED
States Naval Academy, there is a plaque that reads BELICHICK
COLLECTION. Next to it is a library of more than 400 football books, some dating back to the 1890s, behind locked glass cases.
The cases were built and stocked in 2006, long after Bill Belichick's legacy was secure. Belichick did not attend Navy, but his father, Steve, was
a football coach and scout at the school for 33 years. No other coach in
football history could have ever compiled such a library, because there
was nobody like Steve Belichick, a legend in football circles and a collec-
tor of books on the inner workings of the game. From 1938 until 1940,
he was a running back at Western Reserve University in Cleveland—
now part of Case Western—and in 1941, he played for the Detroit Lions,
leading the team with 4.2 yards per carry. After fighting in the Second
World War, Steve decided to be a coach. He worked at Hiram College in
eastern Ohio, where he met Jeannette Ruth Munn, who taught Spanish
and French. Her friends told her not to marry a football coach, but she
did anyway, in August of 1950. Steve's career took them to Vanderbilt—
where, on April 16, 1952, he and Jeannette's first child, William Stephen
Belichick, was born—then North Carolina, and eventually the Naval
Academy.

In 1962, Steve authored his own book: *Football Scouting Methods*,
which was dictated by Steve and written by Jeannette. It was a dry offering that became a bible of sorts for coaches, including his son. It taught
you, primarily, how to exploit weaknesses in your opponents. Bill Beli-

chick's approach to football involved developing winning game plans, but also extended to a deep and ruthless understanding of the human condition. He knew the sport would reveal how the opposing team, and particularly the opposing coach and quarterback, reacted under acute stress. Belichick understood that if he played it right, at some point those other men would revert to their most essential and predictable selves. He compiled comprehensive files on most coaches in the league over the years—detailed histories not only of their schemes, but their personalities, their tendencies, what they were about and why. During a game, while most head coaches stared at a play sheet, Belichick navigated the sideline until he had an unobstructed view of his counterpart, to see how he carried himself in the most critical moments, as though waiting for his opponent to fall into a well-laid trap.

IT'S NOT OFTEN THAT you can point to the exact moment when one man broke another, but it happened just after noon on Monday, January 28, 2002, as Bill Belichick flew to New Orleans to face the St. Louis Rams in Super Bowl XXXVI. He spent the flight preparing for the game. The Patriots were the surprise story of the NFL, coming off a 5–11 season in 2000 and an 0–2 start in 2001, losing their signature player to a near-fatal injury, and reaching the Super Bowl with a little-known and little-regarded second-year quarterback. The Rams were on the verge of a dynasty. They arrived in New Orleans as two-touchdown favorites. They were led by Mike Martz, a brilliant football mind who had helped make the Rams' offense the most potent in NFL history. Everyone called them "The Greatest Show on Turf"—including themselves. For three straight years, the Associated Press MVP had come out of the Rams' offensive huddle: quarterback Kurt Warner in 1999, running back Marshall Faulk in 2000, and Warner again in 2001. Martz had been the Rams' offensive coordinator in 1999, when they won the Super Bowl. He was now the head coach, and the Super Bowl, to be played in the Louisiana Superdome, seemed as though it would be a coronation ceremony for his team.

Martz had earned the respect of many of his peers, including Belichick, because he had won not only in his own style but also by turning an afterthought of a quarterback into a future Hall of Fame inductee.

It's one thing to inherit Joe Montana and Steve Young, as George Seifert did in San Francisco; it's another to *find* Montana and Young, as Bill Walsh had done. But Martz had not just found Warner, he had *invented* him. On Martz's first day with the Rams, Warner came to his office and helped him unpack his boxes. Warner had a rare ability in this task, having worked at a grocery store to make ends meet before his NFL career got going. But Martz had no idea that Warner was the team's third-string quarterback; Warner was so skinny and nondescript that Martz thought he was a Rams staffer. In 1999, Warner's first season as a starter—after a career in the Arena Football League and NFL Europe, and after starter Trent Green went down to an injury in the preseason—he took a team that had gone 4–12 the previous season and threw 41 touchdown passes on the way to a 13–3 record, leading the Rams to a last-minute Super Bowl win over the Titans. He was named the league and Super Bowl MVP and became a civic treasure in St. Louis. What the Rams and Warner had accomplished was so shocking and unprecedented that, when the Patriots pulled off a turnaround with a backup quarterback of their own in 2001 and met them in the Super Bowl, it seemed less an exception than a sign of a new normal in professional football, where salary-cap parity, coupled with luck under center, could allow any team to win it all in any given year.

Neither Belichick nor Martz looked the part. Both resembled professors, brainy and studious, both hailing from unlikely coaching launching points: Belichick from Wesleyan University in Middletown, Connecticut, and Martz from Fresno State. Both men were war aficionados. Martz was a student of the Civil War, interested in how Grant and Sherman worked together. Belichick amassed battlefield strategies from books that included *The Art of War*. The walls of the Patriots' facility were adorned mostly with photos from big wins rather than cliché motivational phrases, but the prophecy from the Chinese general Sun Tzu from the fifth century BC—"Every Battle Is Won Before It Is Ever Fought"—was one of the few signs in the locker room, alongside a blunter Belichickism: "Penalties Lose Games."

Immortality was close for Martz. A Super Bowl win over the Patriots would elevate him into the pantheon of elite football minds. Martz respected Belichick in return, believing New England was the toughest team St. Louis had faced all year. But that November game had been in Foxborough, in cold air and on grass. The season's final game was on artificial turf, where fast players become faster, where the Rams could gain chunks of yards in a hurry and force the Patriots into confusion and doubt. He considered opening with a two-minute offense, knowing that New England couldn't stop them, but "I just decided not to do it," he later said. Still, the night before the game, Martz told the already-immortal broadcaster John Madden that he was going to "blow the roof off this stadium with this offense," unaware that Belichick was already in his head.

ON THE FLIGHT TO New Orleans, Belichick sat with Ernie Adams, one of his best friends. Smart and idiosyncratic and truly obsessed with pro football, a man with a vague and singular title—director of football research—Adams broke down Martz's offense to its essence, which is to say, he broke down Martz to *his* essence. It wasn't complicated. Cut through all the formations, all the dressings and trappings and shifting and motions, and Martz's offense could be boiled down to a handful of simple passing concepts. To say this wasn't to insult Martz. The core simplicity of his offense was what made Martz so proud of it, and Belichick brought the same theory and pride to his defense. As the defensive coordinator with the New York Giants from 1985 to 1990, when he won two Super Bowls under Bill Parcells, Belichick always carried a little note card on game day, not the menu-like trifold playsheet favored by so many of his peers. His rationale was straightforward: if players needed to memorize a million plays, they would think on the field, not react. A football play lasted four seconds. Any hesitation, and you're dead. Belichick called the same defense over and over and asked his players to adjust off it.

Against the Rams, Belichick returned to the premise of a simple and devastating game plan he had run 11 years earlier. Before Super Bowl XXV, Belichick believed the Buffalo Bills would come out throwing—passing teams pass in big games—and so he unveiled a defense that featured only two linemen, with extra linebackers and defensive backs, daring them to run, knowing they wouldn't do it. It worked, and now he revived many of the same tenets—to concede the run, to confuse the quarterback—but with a twist: he was going to key on Marshall Faulk, not Kurt Warner. More precisely, he was going to confuse Warner by all but erasing Faulk from the game, forcing the quarterback to go to his second and third options on every play. In the November loss to St. Louis, New England had blitzed Warner 43 times—mostly a zone-blitz pressure package named "Heavy Cover 8" in Patriots playbook terminology—believing that harassing the quarterback was the key to disrupting the Rams. The strategy played right to Warner's strengths, allowing him to read and throw quickly. Belichick wouldn't make the same mistake twice. New England would hit Faulk on every play, whether he had the ball or not. "Butch the back," Belichick called it. But most of all, Belichick's Patriots would do exactly what Belichick's Giants defense did against the Bills: concede the run, knowing that Martz was eager to showcase his dazzling passing game on the world's biggest stage. In effect, Belichick was using Martz's ego against him.

Belichick was doing what he did best, and doing it better than anyone else ever had, even if few knew it at the time: the son of a pair of teachers, he was cutting through the clutter and presenting football in simple, devastating terms. It was striking for players and coaches to witness. At a fundamental level, Belichick saw the game not just as a series of chess moves and gambits, but as a psychological exercise. For most of his adult life, he had been cast as a tactician, but not a leader, as lacking an essential human touch. And, at times, even he believed a little too much that winning would erase his real or perceived flaws. But here he was, five days before the Super Bowl, standing in front of his team and convincing a group of men that they could pull off the biggest upset since Joe Namath's New York Jets beat the Baltimore Colts in 1969, not merely through tactics, but by winning the psychological battle. All of them had to do it together, starting with him. He confessed that he'd blown it in November with a faulty game plan.

This, he said, would be different. "I'm not going to screw up again."

In 27 years as a coach in the NFL, Belichick had not screwed up often. He was a man who went through each day expecting a lot of himself, and he usually delivered. Decades later, his success in New England had allowed him and some observers to rewrite his career, as if his football life had been a slow and steady and inevitable march toward becoming the game's greatest coach: beginning with the Baltimore Colts in 1975 for $25 a week, continuing in Detroit, then Denver, then the Giants—where he won two Super Bowls—then Cleveland, New England, the Jets, and now back to New England. Belichick's career was founded on skill and hard work, but also on the forces of luck and randomness that he sought to mitigate in each of his beautiful game plans. If not for a freak injury that derailed the career of a promising young running back whom Belichick never coached, there was a good chance his Patriots career wouldn't have happened at all.

5

HANG TIGHT

R OBERT EDWARDS LAY ON A HAWAII BEACH, LOOKING at his left knee. It was disfigured and misshapen and hanging by the skin. People around him called for medical help. His first trip to the Pro Bowl wasn't supposed to end this way. Edwards had been one of New England's two first-round draft picks in 1998, out of the University of Georgia, and he had delivered on the investment, gaining 1,507 total yards and scoring 13 touchdowns in his rookie season. He helped the Patriots make the playoffs, where they lost to Jacksonville, and now was reaping the rewards, taking part in a rookie flag football game that was part of the weeklong Pro Bowl boondoggle. Edwards had jumped to defend a pass and landed awkwardly and at the bottom of a heap, and when the other players were pulled off him, he felt a sharp and hot pain. Players came and went, huddled over him, glancing at his leg, turning away. There were no doctors on site, as nobody had gotten hurt playing beach flag football at these events before. Half an hour passed. Finally, an emergency unit showed up. Edwards had torn all three tendons and dislocated his knee so severely, it had severed an artery. If he had arrived at the hospital ten minutes later, his leg likely would have required amputation.

Forget football—Edwards just hoped to walk again. He flew from Hawaii to Massachusetts General Hospital, where a familiar face soon entered his hospital room.

"Hey, Coach," Edwards said.

"Coach" was what some players called Robert Kraft, the owner of the New England Patriots. He looked like a salesman, short and stocky, and wore a suit so often—usually a three-piece over his signature white-collared blue dress shirt—that he could appear uncomfortable in anything else. He could be kind and idealistic, sentimental and forgiving, but also ruthless and petty. A jagged front tooth at the center of his smile gave him a brawler's edge, and he spoke deliberately, a lifelong boss who provided instruction only once. He was a local kid from Fuller Street in Brookline, outside of Boston; Brookline High class of 1959 and Harvard Business School class of 1965; a better athlete than a glance revealed, who played running back as an undergrad at Columbia University and now tennis on weekends. He didn't own a car until he was 25 years old. He met Myra Hiatt when she was a sophomore at Brandeis University, and after their first date, she proposed. By 1968, he had started his first packaging operation and eventually turned his father-in-law's paper products company into a packaging empire.

Kraft grew up a New York Giants fan, but fell in love with the Patriots in the early 1970s, and one night in 1971, he strode into a room at his Newton home with a leather briefcase, dialed the locks, and showed his sons the Boston Patriots season tickets he had just purchased: section 217, row 23, seats 1–6. The Patriots were horrible, as was their stadium, and the Krafts would sometimes travel to road games to get a taste of a better NFL experience, but he often wondered what it would be like to own the team. Kraft became renowned in Boston for his wealth and philanthropy and shrewdness and, more than anything, winning in business. If you disliked or distrusted him, you still wanted in on whatever he was building or buying. He knew how to hire well and how to make money.

Kraft eventually changed Boston sports forever, but in 1999, as he sat in Edwards's hospital room, he was still relatively new in the league, having entered under strange circumstances and made powerful enemies in a short time. In 1994, Patriots owner James Orthwein was trying to unload the team. No NFL franchise generated less revenue than New England. NFL commissioner Paul Tagliabue had deemed New England's stadium—of which Kraft owned half, by that point—"unacceptable." NFL teams are usually either sold in a bidding war or passed down within a family, but because Kraft partially owned the stadium, had a binding lease with the team until 2001, and controlled many revenue streams on game day, he had rare leverage. He was the landlord. It was as if he owned the owner. Kraft eventually bought the team for approximately $173 million. He and his oldest son, Jonathan, closed the deal in a St. Louis conference room and flew to Boston to deliver the ominous news to Myra that they had paid a record amount for a sports franchise. Even the flight home was a circus. On board, they slipped some cash to passengers so that they could sit next to each other. That night, Robert was explaining the price tag to Myra when the phone rang. A lawyer was on the other end, offering three times what Kraft had paid for the stadium six years earlier, part of a grand plan to move the team to St. Louis.

When Kraft hung up, Myra said, "You're going to take it, right?"

Robert remembered the heartbreak of being a fan of the Boston Braves when they moved to Milwaukee in 1953. A professional sports team mattered to a community. Kraft told Myra that no, he would decline the offer, and as Jonathan later recalled for associates, she replied, "Are you out of your fucking mind?"

A seminal moment in Kraft's life was extraordinarily stressful. He had overextended himself and needed to build a new stadium on top of the cost of the team, with no public money. He threatened to move the team to Hartford, earning a backlash from fans. He also inherited Bill Parcells as his head coach, and the two men immediately rubbed each other the wrong way. Parcells was arrogant and dismissive and had no patience for his new boss, and even less patience for Jonathan, whom Robert had installed as team vice president. Parcells called Jonathan "Harvard Boy," because he had attended Harvard Business School. Jonathan called Parcells "Fatty" behind his back, and later said that he "hated Parcells with a passion." Kraft wanted to learn the business of football and wanted the head coach to report to ownership; he and his son would make organizational decisions. Parcells found that structure untenable.

By 1996, the relationship between Kraft and Parcells was so toxic that Belichick, at the time a Patriots assistant, became a middleman of sorts. Parcells and Belichick had worked together for most of the 1980s in New York, a complicated mentorship and partnership that produced two Super Bowl wins. Parcells had hired him as assistant head coach and secondary coach after Belichick had been fired as head coach of the Browns for reasons both justifiable and extraordinary. He'd had one winning season in five years that were otherwise marked by avoidable public relations blunders. But Belichick had also been the coach amid a fracturing crisis when owner Art Modell announced, in the middle of the 1995 season, that the team would move to Baltimore. In a league where perception is reality, Belichick's reputation was destroyed. He was viewed as a brilliant defensive mind who lacked the vision and personality to be a head coach. But while Kraft found Parcells secretive and defensive, he found Belichick to be open and instructive, a willing teacher who could explain complex theories in simple terms.

If Kraft's relationship with Belichick brought out the owner's best qualities, his relationship with Parcells revealed his worst. The two men were not only at war, they were fighting in the newspapers. Both regularly confided in Will McDonough, the storied *Boston Globe* NFL reporter, until the writer believed Kraft had lied to him over one of the team's draft picks and refused to talk to him for three months. The Patriots reached the Super Bowl in 1996, but rather than burying the problems until after the game, both men put their issues on the biggest stage in sports. On the Monday before the Super Bowl, McDonough published a story headlined "Parcells to Leave," despite his being under contract with New England, citing his dysfunctional relationship with Kraft as the reason. Kraft responded not by ignoring the story, but by upping the ante, stating that Parcells wouldn't leave without New England receiving draft picks as compensation. "He's not as smart as he thinks," Kraft told a *New York Times* reporter—a brazen comment, albeit off the record, with a world championship at stake.

Days after New England lost to the Packers, Parcells essentially accepted a job to be the head coach of the New York Jets—while still under contract with New England. The move blew Kraft's mind. "How does he go accept another job somewhere?" he later said. He suspected the league office had tacitly encouraged Parcells, figuring that having the coach back in New York was good for business. Kraft lost at a game he didn't know existed.

Kraft was in need of a coach. Belichick wanted the job, but Kraft felt so burned by Parcells that he couldn't hire anyone close to him. Kraft took Bill and his wife, Debby, to dinner to explain that he was collateral damage. "I just needed to clean the house of the whole Parcells era," Kraft would put it. Belichick followed Parcells to the Jets as assistant head coach, and actually served as interim head coach for a week while draft compensation for the Patriots, for Parcells's departure, was being worked out. When Parcells was hired, Belichick joked that he was stepping down as head coach with "an undefeated record, untied and unscored upon." Kraft hired Pete Carroll, a promising defensive mind who was as New Agey as Parcells was authoritarian. After his war with Parcells, Kraft wanted everything siloed, limiting Carroll's scope and influence. Carroll would coach, but not pick players or run the building. Kraft elevated Bobby Grier to oversee player personnel and set himself up as the tiebreaker. The approach was destined to fail. Kraft later faulted himself for hampering his new coach. Still, Carroll reached the playoffs his first two years. And then his star rookie running back blew out his knee.

VISITING EDWARDS IN the hospital, Kraft was devastated. "I look forward to you getting back on the field," he said, sitting next to the player. "If anyone can do it, you can."

But Kraft knew that Edwards might be done with football, a first-round pick with a career ending after a single season. Without Edwards, the Patriots finished 8–8 in 1999. Kraft thought the team had deteriorated and decided to fire Carroll and make a run at Belichick. "He grew," he later said, "and I grew." Parcells was preparing to coach the Jets' 1999 season finale against the Seattle Seahawks when he got word from Will McDonough that Kraft wanted to hire Belichick, pay him around $2 million annually, and give him total authority over football operations. No way was Parcells going to let that happen. The previous off-season, he and Jets owner Leon Hess had redone Belichick's contract, both as a reward for good work and as an insurance policy: three years, $4.2 million overall, with a trigger that elevated Belichick to head coach if Parcells were to step down.

And Parcells was burned out. On the Saturday before the Seahawks game, with the Jets already eliminated from the playoffs, he told Belichick that he was "99 percent" sure he would walk away after the season.

This was classic Parcells, down to the use of a percentage. Belichick had heard it all before, going back to 1987 with the Giants, when Parcells promised he would retire after one more year, that he couldn't take the stress anymore. He was a legendary equivocator, always talking in ridiculously precise probabilities: 99 percent, 83 percent, 77 percent, 80 percent, back to 99 again. It was a running joke among his staff. But they understood Parcells would never actually, fully retire, at least not for a long while. He'd walked away from football once, in 1991, not due to burnout but due to health concerns. He was back two years later. Like many driven people, he was happiest when he was unhappy.

Belichick was generally distrustful, choosing to keep emotions and information to himself. He had concerns, but chose to not question Parcells. "I've been waiting for this," he told his boss.

Two nights later, Kraft fired Carroll. On the evening of January 2, 2000, Jonathan faxed the Jets a request to interview Belichick. The next morning, at the Jets' headquarters in Hempstead, New York, Scott Pioli, the director of pro personnel who was married to Parcells's daughter Dallas, handed the fax to Parcells, who crumpled it up and threw it on the floor. He stormed down the hall to a staff meeting. Parcells informed everyone he was stepping down, elevating Belichick to head coach, but would remain with the team in a vague executive role. He then exited the room, leaving Belichick to sort out the mess.

"I'm hearing it for the first time, just like you," he told the coaches, as if his conversation with Parcells just a few days before had never happened.

The Patriots never got an official response to their fax. The answer came in the form of breaking news of the Jets' transition at the top. "They played it that they never got it," Kraft said.

Nothing about it was cute to Belichick, who was desperate to explore the Patriots opening. The Jets head coaching job was less appealing than it had been a year earlier, when Belichick had agreed to the succession plan. For one thing, the Jets now had no owner. Hess had died the previous year. Belichick didn't know either of the two billionaires bidding for the Jets—cable magnate James Dolan and pharmaceutical heir Woody Johnson—but he would later say he "had issues" with both men. Stability mattered—Belichick had learned that the hard way in Cleveland. Each morning, Art Modell would call Belichick and ask him random football questions. Belichick realized that Modell used Tony Grossi's column in the *Cleveland Plain Dealer* as the basis for them. "If Grossi wrote that we weren't throwing a lot of screen passes, Art would call late morning and ask, 'Why aren't we throwing more screen passes?'" Belichick later told a friend.

Belichick despised Modell personally, often saying that the owner didn't know a "football from a golf ball," but what angered him more was that the owner had moved the team. Belichick knew that all NFL owners, from Jerry Jones of the Dallas Cowboys to Al Davis of the Raiders, were a little crazy. You can become a millionaire with your integrity intact, but you can't become a billionaire without kneecapping someone along the way. But he simply refused to work for another Modell.

And then there was the matter of Parcells. They had worked together 14 of the previous 19 years—Big Bill and Little Bill, one the master motivator, the other a master tactician. Everyone assumed they were friends, but while they shared a sort of militant love for each other, they weren't close. They were "both assholes," as Belichick later said, but different kinds of assholes. Parcells was cunning, while Belichick was ruthless. They had generally worked well together, especially in big games, two brilliant football minds singularly focused on winning. Parcells saw the big picture with great clarity; Belichick loved to lose himself in the tiny details of a game plan. When Belichick was in Cleveland and Parcells was on a break from coaching, they spoke almost weekly. But together again on the Jets, the relationship had soured. Parcells openly mocked Belichick, both in front of the players and coaches. During one game, Belichick called a blitz that Parcells hated. When the blitz worked, Parcells blurted into the headset, "Yeah, you're a genius, everybody knows it, a goddamn genius, but that's why you failed as a head coach—that's why you'll never be a head coach. Some genius."

Belichick was at a crossroads. No matter who was to blame for the Cleveland mess, he knew that his next shot at being a head coach would be his last one. He wanted to win or lose on his own terms. He had believed he would get another chance after the Browns fired him, but years had passed and all of these clowns had been hired around the league while he waited. The day after Parcells resigned and promoted himself to an executive role, Belichick approached him in the coaches' locker room and asked for permission to interview with the Patriots, offering the Jets' ownership situation as his rationale.

He got nowhere. "A deal's a deal," Parcells said. "You want out? You're going to pay. Simple."

Belichick thought that, after all their years together, Parcells owed it to him to let him talk with Kraft. A bad situation was getting worse. Around the office, Belichick seemed calm and in charge, but Parcells could tell he was nervous. During a staff meeting, Parcells noticed Belichick's hands shaking as he spoke. On January 4, 2000, the day Belichick was to be introduced to the press as the Jets' new coach, Frank Ramos, the team's director of public relations, spotted him leaving the building in an overcoat and carrying a briefcase. "There's something up," Ramos thought, suspecting that Belichick had made an off-campus phone call to sort out his options.

Shortly before the 2:30 p.m. introductory press conference, Belichick told Parcells and team president Steve Gutman that he was out. He handed Gutman a piece of paper that read, "Due to the various uncertainties surrounding my position as it relates to the team's new ownership, I have decided to resign as HC of the NYJ." Parcells was disappointed, but, after the fax and Belichick's uncharacteristic nervousness, not surprised. Belichick walked to the auditorium, stopping along the way in the defensive meeting room, where Eric Mangini—then a young assistant and Belichick protégé—was buried in player evaluations.

"Hey," Mangini said. "How are you doing?"

"Fasten your seat belt," Belichick said. "It's about to get bumpy."

Belichick entered the auditorium and proceeded to stun the room. He explained his decision over 50 minutes, taking questions and offering rambling answers, blaming the uncertain ownership situation. Most thought the performance was bizarre; Kraft loved it. Belichick's three-year legacy in green and white was unique: "There he was, the two-time head coach of the New York Jets that never coached a game," Pioli later said with a laugh.

Gutman followed Belichick at the podium. "We should have some feelings of sorrow and regret for him and his family," he said. "He's obviously in some inner turmoil."

But Belichick was as resolute about the decision as he was with any in his life, even if he had no idea how it would end. He spent the next few weeks trying, and failing, to void his Jets contract, first with the league office and then in federal court. By Tuesday, January 25, the Patriots still didn't have a head coach. Kraft was on the verge of turning to Jacksonville Jaguars defensive coordinator Dom Capers instead. But he wanted Belichick, despite warnings from friends around the league who told him about Belichick's communication skills, his low mumble, and that he was an introvert in an extrovert's job. Kraft felt philosophically aligned with Belichick. He was one of the only coaches who understood the salary cap; who had developed his own system of measuring the value of each player, relative to scheme and design; who was, in Kraft's view if in few others', a total head coach, expert in coaching defense, but fluent in offense and special teams and able to teach any position; who, unlike most coaches, begging for expensive superstars, knew that a carefully built team could compete every year. After he was hired, Belichick ended up playing a 3–4 defensive front in his first season, not because it was his long-standing preference, but because most of the league played a 4–3, and so players who fit into a 3–4 were available at a discount. Belichick's football ideology was the absence of an ideology.

At around 5 p.m. on January 25, Parcells called Kraft. It was the first time they had spoken since the coach left New England in 1997.

"Hello, Bob," Parcells said. "This is Darth Vader."

Kraft laughed. Parcells offered an apology—to the extent he was capable of one—for their divorce. Then they cut to business: Parcells was willing to trade the rights to Belichick to the Patriots for draft picks. Kraft offered a third-round pick in 2000 and a fourth-rounder in 2001.

No, Parcells replied. The deal had to include a 2000 first-round pick.

Kraft countered with a second-round pick and a third-rounder in 2001. A year earlier, Mike Holmgren of the Green Bay Packers—who had beaten Kraft's Patriots in the Super Bowl and, at the time, had a reputation far superior to Belichick's—had been traded to the Seattle Seahawks for a second-rounder. No way was Belichick worth a first-rounder. But Parcells held firm. Later that night, Kraft was resigned to hiring Capers, but then he thought about Robert Edwards in the hospital bed. What was the actual value of a first-round pick? If the Patriots could lose one to a knee injury so swiftly and suddenly and without recourse, why not spend it on a head coach? What was riskier?

At 10 p.m., Kraft called Parcells with New England's first-round pick on the table, and proposed as well a swap of late-round picks. "I'm going to make a decision here that I don't want to make, because I want this guy as my head coach."

It was the greatest trade in modern NFL history. At the time, though, it didn't only stun the football world. It stunned Belichick when Parcells informed him of the deal. Parcells permitted Belichick to hire a few Jets staffers who were loyal to him: Mangini, Pioli, offensive coordinator Charlie Weis, and public relations assistant Berj Najarian. Belichick quickly called each of them in turn.

"Hang tight," he said. "Things will work out."

IF THE REALITY OF most new jobs never lives up to expectations, the printer was the first sign for Belichick's staff in New England. Shortly after Belichick arrived, the team's lone printer broke. The coaches requested a new one. Belichick's late arrival in New England meant they were a month behind the rest of the league on scouting and free agency and on assembling a coaching staff. The latter fell into place soon enough: a mix of longtime colleagues from the Parcells days, including Charlie Weis coordinating the offense; a few Pete Carroll holdovers, such as Dante Scarnecchia, coaching the offensive line, and Brad Seely, coaching special teams; and some young guys Belichick could mold, including Mangini coaching the secondary. Scott Pioli was named assistant director of player personnel, below Bobby Grier, a holdover from the previous regime whose time was limited from the moment Belichick was hired. The early days for all were both long and not long enough.

Foxboro Stadium, where they worked, was on its last legs, and the new stadium wasn't due to open for another two years. While football coaches tend to complain about everything, it would have been helpful, in the pre-tablet age, to be able to print documents. A week passed . . .

nothing. Two weeks . . . still nothing. Finally, three weeks later, the coaching staff had a new printer. The whole episode seemed like a power move by management, either resentful of Belichick's authority or too cheap to spring for basic supplies. The latter seemed most likely to the staff. Coaches noticed how Kraft sometimes dropped by the weight room to turn off TVs on dormant ellipticals or flick off the building lights while the team was outside at practice. But still, the printer was a warning: they wondered what authority over football operations Belichick truly had if he didn't have the clout to procure a printer.

There were two predominant themes of Belichick's first year in Foxborough: how much shit he was forced to eat and how little he cared what anyone thought of him. "People weren't exactly welcoming him with open arms," Seely recalled. Staffers used to know when Pete Carroll was coming down the hall for a meeting because they'd hear him dribbling a basketball, the bouncing getting closer and closer, the coach an embodiment of looseness and fun. Belichick was all business. Days started at 4:30 a.m. and continued past midnight. If he came off as an asshole, so be it. If he *was* an asshole, so be it. As an assistant coach, Belichick had been approachable. He would hang around the meeting room, giving advice, telling stories, joining in on bitch sessions about the boss. Once, with the New York Jets, Mangini decided to mess with Belichick by emailing him an audio file. Belichick was a technology novice. When he opened the message, his computer screamed, "I AM WATCHING PORN. I AM WATCHING PORN. I AM . . ." Belichick couldn't figure out how to turn the damn thing off. He banged his keyboard. "I AM WATCHING PORN." It echoed down the hall. "I AM WATCHING PORN." Belichick finally ducked under his desk and unplugged his computer, as Mangini and a few others doubled over.

There were no pranks now that Belichick was in the big office. No shooting the bull. No wasted minutes. He had a gatekeeper in Berj Najarian. One meeting tipped into the next; Belichick would blow by you in the hallway without acknowledging your presence, even if you were Robert Kraft—eyes down, mouth folded into a lipless pout, hair vaguely parted to the side. His face was unwelcoming even when he smiled. He had spent his life with his guard up, a cynic who would find a way to believe only after deciding all the ways his team could lose;

who, more than most coaches, measured not just his performance but his self-worth by wins and losses. His friends would insist that there were two Bills: the stern coach and the joyful guy away from the office who would joke and pop a beer and howl to Bon Jovi. But in truth, the deep and maniacal urge to be great at a game nobody could control overrode all aspects of his life. Parcells had once nicknamed him "Doom," and Romeo Crennel, who had known Belichick for decades and was hired as New England's defensive coordinator in 2001, thought Belichick secretly liked the moniker, because "that way, he didn't have to be nice to anybody."

Belichick had learned along the way—from his dad, from studying Paul Brown and Walsh and Parcells—to separate the professional from the personal, that a coach couldn't be a friend to the players, to be unemotional when it came to decisions about the team. And he had taken that philosophy to an extreme. He taught his assistants what he wanted and the unspoken message was: *Go do it—and don't fuck it up.* The hours were long—preparing for football games, breaking down film, teaching techniques—and he would always drop by your office, waging what felt like psychological warfare. *Why the fuck isn't this player doing what we want? Where are we on this project? Watch all of this prospect's games and tell me what you think by Monday.* But if they could just reach the ultimate destination, well—there was nothing like winning a Super Bowl. Belichick knew that to his core. He had sacrificed everything—family time, a discernable level of happiness and self-care—for this moment, and now he would sacrifice even more.

Upon arriving in New England, Belichick immediately fired the team's strength and conditioning coach, Johnny Parker, a man he had known since the 1980s. New England parted ways with Grier days after the first draft, which yielded a group of mostly forgettable picks, aside from the second of the team's sixth-round picks, the quarterback from Michigan. The 2000 season was a disaster. The Patriots lost all four games during Belichick's first month, failing to score more than 19 points in any of them. After ten games, the Patriots were 2–8. Carroll had been fired for losing that many games over an entire season. When the Patriots' plane landed in Foxborough late on a Sunday night after a horrific 19–11 loss to the Browns in Cleveland—during which the fans with long memories chanted, "Belichick sucks!"—Belichick told his staff to go straight into the office.

"I want to meet right now," he said.

Belichick kept them there all night, replaying the game, picking apart each play. *What are we fucking doing? . . . Jesus Christ . . . Goddammit . . . We're so fucking bad. . . . This play is so fucking stupid.*

The Patriots finished 5–11, the worst record of Kraft's tenure as owner, to that point or since. The coaches knew that another losing season would be their last in Foxborough. In July 2001, each player arrived at training camp to find a black T-shirt with white lettering that read WANTED: WINNERS, and included a dictionary definition. Something felt different. Guys seemed to believe. New England had gone on a free-agent shopping spree, not for superstars but for basement bargains, guys Pioli had studied and scouted during his Jets days: 17 signees in the end, for a total of around $2.5 million in signing bonuses, mostly role players, including Mike Vrabel, Larry Izzo, running back Antowain Smith, and defensive end Anthony Pleasant, who were all promised nothing but the chance to compete for playing time on a team that valued love of football first. No politics, no favoritism, just merit. "We built the team on the middle class," Pioli recalled.

Belichick placed a rusty anchor in the locker room to signify the dropping of the dead weight from the previous season. But then the Patriots lost the regular-season opener against the Cincinnati Bengals. A week later, against the Jets, New England looked lost on offense. Belichick was on the way to his 13th loss in 18 games in New England. Kraft was best known as an owner who had threatened to move the team to Hartford, had run off a future Hall of Fame coach in Bill Parcells, and had traded a first-round pick for Belichick, given him total football authority, and then waded into football decisions anyway.

And then, with 5:11 left in the game, down 10–3, Drew Bledsoe dropped back to pass and scrambled right, aiming for the first-down marker. Tom Brady saw him running and instinctively buckled his chinstrap.

6

HOW DO YOU LIKE THAT?

T HE SNOW WAS ALMOST ROMANTIC, BELICHICK
thought. It had a magical quality, falling bright and heavy and
soft in the darkness. The Patriots were hosting the Oakland
Raiders, closing out Foxboro Stadium on January 19, 2002, in a divisional playoff game. Before Belichick could even think about preparing a
game plan for containing Mike Martz's aerial attack, yet another uncontrollable event would remind the football world of the thin line between
glory and obscurity. In the parking lot, fans huddled around fires in
steel cans and drank cold beer. It wasn't a classic New England snow,
dank and swirling and frigid. It was something else, thick and weirdly
warm. The night before the game, Charlie Weis told the quarterbacks, "I
think it's going to snow." The weather held off until a few hours before
kickoff. Belichick ordered the field tarp removed before it started to fall,
allowing the snow to muck up the field, hoping for a slight edge against
a talented Raiders offense—centered on quarterback Rich Gannon, running back Charlie Garner, and future Hall of Fame receivers Jerry Rice
and Tim Brown—that relied on precision and timing. Belichick's decision was the culmination of a weeklong strategy. After practice each day,
he ordered the field watered, angering Adam Vinatieri. "What the hell?
Why do I have to kick in this garbage?" he asked Brad Seely.

Brady took the field to warm up in a T-shirt, trying to show the world
that this California kid was immune to weather. Before kickoff, in full
uniform, Brady drifted over to Kraft and said, in a high and screeching
pitch, "We're gonna get this one! I promise that!"

It took a while, but with 1:50 left in the game, the Patriots down 13–10 and near midfield, Brady looked as though he might deliver. He had shaken off a rough first half, in which he threw for only 74 yards with an interception. At halftime, down 7–0, Brady had turned to a few receivers and given another earnest but effective speech. "If you guys play the best half of your life, I'm gonna play the best half of my life."

Weis had shifted to a no-huddle offense, forcing the Raiders to limit their looks on defense, and with just under eight minutes remaining, Brady scored from six yards out, punctuating his touchdown with a spike so violent—in the spirit of 49ers legend Tom Rathman, he later said—that Brady spiked himself, the momentum causing him to somersault and splash into the snow in slow motion, like something out of a ski movie. At the Raiders' 42-yard line, Brady called Trips Right Slant 68 D Slant. Every receiver, three to the right and one to the left, was to slice inside. Brady approached the line of scrimmage and saw a gaping hole to his left: All of the coverage had shifted to the three-receiver side of the field, leaving wideout Fred Coleman in man coverage. He thought, *God, how can I* not *throw it?*

It was a trap. Eric Allen, Oakland's star cornerback, had overheard Weis and Brady discussing the play on the sideline. "Throw the slant backside," Weis had said. Defensive coordinator Chuck Bresnahan dialed up a perfect answer: he'd dupe Brady into believing that Coleman was in man coverage, but would then drop a defensive lineman into Brady's throwing lane. At the same time, Bresnahan sent cornerback Charles Woodson blitzing from Brady's right side. Brady would never see him coming. It was a brilliant call that worked perfectly, unusual in such an unpredictable game. Brady cocked to throw left, and defensive end Regan Upshaw drifted into coverage. Brady froze and started to bring the ball to his chest—all the hesitation Woodson needed. "My eyes just get big," Woodson said. He rocked Brady. The ball fell and spun in the snow for what seemed like an eternity until Oakland linebacker Greg Biekert smothered it.

Brady walked off the field with his head down, the name on the back of his jersey pulled down and to the side, a portrait of a broken young man. The 2001 Patriots would go down as a nice turnaround story with a looming quarterback controversy between the franchise player who had almost died and the feisty backup who had lost a narrow playoff game and . . .

Referee Walt Coleman announced that the play was under review. The question was whether Brady fumbled or had somehow thrown an incomplete pass. Because the play occurred with less than two minutes left, the officials could initiate a review; if it had occurred mere seconds earlier, the call on the field would have stood and Belichick couldn't have challenged because he had no time-outs remaining. The review seemed like a formality, but when Belichick looked at the replay and saw Brady's arm slightly moving forward as Woodson arrived, he thought New England might have a chance. Earlier in the season, against the Jets, in the game in which Bledsoe was injured, the Patriots had forced what they thought was a fumble by Jets quarterback Vinny Testaverde, when he had gone through the motion of throwing but pulled in the ball at the last moment when he was hit. The call was overturned and ruled an incomplete pass, on the basis of a rarely invoked statute otherwise known as the tuck rule. Rule 3, Section 22, Article 2, Note 2: "When [a player] is holding the ball to pass it forward, any intentional forward movement of his arm starts a forward pass, even if the player loses possession of the ball as he is attempting to tuck it back toward his body."

Halfway across the country, Mike Pereira, the league's director of officiating, was in his St. Louis hotel room ahead of the next day's Rams–Packers playoff game, about two-thirds of the way through a bottle of cheap red wine, when he saw Brady fumble on his television. Relief washed over him. Perfect! Another playoff game down, no officiating controversies that decided the outcome. Then he saw the replay and thought, *Ohh, nooo.* Two weeks before the playoffs, he had sent a videotape to media members explaining how the tuck rule worked. The rule, Pereira later confessed, "was nonsensical," but it made it easier to review on instant replay. That such a strange bylaw existed in the first place revealed what the NFL had become: overregulated, over-officiated, and corporate, quickly losing the spirit that had made it the country's most popular sport, turning what should have been a simple rule book into an 87-page primer destined to foment insanity and controversy. Over the years, Bill Belichick's Patriots would question the rule book, exploit

it, disregard it. Pereira always liked Belichick. They would chat periodically. Belichick would ask about rules, but never tried to bully or push
an agenda or influence refs, as many coaches did. He was always cordial
and fair and friendly, and would remain so until 2007, when he found
himself at the center of a cheating scandal and cut Pereira off forever.

Pereira knew that Brady intended to pull the ball back to his chest.
But intent didn't matter. Only the rule did. Minutes passed. He drank
his wine a little faster, knowing that, as soon as Coleman announced a
reversal, his cell phone would explode.

In Foxborough, the Raiders were beginning to get nervous. "In the
Air Tonight" by Phil Collins blared from the speakers. Jon Gruden, the
Raiders' head coach, had never heard of the tuck rule. Woodson was
dancing on the sidelines in celebration, but was slowing down. In the
press box, Art McNally, the NFL's supervisor of officials, turned to a few
Raiders executives and said, "This is going to be the tuck rule." Amy
Trask, Oakland's CEO, said, "You better call 911, because I'm going to
have a fucking stroke if you overturn this fucking call."

Coleman finally emerged and faced a crowd vibrating in anticipation
of what would be the most controversial replay decision in NFL history:
"After reviewing the play, the quarterback's arm was going forward. It is
an incomplete pass."

Gruden sprinted down the sideline, eyebrows askew, screaming out
of the side of his mouth. Trask and other Raiders executives unleashed
a string of indecipherable obscenities. To take away a playoff game—no,
for the league office, *suits in New York*, to take away a playoff game, was
unthinkable.

Pereira's phone started buzzing, as expected. Nobody knew the rule,
even people in the league office. "Half in the tank, I had to explain it,"
he recalled.

It was impossible to explain. But within seconds, play resumed, and
Tom Brady was about to demonstrate for the first time what would
become an iron law of the NFL for the next two decades: you cannot
give him a second chance. He hit David Patten for 13 yards, and with
less than a minute left, Vinatieri ran out for a 45-yard field goal—in the
snow, into the wind—to send the game to overtime. A South Dakota
kid who'd played quarterback and linebacker in high school, Vinat-

ieri had yet to be known as the greatest-ever kicker in the clutch. Two years earlier, under Pete Carroll, he had blown two fourth-quarter kicks in separate games. Instead of finishing 10–6, New England went 8–8, costing Carroll his job. Vinatieri would now begin a run of incredible game-saving kicks that would transform the reputations of both Belichick and the Patriots and usher in a new era in Boston sports. But this was the hardest kick of Vinatieri's six-year career. He had watched from the sideline as the Patriots marched into range, asking Brad Seely, "Can we get it closer?"

"Adam, we're trying," Seely replied. "It's gonna be as close as it's gonna be, then you're gonna have to go."

Vinatieri jogged on and hit the ball hard. He later wondered how many times out of a hundred the kick would have been good. "Who you kidding, that's maybe a 10 percent shot if you're lucky," he said. This was one of the 10 percent, not that he could see it—the snow was too thick. Crowd noise was a better barometer than his eyes.

In overtime, Brady completed eight straight passes to help move New England into field goal range. Vinatieri was good again. The Patriots sideline exploded. A few players had planned to make snow angels, but they were either too caught up in the moment or they forgot altogether, and so, long snapper Lonie Paxton went at it alone, sprinting to the end zone and falling to the ground in an instantly iconic celebration replicated over the years by other Patriots teams. Brady grabbed onto the back of running back J. R. Redmond and yelled, "We did it!"

Forty minutes later, Brady emerged from the shower in a towel and stood at his locker, beaming after his first playoff win. Stacey James, the Patriots' director of media relations, told Brady that the media were ready.

"They can wait five minutes," Brady said. He put on sneakers and blue jeans and a black leather jacket over a blue polo, topping it off with his lucky Irish cap—very Boston. He turned to a mirror in a teammate's locker and brushed his teeth with notable aggressiveness, as if he knew he might need to combat questions about his "incomplete pass" with a broad smile. Moments later, he stood behind a podium.

So, Tom, did you fumble?

"You know," he said, "he hit me . . . I wasn't sure. I wasn't sure . . ."

Were you throwing the ball?

"Yeah, I was throwing the ball."

The room started to laugh. Brady looked down, knowing where all this was headed. People would imply that he was lucky. That would be an affront to his soul.

"He hit me as I was throwing," Brady finally said. "How do you like that?"

That night, Brady hosted a small party at his condo for family and friends. He sat on the couch next to his roommates with a Jack and Coke, his go-to drink when unwinding, watching the highlights on repeat. The game was national news. The tuck rule was national news. *Tom Brady* was national news. Brady stayed in front of the screen as night turned into morning, too wired to sleep.

7

TURKEY ZERO

EVEN DAYS LATER, BILL BELICHICK WAS HEADED TO his fourth Super Bowl—his first time running the whole show, a man coming into his own. The Patriots won the AFC championship by dominating the Pittsburgh Steelers at Heinz Field, a game exemplary not only of the dynamic team Belichick had built—the Patriots scored two special-teams touchdowns—but of how sports can be beautifully symmetrical. Brady injured his ankle in the second quarter, and Drew Bledsoe entered in relief. Bledsoe had an eerie premonition that he would play. The night before the game, he sat with his father, Mac, discussing life and the difficult season. The next morning, Damon Huard, the third-string quarterback and peacekeeper in the meeting room, seemed to sense his old friend might be called into action. "Hey man, you ready?" he asked. When called on, Bledsoe was more rusty than ready, but he threw a touchdown pass to David Patten with 1:05 left in the first half, putting the Patriots up 14–3 and allowing Belichick to be his most dangerous coaching self: defending a lead against an inaccurate passer. The Patriots intercepted Steelers quarterback Kordell Stewart three times, including on each of the Steelers' final two drives, to seal a 24–17 win that was not as close as the final score suggested.

Bledsoe's performance was sufficiently confident to reignite a quarterback controversy for a few days, enough to allow him to get his hopes up. But as soon as Belichick saw that Brady's ankle had healed enough to practice, he named him the starter. Bledsoe was pissed off all over again, not just at Belichick, but at Charlie Weis, who agreed with the call. It was clear that they simply trusted Brady more than Bledsoe. Both Weis and

Belichick had been assistants on the 1996 Patriots team that reached the Super Bowl against the Packers, and both had watched Bledsoe throw four interceptions, killing any chance New England had of an upset. The Patriots couldn't afford a single turnover against the Rams. Incomplete passes, punts, runs for little gain—Belichick could live with those, and he could live with himself if the Rams beat the Patriots. He couldn't live with the Patriots beating themselves. The offensive game plan was to control the ball, drain the clock, and, most of all, not lose the game. Belichick thought about football holistically and saw better than most, if not all, other coaches how different pieces complemented each other. He knew that if the Patriots could just rough up the receivers and beat the hell out of Marshall Faulk, the Rams would struggle. In practice, Belichick shouted, "Where's Faulk?" so often that some defenders finally told him to shut the hell up. That pleased Belichick; his team understood its job.

On the Friday before the game, Belichick was in his hotel room, talking with Michael Holley, a *Boston Globe* columnist he liked and respected. Holley was searching for ways to write a column that predicted a New England upset, but he told Belichick he couldn't do it, he couldn't make the case. He wasn't alone. When league executives held a meeting with the media relations chief for each team—Rick Smith for the Rams, Stacey James for the Patriots—to discuss how to handle the logistics for the MVP award, they spoke almost exclusively to Smith, barely looking at James.

"Why can't you?" Belichick asked Holley, before adding, "This is taking a fast-break team and turning into a half-court game. They got more talent than us, they're faster than us, they can't beat us in half-court basketball."

THE NEXT AFTERNOON, the Patriots took a team picture at the Superdome in their home blues, then got on the team bus and headed back to the hotel. A few New England videographers stayed behind to set up camera equipment for the game when something unusual happened: the Rams showed up for their walk-through practice. Martz cycled his team through plays, right there, in front of videographers dressed in Patriots gear. Nobody told the Patriots guys to leave, so, for 40 minutes, they watched and took mental notes. At one point, Faulk lined up to return kicks, something he had rarely done. Matt Walsh, one of the Patriots videographers, relayed what he saw to New England defensive assistant Brian Daboll. Years later, when the Patriots' success was no longer viewed as pure, this series of events would throw the Patriots and the league into a full-blown crisis and draw the suspicion of a hard-charging United States senator.

WINNING NFL GAMES requires a combination of preparedness and the perfect call at the perfect time. For the most talented players, it's sometimes about ignoring the coaches. Ty Law was good at that. He liked to freelance, and if he had listened to the coaches, he wouldn't have been perfectly out of position on the play that changed the Super Bowl. It was another example, perhaps, of the role of chance. Early in the second quarter, the surprising Patriots were down 3–0, but in control of the game. New England's defense contested every play, forcing the Rams to be patient and settle for short gains. "We beat the shit out of them at the line of scrimmage," Eric Mangini recalled. The Patriots hit Faulk and Warner so much that, after a shot to the quarterback's head, Patriots linebackers coach Pepper Johnson wondered if they had knocked him out.

On the biggest stage in American sports, Bill Belichick was demonstrating that something more than a football game was at work. A series of subtle strategies within a comprehensive design was translating into the domination of one of the best offenses the league had ever seen. The plan to shadow and hit Faulk not only marginalized him as a weapon, but also as a sophisticated analyst of his opponents. At one point, Faulk was so frustrated, he told Martz, "They know what we're doing." Belichick had created a new reality, and, as he predicted, Martz was slow to adjust. On the sideline, Rams receiver Ricky Proehl begged Martz to run the ball. "Fuck it, I'm going to win it my way," Martz replied. His ego and stubbornness, so often a benefit, was now a weakness, as Belichick had anticipated and as Martz later all but confessed. "It's difficult in a Super Bowl to call runs on third and four, or third and six, even with Faulk as your running back."

It wasn't difficult at all, which Martz learned early in the second quarter. To start a drive, he ran Faulk on consecutive plays for a total of 20 yards. On the third play of the drive—first down from the St. Louis 39-yard line—Belichick countered with one of the best calls of his career. In the Rams' 25 snaps to that point, Belichick had refrained from blitzing, applying the lesson learned from November. This time, though, New England crowded the line of scrimmage with seven players and dialed up what it referred to as "Turkey Zero." It was a version of the famous 46 defense Buddy Ryan had deployed for the Chicago Bears and Philadelphia Eagles in the 1980s, an attacking style based on overloading the interior offensive line. The Patriots had used it once earlier in the season, against the Atlanta Falcons a few weeks before Thanksgiving—thus, "Turkey." The Patriots lined up two rushers, defensive end Bobby Hamilton and linebacker Mike Vrabel, over inexperienced right tackle Rod Jones, and at the snap, Hamilton stunted inside, away from Jones, who hesitated long enough for Vrabel to sprint past him, untouched. "That rocked my world," Martz recalled. Hurried and hit by Vrabel as he threw, Warner lofted a pass outside to Isaac Bruce, who had beaten Law and was wide open.

Law was supposed to be in tight coverage on Bruce, but he played off him, giving Warner the illusion that Bruce was open. A risky decision, but as Crennel later said, "Ty just had a *feel*." He was five yards off, in no-man's-land, but ended up in the perfect place at the perfect time. He intercepted Warner and returned it 47 yards for a touchdown, a play that not only put New England up 7–3, but helped set in motion a dynasty.

THE PATRIOTS REFUSED to let up, recovering a Rams fumble later in the second quarter and intercepting Warner again in the third. Afterward, Warner claimed that the Patriots had gotten away with illegal holding the entire game—"They tackled them all," he said in frustration on the sideline, at one point—believing that Belichick knew the officials wouldn't allow the Super Bowl to be dragged down and decided by penalties. With 1:51 to go, trailing 17–10, Warner pulled off what appeared to be his second game-saving drive in as many Super Bowls. He hit three straight passes for 55 yards, the last a 26-yard touchdown pass up the sideline to Proehl. The score was tied. The drive took only 21 seconds.

On the Patriots bench, Crennel yelled, "I need rushers!" But the Patriots were exhausted and reeling, having held off a faster opponent for as long as they could.

The Rams pinned the Patriots at their own 17-yard line with 1:21 left and no time-outs. One of the closest Super Bowls in history—many prior matchups had been blowouts—seemed destined to be the first to go to overtime. For most of the night, New England's offense had been an afterthought in the chess match between Martz's offense and Belichick's defense. The Patriots had scored only 10 points on offense, both off Rams turnovers. Tom Brady had passed for a meager 92 yards. Twice he had thrown deep. The first time, he was nearly intercepted. The second, he missed a wide-open receiver for what would have been a touchdown. Adam Vinatieri, remembering Brady's magic against the Raiders, told an equipment manager on the sideline, "They screwed up. They gave us too much time." Few agreed. "We didn't know much about Tom Brady at the time," Martz later said. A turnover or quick three-and-out might set in motion a Rams victory in regulation time. Belichick had coached what he would later consider the finest performance of his career and needed to make one more big call: go for the win, or play for overtime.

"What do you think?" Belichick asked Weis.

"Let's start with two-minute and see what happens," Weis suggested. "Proceed with caution."

"Okay," Belichick said. "Call something safe."

Brady stood on the sideline near Belichick and Weis. He had spent much of the morning in his hotel room, watching NFL Films replays of past Super Bowls, marinating in the glory of his heroes winning it all in the final seconds: Joe Montana in Super Bowl XXIII against the Bengals, John Elway in XXXII against the Packers, even Kurt Warner in XXXIV against the Titans. "Wouldn't it be cool if it came down to something like that?" Brady asked Weis hours before the game.

"That would be utopian," Weis said.

Now Brady was facing the moment he had dreamed of, and he seemed to be the only one with absolute confidence.

"Hey!" Weis shouted. "Don't forget your checkdown and don't take a sack!"

Before Brady left for the huddle, Bledsoe shuffled in front of him. It would take the older man years to come to terms with what had transpired in 2001, the fragility of life and of his career. The night before the Super Bowl, speaking with his father, he had a vision that he would come off the bench and lead the team to victory. Now it was clear that wouldn't happen, and he wanted a final word. Bledsoe always loved two-minute situations—the one moment when a quarterback was unchained, liberated from the constraints imposed by the coaches at all other times—and he told Brady, "Fuck that, go out there and sling it."

TOM BRADY HAD the blessings of youth and confidence. He would learn years later how hard it was to succeed consistently in the situation he found himself, but at the time, coming off two bowl games won with second-half comebacks at Michigan, the end of the Super Bowl seemed "like it was a continuation of a lot of things that I had done," he later said. The drive started slowly. Brady twice hit J. R. Redmond for 13 total yards, then spiked the ball to stop the clock. The next three plays decided the game. On second and ten from the Patriots' 30-yard line, Brady hit Redmond again. The running back cut upfield and inside, away from the sideline. With three Rams closing in, Redmond skirted outside, desperately trying to correct himself. If the Rams could tackle him inbounds, the game was probably headed to overtime because the Patriots were out of time-outs and lining up to spike the ball would have wasted precious seconds. Redmond lunged, and his elbow landed on white, by less than a foot. New England had life: first down at their own 41-yard line, clock stopped, with 33 seconds left.

Weis then called an identical play on consecutive downs: 64 Max All In. The first time, the Rams blitzed up the middle. Brady's primary receiver was tight end Jermaine Wiggins crossing over the middle, and his outlet in the event of the blitz was receiver Charles Johnson on the left side, running a slant. Two Rams came free at Brady, but he knew if he threw to Johnson, the receiver likely would be tackled inbounds and the clock would come close to running out, ending regulation. So, he heaved it out of play, burning only four seconds, a deft calculation that some Hall of Fame quarterbacks often fail to make. On the second snap, Weis shifted Troy Brown to Wiggins's spot on the crossing route. This time, the Rams sat back in zone coverage, allowing Brown to run free. Brady scooted away from pressure, his gift for improvisation on display, and fired a dart to Brown, who caught it in stride crossing from right to left and ran upfield and out of bounds for a 23-yard gain.

It all happened so fast, Brady later thought. Just like that, New England was on the edge of Vinatieri's range. Brady hit Wiggins for six more yards, setting up a 48-yard attempt. Brady spiked the ball with seven seconds left. It bounced straight up, and Brady caught it, allowing it to land softly in his outstretched left palm. He held it high and still for a beat, an unintentional championship pose. Then Vinatieri jogged on. He had spent the previous night envisioning this situation, kicking it 100 times in his sleep, imagining how it would feel. Just seconds before, he had told John Hillebrand, the Patriots' equipment man, "When we go out onto the field and kick this game winner, get your butt down there and get this ball for me."

Snap, hold, kick. Cameras flashed. Time seemed to slow. Belichick veered onto the field for a better view of a kick that was high and down the center and never in doubt. The Patriots flooded the field, authors of the greatest Super Bowl upset in 33 years, since Namath's Jets beat the Colts in the third one. Martz stood at midfield for the customary handshake between coaches, searching and waiting for a counterpart that never arrived. *Son of a bitch*, he thought before turning toward the locker room. Vinatieri hugged Hillebrand, who had secured the ball as instructed. Brady was named most valuable player, and from the stage, he scanned the stands until he saw his family. He pointed at them with both hands and shook his head, an innocent smile breaking over his face, as if to say, "Can you believe this?" Through red, white, and blue confetti, Robert Kraft accepted the Vince Lombardi Trophy, and for the first time offered a brief acceptance speech. The meaning of his post–Super Bowl remarks would change over time, as complicated as his team's legacy, but for one night, at least, months after 9/11, with the image of the American flag plastered throughout the stadium, Kraft's words were novel and heartfelt and unified the crowd.

"We are all patriots. And tonight, the Patriots are world champions!"

A FEW HOURS LATER, as Sunday night turned into Monday morning, Tom Brady knocked on the door of Room 533 of the Fairmont Hotel. It was Bill Belichick's room, where he was hosting a small private party, reveling in the day's events. After the game, Belichick had hugged Ernie Adams and said, "Can you believe we won the Super Bowl against the Rams with this team?" Downstairs was the first of many Super Bowl celebration parties, more modest than its future iterations. Attendees were served food on snack trays, not lavish buffets. But there was alcohol, and many of the team's staff were "dead drunk," in the words of one coach.

Brady entered Belichick's room sheepishly. The coach offered him a Corona. They made small talk for 20 minutes or so, two men whose lives had already changed forever. Earlier that week, Brady appeared in a taped Super Bowl television spot, with musicians and others involved in the festivities. He was nervous and asked a few buddies to tag along. Once there, he was inundated with autograph requests. The event became a "Sharpie party," a phrase he would coin. Afterward, Brady and his crew decided to hit Bourbon Street. They didn't even reach a bar before crowds started forming around him. Brady and his friends started jogging away from the masses and ended up ducking into an alley, literally running from fame.

Now Brady had a favor to ask of his coach, and he was nervous about it. As the Super Bowl MVP, he was supposed to be at Walt Disney World the next day. There was one problem: he would have to miss the chartered team flight home. It was important to Belichick that the Patriots arrive and depart together. He had witnessed the drama after Bill Parcells left New Orleans separately from the team after the loss in 1997, signaling that he was no longer part of the Patriots. "Everybody who flies down is flying back with us," Belichick had told his team. As Brady turned to leave, he finally asked, as if it had slipped his mind initially:

"Oh, Coach, by the way—I got asked to go to Disney World. Can I miss the chartered plane?"

Belichick looked at him for a second that seemed to last a minute. "Shit yeah," Belichick said. "How many times do you win the Super Bowl?"

There would be more times. But tectonic forces had already been set in motion: Brady's celebrity was rising. Belichick knew Brady was special; he also knew there were many ways to win a football game, even a Super Bowl. He now had three rings, two with the Giants and one in New England. None of the victories had required a superstar quarterback, and two had been authored by a quarterback who began the season as a backup—Jeff Hostetler in 1990 and now Brady. Later that morning, Belichick and Brady were in a limo, running on little sleep, when the coach said, "Hey, Tom, I just want to let you know—you had a pretty good year." That was about as much of a compliment as Belichick was capable of giving. He had developed an entire system of football based on everyone in the organization being replaceable, except himself. Belichick's infrequent and hesitant compliments are often seen as a natural consequence of his personality, but can also be viewed as an example of his philosophy and ethos, of what he believes matters in football. In the hours after it began, the factors that would drive the dynasty apart decades later were already evident.

WITH HIS PARENTS, Tom Brady went to Disney World and rode on the Magic Carpets of Aladdin in a black mock turtleneck. Tom Sr. and Galynn were on a delirious high from the season, traveling from one end of the country to another on a weekly basis, taking part in something special and soaking it all up because nobody knew when it might end. Brady returned to Boston on Monday night, crashed at his condo for a few hours, then knocked on David Nugent's door at 5 a.m. and asked him if he wanted to work out before the victory parade. Nugent couldn't believe it, but Brady found stability in routine. They drove in the darkness to the stadium and lifted alone together in the weight room.

The victory parade was later that day, 1.25 million people lining the streets of downtown Boston, more than a few women lifting their shirts at Brady. Then he caught a private plane to Hawaii for the Pro Bowl with a few teammates. During a layover, Brady took a call on his cell phone. It was from an aide to Tara Reid, asking if he could meet the movie star for lunch. As soon as Brady hung up, the guys started heckling him. *Ooooohhhhh.*

Brady laughed it off, but something was already different. He was no longer the geeky and skinny backup. He was no longer just a quarterback. He was a sex symbol who would soon be on the cover of *People* under the headline "Those Lips, That Chin—That Super Bowl Win!" When Brady got to his hotel in Hawaii, fans mobbed him. He tried to smile through the swirling insanity, and took it as a clarifying experience. "Our life has changed," he told his parents. "You're gonna change, I'm gonna change."

IN THE WEEKS AFTER the Super Bowl, Brady played golf with John Elway, flew on Donald Trump's jet to be a judge for the Miss USA pageant, visited Barry Bonds and Willie Mays at San Francisco Giants spring training, and met Muhammad Ali. Officials in San Mateo proposed an annual Tom Brady Day. When a blurry few weeks finally slowed down, Brady visited San Mateo for a respite. Arriving at his old home, he saw that his parents had assembled a mass of memorabilia for him to autograph for friends. He was exhausted, but realized he had only himself to blame. He had fantasized and dreamed about the very thing that had just happened, worked his ass off for it, been broken and made himself whole again—and spawned a mania that already was beyond his control.

If a dividing line exists in the life of Tom Brady, a moment in time that separated everything he had ever known from a new, singular life he couldn't begin to understand—what it would give him and what it would strip away—the off-season between the Super Bowl and the next season was it. A few weeks before the 2002 season, Brady and the Patriots agreed to a four-year, $28 million contract extension. He bought a condo in Marina Bay, a neighborhood in Quincy. Needing to fill it, he went furniture shopping with Nugent, buying a big wraparound couch, then drove Nugent back to the old condo in Franklin. They sat in the driveway in the Cadillac Escalade Brady had won as the Super Bowl

MVP. A classic rock station played on the car's stereo. There is no way Brady could have known what his life would become when he pulled away from one home and drove toward another, but in some way, right then, it was all written. Brady turned to his former roommate.

"Nugent, I'm a millionaire."

"I know you are."

"No—I'm a millllllliiioooonnnaaaaiiirre!"

"Black Betty" was on the radio. Brady cranked it, and the two men played some of the sweetest air guitar of their young lives.

8

NO BRIDGES
HIGH ENOUGH
TO JUMP OFF

T OM BRADY IGNORED HIS FATHER'S CALLS.
It was late September of 2003, and the Super Bowl season of
2001 was a hazy memory. The Patriots had just lost to Washington. Brady was pissed off and didn't want to speak to anyone. New England was 2–2, after finishing 9–7 in 2002 and failing to make the playoffs for what would be the first and only time in the Brady–Belichick era when the quarterback played a full season. Both men looked like one-year wonders. For more than a year, the Patriots had both reveled in the glory of their unexpected Super Bowl victory and fought its shadow. Belichick had not only agreed to allow Michael Holley full access for what would be the bestseller *Patriot Reign*, but became a sportswriter himself for the *New York Times* after the Tampa Bay Buccaneers beat the Oakland Raiders in the Super Bowl following the 2002 season, providing a portal into his mind as he struggled to "tiptoe the line between helping your players forget that they're the champions and helping them remember why they're the champions." Belichick occasionally delved into long and honest off-the-record conversations with journalists. But never had he offered such transparency on the fragility of his profession, and even on his own self-doubt. "Your players will stick together, sacrifice, do everything you could ask, and your assistant coaches and scouts will work as hard as they did on the way to Fantasyland. But, impossible as it may seem right now, there could be a time when that's not good enough. No really, it's true."

Belichick had been a surprisingly easy sell when Holley pitched him on the idea of an all-access book, and *Patriot Reign* chronicled a group of men—Belichick, Robert and Jonathan Kraft, and Scott Pioli—who believed they were building a durable and lasting system to transcend the NFL's salary cap–enforced parity during the 2002 season when what actually happened was that they fell victim to it. The Patriots finished in a three-way tie for first place in the AFC East, but lost all the tiebreakers and missed the playoffs. Years later, after general manager Theo Epstein led the Boston Red Sox to their first World Series title since 1918, he called Belichick and asked for advice on how to handle success.

"You're fucked," Belichick said.

AFTER 2002, Belichick wanted more production out of his safeties, and when Rodney Harrison of the San Diego Chargers became a free agent in February of 2003, Belichick recruited him hard, Patriots-style. A Patriots gofer picked up Harrison off his flight and took him not to a fancy Boston steakhouse, but to a burger chain outside of Foxborough called the Ground Round. Belichick greeted Harrison in his usual attire—raggedy sweater and blue jeans—and wasted no time.

"Hey, we want you," Belichick said.

Harrison loved it, and he delivered on his potential so quickly that it allowed Belichick to be his most ruthless. A simmering contract issue between Belichick and Lawyer Milloy was beginning to heat up, with the regular season impending. Milloy's $4.5 million salary-cap number was hard for Belichick to accept, and Milloy wanted a raise. In June of 2003, Belichick and Milloy had spoken about his status and, in Milloy's opinion, reached an agreement for the upcoming year: the safety would play out the season and the contract would be addressed in the off-season.

But in training camp, Harrison and Eugene Wilson, a rookie second-round pick out of Illinois, played well. Belichick saw that the best move was an unpopular one. He liked Milloy personally—Milloy had vouched for Belichick to Robert Kraft before the owner traded for him—but this was business. Belichick told others in the building that he felt he could coach up Wilson to maybe 75 percent of the player Milloy was, and free up millions in cap space to sign complementary players. It was Belichick at his best and coldest. "Other coaches don't think like that," Jonathan Kraft later told a confidant. "They just think, 'Solve Lawyer, in the moment, get the fucking thing done.'"

Nine days before the 2003 season opener against the Buffalo Bills, Belichick called Milloy into his office and offered what the safety would recall as an ultimatum: take a pay cut or be released. Milloy felt blindsided. Belichick gave him the weekend to mull it over. On Monday, five days before the Bills game, Milloy and his agent, Carl Poston, asked for and were granted his release. He signed with Buffalo 48 hours later, joining Drew Bledsoe, who had been traded to the Bills for a first-round pick in April of 2002, to help create Patriots North.

Players were angry, especially Tom Brady, one of Milloy's best friends and after-hours wingmen. In 2002, Milloy had accompanied Brady to the Tourneau store in midtown Manhattan and talked him into the biggest purchase of his life: an IWC watch for "eight or nine grand," Brady later recalled. Brady loved IWC watches so much that, in college, an image of one had been his computer's screensaver. A few months later, in the off-season, Milloy and Brady were at a South Beach bar when Matt Damon and Peter and Bobby Farrelly happened to enter. Over drinks, the Farrelly brothers offered Brady and Milloy cameos in a comedy they were already shooting, *Stuck on You*. Brady and Milloy were cast as two computer nerds. Brady kept on his costume—with thick lamb chops as sideburns—on the flight home, and when the two of them navigated Logan Airport, fans swarmed Milloy while Brady, laughing and trying to not blow his own cover, went unnoticed.

Brady was still somewhat naive to the way the NFL worked—or, at least, to the way Belichick worked. After Milloy received his ultimatum, Brady personally lobbied the Krafts to retain him. It didn't work. Milloy was gone, the first superstar Patriot who had helped them win a Super Bowl to be shown the door. He wouldn't be the last. Moving on from stars was almost a Belichickian first principle, and gave additional meaning to the notion of sacrificing self for team. Milloy's release created a media storm in New England, and revived and amplified the narrative of Belichick as a cold and heartless strategist. Even Patriots assistant coaches found it hard to fathom. Belichick explained the decision to the team— he would later rank it near the top of the hardest moves of his career— but it did little to help. The players didn't "hate their coach," as ESPN's

Tom Jackson said on air—an unforgivable comment in Belichick's eyes because the former Broncos linebacker hadn't spoken to anyone in the locker room. In truth, they were angry with him, and the effects lasted into the season opener against the Bills.

Buffalo obliterated New England, 31–0. Milloy tallied a sack, five tackles, and a tipped pass that led to one of Brady's four interceptions. Brady wasn't himself. In the third quarter, at the Bills' goal line, Patriots tight end Fred Baxter split wide, like a receiver, and Buffalo left him uncovered. Normally, Brady would snap the ball and throw an easy touchdown. But he didn't see it. The coaches wondered if his head was in the game.

New England won its next two games and then faced Washington. Brady threw three interceptions. New England fell behind 20–3 before cutting it to 20–17 on a Brady touchdown pass with 2:10 left. The Patriots got the ball with 1:39 to go, but only gained seven yards on four plays. It was only the second time since high school that Brady had the ball late with a chance to win the game and failed, the first coming in a game against Illinois in college. Brady walked off the field with a dead rage in his eyes.

Tom Sr. called his son a few times over the following days. Tom refused to answer, which was odd: the two of them spoke almost daily. But Tom Sr., ever the persistent salesman, could read his son's mind, even from the other coast. Losing destroyed Brady, sending him to dark places, tortured in ways few knew. Tom Sr. called once more, and this time left a message that he knew his son couldn't ignore.

"There aren't any bridges in Boston high enough to jump off."

Brady called back within a minute.

"You know exactly how I feel," he said.

New England won its next 21 games.

A FUNNY THING about football fans is that almost none of them actually understand what they're watching, because the game some of them played in high school bears no resemblance to the modern, endlessly complicated sport. There are levels of understanding: most fans, who get the basics; talk radio hosts, whose primary gift is carrying on a conversation with themselves; smarter fans, who are wise enough to know that any sport with an oblong-shaped ball has an element of inherent randomness; film guys, who delve into the schematics, often failing to account for the fact that, on most snaps, many players screw up their assignments, which only coaches would know; writers, most of whom at least try to talk to insiders; former jocks; former greats, most of whom know the game, but can't explain it because of how easily it came to them or because it was simpler in their day; NFL assistant coaches; NFL head coaches; winning NFL head coaches; Super Bowl–winning head coaches; and finally, at the very top of arcane knowledge and expertise in a faintly ridiculous corner of American intellectual esotery, Bill Belichick.

One of the most obvious illustrations of this fact came on a chilly November Monday night in Denver, five weeks after the Washington loss, when Belichick not only shocked the fans but also his own staff. A little less than three minutes remained. New England was in trouble. It trailed Denver, 24–23, and was facing a third and ten from its own one-yard line. Belichick had a novel idea, which, if it worked, could prompt a series of events that *might* give the Patriots a chance. Belichick found special-teams coach Brad Seely and said, "We're gonna take a safety here if we don't get a first down."

Seely had coached special teams for 20 years, and he had never heard of a trailing team taking an intentional safety. It was always a move reserved for a team with a lead. *We're going to give them points?* Seely thought.

But Belichick had made his own calculation. If the Patriots took an intentional safety, they would surrender two points and give the Broncos a 26–23 lead—but would then kick off, with the chance to pin Denver deep in its own territory. If the Patriots could then force a Denver punt, they would take over with good field position and a chance to tie the game in the final seconds. It was a long shot. But it was a shot.

No other coach thought this far ahead. No other coach saw how to take control of the game on third and 99. No other coach saw as clearly that the game is a series of sequences, and, if aligned, these sequences could work in concert. Seely told the punt team to expect to run a play called Fast Safety, one of two intentional safeties in the Patriots playbook. The other was Slow Safety, which was reserved for times the Patriots needed to burn time off the clock. In Slow Safety, the punter would take the snap and run around in the backfield, stalling as long as possible, before giving himself up. Fast Safety was to be deployed when the Patriots couldn't afford to waste a second; they'd snap the ball out of the end zone rather than to the punter, preserving as much time as possible.

Brady threw incomplete on third down. It was now fourth and ten. Seely turned to long snapper Lonie Paxton and gave him a final reminder: "Snap it over Kenny's head"—meaning punter Ken Walter. Paxton did, firing it so high that it ricocheted off the upright and bounced in the end zone. It happened so fast that it was hard to process. The crowd exploded, thinking the ball was live. The referees clasped both hands together above their heads, signaling a safety and awarding Denver two points.

MIKE SHANAHAN immediately grasped exactly what Belichick had done. Shanahan was in his ninth year as Denver's head coach and, at the time, was seen, alongside Belichick, as the NFL's reigning genius. He had won two Super Bowls in the late 1990s. He and Belichick were friends who always brought out the best in each other when their teams met. They had faced off in the Super Bowl after the 1986 season, when Shanahan was the Broncos' offensive coordinator and Belichick the Giants' defensive coordinator. Even as assistants, they would meet up after games and talk shop, trading secrets, two young men trying to master their craft. They had both been fired as head coaches by unstable franchises—Shanahan by Al Davis's Raiders in the late 1980s, Belichick by Art Modell—and they had made the most of their second chances. After Belichick was fired by the Browns, Shanahan was asked which assistants should be on the radar for head-coaching jobs. "I ranked him as the top guy," Shanahan later said. "People will see. He'll separate himself." It was rare endorsement at a time when Belichick was at his lowest. He never forgot.

Shanahan was impressed by Belichick's move—"Bill knew exactly what he was doing" with the intentional safety, he recalled—but unfazed. The game was still Denver's to lose: a first down would ice it. Walter punted as a kickoff from the Patriots' 20-yard line. Broncos returner Deltha O'Neal mishandled the ball, recovering at the 15-yard line, costing the Broncos 25 yards of field position. There was 2:46 left, and Shanahan knew the clock, as much as the Patriots, was his opponent. He called two runs that forced Belichick to use a pair of time-outs. On third and six, Shanahan faced a choice: run or throw? A run would force New England to use its final time-out, but likely wouldn't gain a first down. A pass might secure a first down and end the game, but an incompletion would stop the clock, saving the Patriots a time-out, and force Denver to punt—two wins for the opponent on one play. Thirteen years later, Shanahan's son, Kyle, was the offensive coordinator for the Atlanta Falcons and would face the same critical decision, to run or pass with a lead against the Patriots—only with a Super Bowl at stake. This can be said about Shanahans: they always go for the win. "Mike is not afraid of anything," Belichick said. Shanahan called a version of Sprint Right Option, a staple of Bill Walsh's West Coast offense and the play that produced The Catch in 1982. Quarterback Danny Kanell sprinted right, but his pass was dropped.

Belichick always told his players that before they won a game, they had to not lose it. The Broncos were losing it. Denver punted from deep in its own territory, and the Patriots got the ball at their own 42-yard line with 2:15 left.

Tom Brady jogged on. The thing that preoccupied him in two-minute situations was how to manipulate the defense into doing what he needed it to do. Every week, the coaches would give him a breakdown of the coverages the opponent used during two-minute situations, whether the defense was protecting a 21-point lead or a three-point lead. He said to himself, *This is as good a time as any to be a hero.*

The stadium was on its feet and shaking, a giant subwoofer. But Brady didn't hear any of it. He never did, his focus too intense. He dropped back, and did what he always does: he took what was available. "How do I get the defense to give up the plays I want?" he would ask, and then answer: "You've got to complete passes, even short ones. Then you can set the defense up." He hit running back Kevin Faulk three times on the drive's first five plays, for a total of 40 yards. The Patriots had a first down at the Broncos' 18-yard line with 36 seconds left. Well within

Adam Vinatieri's range, New England now was thinking touchdown. Faulk had killed the Broncos on the drive, and so Brady knew Denver would key on him. Lined up in the shotgun, Brady saw that Deltha O'Neal was in man-to-man coverage against receiver David Givens on the left side. Givens was supposed to run an out, but Brady told him to convert it to a back-shoulder fade. Brady slid left to avoid defensive tackle Trevor Pryce and threw to Givens hard and outside, to Givens's back shoulder, a cosmically impossible ball to defend. Touchdown New England—30–26, with 30 seconds left. Brady didn't notice until he watched film of the throw days later that Pryce had come free and that he had shuffled left to avoid him. "A lot of times, I'll watch film later and say, 'I had to sidestep there? I got knocked down after that pass?'" he later told me. "In the game, you're so intent on the situation that you don't even notice. You just react."

CERTAIN LOSSES SCAR COACHES. This one sent Shanahan to a dark place. The Broncos blew it. *He* blew it. Coaches are conditioned to move on from both failures and successes, but Shanahan's staff noticed days later that he was struggling to put the loss behind him, replaying the critical sequences on an endless mental loop. He wasn't alone. Mike Martz never forgave himself for Super Bowl XXXVI. Belichick wasn't immune himself. In a regular-season game in 1988, his Giants defense blew a coverage in the final minute that allowed a touchdown bomb from Joe Montana to Jerry Rice. "Brutal," Belichick said. "I can't get over that play." But more often than not, Belichick orchestrated the moments that haunted grown men, affecting the rest of their lives.

Years after this Monday night game, on a summer night, I met Shanahan at his mansion in south Denver. By then, he was out of the profession, not by choice. I parked in a large circular driveway and the doors were open, as at a country club. Shanahan greeted me with a glass of red wine. We sat at his home bar, and eventually Belichick's intentional safety came up. Shanahan's warm eyes narrowed.

"That game still bothers me," he said.

We walked down the hall, our shoes squeaking on marble floors, to a glass case where his two Lombardi trophies were displayed. They were spotless, but somehow felt like relics. Shanahan had accomplished everything in his career—except become the greatest who ever lived. The gap in accomplishments between Belichick and Shanahan was large, but the differences between the two men were small. Why did one become the greatest in modern history while the other did not? It wasn't as though Shanahan was insufficiently ruthless with personnel or less of a schematic genius in his own way, as an offensive innovator. Maybe it was luck. Shanahan was the head coach of John Elway at the end of the Hall of Famer's career, and Belichick had Tom Brady from the beginning. But New England managed continuously to beat opponents by slim margins. Together, those margins and their consistency added up to a gap. There was Bill Belichick and there was everyone else, left psychologically wrecked, even other Super Bowl champions.

"The line in the NFL is this thin," Shanahan said, holding two fingertips close.

He looked me in the eye, dead serious.

"This thin."

9

CAN YOU IMAGINE?

TOM BRADY WAS STANDING ON THE FIELD OF GIL-lette Stadium a few weeks after the Denver win. It was mid-December of 2003, and he was surrounded by a camera crew from *ESPN The Magazine*, shooting a cover. New England had a 2001 look, though even more so, dominant in its own multifaceted way, and was headed for a 14–2 finish and the AFC's top playoff seed. The worst fears running through the minds of Belichick and Brady—that they would be champions only for a day—seemed alleviated, replaced by a sense of emerging permanence. Belichick, always lukewarm on individual awards in a team sport, had argued publicly that Brady deserved consideration for league MVP, based not on the quarterback's statistics, which were serviceable, but not spectacular—23 touchdown passes against 12 interceptions—but on his ability to win games the way he did against Denver, in difficult moments, diagnosing situation and circumstance with unmatched fluency. "He's been our constant this season," Belichick said. Indeed, the magazine's cover line when it hit newsstands—"Tom Brady Is Just Good Enough to Win It All—Again"—appeared to be both a backhanded compliment and entirely accurate. Brady, only 26 years old, was still learning his craft and suffered through stretches of mortality. The Patriots beat the Cleveland Browns, 9–3, and the Dallas Cowboys, 12–0; they also beat the Tennessee Titans, 38–30, and the Indianapolis Colts, 38–34. Michael Smith of the *Boston Globe* wrote, "There are at least 1,000 ways to win a football game, and the New England Patriots obviously intend on sampling every one." Like the Patriots, Brady was just good enough, just often enough.

Brady had arrived late for the shoot, dressed for the elements, in full uniform under a Patriots jacket and a stocking hat. Photographer John Huet angled around him, using the chilly sunset and the landmark stadium lighthouse as a backdrop. Brady was enamored with Huet's assistant's hair, a dark mass as thick as a rainforest. He kept touching it. Brady was enjoying himself, as loose in front of the camera as he was cautious in interviews. Over the years, he would pose shirtless for *Sports Illustrated* and in a spiked dog collar for *VMan* magazine. He would be shot surrounded by goats for *GQ*. Something about the art and ego of a photo shoot relaxed him. In the months after the Super Bowl win over the Rams, Brady had done a magazine ad for a breast cancer awareness campaign, with a bandana designed by Kate Spade wrapped around his right arm. James Humphrey, who coordinated the shoot for Condé Nast, later said, "He's extremely photogenic. . . . We saw the Polaroids beforehand, and I swear they looked like covers for *Vanity Fair*. I can't believe this kid just wants to play football."

That wasn't quite true. After the Super Bowl, the kid wanted more. He had dreamed not only of winning, but of fame—considered it, fantasized about it, and earned it. And as soon as it arrived, he realized it was something over which he had no control. The 2001 Super Bowl was less than a week past when one of his sisters posited in *People* that he might consider a post-football life as a senator, as though he was a Kennedy. Anyone who knew Brady knew that, while he was in awe of presidential leadership—in awe of what it took to lead a country—he held almost no political convictions. In a family of lifelong Democrats, Brady's political leanings were, as his father later joked, "Californian."

Brady's ambition off the field was defined more by the opportunities he declined or didn't pursue than by those he accepted. He did not cash in, shamelessly hawking various wares the way Brett Favre had. He did not rush out an autobiography, as Kurt Warner had. He definitely didn't open a nightclub and host a talk show, like Joe Namath. This much was clear: whatever Brady did do—judging Miss USA, attending the ESPYs, venturing to the Hamptons for parties with New York socialites, where he witnessed Rihanna driving a car on a polo field and tried to introduce himself to Howard Stern, only to be "big-timed"—he looked good doing it. As Michael Jordan had done, Brady dressed impeccably for postgame press conferences, often in a suit and tie and pocket square, with just enough gel in his hair to let you know he cared. "Tommy's a traditionalist," Robert Kraft later said. "But, he's a what? What do they call it now? That term they use in gossip? Metrosexual?" *People* presented a more direct assessment, listing him as one of 2002's most beautiful people.

Many quarterbacks are labeled pretty boys, but in reality, throwing the football is often their most attractive quality. But Brady was legitimately handsome, legitimately charming, legitimately magnetic, legitimately both at ease and uncomfortable in the spotlight, and legitimately unafraid to display his gifts and doll himself up. He was likely the only NFL quarterback to have his hair professionally highlighted, blond streaks running through an otherwise short and tight light brown crop. "Nice 'do, Elton," his backup, Damon Huard, often said. Brady carried various satchels in the locker room, many of them gifts from Lawyer Milloy, including what looked very much like a black leather purse. "It's a European handbag!" Brady insisted. It all added up to a young man with discernible taste and a desirable look, to the surprise of many. "I knew he'd be a good quarterback," Charles Woodson once told me over lunch in Beverly Hills. "But I didn't think he'd be a sex symbol."

Becoming a star quarterback is arguably as much about the naked desire for adulation as it is about touchdown passes and winning games, and some might have considered it a betrayal, both to the profession and to the aura that Joe Namath helped create for himself and subsequent quarterbacks, if Tom Brady had failed to indulge. So, he indulged—in his own way. In the months after the first Super Bowl, David Nugent would enter the kitchen of 9 Cherrywood Lane and see Brady eating breakfast with Tara Reid—usually delivered from a nearby diner, Brady not being much of a cook back then. Brady was also reportedly linked to Mariah Carey and Britney Spears, and he learned that when you're the subject of Britney Spears rumors, you become the subject of the mean-spirited and misogynistic Britney Spears jokes that characterized the era. "He is such a heartthrob," Jay Leno told a television audience one night, "that Britney Spears said she could see herself married to him for a whole week!" Brady's roommates were in disbelief as the nerd they lived with, the nerd they knew, the nerd who sat at home, surfing the internet, buying clothes online, downloading music and the occasional piece of porn, whose voice elevated to screechy octaves, who often had no game with women, so earnest as to be boring, transformed into this hunk the moment he walked out the door—no, sometimes from the moment he *opened* the door, and saw his steps full of various gifts: cards, letters, requests, candy, cookies, pasta, soup ("Soup!" Brady recalled), proposals, photos, thongs. It made no sense and all the sense in the world: Tom Brady was a quarterback, the coolest job title in America.

Brady lived shielded by two pockets: one on Sundays, staving off a pass rush, and the other whenever he ventured out at night, formed by teammates and friends to wall off a lurching crowd and keep the night's activities out of the gossip pages. The Sunday pocket was more successful. Inside Track, the *Boston Herald*'s version of the *New York Post*'s Page Six, was hooked on Brady like a drug, first calling him the "quarterback cutie" and then tightening it to "QB/QT." Inside Track mentioned him 61 times between his first NFL start and the beginning of the 2002 season. Its sources—usually "A Spy" or "Someone Who Knows"—eyed him "throwing them back" at Whiskey Park in the Back Bay, or caught him and a gal "sucking face" at The Place downtown and concluded, "What can we say? The boy's a player." It noted that Marina Bay in Quincy, where Brady lived, had become the "hottest address in town for swinging single men." It detailed a day at Fenway, where Brady, Kraft, and other Patriots watched a Red Sox game, and extra security was required outside of Box 15 "to keep the gals away from Tom." The Track even tracked down Brady where he was not: in April of 2002, word passed through the coach section of a Northwest Airlines flight that the quarterback of the New England Patriots was in first class. A "gaggle of high school girls" surrounded him for pictures, thinking he was America's new darling. It turned out to be Drew Bledsoe.

Tom Brady was a young man experiencing American celebrity as it usually arrives: at warp speed, without time to process or worry or regret or consider what it was amounting to. "A kite in the wind," he later said. After the photo shoot at Gillette in December 2003 ended, I met him in a small and windowless cell-like room at the stadium. There were two chairs and no table, and just the two of us, knees almost touching as if on a small airplane. The first time we had met, in November of 2001, it felt like we were essentially the same species, young men just getting started. That was long over. Brady's accomplishments had sep-arated him—from his friends, family, teammates, and, as it turned out, from an essential version of himself. It was an experience so singular that even he was still coming to terms with it, and he laid it bare.

"It was like, who am I?" he said. "I didn't like myself. I had changed."

IT WAS TOO MUCH to discuss in one sitting—Brady had to leave to fetch a friend at the airport—so we picked things up the next day in a bigger room at the stadium, over a backgammon board.

In 2003, backgammon had become the New England players' pre-ferred method of passing the time—even in their overscheduled lives, there were dead zones to fill. Brady brought his own board. It was unclear if he was any good. He always felt he was the best on the team, regardless of endeavor. He faced off against Ken Walter in punting com-petitions. If he lost at Ping-Pong, he threw his paddle, sometimes across the room, sometimes at his opponent. When linebacker Rosevelt Colvin arrived as a free agent from the Chicago Bears, he challenged Brady to a quarterback drill. Both men would throw to a net marked with four squares from 35 yards out. "If you're supposed to be as good as you say . . . ," Colvin remarked. They bet $100. Colvin sunk it. Brady didn't. The quarterback paid him in one-dollar bills.

The locker room joke was that Brady had won as many backgammon games as Super Bowls. When he'd lose, he'd hurl the board across the room and storm off. I was unlikely to witness such theatrics. I had never played, so I was reliant on Brady to teach me as we went. His first roll was a three and one; mine was double fours. He made his moves for himself, and then basically made moves for me. All I did was roll—and I was winning.

"You've got to be the luckiest roller ever!" he said. "God help me, I'm losing to a rookie."

He started breathing heavily, mostly through his nose. "You're destroying me," he said. Some moral code within him refused to allow him to throw the game in his favor, so he did a somewhat more accept-able thing: he quit.

"New game," he said.

He was wearing a gray sweater under a leather jacket. His highlighted hair seemed to glow a bit even in the room's mediocre lighting. He rolled double fours. "I like it, I like it. This is starting my way, my friend." He rolled again. Double sixes, stacking his quadrant. "I'm feeling lucky. Here I go."

It seemed like a good opening to return to what he had disclosed the day before. When did you start to figure out—

"When did I get my shit together?" he said.

Fame had distorted everything, leaving him to wonder what was real. He knew what it was like to receive a standing ovation in a restaurant and what it was like to have a car follow him home—or believe a car was following him home, which was the same thing. He'd take back roads, stretching a half-hour commute into an hour or more, trying to shake a set of headlights, real or imagined. At one point, someone broke into his house in Quincy and stole a television. It was a new level of violation, at a time in his life when he felt violated all the time. Who could he trust? There was no road map, and there was no turning back. He wasn't going to quit football. This was the line of work he had chosen. His ambition had not waned after the Super Bowl; if anything, it increased. If Joe Montana could win four, why not him? He found himself wanting more—more of that feeling that came with improving, which he found as addictive as winning itself. Along with it all came more fame, more money, more adulation, more recognition, more power, less control, less energy, more mood swings, more stress, more sulking. "I was worn out," he said. "All the phone messages. Autographs every time I went to a hotel lobby. My dad said, 'It's a great problem.' I thought, *That's so true.* But I wished I could have figured it out for myself."

During the 2002 season, coaches had compiled a reel of Brady's reactions on the field after bad plays. It was a message, in no uncertain terms, that his body language was horrible and unfit for a team leader. "I had accomplished a lot as a player," he said. "But I was setting myself back in terms of growing as a person."

Brady called Greg Harden and, once again, asked for help. He groused about how hard it was to go out, to shop for groceries, how angry he was that he was a recluse, insecure and moody, how he wasn't himself anymore—

"Can I be myself?" Harden interrupted.

"I expect you to be yourself," Brady said.

"You want to be the best in the world, but you don't want to be a superstar?" Harden started chuckling as only he could, deeply and ironically. "I feel *soooo* bad for you! I feel your pain!"

Brady laughed.

"Son," Harden said, "this shit ain't going to last, then they'll have another superstar. Right now, you're the hot cookie. Why don't you do something radically different and enjoy this moment? Right now, you can pick up the phone and change someone's life."

"Ohhhh," Brady said.

"Am I making any sense?"

"You always do."

The TB12 business would not arrive for another decade, but it may have been born right then, in 2002 and 2003, when Brady's fame exploded, out of an effort to control uncontrollables. Brady always needed a plan. He could handle a plan that failed, but he couldn't handle having no plan at all. After the 2002 season, Brady took small steps. His sister Nancy moved to Boston to help manage his life. He carved out regular time to call family and friends, both maintaining a connection to those who mattered to him, but also to the person he used to be. Brady and one of his best friends from childhood, Kevin Brady, road-tripped to Scottsdale for the San Francisco Giants' spring training and then moved to Vegas for a few days of craps and poker. Days before the Patriots beat Jacksonville on December 14, 2003, he and Kevin drove to New York City for the premiere of *Stuck on You* and then Christmas-shopped on Fifth Avenue. The solutions were simple and temporary. But, for the moment, his situation felt manageable. "I've got a life that any 26-year-old would want," he told me. "And I'm finally able to enjoy it."

We played backgammon for another half hour or so. I won again. "Jesus Christ," he said. "You crushed me. I can't believe it. That's it." He had actually crushed himself, but it didn't matter. He started to pack up, but before he left, he mentioned sleep. It had always been hard for him. He was both a night owl and an early riser. During the week, he was sometimes so wired for the upcoming game that he called teammates in the middle of the night, quizzing them on their opponent. He

needed something to turn off his mind. He had recently found it in the
MTV show *Newlyweds*, an outrageous inside look at the first year of
marriage between Nick Lachey and Jessica Simpson. But as he watched,
his eyes would drift to the Super Bowl MVP trophy near his TV. He
would stare at it, and his heart would race at a thought and vision that
seemed unthinkable, yet close enough to touch.

"I want another. Can you imagine? Two Super Bowls?"

10

THANK YOU, PEYTON

THE NEW ENGLAND PATRIOTS DYNASTY ENDED UP lasting so long that it had no true rival team. There were no Los Angeles Lakers to its Boston Celtics, no Dallas Cowboys to its Pittsburgh Steelers. There was only a graveyard. A potential rival would appear every few years: the Jets, Broncos, Dolphins, Colts, Chargers, Ravens, Steelers. All arose and had a crack at the Patriots, before the NFL's legislated gravitational pull brought them down. Some cycled through twice—rising, falling, rebuilding, rising again, sometimes with a new coach and quarterback the second time. They could occasionally beat New England, even win a Super Bowl or two, but not dethrone them. In redefining what it meant to win in the NFL, the Patriots ended up redefining what it meant to have a rival. The closest thing they had to a true nemesis during their extended period of dominance wasn't a team, but rather a single man: Peyton Manning.

Manning was, and remains, a living, walking, talking embodiment of football. He was one of the few quarterbacks in history—joining the likes of John Elway—to endure unrealistic expectations from a young age and not only live up to them, but exceed them. Born in March 1976, Peyton was the second of Archie and Olivia Manning's three boys, between Cooper and Elisha, raised by a family that was a version of Southern royalty. Archie Manning was more than a folk hero from rural Drew, Mississippi, who became an object of affection and obsession at Ole Miss, from 1968 to 1970, where he nearly beat Alabama on prime-time television, was the subject of the famous "Ballad of Archie Who" as a junior, and was eventually named the Southeastern Conference Quarterback of the Quarter Century in 1975. He was an example of how the modern South, still in the shadow of Jim Crow, preferred to see itself. He was a white man who played a white man's position in a game that was increasingly Black, but he was also a legend whose rise was rooted in struggle, carrying a lot of pain within a thin and gifted body. His father, Elisha "Buddy" Manning, put a gun to his chest in the family home before Manning's junior year at Ole Miss. Archie considered dropping out of school to support his mother and sister, but they wouldn't let him. He married Olivia Williams, Ole Miss's homecoming queen; they became blue-collar icons with white-collar appeal. What started in Oxford continued in New Orleans after the Saints picked Archie second overall in the 1971 draft. People from the region referred to Archie and Olivia on a first-name basis, as if they were all neighbors. In a way, they were. Nobody has a story about Archie Manning big-timing a fan, or carrying himself with so much as a hint of self-importance, or taking for granted the admiration people had—and have—for him and his family, even if he sometimes struggled to understand why he was held up as immortal for throwing a football.

Archie Manning was not just a region's hero; he was Peyton's hero. As a kid, Peyton lay in bed for hours, listening to tapes of radio broadcasts of his father's Ole Miss games, dreaming of doing it himself one day, in front of those crowds, honoring his father's legend and the game itself by authoring his own. The problem was that, of the Manning boys, Peyton was the worst natural athlete. His blessings were his last name, his height—he would grow to 6-foot-5, edging out Eli as the tallest in the family—and an obsessive side. At some point before he entered high school, Peyton simply decided he would be a quarterback and willed that dream into reality. He developed his own throwing motion, holding the ball high and at his ear to quicken his release. He had a photographic football memory and could recall obscure college and pro players and statistics on command. Like any gifted student, he displayed a righteous indignation that both amused and annoyed. He once yelled at his youth basketball coach over a strategy disagreement, and Archie forced him to apologize. In 1993, before his senior year at Isidore Newman School in New Orleans, Peyton attended Bill Walsh's quarterback camp at Stanford—a high school junior from San Mateo named Tom

Brady also attended, although neither remembered the other—and complained to Walsh's face that he had shortchanged the campers by not providing enough personal instruction. Manning would later get himself into occasional trouble once the microphones were turned his way, for voicing frank complaints about coaches and teammates for public consumption. But he was usually right. He'd worked his ass off to earn his opinions, and so had no problem sharing them.

Archie was happy that his son had found a passion. That it was football meant he could be of assistance. After throwing four interceptions in a game as a sophomore in high school, Peyton needed help. He asked his father how to study the game. Archie sat him in front of a TV and VCR and gave him game tapes. If you're going to watch film, he explained, do it right. Archie taught Peyton to follow the defense, not the ball. It opened Peyton's mind. He wrote down keys to each game in a notebook that was usually labeled with his name and jersey number, a study habit he continued in college and into the NFL. By Peyton's senior season at Isidore—he wore number 18, in honor of Cooper, who had to give up playing football as a receiver at Ole Miss due to spinal stenosis—he was one of the country's most highly recruited football players, fielding interest from more than 60 schools. Everyone thought he would attend Ole Miss, but he picked the University of Tennessee because he wanted to work with offensive coordinator David Cutcliffe. It was huge news— Peyton held a press conference to announce it—and Ole Miss nearly disowned Archie. Years later, everyone was relieved when Eli decided to attend Ole Miss, where Cutcliffe had become the head coach. Archie might have never been invited back, and he might not have wanted to return, either.

Peyton became a superstar, one of the greatest college quarterbacks ever, as well as an eager football ambassador. You could see all of his hard work each time he dropped back to throw. He looked practiced and programmed, so fundamentally sound, it was as though he was teacher and student in one person. Off the field, he was comfortable in the spotlight, appealing to teammates and grandmothers and children. He wanted to be exceptional at everything. One year, he vowed to local sportswriters that he wouldn't utter a cliché all season. He watched so much film that he moved the VCR he shared with his roommates into his room. When they returned it to the living room, he moved it back. Manning likely would have been the first pick in the draft after his junior year in 1996, but he returned to Tennessee for his senior season—but not before consulting with, and making sure everyone knew that he had consulted with, a staggering lineup of legends including Michael Jordan, Troy Aikman, Drew Bledsoe, Tim Duncan, and Roger Staubach. After he announced his decision to return, a billboard in West Knoxville read, THANK YOU, PEYTON!

In April of 1998, the Indianapolis Colts picked Manning first overall. Unlike the unheralded Brady, he played from the start, and after a difficult rookie year in which the Colts finished with a 3–13 record, he presented offensive coordinator Tom Moore with an audacious proposal: give me the power to audible at the line of scrimmage. If Manning could identify the defensive call before the snap, why not exploit it by switching to a better play?

Most quarterbacks read the defense *after* the snap, as they drop back to throw. Manning wanted to use tricks on offense—pre-snap motion and shifting—to force the defense to declare itself, and then adjust off it before the play began. If Manning could accurately predict the defense, if he could dictate to the opponent, it made too much sense not to allow him to take full advantage.

It was a big *if.* Manning had set a record for interceptions thrown by a rookie quarterback, with 28. Each subsequent year, Manning rooted for a rookie to break the record. Nobody did, although he later joked that if Eli had started all 16 games as a rookie for the New York Giants in 2004, he would have easily surpassed him. But Moore believed he had a generational talent with the "greatest recall of any player I've ever coached," who was willing to be weighed down with more information and more responsibility, in the hope not only of winning, but of perhaps changing how football was played, returning power to the quarterback that had been taken away by the modern, overly regimented version of the sport. Moore gave Manning what he wanted, with a caveat: "Don't surprise me." Manning simply worked harder, combining workday players' hours with work-night coaches' hours, watching film with Moore until they formulated a game plan.

The result was a novel philosophy based on a simple concept. Manning came to the line of scrimmage with three plays, usually two runs and a pass. If the defense had six defenders near the line of scrimmage—"the box"—he picked one of the two runs. If the defense had seven defenders in the box, he picked the pass. Manning developed a system of elaborate hand signals and nicknames for plays, allowing for a no-huddle, hurry-up attack. He would approach the line of scrimmage, hunker down under center, and then, when fans and the defense expected the play, he would pop up, folding his hands into origami, flapping his arms, walking up and down the line, sifting through files in his mind to land on the perfect play or pass route, shouting code words as the play clock wound down. If he yelled "shovel," he was telling the receiver to run a dig route; if he yelled "pistol," it meant run a slant. Many fans were turned off by his theatrics and know-it-all aspect, wondering why he couldn't just snap the damn ball like everyone else. But when he finally did, they were reminded why, all over again.

By 2003, Manning had become a force. He was named co-MVP of the league. He led the NFL in completion percentage at 67 percent, throwing 29 touchdown passes and only 10 interceptions. In one mid-season game against the Tampa Bay Buccaneers—the defending Super Bowl champions, with one of the greatest defenses in history—he led a 21-point comeback in the final four minutes and pulled out a 38–35 win. Manning was stretching the possibilities of what a quarterback could control, becoming a coach on the field, shaping the game down to youth football, where quarterbacks were now using hand signals to change the play at the line of scrimmage. The Colts finished 12–4, waxing Denver, 41–10, in the wild-card round and outlasting Kansas City, 38–31, in the divisional round. Manning completed 78.5 percent of his passes across the two games, with eight touchdown passes and no interceptions. The second victory set up an AFC Championship Game against the New England Patriots in Foxborough—where Bill Belichick figured out a way to use Manning's brilliance against him.

As ALWAYS, the bigger the game, the more sophisticated the opponent, the more Bill Belichick saw football as a simple reflection of human nature. His task was to recognize his opponent's vanities and insecurities and find a schematic way to force them to reveal their worst selves on game day. The fact that Peyton Manning was a one-man show, the Colts' quarterback, game planner, and play caller—"all those things wrapped into one," Belichick later said—made Belichick's job both harder and easier. Harder because Manning was so good and held so much power. One mistake, and he would burn you. Easier because all Belichick had to do was confuse him and "figure out how he sees the game, because in the end, that's going to trump everything else."

Belichick respected Manning so much, and studied him so closely, that he almost knew him better than Manning knew himself. Belichick saw genius at work. The willingness to adapt, to adjust, to search for and exploit weakness was straight out of Belichick's own method. Manning was an offensive mirror image of Belichick, running a limited number of plays—with a talented surrounding cast, from receivers Marvin Harrison, Reggie Wayne, and Brandon Stokley to running back Edgerrin James and center Jeff Saturday—but adjusting off them, tailoring them to take advantage of openings that few others could see. Belichick was complimentary of Manning. "I don't think I've ever seen a team run through the playoffs like they have," he told the press days before the game. He said similar things in private. "They don't do a whole lot," he told the team. "But they're really good at what they do."

But Manning was such a perfectionist, so controlling, so visibly bothered by mistakes, so transparently aware of the stakes and pressure of facing Belichick, Brady, and the Patriots, and plagued by his own personal history of underwhelming play in big games—"You can't prepare enough," he later said—that it left him vulnerable. Belichick's defenses, going back to his days as an assistant with the Jets, had mostly succeeded against Manning. Belichick moved players around aimlessly before the snap, luring the quarterback to audible based on a false look as the play clock ran down, and then his players mugged and clawed at the receivers, disrupting Manning's timing. It drove Manning nuts. New England's defensive players knew Manning well already, the Patriots having beaten the Colts, 38–34, during the 2003 season. They would study Manning on film, watching how easily they could dupe him, and they would mock him, his audibles a source of humor rather than fear.

"We used to laugh at Peyton in the meeting rooms because we used to be able to confuse him so well," linebacker Tedy Bruschi later said.

The week of the AFC Championship Game, Belichick pulled aside backup quarterback Damon Huard and instructed him to watch film of the Colts offense. Huard would serve as the scout-team quarterback, mimicking the upcoming opponent.

"You need to be Peyton Manning this week," Belichick said.

Huard was familiar with the Colts—his younger brother, Brock, was Manning's backup—and studied as if more than a Super Bowl was at stake. Ten days earlier, in a practice before New England defeated the Titans in their divisional playoff game, the coaches gave Huard some snaps with the first-team offense to rest Brady, who had a sore arm and shoulder. Huard had been an invisible, yet invaluable piece of New England's success. He came from a family of quarterbacks—the Huards are kind of the Mannings of the Pacific Northwest—and he knew that the key to being a successful backup quarterback was to be more therapist than threat. He helped keep the peace in the quarterback meeting room during the awkwardness between Brady and Bledsoe in 2001, and he became a resource for Brady during the latter's disorienting rise and amid the pressures of new fame. But Belichick expected players to perform, and Huard was such a disaster with the first-team offense in that one practice, throwing multiple interceptions, that Belichick demoted him.

"Yeah, you're third string this week," Belichick said.

"Fuck, okay," Huard replied.

Portraying Manning was a shot at redemption. Huard attended defensive meetings rather than the usual offensive meetings and spent nights mastering Manning's mannerisms, even his Southern accent and voice inflections. Huard didn't know the Colts' terminology—nobody did, because Manning changed it every week—but he knew their plays. He had Manning nailed when he started to hit deep passes against the Patriots defense in practice, pissing them off and forcing them to study harder. Linebacker Willie McGinest later said that Huard "should have gotten an Oscar."

The game plan that Belichick and Romeo Crennel drew up was devastating and simple, designed to punish Manning physically and mentally.

On passing plays, they would jam and grab the receivers, forcing them to adjust their routes, throwing off the offense's timing and daring the officials to gum up a conference championship game with holding penalties. "Have them in the water cooler," as Patriots players recalled their instructions after the fact, meaning push the receivers out of bounds and into the team benches on the sidelines. At the same time, New England would send an extra pass rusher up the middle, right in Manning's face, knowing that one of his few weaknesses was that he was less accurate throwing on the move than in the pocket. A fundamental component of the Colts offense was an outside running play called a stretch run. Belichick hammered outside linebackers McGinest and Mike Vrabel during practice, ordering them to set the edge and not allow the Colts to run outside, no matter what. It was a risky tactic. Committing Vrabel and McGinest to set the edge meant that the Patriots were vulnerable to runs up the middle. Belichick didn't care. He knew that a player as smart and creative as Manning would grow bored calling runs up the middle. "We *dared* them to run inside," Bruschi recalled.

The night before the game, Belichick added a final, emotional touch. Colts tight end Marcus Pollard had told reporters earlier in the week that if Indianapolis kept up its pace, the league "might as well just hand us the rings." Pollard was simply saying out loud what players say all the time in private—Tom Brady had watched Colts film and told his sister Julie, "We're going to kill these guys"—but uttering it publicly gave Belichick ready-made motivational material. "Nobody hands you a ring. I don't care how much money you have, you can't fucking buy one. You have to play and you have to earn it." Then he pulled out his Super Bowl XXXVI ring and held it up. The room was silent, but vibrating. It was a master class in football leadership from a man once seen as not-quite-head-coach material. Belichick would perfect the formula: he respected his opponent enough to scare his team, he provided a creative but simple path to victory, and he topped it off by reminding them of the reward. "This has to be earned, and there's only one way to do it," Belichick said. "Either they kick your ass or you kick theirs."

On a wet and snowy Sunday, Manning was picked off four times, three of them while scrambling, just as Belichick had predicted. Ty Law had a hat trick with three interceptions. Manning shook his head and threw up his arms in frustration a few times in dismay. The Colts' stretch run was so ineffective that Manning all but abandoned it, allowing the Patriots to cheat on other plays. Bruschi would move around before the snap, feigning a blitz and trying to not laugh. "I was just messing around, knowing we got him," he said.

Still, Manning refused to quit. He fought back from a 15–0 deficit and got the ball with just over two minutes left and trailing 21–14 with 80 yards to go. The comeback went nowhere. He threw four straight incomplete passes. The last two were to Pollard. Both times, Pollard appeared to be held on his route; both times, there was no flag; both times, Manning whined to the officials. The mind game was over, with a clear victor. After New England's 24–14 win, Colts general manager Bill Polian—a future Hall of Famer renowned for his temper as much as his skill at assembling talented rosters—ran down the officials to complain. Polian was a member of the league's competition committee, and Colts head coach Tony Dungy was a member of the subcommittee; both bodies later altered the rules to make sure holding penalties were enforced more often and for lesser fouls. The Patriots' game plan in the win over Manning that year remade the entire sport, turning the NFL into more of a passing league and forcing Belichick to adapt to the new world he had helped create.

In the moment, Belichick was going to his second Super Bowl in four seasons as New England's head coach, validating his methodologies and controversial personnel moves. Nobody cared about Lawyer Milloy anymore. The secondary had held up all year without him, and Rodney Harrison had more than rewarded Belichick's faith in him, becoming a leader and the face of the defense. On the field after the game, as the Patriots waited for a stage to be set on which they would receive the Lamar Hunt Trophy, Harrison found Belichick and bear-hugged him.

"Thank you for believing in me," Harrison said.

"Aww, you bet," Belichick said. "We got one more now."

"Yes, sir."

The postgame locker room was warm and damp, like a ski lodge. Belichick had huddled the team together and recognized Huard for his

Manning impersonation. "One of the most valuable players on the field today didn't play one snap," he said. It was the final word on a masterpiece by Belichick, reinforcing his vision for how a true team operated.

About an hour after the game, the team's lone superstar walked across the locker room. Brady saw his dad near a hallway, and they kissed on the cheek and hugged, holding the embrace for a few beats.

"Can you believe it?" Brady said.

"Two years ago, he didn't know how big it was," Tom Sr. said after his son left to speak to the press. "Now he knows."

The fame awaiting his son scared Tom Sr., who knew that with another Super Bowl, life was about to change again, two years after it had already changed forever. But there was no stopping it. Two nights after the AFC championship, 62 million people watched President George W. Bush's State of the Union address. During one moment, the camera panned up to a fresh-faced guest, clean-shaven in a suit and tie, applauding with the rest of the joint session. It was Tom Brady. It also was jarring. What was Brady doing there? Was he a Republican? A Democrat? Did he really have political aspirations, as his sister had once speculated?

A few hours before the speech, Brady had been in the Gold Room of the White House with 50 or so administration staffers and politicians. Marty Meehan, a congressman from Massachusetts, longtime friend of the Krafts, and Patriots season-ticket holder, accompanied Brady, ushering him from one VIP stage to another, only to find that his task was pointless: Brady was under siege. At one point, Andy Card, the White House chief of staff, introduced himself to Brady—not the other way around. The reception only lasted about 40 minutes, but Brady was in no rush. He wanted to take it all in. Brady was "the star of the room," Meehan later said, until time was up and everyone got into cars heading down Pennsylvania Avenue.

The Patriots were ascendant, but there was a grinding conflict in motion. Their team-first ethos, created and fortified by Belichick, could not fully accept the way society turned quarterbacks into something more than athletes: sex symbols, celebrities, heroes. The coach was obsessed with fame and driven to crush it before it raged out of control. The quarterback was destined to be famous, whether he loved or hated it—or, more specifically, loved *and* hated it. Tom Sr. might have been worried for his son, knowing that, if he won a second Super Bowl, his celebrity would reach even higher levels. But Brady was already the face of the NFL. Before the Colts game, the Bush administration had reached out to the league office and asked for a superstar to attend the State of the Union address. The league offered two names, its two premier players, but asked to wait until after the AFC Championship Game was played before it decided between them. After New England won, and Peyton Manning supposedly had a scheduling conflict, the league sent Tom Brady.

11

THE TROPHY
IS COMING
BACK HOME

NINE SECONDS REMAINED IN SUPER BOWL XXXVIII in Houston on February 1, 2004, with the score between the New England Patriots and Carolina Panthers tied, 29–29. Adam Vinatieri lined up for a game-winning 41-yard field goal—almost a retread of the scenario two years earlier. Tedy Bruschi found Brad Seely on the sideline. It was something of a habit: Bruschi would stand near the special-teams coach before a potential game-winning kick.

"You feeling good about this, Tedy?" Seely asked.

"It's all about the snap," Bruschi said.

IT HAD BEEN all about the snap for more than a month. Long snapper Lonie Paxton had injured his knee in mid-December. Then his replacement went down. Few teams were hit harder by injuries in 2003 than the Patriots. They would use 42 different starters during the course of the year. Now, with the playoffs two weeks away, New England was desperate.

Down in Baton Rouge, at Parkview Baptist School, a 38-year-old former NFL player named Brian Kinchen was teaching bible study to seventh-graders when his phone buzzed, showing a Massachusetts number. He scooted to a corner of the classroom and quietly took the call.

"Hey, Brian," the voice said, "it's Scott."

Scott was Scott Pioli. Kinchen and Pioli had been close years earlier, when Kinchen was a tight end for Belichick's Cleveland Browns and Pioli was a gofer for the coaching staff.

"We wanna get a look at you," Pioli said.

"What?" Kinchen said.

Pioli offered him a tryout to be the Patriots' long snapper. Kinchen was unsure. He had sworn off any more attempts to play in the NFL again, after a few failed tryouts. But when he told his students who had called, a kid in the back of the class said, "The Patriots are 12–2. They're the best team in football right now, and they are going to win the Super Bowl."

An hour later, Kinchen moved class outside and practiced long snaps to his students with a borrowed football. He decided to give it a go. Kinchen called Pioli and accepted the offer, adding that he wanted to see his old friend and coach. "Tell Belichick he better get his sorry butt out of his office and shake my hand."

"No problem," Pioli said.

Within hours, after getting permission from the principal and arranging for his wife, Lori, to substitute-teach, Kinchen was on a flight to New England. The next day, Belichick got his butt out of his office to shake Kinchen's hand—but by then, Kinchen thought he had blown his chance. His tryout, in front of Seely and a camera crew, was awful. For the first time in his life, Kinchen had snapped a ball over the holder's head on a field goal try. Seely didn't want him, but Belichick felt comfortable with a known quantity. Belichick approached Kinchen in the team cafeteria. After some small talk, Kinchen said, "Bill, you know what's funny? Whoever you sign today is going to have the entire season in the palm of his hand."

"That's true," Belichick said. "And it's gonna be you."

"What?"

"Yeah."

"Lori's gonna freak out," Kinchen said.

"Call her now," Belichick said.

Belichick knew Lori from his and Kinchen's Browns days, and so he took the phone and broke the news to her. "Hey, I might be seeing more of you the next couple weeks," he said. She was in class—her husband's class—and the students cheered.

Kinchen started off well. But in the Patriots' divisional-round playoff win over Tennessee, with a windchill of minus-10 degrees, he snapped a ball into the ground. He told himself it was due to the weather. But in the AFC Championship Game, against the Colts, he overcorrected and rifled a snap high. At practice later that week, in preparation for the Super Bowl, something inside him cracked. Two out of his first three snaps sailed high.

"What the fuck?!" Vinatieri said.

Kinchen started to lose it. Until now, long snapping had always been his side job, something he never had to think about. Now, he thought about it—too much. That night, he long-snapped balls down his hotel hallway. But the next day, at practice, he launched a field goal snap high on one play and dropped the ball before he could snap it on another, unable to grip it, as if the ball and the role were too big for him. Belichick screamed, "You're not doing your job!" Kinchen was stunned, confused, scared. It wasn't the yips, a phenomenon known to golfers and base-ball players. It was something else, something weirder. His motion, his release, his power—all of it felt normal. But he couldn't aim. "A mystery," he recalled.

At practice on the Wednesday before the Super Bowl, Kinchen fired another one high. His nerves started to fray, amid visions of blowing the Super Bowl before an international audience. That night, Kinchen called Pioli in a near panic and begged to be released.

"Scott, you gotta send me home."

"No, you're fine," Pioli said.

"Scott, do you see what's happening?"

The next day, at practice, Belichick gave Kinchen a thumbs-up, try-ing to reassure him and set his mind at ease. The effort failed. Kinchen sprayed the ball all over. He and Seely sat in a hotel room that night, watching close-up footage of practice, trying to pinpoint the problem. A devout Christian, Kinchen attended team chapel the night before the Super Bowl and tried to make peace with the idea that "I was going to cost us the game," he recalled. "I had accepted it."

A horrific week got worse the next day at lunch, mere hours before kickoff. Kinchen grabbed a roll to butter and used a steak knife to cut it open. It sliced his right index finger—the most important finger for long snapping—to the bone. Seated near him, Mike Vrabel and special-teams star Larry Izzo started to laugh. When Belichick learned what had happened, he wondered for a moment if Kinchen had cut himself on purpose to get out of playing. Seely tried to help. In the locker room, he told Kinchen, "You're a God-fearing person. God can help you, right?"

It didn't appear so. On the Patriots' first possession, Kinchen snapped low and wide during a field goal try. Ken Walter, the punter who doubled as the holder, snared it and whipped it around for Vinatieri, but the kick veered right. The Patriots were forced to punt on their third possession, and Kinchen bounced the ball off the turf at midfield, kicking up grass on the vast NFL logo, before Walter fielded it and booted it away. Late in the second quarter, on an extra-point attempt, Kinchen dribbled it back. As he walked off the field, he saw Belichick approaching him. He veered toward the bench, trying to avoid the coach.

"Brian," Belichick yelled, "we're in the Super Bowl!"

Kinchen sat alone and did something he had never done before: he prayed for the outcome of the game not to involve him. He prayed that he wouldn't be called on to deliver with a world championship at stake.

BUT THIS WAS A New England Patriots Super Bowl, which meant it was destined to be decided in the final seconds. Nobody knew exactly how the Carolina Panthers, a fast and bruising team, would match up. New England's win over the Colts felt more like the Super Bowl than the Super Bowl itself, similar to the NFC in the 1980s, when the 49ers, Bears, Redskins, and Giants would beat each other up before the victor in a given year destroyed whomever happened to stand between them and the Vince Lombardi Trophy. Belichick, a realist to the bone, both worried about the Panthers and charted a road map to defeat them. He spent the week leading up to the Super Bowl fretting about Kinchen, grabbing the jerseys of Patriots receivers as they ran routes in practice— "This is what they're going to do, they're going to hold you," Belichick said—and, above all, dissecting Carolina quarterback Jake Delhomme, who seemed ready to join Kurt Warner and Tom Brady as the latest in the pantheon of star passers to emerge out of nowhere. Delhomme had been undrafted in 1997 out of Southwestern Louisiana and had spent six years mostly as a practice squad player in the NFL and moonlighting as a star in NFL Europe. In 2003, he signed with the Panthers as a backup. At halftime of the season opener, trailing Jacksonville, 14–0, Panthers coach John Fox turned to Delhomme. He threw three touchdown passes, rallying the Panthers to a win. He started the rest of the way, streaky and clutch, setting a single-season NFL record with eight game-winning fourth-quarter drives.

Something mysterious was allowing quarterbacks to go from obscure to prolific. Had years of scouting malpractice finally been exposed? Was it just randomness? Had the parity created by the salary cap, the NFL's catchall excuse for anything inexplicable, produced this unexpected consequence? Nobody knew, because still, in 2003, nobody could recognize the skill set that produced a great quarterback. Or, rather, nobody could recognize it if it wasn't obvious, if it wasn't packaged like Troy Aikman, and even then, you never really knew, as Bobby Beathard found with Ryan Leaf. The last years of the prior century and the first years of the new one left fans wondering if the faceless new quarterback for their team would be the next Brady, who would lead them to the Super Bowl. And then, like that, it was over. After the Patriots–Panthers Super Bowl, the next ten Super Sundays would feature at least one starting first-round quarterback, guys with slingshot arms and sterling résumés: Peyton Manning, Donovan McNabb, Eli Manning, Ben Roethlisberger, and Aaron Rodgers. It wasn't that general managers no longer missed. Everyone missed, especially the 21 teams that passed over Rodgers in the 2005 draft. But those years, 1999 to 2003, were never meant to last—especially when it became obvious that every draft wouldn't have a Tom Brady.

JAKE DELHOMME WAS not only a strange case, he was a strange player, simultaneously dangerous and careless, even dangerous *because* he was careless. He had thrown 16 interceptions during the regular season, a number he could easily have doubled if opponents had caught his errant passes, Belichick thought. In film sessions before the game, he compiled a reel of all of Delhomme's near interceptions. If the Patriots simply caught the ball when Delhomme threw it to them—and he likely *would* throw it to them—they'd win. "This guy's eminently beatable," Belichick told the team.

The entire Patriots team was odd. It hit Belichick during pregame warm-ups, when he turned to Ernie Adams. "Can you believe we're here? We can't run the ball, we can't punt the ball, and we can't snap for the field goals." But then he saw several Panthers jawing with the Patriots. Few things bothered him more than trash-talking, especially from a team that hadn't won anything. His mood shifted. "They're not us," he told the players before kickoff. "They'll never fucking be us. They'll never be champions. We're the fucking champions, and the trophy is coming back where it belongs."

The first 27 minutes were scoreless, then 24 combined points arrived in a frantic three minutes before halftime. New England led in the fourth quarter, 21–10. The Panthers shifted to a hurry-up offense, igniting a free-for-all. Running back DeShaun Foster ripped through the left side of the line untouched for a touchdown, cutting New England's lead to 21–16, with Carolina failing on the two-point convert attempt.

Back came Brady, calm and precise. He moved New England to the Carolina nine-yard line. A touchdown would essentially end the game, but then, Brady blinked. On second down, he missed David Givens over the middle in the end zone. Then, on third down, he faded back in the pocket, drifted left, and, with a rusher closing in, lofted a pass to the end zone. Panthers cornerback Reggie Howard fielded it like an easy fly ball, giving Carolina life.

It was worse than an inexcusable blunder. For the first time on a big stage, Brady seemed exposed, like Kurt Warner two years earlier against the Patriots. Brady sat on the bench, furious with himself. Joe Montana had never thrown an interception across his four Super Bowls; it was the most salient of all of Montana's excellent statistical accomplishments, a lasting testament to his unparalleled excellence in big games. But the fact was also tinged with fraud. In Super Bowl XXIII, against the Cincinnati Bengals, Montana threw into the end zone for receiver John Taylor, but right into the hands of Bengals cornerback Lewis Billups, who dropped it. Had he caught the ball, the play not only would have changed the game, but it might have altered the entire narrative around Montana's career. His drop gave Montana a second chance, which was more important than the myth of personal perfection. It was a reminder that all of the numbers football fans used to define players weren't real. The only real thing was what happened on the field.

BRADY WAS A perfectionist, and that included perfecting the art of rebounding. Like John McEnroe, mistakes enraged Brady, but also refocused him. On the rare occasions when he had a bad moment, he would always—*always*—bounce back. Four plays after Howard's interception of Brady, Delhomme hit receiver Muhsin Muhammad for a Super Bowl–record 85-yard touchdown pass. Carolina led, 22–21, with 6:53 to go. Charlie Weis called passes on nine of the next drive's 12 plays. Brady completed six of them. "It never entered my mind that he was frazzled," Weis recalled. The final pass, on second and goal from the one-yard line, was a play called 136 X-Cross Z-Flag—a new play, designed for the Super Bowl. Early in the game, Weis had called a short-yardage run with 6-foot-6, 317-pound defensive tackle Richard Seymour lined up at fullback and Mike Vrabel at tight end. The Patriots ran behind Seymour, and the Panthers blew up the play for a loss. This time, Weis inserted Seymour and Vrabel again, but Brady faked a handoff and hit Vrabel on a shallow cross for a touchdown. On his first touchdown pass in the second quarter, Brady had been so pumped that he tackled receiver Deion Branch in the end zone, body-slamming the receiver so hard, he knocked the wind out of him. "Tom, what are you doing?" Branch said. This time, Brady seemed relieved, his penance lifted. After a two-point conversion, New England led, 29–22, with 2:51 left.

Delhomme refused to concede. New England had lost both of its safeties during the game: Eugene Wilson had a pulled groin and Rodney Harrison broke his right arm. A pair of special-teams players were now on the field. "A nightmare," Eric Mangini recalled. "It's like you went from feeling great to wanting to throw up." Delhomme went 80 yards in seven plays, the final blow a 12-yard touchdown pass to Ricky Proehl, the ex-Ram who had scored the game-tying touchdown against the Patriots two years earlier, only to learn that his team had left Tom Brady too much time.

Proehl was about to learn it all over again. Panthers kicker John Kasay botched the kickoff by sending the ball out of bounds, a penalty that awarded New England the ball at its own 40-yard line. Brady took over with 1:08 left, needing a field goal to win. Muhammad watched

Brady take the field and told teammate Steve Smith, "It's not over yet. Not with that quarterback."

Brady hit three passes for a total of 30 yards after a 10-yard penalty, then faced a third and three from the Panthers' 40-yard line with 15 seconds left. He still needed one big chunk to reach field goal range. The Patriots had one time-out, allowing them to throw anywhere on the field without fear of the clock expiring. Weis selected a play with Deion Branch running a deep out pattern. Brady took the shotgun snap, looked left, then glanced to the center of the field, holding the safety in place—a subtle but essential move that wouldn't have been possible without the remaining time-out—and turned back right. He had manipulated the safeties just enough to shake Branch open. Brady hit him on the numbers for 17 yards, setting up a 41-yard field goal attempt.

Off came Brady. On came Vinatieri—and Kinchen, his prayers unanswered. Kinchen had spent the previous few minutes practicing snaps on the sideline, starting to feel sick to his stomach. *There's no way this plays out well for me*, he thought. After Branch's catch, Ken Walter said, "BK, we're on the field!"

Carolina called a time-out. Conventional wisdom held that you could "ice" the kicker. But New England's snapper, not its kicker, was the nervous one. Kinchen paced the field. Walter tried to rope him back into the huddle.

"Brian!" he yelled.

"Shut up!" Kinchen said. "Just let me do my thing."

Most athletes summon up positive memories before their biggest moments, drawing confidence from success. Kinchen invoked failure. He thought about a play from a year earlier, when Trey Junkin, a long snapper for the New York Giants, botched a snap against the 49ers in the playoffs for what would have been the game-winning field goal. Junkin played 19 years in the NFL, but he was remembered for that one mistake. Kinchen decided that no matter what, he would throw this snap as hard as he could. *If this ball is missing, it's missing at full speed!*

New England lined up. Belichick put his hands on his knees. Bruschi found Seely for good luck. Kinchen crouched over the ball, gently rocking his ass back and forth, not enough to draw a false-start penalty, but enough to provide a subtle rhythm, like trying to quiet a screaming baby. Walter flexed out his fingers, calling for the ball.

Kinchen threw hard and listened for a thud. One thud was good news. It was the sound of Vinatieri's foot meeting the ball. Two thuds were bad news. It meant the ball had either hit the turf before Vinatieri kicked it or had been blocked. Kinchen heard one thud. His snap was perfect, miraculously. Walter spotted it with ease. Vinatieri hit it and immediately raised both arms, knowing it was good before the officials signaled it. Kinchen dropped to his knees and screamed.

The Patriots were Super Bowl champions for the second time in three years, vaulting Belichick onto the short list of greatest coaches in football history. Always a self-scout, Belichick thought he hadn't coached well. He had activated only five defensive linemen for the game, rather than six. "Stupid," he said. With its overwrought introductions and halftime show, the Super Bowl was at least an hour longer than most games. The drawn-out nature of the game hit the defensive line hardest, draining the pass rush in the fourth quarter. Belichick had robbed himself of the ability to rotate in fresh legs. He never repeated that mistake again, and he exploited it when opposing coaches committed the same error against him in future Super Bowls.

On the field as the confetti fell, Kinchen shouted at Belichick, who was on the stage to receive the Vince Lombardi Trophy. He caught the coach's eye. "I told ya I'd get it done!" Belichick barely acknowledged him. "I shouldn't even speak to you after what you put Bill through this week," Debby Belichick told him moments later.

The experience nearly destroyed Kinchen as well. "Every nerve in my body was frayed." Even years later, it was both exhilarating and traumatic to relive it. At the team ring ceremony a few months after the Super Bowl, an apparently semi-buzzed Belichick approached him. Kinchen had a weird relationship with his two-time coach, at once wary of him and unafraid to bust his balls. But this likely would be the last time they crossed paths. Kinchen wanted a photo. He pulled Belichick and Pioli in front of a photographer and wedged in between them. Right before the camera flashed, Belichick mumbled something weird but funny, forcing a laugh from all three men.

"A rose between two thorns."

TOM BRADY NAVIGATED a crowd closing in on him at the Super Bowl postgame party at the InterContinental hotel. From the moment he arrived, he was inundated with autograph and photo requests and was at the center of a slow-moving mania, even though Kid Rock and Aerosmith were performing mere feet away. Brady looked for his family between flashes, hoping for an exit ramp. Michael Silver of *Sports Illustrated* handed him a gin and tonic. "This shit better be strong," Brady said. He gave up and forced his way to an elevator, headed up to the second-floor VIP party. As soon as he walked out of the elevator, the crush returned. He felt like he couldn't breathe. "This is horrible," he said. Finally, his family arrived, along with his new girlfriend: Bridget Moynahan, an actress famous for her roles in *Sex and the City* and *I, Robot*. She greeted him with a kiss, and the crowd gave him some space.

The next 48 hours were a blur, though at least a familiar one. After an hour of sleep, Brady, the game's MVP again, left Monday morning for Disney World, then flew back to Boston for the victory parade Tuesday, then to San Francisco that evening. At his old house, sleeping in his old room, his mood seemed to improve. The next morning, Brady drove 105 miles south to Pebble Beach for the AT&T Pro-Am. It was a fun and rejuvenating few days. At one point, Pebble Beach CEO Bill Perocchi handed Brady the latest *Sports Illustrated*, with his photo behind the headline "The Hero (Again)." Brady flipped though Silver's story in awe. Right then, it seemed to hit him. It was a good day to be Tom Brady.

12

EVERY DAY
BUT GAME DAY

W HEN ROBERT KRAFT WAS ON THE VERGE OF
making Bill Belichick's hiring official in January 2000, the
two of them dined at the Capital Grille in Chestnut Hill,
nestled off Route 9 near Kraft's home. The symmetry of the occasion
was not lost on either man. It was the same steakhouse where, three
years earlier, Kraft had told Belichick he wouldn't replace Bill Parcells,
and now he was getting a shot at his dream job.

"Promise me," Kraft told Belichick, "that when we have success, you
won't change."

Belichick tried not to change. His office, at the end of a long hallway on the east side of Gillette Stadium, remained mostly the same
as the Super Bowls piled up, at least until 2014, when Kraft renovated
the building. The office was small by head-coaching standards. There
was a grease board to the left as one entered, and a bookshelf loaded
with binders to the right. The personal touches were few in number and
felt temporary. Framed photos scattered about—of Bill Russell, Bobby
Orr, the 1980 Olympic hockey team, Adam Vinatieri's famous kicks—
weren't even hung. Instead, they were on the top of a couch and propped
against a wall. The room gave a sense that the place was a rental, as if
Belichick were not the head coach of an expanding dynasty and instead
merely the current occupant. But that's how it was in coaching: only the
unwise turned offices into their own. Most kept no more belongings
than would fit into a few boxes, so that when the inevitable dismissal
arrived, at least they could get out of the building quickly, without a fuss
and parade, retaining some dignity.

Nobody knew this fundamental reality better than Belichick, a spectator to his own life's annihilation in Cleveland. But there was another factor at work. Belichick didn't want to be surrounded by relics. At least not at work. There was a paranoia about complacency in the Patriots facility that started at the top. "I don't believe—our team doesn't believe—in living in the past," he later said.

Belichick used two computers. The one to his left had a big screen, better for watching video. A printer sat nearby. The other computer was a laptop, on which he would take notes. He had a CD player, which was often spinning a Springsteen bootleg, courtesy of his friend and former director of player personnel in Cleveland, Michael Lombardi. The furniture in his office—a table under the grease board, another one behind his desk, the bookshelf, a small and uncomfortable couch, and two chairs—was mismatched, but in vague agreement with his cherry wood desk. The carpet was navy blue.

Nobody knew when Belichick's day actually started, because he was often the first one in the building. The early risers on staff would pull into the dark predawn parking lot at 4:30 a.m. and see his office light on.

Belichick was the most successful person in an increasingly unhinged profession. Dick Vermeil was a cautionary tale when he resigned from the Philadelphia Eagles in 1983, having burned himself out at age 46. By the mid-2000s, something about the job was so broken that it seemed only an intervention could fix it. The hours, the pressure, the biological imperative to win—all of it conspired to make coaches believe that if they could just bend time to their will, Sundays would break their way. The job turned good men into assholes, or maybe it self-selected for assholes. Joe Gibbs of Washington once told a story from the 1980s about a time his eight-year-old son, Coy, spent the day at work with him. But Gibbs was so consumed, he didn't realize Coy was there. "Never even thought about him!" Gibbs later said.

Intense media coverage of America's most popular sport began to expose truths about fatherhood and the profession that had long been covered in silence. Fried from the grind, Bill Cowher stepped down in 2007 after 15 years as the Steelers' head coach to spend more time with his daughters and wife. Two of the sons of Andy Reid of the Philadelphia Eagles, Garrett and Britt, were in separate incidents in the aughts involving drugs and, in Britt's case, drugs and guns, which forced Reid to take a five-week leave of absence. Years later, in 2021, Britt was charged with felony driving while intoxicated after his involvement in a car crash left a young girl in critical condition. Belichick would not be immune: both of his sons would be arrested, Brian for underage drinking and Stephen for drugs.

There was a joke in football that every coach was either born-again or an alcoholic. Coaches had few outlets to cope with the stress. A lot of them drank at the office. Divorce rates were high. Excuses for lack of performance weren't tolerated by management. At one point in the 2000s, a group of coaches and general managers quietly approached the league office about setting up some sort of support system for those in football operations. The league suggested that teams hire in-house therapists— as if a coach would risk the perceived weakness of being spotted spending an hour on the couch for any other reason than a quick nap between grinds. All the hours, all the collateral damage, allowed coaches the space to overthink what was, at its essence, a simple game. In most professions, if you took 19 hours to complete each workday, you would be considered incompetent; in coaching, you were glorified. Of course, just because the coaches were at the office didn't necessarily mean they were working. They spent a lot of time on the phone with their buddies, gossiping and speculating about openings. The point was to be at the office 19 hours a day more than it was to work 19 hours a day.

Belichick's 19 hours were different than anyone else's. Oh, he gossiped, with other coaches and general managers, with owners, even with a select few reporters. Or, more specifically, he would engage in what he called "information flow." He listened, stored away knowledge, perhaps to later deploy to his advantage. "You talk to teams that would help you, but don't want to help another team," he later said. "It's more of just knowing what is going on with that team and what's going on with certain players." Weirdly, as he gained stature and despite his reputation, people just told him stuff. Once, before a game against the Colts, Marvin Harrison bitched to Belichick about how little Peyton Manning was throwing him the ball. That a superstar player, moments before a game, would vent to an opposing coach seemed to tickle Belichick.

But Belichick spent long hours at work not for glory, not for pity, but out of necessity as he saw it, to realize his vision for how a team should be run. He was both taking the sport in new directions, operating on a different plane than the rest of the league, and playing by its oldest rule: there are no excuses. "Don't tell me about the pain, show me the baby," Bill Parcells once said. Belichick worked so hard—and worked the staff so hard—that coaches would liken it to being stationed overseas. Wives felt widowed. Belichick would later realize the pressure he put on his players and staff was too much to bear and would hire a version of an in-house therapist, though not for himself. But that was years away. In 2004, he was chasing immortality, even if he had arguably already attained it, seeking to become the first coach to win three Super Bowls in four years.

WHAT BELICHICK WORKED ON for all those hours in that modest office, nobody really knew. The answer seemed to be everything. He could be watching tape of a handful of collegiate offensive guards in preparation for the draft, or replaying all of his team's third downs from a particular game, or jotting handwritten notes. "There's no set formula for me," he said. "I try to coach the entire team because that's what I'm responsible for." The entire football landscape was his arena, and he was a man who enjoyed delving into the minutiae, with a focus so intense, it was jarring. "He has the wherewithal to maintain concentration over an extended period of time," Parcells once said with admiration. Belichick often seemed happiest alone in his office, with a clicker in his hand, a film savant.

The Patriots were known for being secretive, but few understood how that tendency played out within their own facility. Belichick shared exactly what he believed it was necessary to share. Sometimes, staff would learn about the team's transactions on ESPN.com or the NFL Network or in the *Boston Globe*. Belichick would begin a meeting by telling the staff that the team had signed a player to a new deal, but no more. He wouldn't ask the staff how they felt about it. Nobody would talk money. On most teams, the first question after a player signed a new deal was the amount of the signing bonus. Rookies were sometimes forced to disclose it to the vets during training camp, as almost a hazing ritual. Not in New England. It was nobody's job but Belichick's to worry about compensation. He did his job; you did yours. "No more, no less," he later said.

There was always more work to do. That was one thing you learned at the feet of Bill Belichick. Like all the greats, he created work. "It's not do this or do that," he once said. "It's ultimately do everything." The more Belichick analyzed and considered and reconsidered, the more he needed to know. He worked best in the morning and never appeared sleepy. And to think: he hated coffee. Hated the taste and hated the smell. He had tried it a few times, but coffee-flavored anything, including ice cream, didn't work for him. Belichick just had incredible energy. It was one of the qualities that most impressed Kraft: the sheer force Belichick brought to the job. On most days, Belichick would call Kraft on the drive home, at 10:30 or 11, to fill him in on the day's news. If Kraft missed the call, he would return it first thing in the morning, when Belichick would already be at his desk.

Jerry Seinfeld was once asked how he summoned the will to be great at comedy, even after his legend was secure. He replied that it wasn't about will at all. Will was required to pass on cake after dinner; this was love. He loved everything about comedy, from finding the precise language for a joke to perfecting its delivery. Belichick was the same. "I enjoy all of it," he later said. "It beats working." Kraft paid him to handle all football decisions, and that's what Belichick did. From choosing which photos were hung in the hallways to how the team would write contracts, he expanded the notion of what a coach could control and what a football decision could be. The "little things" were set against "the big picture, all connected," Belichick said. He wanted team marketers to feature groups of players rather than just one, in order to keep the locker room tight and stave off jealousy. He designed player contracts to include incentives based on team rather than individual performance. Most teams included a clause that an offensive player would earn a bonus if he made the Pro Bowl; New England's bonuses activated if the team finished first in the conference or in league scoring. Belichick shared credit after a win and assumed total responsibility after a loss. "We're all going to make mistakes," he later said. "And nobody makes more of them than I do." Belichick read most of the words written about himself and his team while on a treadmill each morning. He would be tipped off beforehand about which reporters were attending his press conferences, and he would scan the room upon entering. He was always prepared. The "little things" all added up to the type of culture Belichick had envisioned from the start. By 2004, he had created it, and the results were obvious. During quiet times, even he would marvel at how good the Patriots had become.

Belichick's 19 hours were not taken up just with game planning and player evaluation. He was also a boss, and even if he set the schedule for himself and the team, his day was not his own. He was at the mercy of anything that came up: a breaking news story, a player or coach with a personal problem. He was a man who spent a lot of time both dictating and reacting. "When you're the head coach, too, things come up from time to time within the day that you don't always plan on but you have to allot time for—whether it be player- or coach-related, or league-related, or whatever it is. So, then sometimes you feel like, 'Well I've got a couple hours to work on this,' and then something happens and you don't. That time vanishes, so you have to find some time to make it up."

If Belichick loved his work, people didn't always love working for him. After the Super Bowl win over the Rams, two assistant coaches looked at each other, with the confetti raining down after a historic upset to cap a wild year, and seemed more relieved than euphoric.

"At what price victory?" one said.

It was not a question. It was a lament. The Patriots had shocked the league in winning a game that would launch a dynasty, and within minutes of it being over, these coaches felt relief rather than joy. And, of course, within hours of that win, Belichick was already thinking bigger, telling Jason Licht, the team's national scout, "Now what? We win more."

New England's building was a strange place, even by the standards of NFL team facilities: quiet and lifeless and focused. There were so many meetings to prepare for and so many meetings to attend. Some would last for hours, especially if the team had a bad practice. The staff would convene to watch tape in the early evening, already resigned to a long night that was about to become even longer. Belichick would find every mistake, replaying it over and over and nitpicking the assistant coaches. If a guard stepped a certain way, Belichick would lay into offensive line coach Dante Scarnecchia.

"Why is this guard stepping this way?"

Most coaches had little choice but to eat the criticism. *Sorry, Coach, we'll get it fixed.* Scarnecchia felt that, when the head coach asked a question, he deserved an answer, and it was up to you to explain it. Scarnecchia had been a sergeant in the Marine Corps Reserve and had mostly coached offensive linemen since 1970. He was a loving hardass around the office who remembered the names of everyone's wife and children—"We got too tunnel visioned in that office," he later said. "We need to know each other as people"—and he would become one of the greatest offensive-line coaches of all time. He didn't mind questions. He did mind if the point of the question was just to question.

"Bill, you got a better way?" Scarnecchia often replied. "We'll do it that way."

Belichick would back off. "Oh, no, that's okay. Just do the way you want to do it."

The staff would break for five minutes, during which they'd hustle to the cafeteria, hoping there was food left. Often, there was not. They'd return to the meeting, hungry and exhausted, knowing that the night was just beginning. Belichick would keep digging into every real and perceived error, belaboring every point. "Why the fuck are we doing this? Have we ever coached a down? That's some bad football out there, fellas. Some bad football." Just when the coaches thought it might be over, and they could return to their desks and start on the hours of work that had been delayed, Belichick would signal that nobody was leaving anytime soon. His time wasn't his, but it wasn't theirs, either. He would bend over, untie his shoes, slide out his feet, and—oh, God no—kick them up on the table, planting them there like a centerpiece. It was horrifying. His socks were damp and sweaty. The room was stuffy and small. There was neither an end nor an escape in sight. As bad as these meetings were, they weren't the worst meetings. The worst meetings were also the most fascinating ones. They took place the night before a game, when Belichick would run through how he saw the contest playing out.

THE ASSISTANT COACHES would gather around a table in the hotel where the team was staying, even for home games, at least ten minutes early. That would please Belichick when he entered. Berj Najarian, the coach's chief of staff, would be with him, usually carrying a folder of material and the coach's schedule. Najarian was tall and thin, with an angular face. His organizational skills made Belichick envious. Although some in the building saw him as a glorified receptionist—Drew Bledsoe once sent him flowers on Secretary's Day—he was a power broker in his own right. There was nobody else in the league quite like him. He was Belichick's gatekeeper, handling media requests and appointments. He was often an anonymous source for beat writers. He helped out with scouting players. In 2000, part of his job was to help improve Belichick's image, and so he arranged for what Belichick detested most: long sitdown interviews in which Belichick could relive mistakes and offer suggestions about what he had learned. Now Belichick's fame had exploded, and he was trying to remain unchanged. Najarian changed for him. He would make it harder for assistants to pop in, frustrating the other coaches. But, in truth, everything Najarian did was a reflection of his boss. If Najarian was different due to Belichick's celebrity and the demands it entailed, it meant that Belichick was different, too, at least in some small ways.

Belichick would sit down at the head of the table, sometimes in a suit, often in a gray team hoodie with the sleeves sheared off. This had become his preferred manner of dress, and the look was so sloppy, so odd, so uniquely his own, that it not only became a signature style in New England—the team marketed and sold short-sleeved hoodies, mimicking the most iconic piece of clothing for a football coach since Bear Bryant's houndstooth—but it became central to his identity, speaking for him in a way he couldn't or wouldn't speak for himself. Yahoo! Sports reported that Belichick initially chose the hoodie as a middle finger to the NFL after it signed a deal worth at least $250 million with Reebok and mandated that all coaches wear its apparel. Belichick thought it was absurd for suits on Park Avenue to tell grown men how to dress. So, he picked the ugliest available piece of clothing, one that appealed to both his inner contrarian and inner slob. It was comfortable, the gray hoodie. He liked the pouch, which made it easier to carry stuff. But the sleeves bothered him. "I have short arms," he recalled. "Most of the time, the sweatshirts that I have just would come all the way down past my fingers."

One day, in front of a few staffers, Belichick said, "Fuck this," and cut the sleeves, leaving them raggedy and uneven.

The hoodie—the look—was now his, perfectly suited to fit both his arms and his personality: a gray shield for a gray man. With the hood over his head, he would glower out at the world with a vague resemblance to the emperor from *Return of the Jedi*, an evil and powerful genius. With the hood down, under parted hair and a skeptical face, often with a pencil nestled behind his ear, the hoodie was a reminder that, no matter how much Belichick's fame increased, he would always be known as a coach, just a coach, always a coach, a grinder who wore the only piece of clothing that suited a man who loved to spend quiet hours in the dark with film to dissect and a clicker in hand. Many famous coaches across sports used their platforms to discuss issues beyond the game. Belichick rarely did. He was a daring coach, but a cautious man. As he saw it, he was here to coach the team, not to tell people how to live. The gray hoodie revealed something essential about Bill Belichick. What kind of man was he? He was a man who preferred that you look at his hacked-off sleeves rather than his face.

Belichick began the meeting by announcing the inactive list. He gave a scouting report on the game's officials. Then, the meeting started in earnest. He would turn to special teams, kicking off the meeting as games do, reiterating what he wanted out of that unit—no penalties, no turnovers—and then ask Brad Seely, "What's the first kickoff return?"

Belichick cared deeply about special teams. His first job in coaching, after his apprenticeship in Baltimore, was as the assistant special-teams coach for the Detroit Lions and head coach Rick Forzano. A longtime friend and colleague of Steve Belichick at Navy, Forzano remembered Billy, as he was known then, hanging around practice, emulating his old man in the film room, marveling at one of his favorite players, Roger Staubach. Belichick continued coaching special teams at his next stop, in Denver in 1978, and then when Ray Perkins hired him in New York in 1979. The Giants were horrible that season, and Belichick was tasked with drawing up various versions of a fake punt to give the team's sorry offense more downs. Some of them succeeded. One spectacularly failed, and it was carved into Belichick's memory. Against the Los Angeles Rams, Belichick called for a direct snap to fullback Brian Kelley, who was then to run outside on a sweep. Kelley got the snap and hustled outside. The Rams had it—had *him*—nailed. Before he was about to be tackled, Kelley inexplicably lateralled to punter Dave Jennings, an All-Pro who could throw and run well—for a punter—and, rather than surrendering, he decided to lower his head for the sticks. He was drilled by three Rams, landing near the cheerleaders. "He got killed," Belichick later said. "His helmet was on sideways, he's looking out through the ear hole." Perkins asked Belichick why he was endangering the team's best player. "Look, we're not running any more fakes like that ever again," Perkins said.

As a head coach, Belichick saw special teams as a way to develop toughness, and to set a standard for his program. NFL players often pouted when shunted onto special teams, a forced layover on the way to earning real money on offense or defense. But star Patriots—Troy Brown, Tedy Bruschi, and, years later, future Hall of Fame tight end Rob Gronkowski—played on special teams at first. One of Belichick's favorite statistics was the correlation between winning and a special-teams touchdown: "I'm not sure if it's 90 percent, but it's definitely high," he said. In a league where roughly half of games were decided by a touchdown or less, "if you can get those seven points that you basically can't count on, that tilts a lot of games right there." The first Super Bowl run was proof: Brown's punt return for a touchdown against the Steelers in the 2001 AFC Championship Game provided the margin of difference.

In the meeting, Seely would have his play for the kickoff or return ready. "Sideline return, check with me."

"You think that's the best call?" Belichick said.

A question like that—designed to check for loose screws but sometimes feeling like a preemptive second-guess, after all the long days in a long week, after all the practices and trading of ideas, after all the calls to wives, saying it was going to be another late night—was a signal that the meeting had now truly, officially begun. There was no right answer. What was Belichick implying? That he disapproved? Was he testing the coach's conviction? Nobody knew. Belichick couldn't help it. He wanted to review everything. Seely learned that the best answer was to say, "I don't know, Coach. What do you want me to run?"

Sometimes, Ernie Adams would join the meeting. Even years into the Patriots run, many coaches still had no idea what he did. He was a private man, and would grow even more so over the years, as though he was a clandestine secret weapon, especially after he was a central figure in a massive cheating scandal. Adams and Belichick, friends since they both attended Phillips Academy Andover, had both broken into the NFL in 1975, and while Belichick was known around the league as a young coach on the fast track, Adams had achieved a more powerful position at an earlier age, being named the Giants' director of player personnel at 29. Three years later, he was out of a job. He traded the football world for the finance world, working at Mabon, Nugent and Company, a private investment firm in downtown Manhattan. He was a quiet and diligent grinder at Mabon who brought a brown-bagged lunch every day—sometimes reusing the same brown bag—and he gave others the impression that it wasn't his choice to leave the NFL. But he was a brilliant trader, putting his near-photographic memory and insatiable desire to analyze obscure pieces of information to profitable use. Rumor had it that Adams made Belichick himself a fortune during those years. He left banking in the early 1990s to join Belichick in Cleveland, and then went to New England with Belichick in 2000.

Adams had a goofy aspect, with thick glasses, a thicker mustache, and an awkward Boston accent. But he was genuinely pursuing greatness. More specifically, he was driven to help Belichick achieve greatness. Adams was egoless, both a resource and a security blanket. He spent most days holed up in his office, poring over film—often blurry footage of hand signals used by coaches to call in plays from the sideline—and studying the rule book, searching for loopholes. He was in all of the draft meetings, known for comparing a prospect to someone who had played in the 1970s and for offering advice on the team's value chart— when to draft a player, and when to trade down. Once, Adams called a Rutgers University professor who had researched when teams should try for a two-point conversion. Adams sent him New England's chart— every team had a chart telling them when to go for two—and asked him to analyze it, and to rip it apart if need be. No other team had called the researcher, either because they didn't know about him or were too scared to be questioned. It was Adams at his best.

At his worst, Adams would doze off. Sensing an opportunity, the coaches would try to give him a hard time, asking him if he'd been out "trick-fucking all night." He failed to see the humor. Scarnecchia would stop at Adams's office and yell, "Wake up, Ernie!" When Adams spoke, the coaches were often underwhelmed. Belichick would ask his opinion about whether to go for it on fourth down in a particular situation, knowing Adams had read a paper by a University of California, Berkeley professor that made a statistical case that rolling the dice on fourth and short wasn't a gamble, but a smart decision. Adams would often equivocate. "Well, Bill, if you've got a good play. . . ." It irritated the coaches who wanted him to make a clear argument.

On game day, the Adams experience was even weirder. He sat in the coaches' box, with a stack of notes and a direct line to Belichick's headset. Sometimes, Belichick would ask his opinion about a replay challenge, rule, or a fourth-down decision. Sometimes, Adams would claim to know what play was coming, and would yell into Belichick's ear, "It's Cover 2!" "It's a blitz!" "It's a run here!" He was almost never right. At halftime, while the rest of the staff hustled to meet with players and prepare for the third quarter, Adams would wander around the locker room, munching on a hot dog, maybe two.

Adams was a nerdy man who appealed to Belichick's inner nerd. His cause was as much Belichick as it was the Patriots, his employer. He wanted neither credit nor stature. He wasn't out for Belichick's job. Everyone should be so lucky with a best friend. Adams was once asked to list his favorite books, as a means of glimpsing his motivations and inspirations. His answers included *The Best and the Brightest* by David Halberstam and Robert Caro's multivolume biography of Lyndon B. Johnson. Adams was fascinated by transcendent achievers—and how those men self-destructed. The fragility of greatness was as interesting as greatness itself.

AFTER SPECIAL TEAMS, Belichick would continue around the room. When he got to Romeo Crennel, he'd ask, "What's your call on third and three?"

Belichick was not just asking for a defensive call. He wanted to make sure Crennel knew the opponent's tendencies in short-yardage situations, and that he had an answer in the form of percentages. Belichick was big on percentages. He liked to play the odds. "He wanted us to know what we were going to call," Crennel said, "and not *wonder*." For as many hours as there were between games to imagine possibilities, for as much time as coaches spent at the office, most NFL teams were predictable. Coaches were creatures of habit. Most stuck with what they knew. Which was why Belichick not only wanted detailed scouting reports on opposing teams, but also opposing coaches. Few were smart and creative enough to unveil a surprise each week. That basic reality was a massive indictment of the entire industry, and hard to fathom. Bill Walsh once said that the 49ers' true competition was not the entire league, but rather seven or eight smart teams. Jimmy Johnson, the Super Bowl–winning coach of the 1990s Dallas Cowboys and one of Belichick's good friends, once told him, "If you just stay out of the way, the other 20 teams will screw it up themselves." The Patriots cared little about the infant Houston Texans. The Colts, Broncos, Eagles, Jets, Chargers, Rams, Packers—those were the threats.

One of the first pages of a Patriots defensive scouting report was usually a breakdown of the opponent's offensive performance in three areas, in bold type:

* Down and Distance Tendencies
* Situational Tendencies
* Formation Tendencies

Under each heading were percentages of run and pass, anything that helped "tell the story," as the report later said in bold type. The report was based on seven games that the coaches had dissected, a mix of recent games the opponent had played, games the opponent had played against the Patriots, and games where the opponent had faced teams that played in a similar style to the Patriots. For the Buffalo Bills in 2003, a line in the report looked like this:

* 2nd 1 to 3 = 8R/6P = balanced. This is BIG TIME SHOT ALERT.

Translation: on second and short, the Bills' chances of calling a run or a pass were essentially equal—eight runs versus six passes. And if it *was* a pass, watch out for a throw downfield.

* Red Area 58% pass. Down and distance "Tells the Story" 3rd down is 85% pass ... 1st down is actually more Run than Pass (66% run) ... usually is X Fade (#80).

Translation: the Patriots' breakdowns of the "red area"—when the Bills were inside their opponents' 20-yard line, about to score—were often the most detailed. Belichick considered the red zone the most important part of the field, where a stop on third down would be the difference between a field goal and touchdown, what Michael Lombardi called "a four-point play." This breakdown told the Patriots that the Bills passed more often than they ran in the red area overall, but ran more often than they passed on first down. If they threw near the goal line, the X receiver—Pro Bowl receiver Eric Moulds, number 80—usually ran a fade route, one of the easiest pass patterns to defend if the defender knew it was coming.

* 2-Minute + Hurry-Up = 10R/76P = 88% Pass. Runs are all inside runs mostly Draw 42/43. Overall, all but 8 passes were 6 man protections and dropback passes. They will throw to the back out of the backfield. Only a couple of screens and no boots or dashes.

Translation: when the Bills shifted to a no-huddle offense, they would throw most of the time; if they ran, it was likely to be between the tackles. The key was that the Bills, led by the immobile Drew Bledsoe, called plays that kept him in the pocket. He was a sitting duck, allowing the Patriots to collapse the pocket without fear of him escaping or improvising.

All of this jargon, this complex shorthand for a language few spoke fluently, was a key part of the "mosaic" of information that went into game plans, as Belichick put it. As usual, he was ahead of the rest of the league. Twelve years later, toward the end of New England's dynasty, a writer named Warren Sharp began publishing an annual book of each team's tendencies, based on personnel and circumstance. Coaches bought it, believing they had acquired proprietary information. But the book was exactly what the Patriots were doing more than a decade earlier. "If I were to show you some of the sheets that he brings in, oh God, it's incredible," Brady said of Belichick. "I think he knows what their defense is doing more so than their defensive players know what they're doing. And to have him come in each day to break down film with us, to understand why teams are playing certain coverages, certain schemes each week, you go into a game realizing, 'Hey, there's nothing this defense can do to surprise us because we've seen it all.'"

Saturday night meetings concluded only after Belichick felt confident in his coaches and the overall plan. And then, the next day, what Belichick expected to happen usually did. Once, before facing the Jets, Belichick told the coaches during the Saturday night meeting how New England would be attacked. He told the defensive coaches that the Jets would test New England with seam passes and throw to the tight end in the red area, and he told the offensive coaches not to run deep sideline routes at cornerback Darrelle Revis, because the future Hall of Famer covered them particularly well. Sure enough, the Jets attacked with seam passes—and hit them. New York's tight end scored a touchdown. Brady tested Revis deep, and Revis picked him off. The Patriots lost. Nobody, not even a coach as astute and as weathered as Bill Belichick, could control for everything. It was why, despite his outward stoicism, Belichick was still nervous in the moments before kickoff. "Every year, I walk on the field before the game and I think, 'This will be a little better this year,' and it never is. . . . But the buildup, the anxiety, the butterflies—that's the perfect word for it, because that's what they are."

New England's system earned a name among football writers and fans: the Patriot Way. The term was defined as the emotionless pursuit of victory, but also as a team-first ethos, and as arrogance. In truth, it was a combination of the three. A phrase rarely if ever used inside the building, the Patriot Way was studied in business schools, a catchall term for a system that evolved each year, each season, each week. Players on other teams would talk about how their game plans were presented on Wednesdays during the season. In New England, a version of the plan was installed on Wednesday, and it would undergo several revisions and tweaks and adjustments until the game itself ended, a malleable theory more than a rigid conclusion. This was possible for one reason: Bill Belichick. *He* was the system. One day, after New England's second Super Bowl, I stood on a practice field with Michael Lombardi. Talk turned to Belichick. As the Patriots continued winning, Belichick's assistant coaches were in demand around the league, with team owners trying to tap into Belichick's system, his methodology—most of all, his mind. Both Romeo Crennel and Charlie Weis had received feelers from teams in need of head coaches. It seemed inevitable that 2004 would be their final year in New England. I wondered how those potential losses would impact the Patriots. Lombardi shook his head.

"It's all Belichick," he said.

IT WASN'T ALWAYS all Belichick. Until he won a Super Bowl with Bill Parcells, Belichick was best known for being the son of a football legend. Football coaches have a militaristic obsession with stripes earned and dues paid. Belichick had grown up watching film with his dad, absorbing a career's worth of knowledge by his 20s. But that didn't count. When Bill first arrived at the New York Giants in 1979, players were more in awe of his father than of him. Bill inherited his father's understated manner, his relentless discipline, his passion for finding football's overlooked details. Unlike his father, Bill was not a child of the Depression, but he worked as if he were one from the start. When Bill was in high school, Steve held football camps in the summer. Bill would help out. He met a lot of good coaches, including George Boutselis, with whom he would later work on the Baltimore Colts staff. During football season, Bill followed his father around Navy's campus. When he revisited Navy as an adult, he still heard the sounds of the team's cleats on the sidewalks echoing through the yards.

Steve "didn't have much patience," Belichick said. But he was fair, and he wanted to help. Steve either knew every powerful figure in football or knew someone who knew them. He helped his son gain an audience with Ted Marchibroda that led to his first job with the Colts in 1975. After his first few years with Baltimore and Detroit—after both staffs were fired—Bill was at a crossroads. Steve helped arrange a phone call with Don Shula, then the coach of the Miami Dolphins. Belichick was hoping for a job, eager to learn at the feet of a future Hall of Famer. On the call, he offered to break down film so that coaches could focus on bigger items. Shula apologetically replied, "I'm afraid you're exactly what I *don't* want." Belichick was stunned. Shula explained himself. "I don't want someone like you doing film. I want my coaches to do it themselves."

It was a compliment wrapped in rejection: Belichick was too advanced. In the 1970s and 1980s, many coaches were former players, at the very least at a major college program, if not the NFL. Having played at a high level was one of the few ways to earn the respect of the locker room. Steve Belichick had played football. For all practical purposes, Bill Belichick had not. Division III Wesleyan, where he was a center and tight end in the early 1970s, didn't count in this world. When Belichick arrived in New York, players knew him as a former lacrosse player who was "riding his dad's coattails and hadn't earned the right to be in the NFL," defensive end George Martin said.

Giants players did not just defy Belichick; they were dismissive of him. If he ordered them to hit the weight room, they walked slowly. If he asked someone to flick on the lights during a meeting, nobody did. In one meeting, Belichick shifted the dynamic, from the players' turf to his own. He noticed Gary Jeter, a talented but underperforming defensive lineman, carrying on a conversation. Jeter wasn't trying to test Belichick; he simply didn't care about anything the coach had to say. Belichick lost his cool. "Hey, Jeter—one of the reasons you fucking guys were [6–10] last year was because your special teams stunk, and so, if you want to laugh about it, if you think it's a joke, you can get the hell out of here." Jeter ended the side conversation. It was not a watershed moment, with Belichick now suddenly in command, but it was a small step.

In 1985, Bill Parcells officially handed off the defense to Belichick. Many players were furious, including the most important one.

"You gotta be kidding me," Lawrence Taylor told Parcells.

In the early 1980s, the Giants had underachieved. Jobs were on the line. Parcells knew the culture had to change. *He* had to change. He loved hanging with the guys in the locker room—he was a gifted and cutting conversationalist—but in 1986, he stopped, and started channeling his inner asshole. Nobody was spared, the coaches least of all—and among the coaches, Belichick least of all. Parcells believed he had given Belichick a gift in the form of the Giants' talented defensive roster, from Taylor to Martin to Carl Banks. He seemed to be telling Belichick what Belichick would later tell his own assistants: "I've given you all you need—don't fuck it up."

The two of them often screamed at each other on the sideline during games. Sometimes, Belichick ignored Parcells. Sometimes, he redirected the abuse onto the defense. "If I have to take it, you have to take it. Shit runs downhill." Once, after Belichick pushed back on Parcells, the head coach told him over the headset, with all the coaches listening, "Don't you give me any shit, Belichick. Your ass will be out in the parking lot."

"Sensitivity really wasn't in play," Parcells recalled.

Parcells had all kinds of catchphrases, known as Parcellsisms. One of his favorites was to say, "Just because you've identified a problem doesn't mean you're any closer to solving it." But Belichick was starting to solve problems—and both Parcells and the locker room noticed. In 1986, Belichick came into his own as a coach and the Giants came into their own as a team. New York won the Super Bowl, going a combined 5–0 against Bill Walsh's San Francisco 49ers and Joe Gibbs's Washington Redskins. A 17–0 shutout of Washington in the NFC Championship Game earned Parcells a Gatorade bath and Belichick a victory ride off the field on the shoulders of two players. "Nothing you can do about it," Belichick later said of being lifted. "Nothing you want to do about it." Barton Silverman of the *New York Times* snapped a photo of Belichick lifted high and smiling, and it made the upper fold of the front page on January 12, 1987, his first time on the front page of the world's most important newspaper. "I must have had 100 copies of it," he said.

Years later, with his legacy secure but still in progress, Belichick toured Giants Stadium before it was demolished, followed by a camera crew. He walked through the old, dank hallways, past the coaches' locker room and the racquetball court where he would play, and often beat, Parcells. Before the tour ended, he stood in a hallway and glanced at his old office. The nostalgia got to him. He teared up. That office was where he had sharpened himself, killing what made him weak to the players and strengthening what made him respected—where he had entered as the son of a great football man and left as one himself.

13

20/20S

FOR YEARS IN NEW ENGLAND, A PIPELINE WAS AT work.

From the moment Belichick hired Charlie Weis and Romeo Crennel and even Scott Pioli, he was grooming a pool of candidates to replace them: Eric Mangini, Josh McDaniels, Brian Daboll, Nick Caserio, Thomas Dimitroff, and Matt Patricia. He loved few elements of football more than molding an army of young men. One of the non-football books that shaped Belichick was *Jack Welch and the GE Way*. Welch's philosophy about the dual loyalty involved in hiring and training—invest in a young staffer, and the young staffer will run through a brick wall to reward the show of faith—reinforced not only what Belichick believed, but what he had lived rising up the ranks. It was easier and cheaper to hire young and teach novices how the New England system operated than it was to bring in an older coach who was set in his ways. Belichick had employed the same approach in Cleveland, where he hired Mangini, Pioli, Dimitroff, and Jim Schwartz, all of whom would end up as NFL GMs or head coaches in the coming decades. They were called "Slappies," short for "slapdicks." Their jobs ranged from making copies and runs to the airport to mowing the lawns of coaches. All of them had varying stories about how they entered Belichick's world, but Pioli's stood out. They had met in 1987, before Pioli's senior season at Central Connecticut State University. The Giants had just won their first Super Bowl, and through a mutual friend, Pioli gained an audience with Belichick during training camp. Pioli wanted to work in football, and was driving 90 minutes each way a few times a week from the Hartford area to Madison, New Jersey, where the Giants held camp, to meet coaches and learn. Belichick could sense his passion, and when he learned that Pioli was commuting—"You're driving back and forth?"—he invited the young man to bunk with him and another coach. Pioli slept on the couch and followed the two coaches from practice to the film room, an astounding football education. Years later, Belichick offered Pioli a chance to join the staff in Cleveland. "I don't know what the job is yet, but I'm offering you one." It was for $16,000 a year—$8,000 less than a competing offer Pioli had from the San Francisco 49ers, who at the time were the league's reigning dynasty. He chose Cleveland.

Pioli followed Belichick to the Jets, then to New England as assistant director of player personnel, eventually being promoted to vice president of player personnel. Kraft initially wasn't going to let Belichick hire Pioli—who had married Bill Parcells's daughter—but he relented. Pioli developed into a perfect lieutenant, carrying out what Belichick asked him to do each day, and although Belichick had final say over football decisions, Pioli was instrumental in helping him clean up the salary-cap mess left by Bobby Grier. Belichick had pledged to develop the team through the draft, believing this to be the efficient and cost-effective way forward, but the draft was a crapshoot, even for him. By 2004, only Tom Brady, fullback Patrick Pass, and offensive lineman Adrian Klemm remained from the 2000 draft class. Where New England under Belichick and Pioli excelled was in free agency. After the Patriots emerged as a dynasty, there had been a whitewashing of Belichick's Cleveland tenure, as if he had done nothing wrong in a five-year run with one winning season. That was partly true—it wasn't his fault that Modell moved the team—but Pioli, ever the self-scout, believed they had made a critical mistake with the Browns in free agency. They had wanted blue-collar men who loved football more than money and fame. But, under pressure to win, the Browns had signed players who were the opposite of the ideal type. Free agents visiting Belichick's Browns would arrive at the airport to a waiting limo, in which they were ushered to the best hotels and fed at a steak house. Pioli felt it was inconsistent with Belichick's personality. At one point in New England, Pioli said, "Let's just tell people who we are and what we do. Why are we blowing smoke up their asses when that's not what we're going to do when they're here?"

From Rodney Harrison to Corey Dillon, a talented and bruising but troubled running back the Patriots signed for the 2004 season from the Cincinnati Bengals, nobody got the star treatment after Belichick got his second chance to run a team. It was work, not a college-recruiting visit. Pioli would win two NFL executive-of-the-year awards in his first five years on the job, establishing a template for all of the Slappies.

In New England, Slappies were called "PHDs"—poor, hungry, and driven—or "20/20s": young men who worked 20 hours a day for $20,000 a year. The interview process was daunting. The candidate would be put in a room with the coaching staff, as if in front of a firing squad, a test of how badly you wanted to be part of something great. One interviewee pledged to live in a motor home parked in the stadium lot, promising to leave only to walk his dog. In 2000, Belichick brought in Daboll, who had worked at Michigan State as a graduate assistant under head coach Nick Saban, Belichick's former defensive coordinator in Cleveland, who later became one of the greatest college football coaches in history, winning seven national championships. After the coaches interviewed Daboll—they fired verbal darts at him for an hour—Scarnecchia asked Daboll a question that indicated he had passed the hazing ritual. It was about his salary expectations.

"Seventy thousand," Daboll said, laying out a rationale based on his previous experience and research he had done on the internet. The coaches were impressed. Daboll was resourceful—and delusional. Everyone started snickering.

"Would you do it for $20,000?" Scarnecchia asked.

"Yep," Daboll said.

"Would you do it for $12,000?" Seely asked.

"Yep."

And so it went. Belichick had broken into the league at $25 a week; he always lowballed when hiring. Once in the door, no task was too menial. "The more you can do," Belichick liked to say, "the more you can do." If you worked in scouting, your job was to turn the room lights on and off during long film sessions. If you worked in the video department, your job was to do whatever video director Jimmy Dee said, including the odd and furtive task of videotaping the opposing sidelines during games. If you worked in coaching, your first job was to write down the daily practice schedule on a grease board. Daboll did it for a while, though his script was often illegible. One day, Belichick saw the scribbled mess and shook his head.

"Sit the fuck down," he said, more playful than angry. He turned to McDaniels. "Josh, you do that."

McDaniels wrote out the schedule in perfect penmanship. It was his job the rest of the way—and one of the tiny moments that launched his career.

The coaching staff was both tight-knit and intensely competitive, all exhausted, all underpaid, all tagged with the blessing and curse of being deemed "smarter" than the rest of the league, all riders on a shotgun dynasty that arrived out of nowhere, all pushed to the edge by Belichick, but in awe of him. Belichick worked them hard—once, an assistant petitioned him to allow families to visit the facility on Thursday nights for dinner; Belichick said no—but there was a benefit not captured in the salary or even in all the winning: he provided them with a measure of job security. Belichick rarely fired coaches; once you were in, you were mostly in. The idea of stability in an unstable profession was deeply personal to Belichick. He was too young to remember when his parents sat in an empty, rented house in Nashville after Vanderbilt fired the football staff, including his father, all of their furniture in storage, waiting and wondering when the next job would arrive, but that experience stuck with him nevertheless. And he was scarred decades later, when Modell destroyed the lives of the families of the football staff Belichick worked so hard to protect.

"When you're the head coach, there are a lot of people that are dependent on you," he later said. "It's important to me to be able to hopefully provide some stability to the other members of the coaching staff." The coaches might work all hours, but their kids could at least attend the same school for multiple years. They could make friends and live in the same house. Those were no small things in this line of work. Belichick would reward the coaches who made little, out of his own pocket. During the season, he gave out what were called "green balls," wads of cash that could reach thousands of dollars. After the season, he would write a personal check to staffers who had overperformed—sometimes up to the six figures.

WINNING BROUGHT EXPOSURE. By 2004, Crennel and Weis had more than paid their dues. Crennel had known Belichick since the Giants days in the 1980s and they were entering their 18th year together. There was a mutual respect and trust, even if Crennel was in the strange position of being a defensive coach working for a transcendent defensive mind. He had a big, broad smile and was "a joy to work for," Mangini later said, so much so that on the rare occasions when he erupted, the coaches and players took it seriously. He was one of the few coaches who could both command a room—he came from a military family—and could be a soothing presence. Whenever Belichick was antsy, Crennel would say, "Don't worry, Coach—we'll get it fixed," and it mostly set Belichick at ease.

Weis was more transparently ambitious than Crennel. He wanted to be a head coach. He was always pulling assistant coaches into his office, telling them about all the interest in him his agent had received. There's an inherent tension between a head coach who specializes on one side of the ball and a coordinator whose expertise is on the other. Weis called the offense, but it was Belichick's offense, not only in philosophy—he had assembled a playbook over the years, taking concepts from Joe Gibbs's Redskins, Bill Walsh's 49ers, and the stuff the Giants ran—but in execution. One of Belichick's most vital weekly tasks was to make sure that he was aligned for the upcoming game with his most important player: Tom Brady.

IT BEGAN ON August 6, 2001, when Belichick entered a staff meeting and said, "Dick Rehbein passed away today." Rehbein, the team's quarterbacks coach, had a preexisting heart condition and had died during a stress test. Belichick picked up Rehbein's workload. When Weis missed a few days of training camp in 2002 due to his recovery from gastric bypass surgery—an operation that nearly killed him—Belichick took over meeting with the quarterbacks daily again. By then, it was clear that Brady was the Patriots' future, and so Belichick also met with him twice a week, a ritual that would continue until the end. Although the backup quarterbacks were allowed to attend the Brady meetings—these were high-level scouting conversations, where Belichick strategized on attacking opposing defensive backs—Weis was not. Weis would have liked an invite—"They would have been informative," he later said—but Belichick preferred that time with Brady alone, or at least without any other coaches in the room.

Belichick was training Brady to coordinate the offense no matter who held the title of offensive coordinator, and creating a partnership that transcended circumstance and change, immune to roster or staff. It was also a relationship that really worked during the early years, perhaps the best years of their shared time together. Both men collected slights alongside their scars, and both loved proving people wrong. They did it in different ways—Belichick with a scowl, Brady with a smile—but it was the same urge and behavior, the same rush of triumph. Brady thought Belichick could be an asshole, but he was so eager to learn, and win, and win more, that he didn't care. Belichick knew that to be great in football, you needed luck. Brady had fallen into his lap and was the perfect vessel for the program he wanted to build, willing to take hard coaching. Tom Brady and Bill Belichick were two special talents who knew that they needed each other—and knew how different it all could have been, had they not found one another. Brady often wondered what his life might have been like if, say, he'd been drafted by the Arizona Cardinals. He likely would have been successful. But would he have been great, a Hall of Famer, one of the best ever to play the game? Their shared fortune was a powerful bond, and motivator.

And it left Weis in a weird spot, working his ass off on a team where the head coach and the quarterback got all the credit. Weis was in Belichick's inner circle, but not the innermost one. He wasn't Ernie Adams, who also met alone with Brady, an overlooked mentor in the quarterback's development, telling him to "make them defend every blade of grass." Belichick had set up a brain trust that could sustain losses at key coaching positions, which called into question the entire notion that they were key coaching positions. Belichick always made a staffer prove he could do the job before he was awarded the title and compensation. Belichick went one year in Cleveland with no offensive coordinator and would do the same in New England. Titles mattered less than performance. And so, Weis was both an important coach, able to handle the offense, and a replaceable one. Still, Weis admired what he termed Belichick's "insight and foresight"—insight for how he planned for games, with no detail viewed as inconsequential; foresight for how he could see the big picture with stunning clarity and could anticipate issues months or even years beforehand, related to salary cap, roster—or coaching staff. Belichick often joked that the time between today and the next game was "long term for me," but nobody since Bill Walsh had been more prescient.

Weis and Crennel were now part of their boss's foresight. Belichick's plans to replace them—and the jockeying for jobs after their assumed departures—had started in 2003.

Of all the candidates, Mangini and McDaniels were clearly the favorites—and the favored sons. A college quarterback and receiver at John Carroll University and son of Thom McDaniels, a renowned high school coach in Ohio, McDaniels had arrived on a recommendation from Saban, who had hired him at Michigan State, as an assistant to break down film for the defensive staff and work in scouting. McDaniels was smart and ambitious and handled everything Belichick threw at him—and Belichick threw a lot at him. After the 2002 season, the Patriots needed help in the secondary. Belichick told McDaniels to evaluate 35 defensive backs eligible for the draft and compare them against available free agents. McDaniels did it, and helped find a pair of starters in the 2003 draft: Eugene Wilson, out of Illinois, and Asante Samuel, out of Central Florida. Of course, Belichick saw the study not just as a way to scout players, but also to scout McDaniels. He wanted to know "what kind of guy do I have here?" McDaniels recalled. "Is he going to be a trustworthy, top-notch guy who can assist me? Or is there a ceiling? He always tried to push you."

Belichick had deemed McDaniels proficient, and so he started to move him around, from defense to offense, giving him the full football education that his program both offered and demanded. "Once they get the experience," Belichick said, "they get how our system fits together." Belichick gave McDaniels another research project. The Patriots had whiffed on several receivers in the draft—wideout was a blind spot for Belichick; nobody could explain why—and Belichick asked McDaniels and Nick Caserio, who had played college football with McDaniels at John Carroll and who worked in the Patriots' scouting department and with the receivers, to break down every non-Patriots defensive back in the AFC East and reimagine job descriptions for receivers based on the skill set required to face them. Belichick wanted the two to look at how the corners covered receivers as they lined up on the strong side, on the weak side, in the slot, on the perimeter, in zone, in man-to-man, and in combination coverages; then to dissect the receivers who had success against them, in terms of size, speed, quickness, and ball skills; and, finally, to rank which skill and trait the Patriots should prioritize. The report took three months. But Belichick was so impressed with the results that he used it as a template for rewriting the Patriots scouting manual for receivers. By the 2004 season, Belichick had promoted McDaniels to quarterbacks coach.

Mangini was more than a favored son: it was as if he were an actual son. Like Belichick, Mangini had not only attended Wesleyan, not only played football, but had been a member of the same fraternity: Chi Psi. Mangini was working as a ball boy and PR intern for the Browns when Belichick saw something special in him and moved him to football operations. He gave him a project: to analyze the fumble history of every free-agent running back. Mangini aced it. He joined Belichick with the Jets in 1997 as a defensive assistant. They would spend hours together in the film room, Mangini earning his football doctorate. They grew close: Belichick read a poem at Mangini's wedding, and Mangini named his secondborn son Luke William. Mangini was one of the few coaches unafraid to battle with Belichick over personnel or scheme, even if in vain. In 2003, Mangini had lobbied hard for the team to draft Asante Samuel. The Patriots had two fourth-round picks, and Mangini was convinced Belichick would use one of them on Samuel. After Belichick picked Dan Klecko, a defensive lineman out of Temple and son of Joe Klecko, the former Jets Pro Bowl defensive end, Mangini was so angry that he threw food against a wall. Belichick drafted Samuel with the Patriots' next pick.

Mangini was more than a pupil or even an adopted son; he was a friend, one of the few people in the building who looked out for the boss. "You need someone to tell you if you have spinach in your teeth," Mangini recalled. Belichick gave Mangini lessons in both life and football. Most coaches wanted long-term contracts, thinking mainly of job security, but Belichick always advised him to sign one-year deals. "Have faith in yourself," Belichick often said. It was the best way to get bigger raises—and to be free to leave for the right opportunity.

The three young men in whom Belichick had invested the most—Pioli, McDaniels, and Mangini—would all eventually leave for what they saw as the right opportunity, carrying with them the lessons they'd learned in New England and saddled with impossible expectations. But during the 2004 season, as defending champions and two-time Super Bowl winners, they were united in common purpose. One day, Mangini reached the end of his rope with Ty Law's freelancing during games. Law was doing whatever job he wanted, no matter how often or how loudly the coaches criticized him. At the heart of it was money. Law felt underpaid and went to Michael Smith of the *Boston Globe* to talk his way off the team, saying he felt "lied" to by Belichick and Pioli and adding, "I no longer want to be a New England Patriot."

Mangini sat in Belichick's office and discussed options for how to handle Law.

"He's not listening," Mangini said.

Belichick smirked his famous smirk, letting you know there was a joke inside his head that would remain untold.

"That's why you have a C on your shirt," he said—for *coach*. It was Mangini's job to solve problems, just as Belichick had solved them. He had coached Lawrence Taylor in the 1980s, when the linebacker was as dominant as any defensive player in the NFL history—and when he was saddled with drug and alcohol issues. Taylor arrived at one meeting wearing handcuffs, which a woman had placed on him before leaving their hotel room and taking the key. But Taylor always showed up on Sundays and had a gift for making game-changing plays. Sometimes, a coach simply had to allow superstars some leeway.

"Fuck," Belichick told Mangini. "Here's the fucking deal: Ty Law will be here long after you're fucking gone and long after I'm fucking gone. So, figure it the fuck out."

Law would miss most of 2004 with a foot injury. A year later, in February 2005, Belichick finally let him go, another discarded superstar. That day, Mangini entered Belichick's office with his arms raised, as if he had scored a touchdown.

"Look," he said. "I'm still here!"

14

THE SLEEPER

C HASING A SECOND-STRAIGHT SUPER BOWL, THE 2004 Patriots tore through the regular season, finishing with the same stellar record as the 2003 team: 14–2. If there was a pivotal moment, it came on November 7, in St. Louis against the Rams. A week earlier, New England had lost to the Steelers in Pittsburgh, 34–20, a game that ended its 21-game winning streak. Worse, New England was down both its starting cornerbacks. New England was traveling to St. Louis to face Mike Martz and his pass-heavy offense for the first time since Super Bowl XXXVI—a stunning loss the Rams had never recovered from, and Martz had always suspected that something suspicious happened that day. He wanted revenge.

Belichick needed to be resourceful. He had planned ahead, seeing a contingency where other coaches would not have. One day in training camp, Eric Mangini approached Troy Brown and handed him notes on playing cornerback, in case of an emergency. Brown was surprised. He was 33 years old. He hadn't played defensive back since his college days at Marshall. But he did as he was told, lining up at corner. It was a mess; Brown was beaten all day. Charlie Weis happily called it a "one-day" experiment. During his first three games of 2004, Brown played receiver and on special teams, his normal roles, but after the Steelers loss, with New England thin in the secondary, Brown suspected he might be called on. He was right. He took some snaps at corner in practice, with the coaches hoping he wouldn't be needed. They told Brown that, if the team could gain control of the game by the third quarter, he wouldn't be called on to play defense.

On the Rams' second offensive play, cornerback Asante Samuel injured his right shoulder. "You gotta be kidding me," Belichick said. In went Brown: he was now a receiver, returner, *and* defensive back, joining a secondary that included two undrafted free agents. With New England up 19–14 in the third quarter, Tom Brady hit Brown for eight yards to set up first and goal. But the drive started to stall. Belichick was fed up with settling for field goals.

"Let's run the Sleeper," he told Brad Seely.

The Sleeper was a fake field goal play that Belichick had first seen in 1962, when Navy ran it against Pittsburgh. A receiver stays out of the huddle and drifts toward the sideline, hoping to go uncovered. Whoever receives the snap throws to him. On came the field goal team and Adam Vinatieri. Brown shuffled to the left sideline, unnoticed by the Rams. Vinatieri took a direct snap and fired outside to Brown, who was alone for a four-yard touchdown—starting an avalanche of points in what would be a 40–22 Patriots win. Brown finished with three catches, three tackles, and a pass defensed, which could have been an interception. It was an embarrassment for Martz. New England had whipped him with a bunch of nobodies and a backup receiver in the secondary.

AFTER THE GAME, I walked with Brady from the locker room to the team bus. We talked about Peyton Manning, who was having the most prolific quarterback season in 20 years. Manning would finish with 49 touchdown passes, beating Dan Marino's record of 48. A narrative had emerged: Brady was the Joe Montana of his generation, an unspectacular winner and dynamite in the clutch, while Manning was a version of Marino, lighting up the box score without much postseason success. It bothered both men and their families even more, but as Manning often said, in the NFL, "perception is reality."

Brady and Manning were a strange pair—Manning calculated and polished, with a one-liner always at the ready; Brady cautious, most comfortable in the background—but they had become buddies, two football nerds, as if they knew from the beginning that they would be forever linked as their generation's defining quarterbacks. Brady's first start, in September 2001, was against Manning's Colts, and he had introduced himself to Manning on the field before the game. "I know who you are," Manning replied. *Man, that's really cool!* Brady thought. *Peyton Manning knows who I am!*

In 2002, Manning invited Brady to join him at the Kentucky Derby. They attended the Barnstable Brown Gala the night before, one of America's most exclusive parties. Kid Rock chatted them up. So did Sean Combs. And Janet Jackson. And N'Sync. And Ashton Kutcher. The two of them would meet up a few times a year, "discussing football, trying to improve our games," Manning recalled. In the coming years, they partnered on a successful campaign to change the league's rule about the preparation of game balls. The rule had required that the home team break in 36 official Wilson footballs, which both teams would use. Quarterbacks hated it—especially Brady. He compared it to Derek Jeter being forced to use a new mitt before each game. Brady and Manning persuaded 20 other starting quarterbacks to sign a petition to change the rule to allow each team to break in 12 footballs before every game. "I can tell you there've been nights before road games when I have had trouble sleeping because I'm thinking about what kind of footballs I'll be throwing the next day," Brady told Peter King of *Sports Illustrated* in 2006. It was a surprising statement from a quarterback who refused to allow himself an excuse, and the words later boomeranged.

Each off-season, Brady watched all of Manning's snaps from the prior year and kept a running file of notes on how he orchestrated his offense. But as much as Brady admired Manning's football savvy, he was in awe of the mental toughness required to carry such massive expectations and not only live up to them, but exceed them. "I actually think it was harder for those guys who are the first-round picks and the top-overall pick because the pressure is on right away," Brady later said. "You have no time to learn. They throw you in there and you go. 'Okay, let's see how well you do.' Usually, it doesn't go well. How could it? There's just too much for you to learn in too short a period of time."

It was a longer walk to the bus than either of us anticipated. After about ten minutes, we saw taillights at the base of a large ramp. We finished talking, near whirring engines, then rounded a corner—and then it got loud. There was a crowd, maybe 50 deep, of fans in Patriots gear who had lain in wait for Brady, holding helmets and posters and shrieking now that he was in view.

"Oh, wow," Brady said.

People always wonder what it's like to be famous. This was it: you're alone, it's quiet, there's space, and all of a sudden, it's as if you've entered a surprise birthday party thrown for you by strangers. Brady had spent a lot of time in the past year desperately trying to draw boundaries, and had learned that it was impossible, at least in Boston. He wanted—needed—to get out of the country. In the months after the Super Bowl win over the Panthers, Brady and Bridget Moynahan vacationed in Europe. One night in Florence, they shared a table at a trattoria with two other couples, one from Belgium and one from Singapore. Neither couple had any idea that Brady was twice the star of America's most-watched television event or that Moynahan had been in one of 2004's highest-grossing movies worldwide. They just dined and talked for hours like normal humans, without the customary disparity in scale. It was one of the last times in Brady's life he would do so.

Brady was in a familiar bind: sign for those who'd waited an hour, but keep the bus waiting, risking Belichick's scorn, even risking that the coach might order the buses to leave—or stiff the crowd?

He handed his roller bag to an aide and waded into the noise, disappearing into a flurry of posters and flashes.

BILL BELICHICK HAD a last-minute idea. It was the night before the Patriots played the Indianapolis Colts in a divisional playoff game in January, and he was running a defensive meeting. Robert Kraft had noticed that Belichick had been uptight all week, more than usual before a big game. Once again, the Colts arrived in Foxboro hot. In Indianapolis's 49–24 win over the Broncos in the wild-card round, Manning threw four touchdown passes and a mere six incompletions. This would be the fourth time in 13 months that the Patriots were facing Manning, after a November win in 2003, the AFC Championship Game, and the 2004 season opener. They had won the latter game, too, but it had been a close-run thing, as it was hard to repeatedly fool such a cerebral and skilled quarterback. Manning gashed New England's defense, which had stayed mostly in Cover 2, a coverage package designed to rough up receivers and erase big plays downfield, forcing the quarterback to be patient. Once he unlocked the Patriots' game plan, New England had no counterpunch. "I screwed up," Belichick later said.

For the divisional-round rematch, Belichick and Crennel installed a Cover Four defense that masqueraded as Cover 2. Both defenses were designed to prevent deep passes, but had different vulnerabilities. In a Cover 2, the middle of the field could be exploited; in a Cover 4, the outside was open. The Patriots planned to trick Manning into throwing inside to a Cover 4—allowing the Patriots to tackle Colts receivers after modest gains, keeping the clock moving and shortening the game.

It was such a good design that, the night before the game, in the defensive meeting, Belichick had an idea for another defense to use if it worked as well as New England anticipated. It was a look with only one down pass rusher and nine or ten defenders in pass coverage. No defensive linemen would be on the field, only linebackers and defensive backs. It was unheard of. Belichick wanted to use it if the Patriots were up big late in the game and needed to run out the clock. A 1–10 defense would allow New England to double-team every Colts receiver downfield. Manning would either have to dump off the ball to a running back for a short gain or run the ball himself, both winning scenarios for New England, with Manning perhaps even slower than Brady.

The staff was in disbelief. "I had never heard of anything like it," Mangini later said. "I had never seen anything like it. When would we possibly ever run this?"

Sure enough, on another wet and cold Foxborough day, New England dominated the Colts. After leading the league with 522 points in the regular season, Indianapolis managed only a field goal. Manning threw 42 times for a pathetic 238 yards, 5.7 yards per pass, almost four yards below his season average. With 2:53 left and the Patriots up 20–3, Belichick inserted the 1–10 defense. It worked exactly as Belichick drew it up: Manning completed passes that drained the clock—and his last one landed in Rodney Harrison's hands with four seconds left. Bill Belichick was a man at the peak of his creative and psychological powers, and a week later, the Patriots beat the Pittsburgh Steelers in the AFC Championship Game, avenging the midseason loss and sending themselves back to the Super Bowl, this time against the Philadelphia Eagles.

15

SOMETHING
VERY SPECIAL

THE DISTANCE BETWEEN VERY, VERY GOOD AND great in the NFL is measured in increments so small that it is almost impossible to quantify. From 2001 to 2004, New England and Philadelphia each produced 48–16 regular-season records. The Eagles did everything right. They were a smart and innovative team, constructed both methodically and radically. In 1994, a year after Robert Kraft had outbid him for the Patriots, movie producer Jeffrey Lurie bought the Eagles and hired one of his best and oldest friends, Joe Banner, as a top-ranking executive. In 1999, the team needed a new coach. Head coaches always seemed to be chosen from a list of successful coordinators, and Banner saw a flaw in the process, especially after so many coordinators were exposed in the top role as little more than glorified play callers, lacking the leadership and organizational skills to run a team and manage an unpredictable, maddening game. He culled a list of 16 elite coaches who had appeared in at least two Super Bowls and analyzed them, looking for shared traits. To his surprise, seven of the 16—including three Hall of Famers, Tom Landry among them—hadn't been NFL coordinators. And others, like Bill Parcells, had been coordinators for only a brief and uneventful period. Banner later said that the process "liberated" him to expand his pool of candidates beyond coordinators. He ended up hiring Andy Reid, the quarterbacks coach for the Green Bay Packers, who had never called plays—and who became one of the premier coaches of the next two decades.

Months after hiring Reid, the Eagles drafted Syracuse quarterback Donovan McNabb with the second-overall pick. Almost six years later and headed to the Super Bowl, McNabb was one of the best quarterbacks in football, a runner and thrower who had completed 64 percent of his passes in 2004, with 31 touchdowns and only eight interceptions—better numbers than Brady had ever produced to that point. McNabb and Brady had a short but notable history. In 1998, Michigan played Syracuse. McNabb was a fifth-year senior and Heisman Trophy candidate; Brady was a placeholder for Drew Henson, making his second career start. Brady threw an interception on his first drive, was briefly knocked out of the game, and was finally benched for Henson. McNabb threw a touchdown wearing only one shoe, after a defender pulled it off. Syracuse's 38–28 win was what Brady later called "probably the worst defeat I've ever had."

The Eagles had done the hard part. They found two organizational cornerstones, at the most difficult and vital jobs. And yet, there was an ineffable difference between them and New England. No matter how groundbreaking Banner's study was, it failed to yield the greatest coach in modern history—he was buried on the Jets, waiting for a second chance. No matter how many Pro Bowls McNabb was selected to, the humiliation Brady suffered at the hands of Syracuse mattered more. The Eagles reached four straight NFC Championship Games, losing three before finally winning one, against the Atlanta Falcons. The Patriots, by contrast, were on the verge of making history, of doing what few other teams had ever done. Nobody on either team did anything wrong. It was randomness. It was the unpredictable confluence of events. It was luck.

If the Patriots needed more motivation—if playing for history wasn't enough—Belichick deployed one of his reliable methods the day of the game. He stood before the team in a hotel ballroom, the shades drawn, and presented details from a Philadelphia newspaper of the Eagles' planned championship parade route. "Let me just read you a little something here. I thought this was kind of interesting. At first, I couldn't believe it, but it's actually true." His head was down, his voice measured but tinged with anger—maybe mock anger. "I'm talking about the Philadelphia parade after the game, all right? It's 11 o'clock, in case any of you want to attend that." He looked up at his team, then back down, and explained the parade's precise route, down to the street.

"The Willow Grove Naval Air Station is gonna fly over with their jets, too—in case you're interested in that," Belichick said.

It was a classic piece of performance art, cheap but easy and effective inspiration. Belichick riled up the team and then brought everything back to his trademark details, all business. "Do your job. Do your job. Just take care of your assignment. Know what it is, execute it, and get it taken care of. This is over six months now we've been working at this, and today, you've got a chance to do something very special."

On February 6, 2004, on a clear but nippy day in Jacksonville—it didn't feel like Super Bowl weather—Lurie and Kraft chatted and even engaged in an awkward bro hug for the cameras on the field prior to kick-off. It hid some hard feelings well. After Lurie had lost out on the Patriots a decade earlier, he disconnected, traveling the world. "Depressed," is how a confidant put it. Lurie and Kraft later become close. But this week, Lurie was antsy leading up to the Super Bowl, as though the game were part of a revenge fantasy.

At one point, Lurie said with wry seriousness, "We better not lose the game to this son of a bitch."

IT WASN'T JUST LUCK or circumstance with the Patriots, of course. They destroyed all kinds of myths during their reign. One was the NFL's meathead-warrior ethos. The "bull in the ring" is one of football's most barbaric drills, and in the hours before Super Bowl XXXIX, it provided an early tell that New England was operating on a different level than the Eagles. In the drill, two players square off and try to block one another out of a small circle, almost like in wrestling. It's taxing and brutal and normally reserved for training camp, when coaches try to instill toughness, not hours before the biggest game of the year. During warm-ups, the Patriots coaches noticed the Eagles players on the field, engaged in the bull in the ring. It was a first-timer's mistake. The Patriots had learned from the Panthers Super Bowl a year earlier, when the defense ran out of gas in the fourth quarter, how the game saps energy like no other, how precious it is to hold as much in reserve as possible. Belichick not only corrected his mistake from the prior year by carrying extra defensive linemen for this game, ensuring the pass rush would be fresh late in the fourth quarter, but he implored players to drink extra fluids Sunday morning, during pregame, and during the game itself. As the Eagles locked horns with one another, the Patriots coaches told their players, "Don't do much in warm-ups."

Of the nine Super Bowls New England took part in during Brady and Belichick's run, XXXIX was both the weirdest and the least dramatic. The Eagles scored first, on a touchdown pass from McNabb to tight end L. J. Smith. Midway through the second quarter, after the Eagles' blitzes had rattled the Patriots—New England had two false-start penalties and just one first down with 9:49 left in the first half—Charlie Weis called consecutive screen passes to Corey Dillon, which went for a combined 29 yards. The plays both gave the Patriots life and forced the Eagles to hesitate. After that, the Eagles "went to a little more zone coverages," Brady later said. "They started to drop back, and then we made the plays we needed to make." Most of those plays went to receiver Deion Branch, who caught 11 passes for 133 yards and was named the game's most valuable player.

The Eagles felt something else was at play. Philadelphia defensive coordinator Jim Johnson told his staff, "They're getting our signals. They know when we're blitzing." Steve Spagnuolo, the linebackers coach, didn't believe Johnson. Sign stealing was common in football, but how could the Patriots get the signals in real time and relay them to Brady? *I don't think so, Jim,* Spagnuolo thought.

With 5:40 left in the fourth quarter and New England up 24–14, the Eagles took over at their own 21-yard line and authored one of the strangest drives in NFL history. The Patriots expected a hurry-up attack, but the Eagles showed so little urgency—methodically huddling after every play and milking the clock, as if they were up two scores, not down two—that even Belichick was confused, left to wonder whether the scoreboard clock had malfunctioned or he had slipped into an alternate reality.

"What the hell are they trying to do?" he asked.

Eagles players wondered the same thing. Something was wrong with McNabb. He was panting and struggling to call plays. He'd either had the wind knocked out of him from a brutal Tedy Bruschi hit or was running out of gas—the exact scenario Belichick had warned his own team about. Some Eagles would insist that McNabb had vomited on the field, which he denied. Whatever was happening to McNabb, he was sluggish and fading in the biggest moment on the biggest stage. Superstar wide receiver Terrell Owens, who had valiantly played on a broken leg, later took a shot at him, saying, "I'm not the one who got tired in the Super Bowl."

With two minutes left, Belichick told the coaches, "If we can just hold them here . . ."

On the next play, the Patriots lined up in the wrong coverage. McNabb threw a 30-yard touchdown pass, cutting the lead to 24–21 and giving the Eagles a prayer. Philadelphia got the ball back with 46 seconds remaining, but McNabb threw an interception to Rodney Harrison. It was over: 24–21, Patriots.

Belichick leapt into the air. He hugged Weis and Crennel, knowing it was the last time the three of them would share a sideline. Weis was off to be the head coach of Notre Dame, while Crennel was set to become the head coach of the Cleveland Browns. "You can be the richest man in the world and not be able to buy moments like this," Belichick told them.

By a total of nine points across three Super Bowls, Bill Belichick had authored a dynasty. Steve Belichick was on the sideline, locking arms with his son as a cooler of water was emptied on their heads. An Associated Press photographer named David J. Phillip caught a shot of them after they were doused, and they both have the same expression, mouths open, as though surprised by the least surprising shower in sports. Belichick had watched his 86-year-old dad in pregame warm-ups and sensed the preciousness of the moment. Steve walked the field, chatted with Paul Tagliabue, and relived old memories. He had seen his first football game in 1924. "A long time ago," he said, a classic bit of Belichickian understatement, his mouth curving ever so slightly and subtly at the edges as he tossed around the humor in his mind. It's hard to imagine Bill Belichick happier, professionally and maybe personally, than he was on that field after the game. He had achieved excellence in a league designed to destroy it, and his old man witnessed it at his side. Steve was entering the final year of his life; he would die on November 19, 2005, in his living room, after watching USC play Fresno State. Bill Belichick coached football for himself, first and foremost. But he also seemed to coach for his dad—as a way to both honor him and be with him, as if he could feel his father's presence on a field. His father taught him to work hard, regardless of circumstance, and to chase a passion rather than a job. Those lessons sent him into coaching—and maybe explained why he couldn't stop.

IN THE WEEKS AFTER the third championship, even Tom Brady's truest believer couldn't believe what had unfolded. Tom Sr. was on the phone with me, reading off his son's superlatives. Brady's record as a starting quarterback was a staggering 57–14—an 80 percent winning rate, placing him alongside Otto Graham's 80 percent with the Cleveland Browns in the 1950s and '60s. Brady was 9–0 in the playoffs. The Patriots' accomplishments over only four years were incomprehensible, as was how quickly so many lives had changed. The wildest fact wasn't a statistic. It was almost too mind-boggling for Tom Sr. to say out loud. It was that Tom Brady—a quarterback who entered college and the NFL with his team's coaches not expecting him to ever emerge as a starter—had all but clinched a spot in the Hall of Fame at age 27.

"We're in Otto Graham territory, babe!" he said.

Brady, of course, was concerned only with his own territory. With Weis gone, he was in transition. Weis and Brady were close, a bond forged out of both the football emergency of 2001 and the life emergency of 2002. Brady had stayed at the hospital and at the Weis home for days with Maura Weis, not knowing whether her husband would leave the building alive. In one quiet moment, he asked her, "Do you think that this will mean that he won't yell at me as much?" The answer was no. But after the Super Bowl win over the Eagles, there was no need to yell. They were together at 4 a.m., downing adult beverages. Weis's departure hung in the air.

"What am I going to do?" Brady said.

"You don't need me anymore, big boy," Weis said. "I'm passing the torch!"

Brady seemed to be searching for something. For what, he wasn't sure. "It's got to be more than *this*," he often said. And he didn't mean more rings, although at the Pro Bowl, a week after the Super Bowl, he said to Tedy Bruschi, who still had confetti in his pocket, "You know, nobody's ever won three in a row." Brady was in transition, exploring the world, meeting the Pope—and still a sixth-round pick who, in one corner of his mind, felt he hadn't done *anything*.

Whenever someone told him he was the best quarterback in the NFL, Brady smiled. Whenever someone asked him if he believed he was the best in the NFL, he'd reply that it was the kind of statement that sounded better coming from anyone other than him. As for money, Brady didn't want to be the highest-paid quarterback in the NFL. He wanted to be the quarterback of the New England Patriots. After the Super Bowl, Brady signed a new six-year contract worth nearly $60 million. It was intentionally team-friendly, providing Belichick maximum flexibility in salary-cap maneuvers. Belichick had a quarterback who could cover up holes on the field; that alone was an obscene advantage. Brady allowed Belichick to win with spare parts, but no one could win with spare parts forever, and Brady's contract freed Belichick to spend when necessary in the future, giving the Patriots a shot of keeping the dynasty going. Brady's display of unselfishness was also a naked display of fear. He watched Belichick mercilessly cut star players—Pro Bowl receiver Terry Glenn, Lawyer Milloy, Ty Law—and knew it could be him, particularly if he was seen as overpaid. In the months after the Super Bowl, Brady was the subject of a *60 Minutes* profile. It was a classic Brady story, shot in Boston and San Mateo, covering a handsome young man who had made history through sheer will and with the support of his family, and who wasn't anywhere close to being satisfied. But the most revealing moment, which would explain so much to come, was overlooked. Steve Kroft asked, "Anything that really scares you? Anything that intimidates you?"

"The end of my playing career," Brady said.

16

ALL YOU HAVE
IS YOUR NAME
AND REPUTATION

I N THAT ERA, YOU KNEW YOU HAD REACHED A CERTAIN pinnacle in American life when David Halberstam decided to write a book on you. Bill Belichick had attained the requisite status, not just because he had won three Super Bowls, but because Halberstam, a lifelong New York Giants fan, found him to be something nobody else had: not just a fascinating coach, with clever game plans, but a fascinating American character. At first, Halberstam just wanted to meet Belichick. Both men summered in Nantucket. Halberstam, weighing the merits of a cold call, looked up Belichick in the phone book. He was unlisted, of course. Halberstam got wind that Belichick was interested in a book of some sort, and a mutual friend introduced them. Over dinner, Belichick started to back away, explaining that it would be hypocritical for him to participate in a project about himself and not the team—even though he had already participated in many projects about himself and not the team and would participate in more in the next decade, with his reputation in need of repair. Halberstam reframed the idea, deploying the surest method for getting Belichick on board: by treating Belichick's life and experience as a means to speak to something larger. Halberstam saw Belichick not only as the son of a father who was a coach, but as the son of a mother who was a teacher; not only as a successful football story, but as a successful American immigrant story; and it all manifested in a generational football education, the rewards of which the country saw on Sundays in the fall.

"That's a really good idea," Belichick replied.

In May and June of 2005, the two men convened for a few marathon interview sessions. Halberstam wasn't a ghostwriter, but Belichick was a partner and the book would be told from his perspective. Halberstam agreed to donate a share of the royalties to one of Belichick's favorite charities. It was a new arrangement for Halberstam, a dogged and brilliant reporter who had won a Pulitzer Prize for his coverage of Vietnam and fearlessly pursued stories regardless of access. His books looked and felt like definitive historical studies, thick and dense and on pages destined to become yellowed and warped. This would be his 20th book, not his first on American sports, but his first on football. In November of 2005, *The Education of a Coach* was published. It was small and thin by Halberstam's standards, fewer than 300 pages, leisurely rather than muscular. Halberstam was drawn in by the romance and momentum and inertia of the Patriot Way, which made the hearts of many football fans full and strong, like Vince Lombardi's Green Bay Packers once did, and he wrote fast.

THE PATRIOTS WERE so dominant that every other team's talent, strategy, and success could be viewed only within the context of New England's superiority. In the summer of 2005, the Patriots were in the heads of every other team in the league—none more so than those of the Indianapolis Colts. "Everyone wants to know, 'Why can't you beat the Patriots?'" defensive end Dwight Freeney told me. "It gets old. But it won't end until we beat them." Freeney began experimenting with new ideas, and it was hard to keep a straight face as he described them. He tried to refrain from putting his hands in his pockets, because his trainer told him that it caused his back muscles to contract, which slowed recovery. He adhered to the Sari Mellman diet, consuming foods based on what he had been told his body best processed, eating steak with only sea salt and water with no lime. Freeney—and the Colts—were that desperate. In the two meetings against New England during the 2004 season, Freeney was in Brady's face regularly, but only came away with two sacks. "You almost got me that time!" Brady said after Freeney missed by a fingernail. New England kept him away with a creative mix of quick passes and surprise blockers. During the Colts' loss in the divisional round, Freeney took a blindside shot, knocking him off course. He looked up and was stunned to see that it was wide receiver, David Givens, who had hit him.

"What are you doing fucking with me?" Freeney said.

"I wish I weren't," Givens replied.

In the 2005 season, the Colts finally beat the Patriots. Manning threw three touchdown passes, helping the Colts to a 28–7 lead on the way to a 40–21 win in Foxborough on November 7. The Patriots still won the AFC East and dominated the Jacksonville Jaguars in the wild-card game, but arrived in Denver for the divisional-round game lacking their signature confidence. The Patriots had faced every team's best effort for years, had drafted late, and now, with nobody able to beat them, the league was raiding their staff and roster. Before the Denver game, the New York Jets began to court Eric Mangini to be their head coach. He was only 34 years old and still in his first year as a defensive coordinator. Belichick had a vindictive streak—and hated few things more than the Jets. He tried to convince Mangini to pass, reminding him that other jobs would open up, and he'd help him get one. But Mangini viewed the Jets as a transformational opportunity for himself, and a chance to work with executive Mike Tannenbaum, a good friend, at a huge salary, reported to be $2.5 million. Belichick refused to offer him a raise as a means of keeping him in New England.

But first, New England had a playoff game against Mike Shanahan's Broncos. Down 10–6 in the third quarter, New England showed life. But on third and goal, Brady sensed a Denver blitz and started to audible. Facing a Mile High crowd so loud that the stadium was shaking, Brady stepped forward, trying to sort out the protection scheme, then looked up. The play clock was dripping down, inside five seconds. Brady had fallen into the trap that Belichick always set for Peyton Manning: by trying to audible as the play clock ran out, he gave the defense a chance to jump the snap. Sure enough, Denver's rushers fired off the ball so fast, they were almost offside, forcing Brady to roll right. Off his back foot and fading away, Brady unleashed one of the worst passes of his career, underthrowing Troy Brown on an out route. Denver's All-Pro cornerback Champ Bailey fielded it easily and took off down the sideline. He was inches away from the end zone—and a 101-yard return for a touchdown—when he eased up, running out of gas. It allowed Patriots tight end Ben Watson, who had raced across the field, to drill Bailey and jar the ball free.

The ball either went out of bounds, which meant Denver's ball at the one-yard line, or out of the end zone, a New England touchback.

Belichick thought Watson had made a game-changing play to negate a game-changing play. He threw a red challenge flag and told referee Jeff Triplette, "We believe the ball went through the end zone."

Belichick had a good relationship with Triplette. He got on well with most officials. But they'd had words earlier in the game. Belichick had wanted a measurement on a fourth and one deep in his own territory, as if he wanted to go for it. Triplette knew that Belichick was posturing; no way would a coach gamble so close to his own end zone. "You're not getting a measurement," Triplette said.

"You gotta give me the measurement," Belichick protested.

"I don't have to," Triplette said.

"This is bullshit," Belichick said.

Belichick was a notorious grudge holder, but with officials, he would let go. In the next few years, whenever Belichick saw Triplette, he said with a smile, "Okay, so tell me the day when I'm going to get a measurement."

Triplette reviewed the Bailey fumble. It was inconclusive. There wasn't a good angle showing clearly where the ball went out of bounds. Belichick later used the play as an example of why the league should have goal-line cameras. "Maybe we could have a bake sale to raise some money for the cameras. We could do a car wash," he said, tweaking a league that loved to brag about its multibillion-dollar profits. Officials awarded the Broncos the ball at the one-yard line. Denver scored on the next play and went on to win, 27–13.

It was Brady's first playoff loss in 11 starts, and Belichick's first since 1995. Belichick dropped by Shanahan's office to personally congratulate him. Shanahan's son, Kyle, was sitting with his dad. Kyle was just getting started in his NFL coaching career, following in his father's footsteps, and was in awe of the fact that Belichick had come to see his dad after such a painful loss. He couldn't wait to hear what the two men would discuss, what football secrets they would reveal, expecting a high-level back-and-forth between high-level minds. But his dad gave him a nod, telling him he needed to step outside. This conversation was privileged.

IF THE MOMENTS AFTER a tough loss to Shanahan showed Belichick at his most elegant, the next few days revealed him as his most savage. Mangini accepted the Jets' offer, and Belichick took it as a personal betrayal. He revoked Mangini's key-card access and had his office boxed up, sifting through his files before returning them. Mangini was prepared: he had already copied his hard drive and offered jobs to many Patriots staffers and coaches—exactly what his mentor would have done. Belichick's behavior was so swift and ruthless that it left even those close to him at a loss and shook members of the coaching staff. If he could do that to Mangini—his boy, the guy on staff who always had his back—he could do it to anyone. His friends wondered why Belichick could be alternately so kind, writing handwritten notes, giving hundreds of thousands of dollars out of his pocket, and so indifferent about the closest relationships in his life. Was it his only-child upbringing coming out? Did he only need himself? "He doesn't hold grudges," a friend of Belichick's had once said. "He holds death. With a grudge, there's a chance of reconciliation. With death, there is no chance."

FOR *THE EDUCATION OF A COACH*, Belichick had only one condition: he refused to promote it. If he deviated for even 20 midseason minutes to shill for himself, it would be an affront to everything he stood for. But Belichick agreed to do one event after the season ended. On April 11, 2006, he delivered the annual Fusco Distinguished Lecture at Southern Connecticut State University, on a stage that had also featured Colin Powell, Madeleine Albright, Walter Cronkite, Christopher Reeve, and Rudy Giuliani.

Belichick arrived onstage to an ovation so thunderous and sustained that it became awkward. He was in a suit. His hair was brushed to the side, perhaps gelled. He carried no notes. He gently waved his arms to quiet the crowd, the way his friend Jon Bon Jovi would do before an acoustic song. He was happy and relaxed and seemed in his element on a college campus, speaking to a young crowd at that age when lives were about to begin. He began by telling the students to follow their hearts, to chase not money, but a job that was a continuation of a passion. One of the proudest moments of his life was when he passed on a career in finance and moved to Baltimore to do whatever the Colts asked of him. At one point during his brief negotiation, if one could call it that, he offered to work for free as long as he could learn about his craft. He wanted something real.

He had told all of these stories before, but something about them seemed different now, with the passage of time and in this forum and Belichick now a cultural force who, in 2004, had been named one of *Time*'s most influential people in the world. Nobody could touch him. It was "B.C.," he said—"before cell phones." He had a job in football, an undying passion, and could look forward to endless magical moments when he was in the film room with piles of work to do, when time seemed suspended, hours blurred together, just him and questions he would spend the rest of his life trying to answer.

Belichick confessed to the audience that it was hard for him to mold a group of individuals into a team, which was perhaps surprising, given his power and stature. A few years earlier, he said, a few of the rookies had a problem arriving on time to morning meetings. Belichick moved up the meetings an hour each time a player was late, from 8:30 to 7:30 to 6:30, until the meetings started at 5 a.m. "That was the crossroads," he said.

Everything was earned in New England. In 2004, during the doldrums of training camp, offensive tackle Matt Light asked on behalf of the team for a night off, promising everyone would be fresh the next day. "Light, look, it doesn't really work that way," Belichick said. "You don't get something for nothing."

What do we have to do? Light asked.

Catch a punt, Belichick said. If Light caught it, the players would have the night off. If he dropped it, they would run 20 extra sprints. Light backed up to field the kick. The team looked on. The ball was launched into the air and then nose-dived down. Light drifted under it as it swirled into his arms. The team exploded and Light held the ball high, as though he had scored a Super Bowl–winning touchdown. "There was some real team bonding there," Belichick told the audience. "That might have been the single happiest moment of the entire season."

You could see all of it starting to sink in, by looking at the faces in the auditorium, as Belichick opened minds and spoke of his own limits. He took questions from the crowd, and a young woman asked about opportunities to work in football operations. He had a chance, right there, to open a previously closed door, or at least to answer the same way he would a young man. No coaching staff had women on it—that was a decade away—but if anyone wanted to be the first, Belichick had the power. He later was involved in a league event called Women's Careers in Football Forum. But in 2006, that wasn't him.

And then, a kid in a Brady jersey asked why Adam Vinatieri was no longer with the team. Vinatieri had been a free agent after the 2005 season. New England could have kept him by deploying the franchise tag—a designation to prevent a player from hitting free agency—and paying him around $3 million. But Belichick believed the team could force the player who had won two Super Bowls with last-second kicks into accepting a hometown discount, betting that he wouldn't leave a region that adored him. It backfired. Vinatieri left for the Colts. It was another ugly contract fight with a superstar, and first of a few in 2006 alone. Belichick refused to engage the young questioner, stiffing him as though at a press conference.

A question from a young fan about a kicker cut to the essence of Belichick as a coach and as a man. It wasn't enough for him to win. Somebody had to lose. Why was that the case? Had he always been that way, or was his approach simply a necessary path to winning, learned from Paul Brown and Tom Landry and Bill Walsh, amplified by his own drive and ambition and vanity? In truth, he loved his players, but refused to allow himself to show it. When Tedy Bruschi suffered a stroke nine days after the Super Bowl win over the Eagles, Belichick called him, but didn't visit him in the hospital. Only after Bruschi retired did Belichick permit himself to show a measure of affection for one of the greatest players in team history. As long as Bruschi was on the roster, Belichick couldn't budge. Winning football games could hide the flaws of a team. It was another question entirely whether it could hide the flaws of a man.

BEFORE ENDING HIS SPEECH, Belichick told the crowd, "All you have is your name and reputation. And your reputation is earned."

At that moment, Belichick had both. Halberstam later said that Belichick had an admirable "inner honor" and an "ethical sense." During one meeting, Halberstam asked Belichick if he had ever read any of his books.

"Yeah," Belichick replied. "I've read them all."

The Best and the Brightest had been the first one Belichick read, on the recommendation of his friend Bobby Knight, the legendary college basketball coach. The story of how John F. Kennedy's brilliant cabinet led the country into the morass of Vietnam resonated with Knight. In the 1980s, he was the best basketball coach in the world, at Indiana University and for the Olympic team. Only he could stop himself, and he eventually did, self-destructing with angry tirades that culminated in a fit of rage in 1997, when he grabbed the neck of guard Neil Reed in practice, which helped cost him his job three years later. Knight seemed to see a glimpse of himself in Belichick, recognizing his ambition—and all of the dark places you might go, the clear lines that become blurry when you want something a little too much. That was why Knight recommended *The Best and the Brightest*.

It's the best book ever, he told Belichick, on screwing up.

PART II

THE
HIGHEST
PLATEAU

2006–2015

17

PROTECT
THE SHIELD

HERE WAS NO WAY ROGER GOODELL WAS GOING TO lose. Most of the owners wanted him. All of the reporters knew he was next in line for the top job. It all felt preordained, the vote a mere formality. The owners convened in early August of 2006, at the Renaissance Chicago North Shore Hotel, to make the generational choice of a new commissioner. Paul Tagliabue had decided to call it a career, after 17 years running the league. Robert Kraft was friendly, but not particularly close with Tagliabue. Nobody was. Pete Rozelle, the league's legendary fourth commissioner, vacationed with owners; Tagliabue purposefully kept his distance from them so that he'd never be accused of favoritism. But since the 1990s, Kraft had been close with Goodell, the son of a former United States senator who had started at the league in 1982 as an intern and rose to executive vice president and chief operating officer. Goodell was 47 years old. His parted hair could alternate between auburn and blonde, depending on the light, and his face could alternate between pink and red, depending on his mood. Unlike Rozelle, Goodell was not tanned and polished. Unlike Tagliabue, he was not lanky and professorial. Goodell was tall and sturdy, a jock from Westchester County, New York, who as a child slept with a football and as an adult woke up before dawn to lift weights. Stiff and scripted behind a podium, he was loose away from it: cussing every now and then, slapping executives on the shoulders for a job well done, a quarterback in his own vast huddle and a man forever ready to mix it up—a trait that would help and haunt him over the next decade.

For years, Goodell had positioned himself to succeed Tagliabue, inside and outside the walls of the NFL's Park Avenue offices. He became the executive everyone—staffers, owners, reporters—called to solve their problems or to trade gossip. Long before Tagliabue retired, NFL public relations executive Greg Aiello invited a few reporters who were in Indianapolis for a playoff game for an off-the-record dinner with Goodell at St. Elmo Steak House. It was billed as a night with "the next commissioner."

Now Goodell found himself at the nexus of a league that was changing, both structurally and philosophically, mostly at the hands of a group of men—Kraft, Jeff Lurie, Jerry Jones of the Dallas Cowboys, Dan Snyder of the Washington franchise—who were called the "New Guard" or "New Money" owners. They comprised the sports bloc of a larger movement that was invading the halls of political power and finance, their zero-sum mentality foretelling a changing way of being an American in the world. It started, as so much of the modern NFL did, with Jones. He had helped to usher a new mentality in 1995 when he cut a sponsorship deal between the Cowboys and Pepsi, breaking away from the existing league-wide sponsorship deal with Coke. Owners were furious at first, then envious. They copied him, striking their own deals without league approval or against the league's interests. Jones would end up as the face of a group unafraid to anger the traditionalist owners, the "Old Guard"—Wellington and John Mara of the New York Giants, Dan and Art Rooney of the Pittsburgh Steelers, Lamar and Clark Hunt of the Kansas City Chiefs, Ralph Wilson of the Buffalo Bills—whose families had entered the league early, or helped create it in the first place, operating their teams as vanity items but still finding opportunities to collaborate. They were not only wary of the NFL so transparently chasing revenue at any nonfinancial cost, but also frustrated that a lot of the new money wasn't being redistributed across all owners. A league built on foxhole loyalty was now becoming something else entirely.

Goodell had fashioned himself as a capitalist voice for capitalist owners, a man who understood that many of them had paid hundreds of millions of dollars for their teams and were mired in stadium debt and demanded not only high revenues and high profits, but high franchise values. The league needed to modernize. For most of its history, the large-market clubs had propped up the small-market teams. Now, that philosophy had shifted, despite the mitigating forces of the salary cap and free agency. A new round of collective bargaining with the players' union was coming in 2011. Tagliabue had just completed an agreement in 2006, in his last major act as commissioner, and owners felt Tagliabue had given away too much. This time, they wanted to lead the fight. The NFL was about to transition from a league run by the commissioner to a league run by owners. Few could stomach dealing with 32 bosses, all brilliant and crazy and accustomed to leverage in every room they entered. Goodell loved it.

There was one problem, which only the modern NFL could create: Goodell was so favored, it created an optics issue. It looked like the fix was in. The owners had to find other strong candidates, but not strong enough that they would win.

FORTUNATELY FOR THEM and for Goodell, team owners are diabolical geniuses at reverse-engineering to a desired outcome. There are processes they're technically supposed to abide, but in reality, they play by their own rules, when they're not creating them as they go. Robert Kraft was a master at finessing such conundrums. In the words of a rival executive, he "could walk through a minefield and avoid all the mines." He wasn't Jones, all oratory and affect and illicit charm; Kraft was quieter, smoother, refusing to impose his will on other owners, preferring to achieve consensus behind the scenes. He had a way of making everyone feel like they had won. As his team became a dynasty, Kraft had transformed from the new guy to one of the most powerful owners, in terms of influence and as chair of the broadcast committee. He could seem pious at times, but nobody doubted he was one of the kings. Winning did that.

So, it was Goodell—and who else? The other options "had to be real choices," Tagliabue recalled. "They couldn't be sham candidates." The league had commissioned a search committee, and it suggested three outside candidates: Robert Reynolds, COO of Fidelity Investments; Cleveland attorney Frederick Nance, who negotiated with Goodell to bring the Browns back to Cleveland in the '90s; and Mayo Shattuck III, chairman of Constellation Energy. None of them gained traction. On

Tagliabue's suggestion, the search firm found several internal candidates beyond Goodell, including Jeff Pash, the league's general counsel. Pash was brilliant and reserved, with degrees from both Harvard College and Harvard Law. He had helped and angered many owners as they tried to finance new stadiums—especially Kraft—but he never took those disagreements personally and would be calm and professional in meetings, regardless of raw feelings. Behind a podium, Pash was less polished than Goodell, but his command of legal issues, from the union negotiations to revenue sharing, was unrivaled.

Goodell encouraged him to run, believing that he would be a good commissioner. But Pash wasn't going to win. All the owners knew that— and it worried them. If Pash lost, he might leave the league. Nobody wanted him gone, especially with a looming collective bargaining fight with the union. So the owners also put up Gregg Levy, a sharp attorney from the Washington law firm Covington & Burling who had worked on an array of league issues. Levy and Pash effectively canceled each other out—two brainy lawyers—and because Levy was a legal consultant to the league and not an executive, nobody worried about him leaving, or beating Goodell. It was ruthless, toying with the careers and reputations of proud men, but that's the way some owners worked. The search committee chose five finalists. Pash didn't make the cut; Levy did. It was soon Levy against Goodell—which left the New Guard optimistic and the Old Guard angry, not only at the choice but the process.

ON AUGUST 8, in suburban Chicago, Goodell stood before the owners in a pin-striped suit and blue-striped tie, similar to the one his father, Charles, wore in 1969 when he delivered a career-defining rebuke of the Vietnam War on the Senate floor, a stance that would cost him reelection. Goodell gave the defining speech of his own life, speaking the language of his base, of consolidation and profits and red tape eliminated. He had merged three different league business units into one, he explained, improving club payouts from $81 million in 2001 to an astonishing $770 million in 2006. He bragged not only about revenues, but about a showdown with the Rolling Stones over the Super Bowl halftime show. "In a little-known story, on the Thursday before the last

Super Bowl, the Rolling Stones were threatening to play two songs that were not appropriate. I told our people to tell the Rolling Stones they would be replaced by Stevie Wonder if, by the next morning, they did not agree to change those songs and present a show that reflected well on the NFL." A compromise was reached: the Stones ended up playing the songs—"Rough Justice" and "Start Me Up"—but the audio was dropped during certain lyrics.

Goodell promised he would treat each team with "fairness and integrity."

"You know my priority is not Roger Goodell," he said. "You know my priority is the NFL. I live and breathe the league—your league. I know how to get things done. I am ready."

A vote was cast. A two-thirds majority was the necessary threshold. The first ballot was returned, and it was a shock:

Goodell, 17; Levy, 14.

Some of the Old Guard owners were protesting the process, and refused to back down. All the owners immediately voted again:

Goodell, 17; Levy, 14.

What was going on? The Old Guard felt the New Guard had rigged the entire thing. The owners took a break, retreated into their corners, and lit into each other. Jones made an emphatic plea for Goodell.

Another vote:

Goodell, 21; Levy, 10.

They voted again, for a final time:

Goodell, 23; Levy, 8.

The league had a new commissioner. Dan Rooney went up to Goodell's hotel room to tell him the news. It was just after 5:30 p.m. Back in 1960, Rozelle was in the bathroom when he learned he had been elected. Goodell was not, though he had taken off his suit pants at some point during the hours that he waited, not wanting to wrinkle them, and when the knock came, he joked to himself, *It's a good thing I just put my pants on.* There was Rooney, the 74-year-old owner of the Steelers and one of Goodell's most trusted advisors, smiling and saying, "Mr. Commissioner." Goodell hugged him, and in the coming days, moved quickly to heal the wounds left by the process. He elevated Pash, making him his closest aide and confidant. Over the next decade, the two of them would go to war together in an effort to, as Goodell often said, "protect the shield"—against former players suffering the long-term effects of head injuries from football, against the union, against broadcast partners, against superstars like Michael Vick of the Atlanta Falcons for his involvement in dogfighting, against afterthoughts like defensive tackle Tank Johnson for gun-related charges, against the New Orleans Saints for a bounty scheme, and, most famously, against the league's dynasty.

18

WHO DOES THAT?

THE CALL ARRIVED IN THE MIDDLE OF THE NIGHT. IT was April 28, 2007, a Saturday. Randy Moss was in line outside a nightclub, hat pulled low, hoping to remain unnoticed, when his phone buzzed, showing a Massachusetts area code. A tall and lanky wide receiver with elite speed and an unparalleled ability to levitate for jump balls—one of the greatest matchup nightmares in the history of sports—Moss had just finished his second season as a member of the Oakland Raiders. It was the worst of his career: he caught only 42 passes and scored only three touchdowns for a 2–14 team. He once was an All-Pro and a pain in the ass—an unstoppable force for the Minnesota Vikings who had alienated his mentor, Cris Carter, pretended to moon Green Bay Packers fans, and bumped his car into a traffic cop— and now he was neither. When he was first traded to the Raiders from Minnesota, Moss remade his image, from a diva to one of the team's hardest workers. But in 2006, Moss was lost in Oakland's morass. He wanted out.

Moss didn't recognize the number, but answered it anyway. "Hello, who's this?"

"Hey," the caller said, low and mumbling. "This is Bill Belichick."

"Who?"

"This is Bill Belichick."

"Man, stop playing on my phone."

Moss hung up. Back in Foxborough, Belichick waited a minute, then called Moss again. The first day of the 2007 draft was nearing an end. Belichick had spent much of the previous month on the phone with the

Raiders, believing he had the pulled off the steal of the decade. Al Davis thought Moss had lost a step and had given the green light to first-year head coach Lane Kiffin to deal him. Michael Lombardi, at the time Oakland's senior executive, convinced Belichick that Moss was still dangerous and would fit in well in New England. Belichick and the Raiders agreed to send Moss to New England for a sixth-round pick. When Davis got wind of it, he was furious. He felt Lombardi had undermined the Raiders' leverage by selling Moss too cheaply to his pal. He would later use it as cause to fire Lombardi. Davis called Belichick, whom he considered a friend, and accused him of trying to fleece his team. Belichick responded that he had merely accepted an offer presented to him and asked Davis what the price would be.

A fourth-rounder, Davis replied.

Done. Moss was one of the few players Belichick often had to design an entire defensive game plan to stop—and sometimes still couldn't. Before the 2005 season opener against the Raiders, Belichick told his players that Moss would tip off the play by his body language: when it was a pass, he would put in his mouthpiece; when it was a run, he would leave it out. In the second quarter of that game, Moss still burned the Patriots for a 73-yard touchdown. Despite his physical gifts, Moss "approached the mental part of the game like an underdog always looking for an edge," Lombardi said.

Outside the club, Moss's cell rang again. He answered it again.

"No, Randy, this is Bill."

Belichick told Moss that he was now a New England Patriot. For the first time in his career, Moss would play with a future Hall of Fame quarterback. He apologized to his new boss. The bouncer spotted him and waved him inside.

"WE'RE ALL LOSERS," Belichick told his players.

It was the first team meeting after the 2007 draft, and he let that message wash over the players, gathered in the auditorium. Outside, the Patriots were billed as a super team, loaded on both sides of the ball, and Belichick was all too eager to play the role of buzzkill. The 2006 season had started with Tom Brady realizing once again that his power within the Patriots building had limits and ended with New England blowing a 21–3 lead in a loss to the Indianapolis Colts in the AFC Championship Game. In August of that year, Deion Branch held out for a better contract through the minicamp and training camp. Brady loved Branch; the 2002 second-rounder out of Louisville had been one of the few receivers the Patriots had drafted and developed well. It was especially difficult to play receiver in New England's offense because each one needed to know everyone's routes on every play, and each play contained route variations depending on the defense. Branch's salary entering 2006 was just over $1 million. Both sides realized he was underpaid, but he wanted better than the three-year, $18.75 million offer from the Patriots. One of the iron laws of professional sports is to not get involved with another player's contract situation, but with the season nearing and both sides at an impasse, Brady dove in, for the first time publicly since Lawyer Milloy. Brady made clear to Michael Silver of *Sports Illustrated* that he was "mad as hell," Silver wrote. "Deion is the most important player on our offense," Brady said.

That argument failed to convince Belichick, who knew that his quarterback could win with nearly any surrounding cast. Brady was so great, it worked against him at times. His pleas created a stir outside the building, prompting a few days of talk radio and newspaper coverage. But inside, they went nowhere, another reminder that he was an employee, regardless of stature, accomplishment, and especially fame. A day after a season-opening win over the Buffalo Bills, Belichick traded Branch to the Seattle Seahawks for a first-round pick. Brady was unhappy with the remaining talent around him. As Tom Sr. recalled, "We didn't have anyone at a Pro Bowl level on the offensive side of the ball." Brady got revenge by working his yard-sale group of wideouts—Reche Caldwell, Jabar Gaffney, and an aging Troy Brown—into the ground. "You could see his frustration with some of the decisions within the organization," cornerback Ellis Hobbs recalled. "He would take it out on the receivers, always trying to get extra time with them."

The work paid off. Brady produced what many believed at the time was the best season of his career in 2006, leading New England to a 12–4 record. The Patriots whipped Eric Mangini's Jets in the wild-card round of the playoffs. Brady was both clutch and careless in the next two games.

Against the San Diego Chargers in the divisional round, he threw three interceptions, including one to Chargers safety Marlon McCree with 6:25 left and New England down, 21–13. It should have ended the game, but rather than simply hitting the ground, McCree tried to return the ball, and Troy Brown ripped it free. New England recovered it. Brady led the Patriots to 11 unanswered points in a 24–21 win. The following week, New England traveled to Indianapolis for the AFC Championship Game. After years of devastating losses, Peyton Manning's Colts had started to solve New England, winning two straight regular-season games in Foxborough. The Patriots raced to an 18-point lead and had a chance to put the game away, driving to the Colts' 28-yard line midway through the second quarter, before they self-destructed. Two consecutive penalties and a sack cost New England 21 yards—and gave the ball back to the Colts. Indianapolis scored on four consecutive drives, and late in the fourth quarter, down 34–31, Manning took over. What followed was one of those precious moments in sports when a transcendent athlete comes into his own.

On second down, with 2:08 remaining, Manning drifted out of the pocket—exactly what Belichick had wanted him to do for so many years, a rare weakness the quarterback had now ruthlessly identified and fixed—and lofted a beautiful deep throw to tight end Bryan Fletcher for 32 yards. Four plays later, running back Joseph Addai scored from a yard out to put the Colts up 38–34 with 1:02 left. Brady took over and completed two passes for 34 yards, moving New England to Indianapolis's 45-yard line. On the next play, Brady, under heat from Dwight Freeney, threw over the middle into double coverage and safety Marlin Jackson snared it and, unlike McCree a week earlier, hit the turf. Manning watched the play on the stadium's jumbotron and stood up when it was over, trying to throttle his excitement. Belichick took off his headset and hung his hands around the neck of his gray hoodie, mouth clenched. It was the third game-changing interception Brady had thrown in four playoff games. The Colts easily won the Super Bowl over the Chicago Bears two weeks later, forever erasing the nonsensical notion that Manning failed to deliver in big games, and only further raising the stakes for all future matchups with the New England Patriots.

IT MIGHT HAVE BEEN a year too late, but Belichick realized that, in the era of relaxed passing rules—an era he helped usher in with his brutalizing of Manning's receivers in prior seasons—his offense needed more talent to compete with the Colts, especially on the RCA Dome's turf. He acquired Wes Welker of the Miami Dolphins in early March for second- and seventh-round draft picks. Welker was a small, versatile, darting slot receiver who had earned Belichick's respect the best way: by beating him. "We couldn't cover him," the coach later said. Less than a week after Welker arrived, the Patriots signed Donté Stallworth, a 2001 first-round pick out of the University of Tennessee. Add in Moss, and Brady was surrounded by mismatches for the first time in his career.

In that first team meeting after the 2007 draft, Belichick played film of the loss to the Colts. He replayed a clip of Brady missing an easy throw, remarking that "Johnny from Foxborough High" at the nearby high school could have hit it. The message was clear: nobody was above criticism. "It was where all that humble pie started," Brady later said. In camp, safety Brandon Meriweather, a rookie first-round pick out of Miami, lined up over Welker. He told the *Boston Herald* it was an honor to cover "one of the best slot receivers in the league," an innocuous compliment. But in a team meeting the next day, Belichick read the quote aloud and said, "Brandon Meriweather thinks Wes Welker is one of the best slot receivers in the league. How the fuck would Brandon Meriweather know! You don't know anything, so shut the fuck up."

But no matter how hard Belichick tried to keep the team grounded, 2007 was destined to be different. In one meeting he explained how the Patriots offense planned to attack single high safety coverage, a defensive alignment designed to stop the run, not the deep pass.

Moss tried not to laugh. "You ain't gonna see any more single high safety. You can forget about that." Nobody was going to worry about the Patriots' running game in 2007. Moss was right.

The season opener against the Jets, at the Meadowlands on September 9, 2007, offered a glimpse of both the brilliance and the troubles that would define the season. On a play late in the first quarter, Stallworth's job was to run a 20-yard curl route. When he broke for the curl, he saw that he was double-teamed. He looked to Brady in the pocket. It was his first regular-season game with the team, and Stallworth was desperate to impress the quarterback. During a preseason game, Stallworth was assigned a "clear" route, meaning his job was to take defenders with him and open up space for another receiver—he wasn't a target. But Brady threw him the ball anyway, and it was intercepted and returned for a touchdown. "My bad," he told Brady on the sideline. Brady didn't say anything. He just stared at Stallworth, and stared, and stared, leaving Stallworth anticipating an explosion. Brady just held his glare, an invisible line of tension, until finally looking away.

Stallworth now saw Brady subtly flick his thumb, motioning to him to cut to the sideline. Stallworth did, and Brady threw to him, a 19-yard completion. "Good job seeing my thumb," Brady told him. Stallworth thought to himself, *Who does that?*

Early in the second quarter, Brady was hit as he fired to Moss on third down, throwing high and outside toward the sideline. He figured it was incomplete. Then he heard the crowd groan in unison and saw Moss with the ball.

Holy shit, Brady thought.

Midway through the third quarter, the Patriots called a play for Moss in which he had a three-way go route. The entire deep part of the field was his canvas; where he ran was his choice, based on the coverage. Moss told Brady that if the Jets played him in man coverage, he was going to sprint diagonally across the entire field. "Just wait on me," Moss said. Brady dropped back and saw that Moss had three Jets on him. Brady stalled as long as he could before throwing deep to his left, from one hash mark to the other, hitting Moss at the goal line for a 51-yard touchdown.

The Patriots won, 38–14. The next morning in Foxborough, as players passed in and out of the locker room, Ellis Hobbs saw members of the local media approaching him. He had set a record with a 108-yard kickoff return for a touchdown. He stood up, anticipating a discussion about his record, but the first question caught him off guard. It was about the Patriots' cheating.

19

REMAIN INCONSPICUOUS

THE JETS HAD GOTTEN THEIR ASSES KICKED, BUT they had one comically unfair advantage. His name was Steve Yarnell. He was the team's security director and a former FBI agent and Army Ranger. He had slits for eyes and a pony keg of a head atop broad shoulders, and he had a special job against the Patriots, aside from protecting Eric Mangini. General manager Mike Tannenbaum, with the blessing of owner Woody Johnson, had instructed him to keep an eye out for a cameraman filming the Jets' sideline. Belichick made it easy for him. The cameraman was Matt Estrella, a young man no different than those who had preceded him. He was 26 years old. He was disguised in a red media vest and had used tape to cover the New England Patriots logos on his shirt. He was told to alternate between scoreboard shots of the down and distance and aiming directly at the opposing team's defensive coaches as they signaled. He knew, as did his bosses, that what he was doing was a violation of league rules. "Videotaping of any type, including but not limited to taping of an opponent's offensive or defensive signals, is prohibited on the sidelines, in the coaches' booth, in the locker room, or at any other locations accessible to club staff members during the game," the relevant statute read. And so, he was armed with alibis, should anyone try to remove him from the field, as the Green Bay Packers had done a year earlier at Lambeau Field.

Toward the end of the first half, Yarnell spotted Estrella, down near the end zone. He alerted NFL security. Just before halftime, Estrella rushed into the bowels of the stadium, toward the Patriots locker room—and ran right into a waiting Yarnell. He confiscated the camera and tape, and soon Estrella found himself in a small room with a few other security officials. Estrella knew he was busted. They asked Estrella who he worked for.

"Kraft Productions," Estrella replied, deploying one of his excuses.

He was sweating. Someone handed him a cup of water, and he was shaking so severely that he spilled it on himself. Everyone started arguing. Yarnell characterized the Patriots' spying as corporate espionage. After about a half hour of fighting, Bob Bukowski, an FBI agent on site who started working games after 9/11, placed the camera in a box, sealed it up, and gave it to Rodney Davis, an NFL security representative. That night, Davis drove the box under the Hudson River to NFL headquarters on Park Avenue. The next morning, the story broke that a camera and tape had been confiscated from the Patriots. NFL spokesman Greg Aiello confirmed that the league was investigating the Patriots for a rules violation, and his explanation—"Clubs have specifically been reminded in the past that the videotaping of an opponent's offensive or defensive signals on the sidelines is prohibited"—was a dead giveaway that New England was in serious trouble.

FIVE THOUSAND MILES AWAY, a 31-year-old assistant golf pro in Maui named Matt Walsh saw news of the league investigating the Patriots' videotaping and wondered if he would get a call. Walsh was Estrella before Estrella, and as he learned the details of the accusations against the Patriots—cameras, hand signals, covert operations—it was as if he was reading an account of his old life. In August of 2000, before a seemingly meaningless preseason game against the Tampa Bay Buccaneers, Jimmy Dee, who ran all of the Patriots' video operations, told Walsh to stand on the sideline and aim the camera at the Bucs' offensive and defensive coaches as they signaled plays. Walsh was confused. Dee was, too—"unsure himself of what specifically it was that the coaches wanted me to film," Walsh later said. At the time, Walsh didn't know that the NFL game operations manual forbade taping signals from the sidelines. He did his job and gave the tape to Dee.

Questions were answered a few weeks later, as the Patriots prepared to face the Bucs in the season opener. It was Belichick's first game as

the Patriots' head coach, which he memorialized by giving Kraft a photograph of Ted Williams and Babe Ruth that he had signed himself:
*Thanks for giving me the opportunity to coach your team. Let's hope we
will be as successful as these two fellas.* Days before the game, backup
quarterback John Friesz was called into a meeting with Belichick, Charlie Weis, and Ernie Adams. He was given Walsh's tape of Bucs defensive
coordinator Monte Kiffin's signals and told to memorize them. During
the game, Friesz's job would be to stand next to Weis and help decode
the defense, giving Weis a chance to exploit it with his play calling.

Sign stealing had been part of football for decades. In his 1931 book,
Coaching: The Complete Notre Dame System of Football, Knute Rockne
suggested that the huddle was invented to prevent teams from stealing signals. As a freshman at Washington State, Drew Bledsoe had won
a team award for decoding signals in a win against Cal Berkeley. The
Patriots bet that, with so little time between the preseason game and
the first game of the regular season, it would be too complicated for the
Bucs to change their signs. Taking it up a level, the Patriots decided to
deploy a hurry-up offense, forcing Kiffin to signal plays quickly—and
before the 15-second mark on the play clock, when coach–quarterback
radio communication cut off. It was a clever strategy, perhaps informed
by what Belichick had watched Bill Walsh do against the Giants in the
1980s. Walsh scripted the first 15 offensive plays, and then, early in the
game, the 49ers' headsets mysteriously cut out, triggering a rule man-
dating that the league shut down both teams' headsets. The advantage
was clear: the 49ers had rehearsed the situation, while the Giants were
left scrambling.

The Patriots lost to the Bucs, but Weis confessed to Kiffin that New
England knew all of the Bucs' plays. It was a potent scheme. Friesz later
told Matt Walsh that the Patriots knew 75 percent of the Bucs' defensive
calls before the snap.

Anticipation was everything in football, and so it was everything to
Belichick. If the coaches could force the opposition into a predictable
defense, it could decide a game. The Patriots knew they were on to something, a clear edge in a sport that offered few. They expanded the scope
of the operation and tightened the circle of those privy to it. The quarterbacks were cut out. Now only Adams, Weis, Belichick, a few coaches,

and the video department were involved. Adams, with his direct line to Belichick during games, would sit in the press box with binoculars, watch the signals, and alert the head coach if he recognized a defense. Belichick, in turn, could then suggest a play call to Weis.

The entire system was dependent on the lowest man on the totem pole—Matt Walsh—not only doing his job, but doing it covertly. He was given an older camera with a broken red light, so that nobody could tell if it was filming. He outfitted Walsh in a media vest, so that he would blend in with other photographers. And Dee drilled cover stories into Walsh. One was to tell security he was shooting celebratory footage in the stands. Another was that he was assigned to get tight shots of the Patriots' own quarterbacks and kickers. The credentials on the sideline pass Walsh wore around his neck changed: Kraft Productions sometimes, Patriots TV at others.

"Remain inconspicuous," Dee told Walsh.

At first, the Patriots rolled out the spying system only at their home stadium, where they had more control over access and security and were less likely to be caught. Over the seven years they spent illegally videotaping signs, the Patriots never ran into trouble in Foxborough. All of the problems occurred when they taped on the road. Walsh taped four games in 2000, all against AFC East opponents. The Patriots played divisional teams twice a year, and the coaches knew that, like the Bucs, these opponents might not change signals between games. In 2001, Walsh filmed seven games, broadening the scope to include teams New England thought it might meet in the playoffs. Walsh taped the San Diego Chargers on October 14, 2001—the game that yielded the initial glimpse of Brady's greatness. He shot the St. Louis Rams on November 18, a Super Bowl preview. Sometimes, Adams or Dee asked Walsh to film more than signals—against the Indianapolis Colts, they wanted Peyton Manning's hand gestures—but little changed from game to game. Walsh would shoot the down, distance, signal, and then a peek at a cheerleader's top or bottom, as an in-house joke.

After a game, Walsh gave the tape to Adams, who spent hours decoding it, matching signals to plays alone in his office. The tapes were edited down to rapid-fire clips: down and distance, signal, play. Soon, an entire library had been amassed, with files on every team and coach. Walsh felt as though he was part of the team, helping coaches and players prepare, especially after the Patriots started to win. In one game, against the Jets, Walsh saw what appeared to be a Jets employee with a camera aimed at Romeo Crennel. "They're doing to us what we do to them," Walsh told Crennel.

Every NFL team had an advance scout who took notes on upcoming opponents' signals. Some teams tried to steal signals in real time. Manning sometimes looked to the sideline shortly before calling for the snap, and one of the Colts assistants would relay a sign to him if he had a read on the opponent's signals. But videotaping took the practice to a new realm, not only because it was illegal, but because it made decoding signals more efficient and accurate. No other team had a weapon like Adams analyzing its opponents' signs. Walsh was astonished by Adams, with his photographic memory and amazing stories of the lengths teams would go to so as to stretch, if not break, the rules. When Adams and Belichick were with the Browns, Adams told Walsh, they would outfit a staffer in an NFL Films T-shirt and assign him to film the opposing team's sideline discussions from behind the bench.

One day, Walsh asked Adams, "Are the tapes up to standards?"

"You're doing a good job," Adams replied. "But make sure that you get everyone who's giving signals, even dummy signals."

The stakes were high the first time Dee asked Walsh to tape the signals on the road. It was 2002, and the Patriots were playing the Pittsburgh Steelers in the AFC Championship Game. Walsh turned his sweatshirt inside out and filmed the game. Apparently, no one noticed him. Later that year, Walsh was promoted to scouting. He hated it. He missed video. He missed being around the guys, missed being part of a team. Scouting was lonely. He was eventually fired. Walsh spent the next few years in the New England area, unsure of what to do or where to go. One of his friends worked in security for the Red Hot Chili Peppers, and so he finagled his way into the band's entourage and followed them on tour, playing golf during the day and watching shows from backstage at night. He kept his Patriots season tickets and attended a few games a year. Against the Dallas Cowboys in 2003, Walsh sat in the seats and scanned the sideline until he saw a familiar young man with a familiar pose. It was Steve Scarnecchia, Dante's son, who had assumed his role in the video department, on the field in disguise, with a camera fixed on the Cowboys' sideline.

BILL BELICHICK LIVED within his own definition of the guardrails, hyper-aware of where the line was and where it could be crossed, and how far beyond it he could go when he did. It wasn't a question of a moral compass; it was part of the everyday reality of his profession. To win football games, you sometimes had to be less than honest. You had to manipulate. You had to keep secrets. You had to be unafraid of using people, even those you cared about. You had to be willing to hold grudges. You didn't wade into the gray area; you lived in it. "Do business as business is being done," Belichick always told his players. Business in the NFL was often dirty; Belichick knew that better than anybody, having studied the greats, beaten and lost to many of them.

Belichick was barely out of diapers in 1956 when the New York Giants used a high-powered audio receiver to intercept helmet radio communications between Cleveland's Paul Brown and his quarterback, George Ratterman. Years later, Belichick would be suspected of a similar practice, when the radio headsets at Gillette Stadium seemed to go out during pivotal moments for the opposing coaches. George Allen was famous for sending a scout to a hotel room overlooking the Dallas Cowboys' practice fields. Al Davis would order his grounds crew to let the field grass grow if a fast team happened to be the upcoming opponent, and he was suspected of planting listening devices in light fixtures in the visiting team's locker room. There was a dark side to all instances of NFL greatness.

Patriots coaches became accustomed to receiving a script or play sheet moments before kickoff that had been swiped from the visitors' locker room. Former Patriots linebacker Ted Johnson told *USA Today* that, an hour or so before games, a piece of paper listing the opponent's audible mechanisms would somehow appear at his locker. The sheets amused the coaches—rarely did the teams adhere to the scripted plays, so their effectiveness was limited—and enraged the opposition. In 2006, after Eric Mangini was hired as the Jets' head coach, he met with special-teams coach Mike Westhoff, a holdover from the previous regime. Westhoff was a respected coach who poured every ounce of himself into his scouting reports, which sometimes ran to 80 pages. He was so proud of them, and he gave one to Mangini in that first meeting, not only out of pride, but because he thought it might help him retain his job. Mangini perused it and, according to Westhoff, said, "Yeah, I know, Mike, it's good. I've seen it before. We had it in our facility."

"What did you say?" Westhoff said.

"I've seen it."

Westhoff was livid. How did New England get hold of his report? He never asked, and Mangini never said.

Looking back, it's startling how reckless Belichick was, putting his reputation in the hands of low-level staffers. The interns and Slappies would go through garbage cans in the boxes reserved for opposing offensive and defensive coordinators in the upper reaches of Gillette Stadium, searching for any thrown-away material that could be used at a later date, a task Belichick assigned one of his scouts to carry out back in Cleveland, and something Belichick himself once did as a member of the Giants after a playoff game. The paranoia other teams felt toward the Patriots—that they might be bugging, stealing, and videotaping— was matched only by the paranoia *within* the Patriots. New England football operations staffers were tasked with shredding football-related documents, sweeping hotel rooms and coaching boxes for anything left behind—and watching for opposing teams trying to tape the Patriots' signals.

Belichick insisted that other teams videotaped signals, too. The difference was that he had the foresight to hire his best friend, a man who would never burn him and was not out for his job, to study the rule book and find all the loopholes, the way an accountant would the tax code. Coaches sometimes entered Belichick's office to see Adams explaining to Belichick all of the ways they could bend rules.

"Okay, Ernie," Belichick replied, as though he wanted Adams to leave.

There was a sense around the league that the Patriots, from coaching to ownership, felt they were above the rules. There were some, within the Patriots and beyond, who found Belichick's deviousness understandable. Belichick was smart, yes, and ruthless, yes, and pathologically driven, yes, but if opposing coaches were dumb enough to leave playbooks and play sheets in the locker room, or to never change signals, or to leave valuable information in a garbage can, maybe Belichick owed it to himself and to his team—and his profession—to take advantage. It wasn't just that Belichick was one of the smartest coaches in NFL history. It's that many others were so stupid.

OVER THE YEARS, New England's secret taping system became less of a secret. Jets coach Herm Edwards and defensive coordinator Donnie Henderson once spotted the Patriots cameraman and waved. Pittsburgh Steelers defensive coordinator Dick LeBeau told his staff, "They're filming you," and so they started to outfit their defensive play caller with a wristband with play calls to make it harder to decode their signals. When Ernie Accorsi, the Giants' general manager, learned that the Patriots had likely illegally taped New York's signals in a 2006 preseason game, he was flattered that Belichick thought the Giants were worth breaking the rules over. Tom Brady later said that players "weren't privy to what goes on" with respect to the taping, but some of his teammates not only knew of it, but also participated. The Patriots would sign recently cut players from upcoming opponents and ask them to decipher defensive signals. One year, New England signed a defensive player and led him to a room where Adams was waiting alone. He took a seat. The door closed behind him. It was unnerving. Adams played a compilation tape of the player's former team that matched signals to plays. Adams asked how many were accurate. The player replied that Adams had about half of them correct, and then helped fill in the details of some of the more exotic blitzes.

Belichick lived in the heads of his opponents, which he enjoyed almost as much as beating them. Worried about listening devices, Peyton Manning held pregame conversations at Gillette Stadium in hallways. The scrambling and jamming of the opponents' coach-to-quarterback radio line occurred so often at Gillette that, for a 2002 game, the Kansas City Chiefs asked a league official to sit in the coaches' box and wait for it to happen. Sure enough, on a key third down, the headset went out. In January of 2006, the Jacksonville Jaguars headsets were offline for the entire first half in a 28–3 playoff loss, leading to a pair of delay-of-game penalties. Bill Polian, a member of the NFL's competition committee, fielded complaints about New England, with coaches—especially from the AFC East—arguing that the cheating was affecting their livelihoods. Something had to be done. In 2006 and 2007, a rule was proposed to allow radio communications to one defensive player on the field, as was already allowed for quarterbacks. If it passed, it would all but eliminate defensive signals. It failed twice, with Belichick voting against it each time.

On September 6, 2006, NFL executive vice president Ray Anderson sent a letter to all 32 team owners, general managers, and head coaches, reminding them that "videotaping of any type, including but not limited to taping of an opponent's offensive or defensive signals, is prohibited from the sidelines." Before the 2007 season, the Patriots and the rest of the NFL were again warned in writing not to videotape from the sidelines. The practice was starting to anger many Patriots coaches, who felt cheating was unnecessary. There was a league-wide suspicion that the Patriots' videographer gave the tapes to Adams at halftime, allowing him to translate the signals in real time and prepare the Patriots for the second half. New England coaches rolled their eyes at that accusation, not only because it would be nearly impossible in the videotape era to match the signals to plays in the 12-minute intermission, but because of Adams's halftime ritual of downing hot dogs.

Mangini, of course, knew all of Belichick's tricks and used them against him, honoring his mentor by showing that he had learned all too well. A Jets aide left fake playbooks in the locker room for the Patriots to swipe. Mangini had three coaches signal in plays, and messed with Adams by changing signals on game day after the latter had spent weeks decoding the prior set of signs. A part of Mangini hoped that time would bring a thaw in their relationship—he cared deeply about his mentor, despite the acrimony following his decision to take the Jets job—but Belichick refused to relent. He often wouldn't refer to Mangini by name, whether behind a podium or in staff meetings, and after games, he gave Mangini such limp handshakes that it became an event in its own right, with dozens of cameramen sprinting to midfield to watch what was once a meaningless ritual that now meant everything.

By 2007, all of it—the handshakes, the pettiness, and the taped signals—was getting old. "He's pissing in my face," Mangini told an aide. He let it be known to many Patriots staffers that he wouldn't tolerate filming.

"We know you do this," he said. "Cut this shit out."

Yet, when Mangini learned after the season opener that Jets security, backed by Tannenbaum and Johnson, had blown the whistle on the Patriots, he was furious. Security was supposed to kick the photographer off the field, not start an unwinnable war against a shrewder, pitiless opponent. Mangini knew who would win that fight, in the end.

TELL THE TRUTH, Kraft told Belichick.

Goodell was due to call Belichick on Wednesday, September 12. The Jets had sent a letter to the Patriots asking them to preserve any evidence, part of the process of filing an official grievance. Kraft denied any knowledge of the filming to the league and ordered Belichick to cooperate with the investigation. In the days before the call with Belichick, Goodell set himself an impossible task: he tried to educate himself on the advantage the Patriots had accrued in the seven years they had been taping their opponents. He called around the league, including to Mike Shanahan.

"What's going on here?" Goodell said.

"I *wish* I had thought to videotape signals," Shanahan replied. "I'm disappointed in myself."

It was a sobering glimpse into the mindset of the best of the best. Unlike many in the league, who took the opportunity to pile on Belichick when talking with Goodell, here was a two-time Super Bowl champion responding with honesty—and envy.

"Roger," Shanahan continued, "first of all, people are always trying to steal signs. Peyton Manning is the best. If you don't change your signals, you're dead."

Goodell understood, but thought that taping them illegally was different. The rule was the rule.

"You can't say that Bill Belichick is a bad guy," Shanahan said. "Bill is just better at it than most are." He took it a step further, arguing that taping signals was worth the risk because there was no precedent for punishment. If nobody knew what the penalty was for crossing the line, why not cross the line?

It seemed to hit Goodell that this went beyond the Patriots. "It's really been going on for that long?" he said.

"I can promise you," Shanahan said.

With the Shanahan call as a backdrop, Goodell and Belichick spoke by phone for 30 minutes. The coach repeated to Goodell a refrain that he had expressed privately: that, despite all of the warnings issued by the league, he believed he had merely misinterpreted a rule. He argued that the rule book permitted him to tape signals so long as the material wasn't used in real time. Goodell didn't buy it. Belichick confessed that he had been engaging in the practice of taping signals for "some time" and that, "at most, he might gain a little intelligence." Belichick didn't volunteer the total number of games in which the Patriots had recorded signals, and Goodell didn't ask. "Goodell didn't want to know how many games were taped," a source with direct knowledge of the investigation later said, "and Belichick didn't want to tell him."

That day, ten minutes before his regularly scheduled daily meeting with the media at the Patriots' facility, Belichick released a 66-word statement, taking responsibility for the videotaping, but refusing to admit that he had broken the rules, sticking to his story that he had misinterpreted a bylaw, offering an apology to "everyone who has been affected, most of all ownership, staff and players," and vowing to address the issue in more detail only after the league had concluded its investigation. When Belichick took the podium in an overflowing media room, he deflected questions about the taping for a few minutes, all but begging for football questions. He eventually walked off. Goodell was furious and felt "deceived," he later said. He thought Belichick would apologize verbally, not stonewall.

In a public letter to the Patriots on September 13, the NFL announced it was imposing a $500,000 fine on Belichick, a $250,000 fine on the team, and the loss of a first-round draft pick if the team made the play-offs or a second- and a third-round pick if it did not—a historic penalty, but one that many teams felt was light. Later that day, Belichick addressed the coaching staff. They had seen him angry before, but he was on another level now, wounded and seething.

"This is bullshit," he said.

GOODELL NEVER CALLED Matt Walsh. But a few football writers did, with questions about a more explosive accusation than taped signals. A rumor had floated in league circles for years that the Patriots had videotaped the St. Louis Rams' walk-through practice in the Superdome on the Saturday afternoon before Super Bowl XXXVI. If true, it would not only invalidate the Patriots' championship run; it might destroy the league, a Chicago Black Sox scandal on steroids. Belichick was aware of the rumor—and had been told by people within the Patriots building that Walsh admitted to videotaping the walk-through. Walsh played coy now with reporters, refusing to confirm or deny. He wanted to say more, but feared for the safety of his family and a lawsuit from the Patriots for possibly violating a confidentiality agreement. During quiet moments at the Hawaii golf course where he worked, Walsh would visit a cliff called Black Rock. Sharks swam in the cove below. A ritual occurred each night: a local would lift a torch to salute the sky and jump off the cliff, risking death. The ritual and its implications were profound to Walsh. Right now, at least, the leap wasn't worth it.

THE SCANDAL WAS quickly called Spygate, and it became an instant obsession, not just among fans but around the league. Several owners, executives, coaches, and general managers were furious at the expediency of Goodell's investigation. The Sunday after the punishment was announced, Fox aired a few seconds of leaked video of the Jets' defensive coaches signaling plays, and the investigation blew up in Goodell's face, unleashing a new round of league-wide fury and forcing him to reopen the matter he had so quickly and summarily closed. Goodell ordered the Patriots to hand over all notes, tapes, and related materials, and, for good measure, he dispatched a squad of executives to Foxborough.

On September 18, Jeff Pash, Ray Anderson, and director of football operations Ron Hill arrived at Gillette Stadium for a series of unprecedented meetings. Never in modern NFL history had the league tried to investigate a cheating scandal involving espionage. The inexperience showed. The executives interviewed Belichick, Dee, and Adams. For the second time in a week, nobody from the NFL asked how many games had been recorded or attempted to determine whether the spying had ever swayed a game. The Patriots told the league officials that they possessed eight tapes of game footage and a half-inch-thick stack of notes about signals and other scouting information. All of it belonged to Adams. The officials watched portions of the tapes in a Patriots conference room. Pash called Goodell, explained what he had seen, and asked what the commissioner wanted him to do. The Patriots didn't want any of the evidence to leave the building, arguing that some of it was obtained legally and thus was proprietary.

Goodell ordered the tapes and notes destroyed.

Pash put the tapes on the floor and stomped them into small pieces, leaving the shards of plastic on the floor for Robyn Glaser, vice president of the Kraft Group, to clean up. The officials fed Adams's notes into a shredder.

Goodell's decision haunted him—and the Patriots—for years. When word got out that the evidence had been destroyed, other teams were outraged and assumed the worst. What was on those tapes? Practices? Walk-throughs? "I wish the evidence had not been destroyed, because at least we would have known what had been done," Bill Polian later said. "Lack of specificity just leads to speculation, and that serves no one's purpose—the Patriots included." Roger Goodell went from enforcer to accomplice, in the eyes of many, from someone seeking justice to someone obstructing it. Under the guise of protecting the integrity of the game, Goodell had left its integrity in pieces on the floor with those smashed tapes.

SPYGATE FORCED BILL BELICHICK and Tom Brady to consider their football mortality. Their careers might be fleeting, the player's more than the coach's, but their legacy, once assured, was now fragile and up for debate. It was breathtaking how fast it all started to come undone, how quickly those who once believed in the tale of a discarded coach and a sixth-round quarterback winning three Super Bowls now turned on them. After watching NCAA champions vacate wins due to infractions, and after witnessing Mark McGwire and Barry Bonds break home run records, only to later squirm under oath when asked if they had received illicit help, cynical fans suspected that behind any major success was a looming scandal. After Spygate, both Belichick and Brady relied even more on the hardened will that had sustained them their entire lives, and they buried themselves in the redemptive power of work—two men ready to unleash hell, regardless of opponent.

In the first team meeting after Spygate broke, Belichick stood before his players. It was tense. Always willing to admit a schematic mistake to his players, he was now confessing an ethical one. His manner was neither conciliatory nor repentant. If anything, he was emboldened.

"There were some things that happened," he said.

Did we do anything that anyone else hasn't done? he asked. No—and he vowed to continue to prepare the team as best he could. He asked for questions. There were none.

"I don't want to hear about it," Belichick said, ordering players not to discuss the taping, the investigation, or the scandal with the press.

Tedy Bruschi and Mike Vrabel were visibly fuming. Tom Brady was angry but stoic. At the end of the meeting, Bruschi said, "We have 16 one-game seasons!"

In their next game, a mere six days after the scandal broke, with preparation for game-day grinding on as always, the Patriots dismantled the San Diego Chargers in Foxborough, 38–14, in front of a crowd baying for blood. As the seconds ticked down, Bruschi and Brady hugged Belichick. The coach walked off the field into a tunnel, fans clamoring at the railings above for a glimpse or even a touch of him. In the locker room, players awarded him the game ball. The message from inside Gillette Stadium, and from an entire region of the United States, was clear: Bill Belichick may be a cheater, but he's *our* cheater. It was a strange position for Belichick. He was used to a productive layer of friction between himself and the players. He never cared if they disliked him, as long as they knew he was trying to get the best out of them. Now that the team had lined up definitively behind him, he faced a new challenge: he had to manufacture friction again. Belichick being Belichick, it turned out to be easy.

20

18-0*

O N Saturday nights before each game of the
2007 season, Tom Brady held a 20-minute meeting for the
receivers and tight ends. He stood at the front of the room
with a list of items to run through, making sure that everyone was on
the same page. Sometimes, he used video. Josh McDaniels, who had
been promoted to offensive coordinator in 2005, would attend as well.
Donté Stallworth had never seen anything like it. Brady was almost a
coach, and the one players feared most and were most afraid of letting
down. Brady's willingness to be weighed down with work and responsibility made everyone's jobs easier, including Belichick's. It was Brady's
offense, and it was distinctive. It wasn't a numbers-based system, like
Don Coryell's offense. And it wasn't Bill Walsh's West Coast offense,
based mostly on timing concepts. It was based on Brady, and his ability
to find the open receiver. Brady refused to throw to a receiver if he ran
the wrong route. He had to know, within an inch, where everyone would
be at every moment, or he couldn't trust what he saw.

Nobody needed to spell out the consequences if a receiver failed to
catch on. "He isn't an asshole," Stallworth recalled, "but he is a perfectionist." If a player couldn't perform, Brady wanted him on the sidelines.
During one 2007 game, Wes Welker was hit hard on the head, and when
he returned to the huddle, Brady recognized a familiar daze in his eyes.
"Wes, you all right?" he said.

"Yeah, I'm fine."

"Maybe you should take a play off."

"Nah, I'm all right."

Two plays later, Welker ran the wrong route. "Wes, I asked you if you were fucking all right!" Brady yelled. "If you need to take some fucking plays off, take 'em off!"

The Patriots, known as a well-rounded or even a defensive team through the first three Super Bowls, emerged in 2007 as a machine-like and devastating offensive force. Brady would throw 30 touchdown passes in the first eight games, eclipsing his previous total for an entire season. All of the routes his pass catchers ran were iterations on conversion routes, designed to exploit open space. The 2007 Patriots used the shotgun on 49.4 percent of their snaps, a high mark that later became a common feature across the league. From the immediately widened view afforded by shotgun, Brady looked for dead spots in the defense, knowing which receiver would soon fill it. The Patriots were not just winning; they were humiliating teams, beating Buffalo by 31 in week 3, Cincinnati by 21 in week 4, and Cleveland by 17 in week 5.

For all their precision, the Patriots sometimes played a football version of streetball. On a second and one against the Bills, up 31–7, McDaniels radioed in to Brady to call a run, hoping to get a first down. Brady instead told Moss to go deep, and he tossed it up to him for a 45-yard touchdown. "Holy shit," McDaniels told Brady on the sideline. Here they were, just hoping to move the chains, and Moss scored anyway. "In 2007, for the first time, our offense could support our defense," Brady recalled. "It was a nice feeling."

On October 14, the 5–0 Patriots arrived in Dallas to face the 5–0 Cowboys. It was billed as a midseason collision of Super Bowl contenders, with plenty of subtexts, from Jerry Jones facing off against Robert Kraft, to Brady versus Tony Romo, a pair of quarterbacks who were draft-day afterthoughts and now were not only superstars but sex symbols, to Randy Moss versus Terrell Owens, a pair of moody but game-breaking receivers. "The game was hyped up more than it should have been," Ellis Hobbs later said. "We knew that if we hit them, they'd fold like a tent."

New England attacked through the air. In the first quarter, with the Patriots already up by seven, Welker ran upfield, planning to fake outside and spin inside. But as he cut, he saw a hole: Cowboys safety Ken Hamlin had hustled down from the secondary, forming a bracket of

Cowboys around him, one inside and one outside. Rather than stop, Welker bolted deep—Brady loved Welker because he could read and react "at full speed"—and Brady found him in the clear for a touchdown.

By the fourth quarter, the Cowboys had made a game of it and trailed, 31–24. Brady called a play that Stallworth was unsure of how to execute. "I was 90 percent on it," he later said. "But that's not good enough." Earlier in the week, Stallworth had considered asking Brady for help on the play, but didn't.

Now he wished he had. *Oh shit*, Stallworth thought.

As the huddle broke, Brady sensed that Stallworth was unclear about his job. "What do you want me to do?" Stallworth asked.

Brady looked at Stallworth, looked at the defense, then looked back. "Go deep," he said.

Stallworth exploded down the middle of the field. Brady faked a handoff and threw hard and in rhythm, hitting Stallworth in stride for a 69-yard touchdown, in what would be a 48–27 win. When Stallworth got to the sideline, he found Brady and laughed. Brady had always been bloodthirsty, but now he was on another level, out to avenge every slight, real or perceived. The attitude was contagious.

BELICHICK REFUSED TO LAUGH. Or let up. The more the Patriots won, the harder he coached. The winless Miami Dolphins were next after the Cowboys, and on the Friday before the game, in the middle of a sloppy practice, one of the worst of the season, Belichick got fed up.

"I'm sick of this shit. I'm sick of looking at this shit."

He turned to Brady and Rodney Harrison. "Brady, Rodney, this is your team. I'm not looking at this shit anymore. I'm going in."

Coaches handed practice scripts to Harrison and Brady, then went inside. "Hey, y'all know what we need to do," Harrison told the team. "OK, we had a bad practice. This shit happens. Let's finish the practice."

Still disgusted the next day, Belichick went after the players again. He showed video of a *Monday Night Football* game from 2004, when the two-win Dolphins upset the Super Bowl–bound Patriots. "If you go out there and bullshit," Belichick said, "Miami can beat us."

It worked, mostly. The next afternoon, New England was up 42–7 in the fourth quarter. But Belichick gave some of the starters a rare rest—and the wheels began to come off. After backup quarterback Matt Cassel threw a pick six, cutting the Patriots' lead to 42–21 with 10:30 left, Belichick inserted the entire first team, including Brady. He would rather risk injury to his stars than allow anyone on the team to think that a lack of focus was acceptable. In the locker room after the 49–28 win, Belichick was salty—and the players were starting to lose patience.

"Hey, Bill," Hobbs said, "you said we'd come out and get our ass beat. You saw what happened." He lobbied for an extra day off.

"Yeah, don't press your luck, Hobbs," Belichick replied.

The Patriots had no demonstrable weaknesses. The next week, they destroyed Washington, 52–7, the game over from the first snap. The Patriots were winning so much, and by such large margins, that their sportsmanship became as much of a talking point as their dominance. A few Washington players accused the Patriots of running up the score. Spygate was the subtext of it all. "People thought Bill was giving Tom all the answers," linebacker Rosevelt Colvin later said. "So it was a matter of, 'We're not just going to stick it to you. We're going to stick it to you a little more than we usually have. We're going to prove a point, and prove it hard.'"

Belichick had a few points of his own he wanted to prove, but he had to walk a fine line. There was no better way to convince the world that Spygate was irrelevant than by going undefeated after the taping stopped, but in his mind, the only way to do so was to convince his team that, on any given Sunday, it could be beaten. He surpassed himself in coming up with motivational techniques. After the offensive linemen lobbied Belichick to go for it more often on fourth down, he showed the entire team a clip of them unable to move the pile on fourth and short, rewinding it again and again like "the Zapruder film," Stallworth later said.

"We can't get two inches," Belichick said. "Fourth and inches. Fourth and inches. Fourth and two—not even two inches, fourth and *the size of my dick*, and we can't get the first down."

Nobody knew whether or not to laugh.

Whenever a player hinted at his or the Patriots' confidence to the media, Belichick would humiliate him before the team. "We don't need any more State of the Unions. Shut the fuck up. How about that? Just shut the fuck up." On some days, he left players more confused than angry. The offense kept fumbling in practice, so Belichick ordered all of the footballs soaked in water. "Wet that shit up," Belichick said. "I want it so oily that you can't hold on to it, like your mom's tits." Nobody knew what that one-liner meant, and nobody cared. It was professional football. People said weird stuff, and whether it was funny, politically correct, or even made sense, it helped players get through long days, which were so full of criticism that some Patriots wondered if the undefeated team was even good. Belichick dismissed anything positive an outsider might say about the team—or for that matter, even an insider. In early November, Stallworth was making an appearance at a local event, when a reporter from the *Boston Herald* showed up. The reporter was working on a glowing story on Randy Moss's unprecedented year. Stallworth had been avoiding the reporter for days, worried that if he spoke publicly about anything other than the next game, Belichick would notice—and would let him have it in front of the entire team. The reporter told Stallworth that every other Patriots receiver had cooperated, so Stallworth decided to give a few kind quotes about Moss.

The day the story ran, Belichick arrived at the team meeting holding it. He was in a foul mood. "What was one of the first things I told you fucking assholes at the first meeting? Speak for yourself. There's one group that doesn't understand what the fuck that means—the receivers."

There was nowhere for the wideouts to hide. What had been said couldn't be unsaid. They had no choice but to take what was coming. Belichick proceeded to rip each receiver who was quoted in the story by name, as if checking a list. Welker. Stallworth. Jabar Gaffney. When Belichick reached Chad Jackson, a disappointing second-round draft pick from 2006, he said, "Chad Jackson, you haven't done shit all year. You're not talking to the media the rest of the year." After a few minutes, Belichick added, "I told you assholes to speak for yourself. If you want to blow Randy, do it on your own time. Don't do it here."

Belichick later returned to the metaphor, going on about how "they're gonna start blowing you in the media. Don't believe that crap."

After a few seconds, Mike Vrabel raised his hand.

"Coach?"

"Yeah?"

"What was that you were saying about blow jobs?"

The entire room busted up, including Belichick.

SOME OF THE season's most competitive moments weren't on Sundays. They came on Friday afternoons, when the Patriots would practice the two-minute drill, one of the rare times when the first-team offense and first-team defense faced off. It was so fierce, almost sociopathic, with trash-talking reaching destructive levels. Mike Vrabel, Rodney Harrison, Asante Samuel, and Ellis Hobbs would taunt Brady mercilessly. Vrabel would sometimes line up at safety to get extra conditioning work in. "He always knew what plays were coming," fullback Heath Evans later said. "Brady couldn't stand it." One Friday, Colvin sacked Brady, but because hitting quarterbacks was off-limits, Colvin yanked Brady's shorts as Brady threw, trying to de-pants him in front of the team. Even Belichick would join in, calling bogus penalties on the offense to make Brady's life tougher, just as Phil Jackson used to do with Michael Jordan, testing the boundaries of an intense competitor's patience and composure. Brady's face would turn red, his voice screechy. Never a gifted shit-talker, Brady would just scream, "Fuck you!" and stalk off the field.

Teammates, even those within the offensive huddle, became enemies. Once Moss ran out of gas during the two-minute drill. Brady benched him. "Put somebody else in there," Brady said, motioning to a backup. Moss yelled at Brady, who yelled back. All the defensive players laughed.

"Fuck this shit," Moss said. "Come on, Tom, let's get their ass."

Samuel was locked on Moss man to man. Moss ran a slant and go, hoping to end practice with a deep touchdown. Brady threw it, but Samuel outleaped Moss—*nobody* outleaped Moss—and came down with the interception. He spiked it in Moss's face. Brady threw his helmet. After practice, Samuel removed the nameplate on Brady's locker and replaced it with his own.

On another Friday, after the defense had won again, Belichick benched the first-team offense. Brady begged for another chance. Belichick relented, and Brady told his receivers, "Hey, we're going back out, so make sure you're ready!" The defenders thought it was absurd to give the offense a second try after the defense had already won. In the huddle, Brady looked at Moss and said, "I'm going to the end zone. Let's end this shit." This time, Moss caught it for a touchdown, and Brady ran down the field, hollering at the defensive backs. The Patriots had an inside joke about celebrating touchdowns in practice in a way that would draw fines during games. Brady raised his arms and pretended to fire bullets, mimicking the cannon fired at Gillette Stadium after a touchdown. Then he mock-slashed his neck and dropped to his knees, lobbing fake grenades. A few members of the defense came after him, ready to throw down. "We felt they were cocky bastards," Harrison later said. Harrison confronted Brady and told him to cut it out before things got ugly.

WHEN THE PATRIOTS VISITED the Baltimore Ravens on the Monday night in week 12 with an 11-0 record, there was a feeling in the air that New England might be handed its first loss. You couldn't play scared against the Patriots if you hoped to beat them, and the Ravens were one of the few teams unafraid to brawl. Baltimore was only 4–7, but had a ferocious defense, led by a pair of future Hall of Famers in linebacker Ray Lewis and free safety Ed Reed. Belichick loved both of them. In 1996, before Modell fired him, Belichick had planned to draft Lewis, a star at the University of Miami, and later, as an assistant in New England under Bill Parcells, wanted to draft him, but the Ravens picked him first. Reed was another former Hurricane, and had such phenomenal instincts that Belichick believed he was the greatest free safety in history. He was so complimentary that Brady referred to Reed as Belichick's "son."

The crowd was in a frenzy despite the cold and wind. Belichick had spent the previous day in his hotel room, overlooking downtown Baltimore. Memorial Stadium, where he got his break for the Colts in 1975, was now a youth baseball field. Still, it brought back memories. He worked in a broom closet with a projector and a chair, his career in front of him. There were only seven coaches: three for offense, three for defense, and one for special teams. "I was like the eighth guy," Belichick later said. "I didn't know anything, but at least I was a warm body." The

Colts didn't even have a regular practice field. They started at Goucher College, then moved to the McDonogh School, a private campus in the suburbs, then moved downtown to Eastern High School. The entire team would leave the locker room at Memorial Stadium, shuffle to the intersection at 33rd Street, hit the walk button, cross, and then practice at Eastern, "which had two blades of grass, dirt, glass, rocks, you name it," Belichick later said. He was both animated and relaxed in his hotel room, as if the purity of the beginning of his football life meant more now, his reputation up for debate.

Both teams were feisty and jawing and refusing to back down. At one point, after a Patriots interception, Rodney Harrison mouthed off to Ravens head coach Brian Billick, who returned fire by blowing Harrison a kiss. With the Ravens leading, 24–20, and 1:48 left, the Patriots faced a fourth and one at the Baltimore 30-yard line, the game and the undefeated season at stake. New England called a quarterback sneak to the left side, but Lewis single-handedly destroyed it, colliding so hard with the scrum that he knocked two Patriots, including Brady, back three yards.

It should have ended the undefeated season. But, before the snap, Ravens defensive coordinator Rex Ryan had called time-out, negating the play. Ryan was one of football's smartest and brashest coaches, and he loved to take aim at Belichick. Like many in the profession, Ryan felt Belichick was a good coach who had became known as a great one because he got lucky at quarterback. But one thing Belichick never did was crack under pressure—he was a master of letting situations play out—and Ryan had just panicked, costing his team a victory over the best team in the league. The Ravens' defensive players yelled at him from the field.

"We called that Rex's 'wanna get away?' moment," Brad Seely said.

On the next play, fourth and one, the Ravens again stopped the Patriots, this time on a handoff to Heath Evans, who was hit in the backfield almost as soon as he took the ball from Brady. But the Patriots had committed a false start, erasing the play, a rare instance when a penalty helps the offending team. Now, on fourth and six, Brady stepped up in the pocket, saw a lane, and ran for an easy first down. Four plays later, the Ravens stopped the Patriots for the *third time* on fourth and undefeated on the drive—but were flagged for defensive holding on a receiver away from the throw, giving New England a first and goal. The iron law of facing Brady was to never give him a second chance; he was now on a fourth. With 44 seconds left, Brady hit Jabar Gaffney to put the Patriots up 27–24. The Ravens refused to concede: as time expired, receiver Mark Clayton caught a Hail Mary—but was tackled three yards short of the end zone. The Patriots were 12–0.

Belichick was predictably miserable. "This performance is not going to be good enough," he told the team. Several players were starting to lose patience. The endless carping, the unrelenting pressure, the steadfast refusal to be proud of the team or to acknowledge how remarkable its accomplishments were—it was all getting old. "We thought that was bullshit," Hobbs recalled. "We were angry at Bill. We were trying to prove to him, this shit is hard."

Belichick, of course, knew it was hard. At one team meeting, he seemed to acknowledge the toll. "You guys have paid your debts. Your family is suffering. Your parents are suffering. Your bodies are suffering. Wanna know what cures it? Winning. Winning cures everything." But it wasn't curing everything. It was draining them. Belichick was draining them. Opponents were catching up. Success in the NFL requires peaking at the right time. A loss can be a boon, serving as a chance to refocus and reset. Belichick refused to let it happen. Wins had to serve as losses. History was too close.

A FEW DAYS AFTER the Baltimore game, Belichick walked over to Stallworth in the locker room.

"Hey, do you plan on playing this week?" he asked.

Belichick rarely cruised through the locker room, especially during the players' free time. The Pittsburgh Steelers were up next, a talented team that never had an answer for New England on the biggest stage. After their two losses to the Patriots in the AFC Championship Game, the Steelers viewed themselves as the primary victims of Spygate. The team's star receiver Hines Ward had vented that the Patriots players "were calling our stuff out" during games. The cheating storyline, which had somewhat faded as the wins piled up, now resurfaced. Belichick's tone was flat, as always, leaving Stallworth with no idea what he was getting at or why he was there.

"Yeah," Stallworth said.

"It's not going to matter anyway, according to Smith."

Smith was Anthony Smith, the free safety for the Steelers. At the precise moment when the Patriots were tired and pissed off at their coach—at a moment when the Patriots seemed ripe for a loss—Smith had delivered motivation on a platter. "We're going to win," Smith had told Pittsburgh reporters. Belichick deployed it like a dusty club in the bag, reading Smith's comments before the entire team, pausing to let each word sink in.

"This fucking asshole," Belichick said. "This is the way he feels about you guys."

On game day, the Patriots didn't just target Smith; they derailed his career. Twice, Brady threw long touchdowns over Smith's head—one a deep post route, the other a trick play where he threw behind the line of scrimmage to Moss, who passed back to Brady, who launched a bomb to Gaffney, rubbing it in Smith's face. Even Belichick, for the first time all year, revealed his true feelings at the podium. "We've played against a lot better safeties than him, I'll tell you. The safety play at that position was pretty inviting."

A week later, New England slogged out a win over Mangini's Jets in the rain, sweeping the whistleblowers to move to 14–0. The 1–13 Dolphins were next. If the Patriots won, they'd be 15–0, passing the only undefeated team in league history, the 14–0 Dolphins of 1972, in regular-season wins. Once again, Spygate was at the center of the week's storylines. Don Shula had told the *New York Daily News* earlier in the season that the Patriots deserved an asterisk and later coined the phrase "Belicheat." Those words were harsh. Shula and Steve Belichick had been friends; Bill had once spoken to Shula about a job. Belichick, though, refused to entertain either narrative—the cheating or the 1972 Dolphins.

"I don't want to hear it," he told players. "If I hear it, you'll be fined for conduct detrimental to the team."

The tenser the atmosphere, the more Wes Welker hunted for a good prank. He once got Brady with a fake rat, causing the quarterback to scream. One morning before the Dolphins game, Welker and Larry Izzo carpooled to work. Izzo did a radio interview during the ride, during which he was constantly asked about the 1972 Dolphins. Izzo did his best to dodge the questions, but the issue was unavoidable. He had to engage. After the call ended, Izzo was nervous.

"Dude, should I have said that?" he said.

"No big deal," Welker replied.

Welker had an opening. Izzo was an easy target, a perfect combination of high-strung and gullible. At the stadium, Welker told Brady what had happened and asked him to bring Belichick in on a prank. Brady was in. So was Belichick. After practice, Belichick addressed the team as usual, the players encircling him, and was demonstrably angry, even by his own standards. He spoke to the team, but stared at Izzo with "cold eyes," Izzo later said.

"I told you earlier I didn't want to hear anything about this," Belichick said. "I don't want to hear about the Dolphins!"

Brady and Welker were trying not to laugh. Izzo was terrified to the bone. "Freaking out," he recalled. "I was so mentally fucked up. You don't want to be the guy who brought something up and that's the reason you lose."

On the drive home, Izzo feverishly surfed the sports talk radio stations to see if his words had created buzz. He barely slept. The next day, he was still shaken. Brady decided to put him out of his misery.

"Buddy, relax. He's just fucking with you."

Izzo didn't laugh. "It was total mental sabotage," he recalled.

It didn't matter. The Patriots creamed the Dolphins, 28–7, leaving only one obstacle between them and the NFL's first undefeated season in 35 years: the New York Giants in the Meadowlands. Belichick's former team, in a stadium he revered, with one of his old Giants colleagues, head coach Tom Coughlin, on the other sideline. On paper, the game was meaningless. Both teams had secured playoff spots. But Bill Parcells had raised both coaches. You came hard or not at all. With 11 minutes left, New York led, 28–23. It set the stage for one of the most indelible moments in Patriots history. Brady threw deep to Moss, who had separated from the defense, but the ball was underthrown and Moss couldn't secure it.

"We'll get 'em again," Brady told Moss in the huddle.

On the next down, the Patriots called a version of the exact same play. The mentality of the 2007 Patriots was distilled into those two plays: they were afraid of nothing and nobody. Brady dropped back and looked downfield to Moss, throwing just before he took a helmet to the chin. He hit Moss in stride and down the sideline for a 65-yard touchdown, breaking two NFL records at once—Brady's 50th touchdown pass and Moss's 23rd touchdown—and reclaiming the lead for good in what would be a 38–35 win.

"I told you, baby!" Brady said on the sideline. "I told you we'd get 'em, baby!"

New England had finished 16–0. On the field after the game, Giants tight-ends coach Mike Pope found Belichick and told his former colleague, "I'll tell you what—that's an incredible thing. Nobody does that." Pope was right. The 2007 Patriots set 17 NFL records, including most victories in a season and most points scored. The Associated Press named Belichick coach of the year and Brady most valuable player. It was, Tom Sr. recalled, a "watershed year. . . . Tommy always knew he could perform at the highest level, and that year he performed at a level that had never been attained before. That provided him a stepping board to believe that there are really no boundaries on what he can accomplish."

Outside the locker room, Belichick bumped into Giants owner John Mara and told him he expected to face them again in the Super Bowl. Belichick meant it. He knew that Coughlin's Giants were uniquely suited to give the Patriots problems, with a ferocious defensive line and with Eli Manning, the rare quarterback who could read the entire field, making it hard for Belichick's defense to shade to one side.

The Patriots looked invincible to the outside world, but were running on fumes. Kraft could see other teams closing in, the weight of an undefeated record saddling his players. The team sat in the locker room after the Giants win, amazed at their accomplishment. Belichick knew better. So did Brady, and as he left the locker room, it was clear to his teammates that he had already moved on.

"Nothing's better than the Super Bowl ring," he said.

21

GIRLIE MAN LIMPS HOME

Tom Brady walked slowly through the locker room a few weeks later, after the Patriots had beaten the San Diego Chargers in the AFC Championship Game to set up Belichick's predicted rematch with the Giants in the Super Bowl. Something wasn't right, and it went beyond the fact that he had thrown three interceptions in a nine-degree windchill. Normally after conference championship wins, he was elated, hugging friends, family, teammates. Now, he looked serious and worried—seriously worried. As Brady stepped off the platform after his press conference, his right leg buckled, as though he was rolling it after coming down with a rebound. He hobbled away before disappearing behind a closed door, in obvious pain. He had been nursing a high-ankle sprain—which ranked near the top in the rankings of brutal injuries that aren't excuses for missing game time—and had spent the year in more pain than usual. One night, his parents went to his room to see if he was ready to go out to dinner. Brady was in bed, his leg in an Aircast and hanging from a contraption in the ceiling. "Blood red from hip to ankle," Tom Sr. later described it.

"It hurts pretty bad," Brady told his father.

"Looks like we're not going to dinner," Tom Sr. said.

No, Brady replied. "We're going to dinner."

In the days after the AFC Championship Game—and after a stalker threat led to police being stationed at his Back Bay townhouse—Brady went to New York for a few days to escape the Boston bubble. Paparazzi hunted him. That Monday, Brady was photographed on the sidewalk in black sunglasses and a black hoodie, carrying a bouquet of flowers, with a walking boot on his right foot. The *New York Post* put him on the cover with the headline "Who's Afraid Of Tom Brady Now? Girlie Man Limps Home."

His celebrity had reached a new level. He was now famous enough to mock.

TOM BRADY HAD always seemed to view fame as a tool, something to be used in the right circumstance, rather than a block on which to build. He was judicious in selecting his few endorsements, and unlike Peyton Manning and Michael Jordan, he viewed his ads not as a platform to control his image, but as cool experiences to share with his buddies. His best-known commercial, a Visa spot, was memorable only because he insisted that his linemen appear in it alongside him. He seemed to be carefully managed, as if each choice was part of a grand strategy, but that wasn't really accurate. In truth, he felt overexposed. If someone mentioned an item from the gossip pages to him, he usually replied, "There has to be something more interesting in this world."

Until 2006, Brady was famous in Boston—Inside Track famous. But in Los Angeles, TMZ had yet to obsess over athletes. In New York, Page Six had bigger fish to fry. In Europe, nobody cared about quarterbacks. All of that changed in December of that year, when Brady's friend and manager, Will McDonough, offered to set him up on a blind date with a celebrity many magnitudes more famous than him. Brady knew that if they met in Boston, there would be a scene, so they decided on New York. On a night off from football, he walked through Greenwich Village until he reached Turks & Frogs, a wine bar on West 11th Street, and entered the warm darkness, with no idea how much his life was about to change.

Brady made his way toward a small table at the back corner. Soon, the world's most recognizable model joined him. Although Gisele Bündchen had previously told an interviewer she thought Brady was "definitely not too shabby" and "pretty cute," she had limited this night to a drink. She was tired of blind dates. This was her third in a short time. The other two had been long dinners—too much of a commitment. She wanted to have an escape hatch. But then she saw him—saw his "kind eyes," she later said—and felt herself falling in love right away. Although

Brady had called her to ask her out, and although he later said that, when he first made eyes with her, "she was the most beautiful thing I had ever seen," it wasn't love at first sight for him. Or, more precisely, it was and it wasn't. He soon fell for her, but was wary of a relationship. He and Moynahan had just ended their two-year run. He wanted to be single. Brady loved his family, but he was in no rush to begin one. He had noticed that quarterbacks tended to fall off in their late 30s, weighed down by parenthood. He vowed that wouldn't be him.

A few weeks after the blind date, Bündchen was in San Diego to watch Brady lead a playoff comeback over the Chargers. She waited for him in the low tunnel at Qualcomm Stadium. In January of 2007, word broke that they were an item. Brady—who, when he was at Michigan, once attended a friend's wedding and asked a girl to dance, and she responded by reaching into her purse, dabbing her nose, and then saying no—was now with Gisele Bündchen.

Celebrity relationships almost never work, with every public interaction, utterance, errand, and facial move turned into tabloid fodder. Theirs got complicated two months after they started dating, when Brady informed Bündchen that Moynahan was pregnant. The baby was his. The news became public the next day. "I felt my world had been turned upside down," Bündchen later said.

An entire layer of drama had been added to an already dramatic situation, not only putting Brady in the gossip pages between his beautiful pregnant ex and his beautiful new girlfriend, but introducing a new side to a young man the country largely admired. Brady had not only fathered a child out of wedlock, he was the type of guy who left a pregnant girlfriend. Brady later said he didn't know that Moynahan was pregnant when they broke up, but the optics were horrible. In August of 2007, Brady left training camp on Robert Kraft's plane to fly to LA and welcome his first child, Jack, into the world. Weeks later, Spygate broke, and Brady was not just seen as an asshole who had left his pregnant ex, but also as the chief beneficiary of a massive cheating scandal. He felt the outside world had built him up to knock him down, the old celebrity refrain. He couldn't control his fame, but he could try to limit his own exposure to it. He distanced himself from everything except football, his son, his family, and his girlfriend, in varying order.

Belichick, of all people, helped ease a confusing and complicated time in Brady's life, allowing him to fly to California twice during the regular season so that he could see his son. Brady would return to Foxborough "with a little glow on his face," Stallworth later said. But it was hard. "I didn't envision myself being a parent that wasn't with my son all the time," Brady recalled. Brady had always admired his own father's selflessness. Once, he and Ben Watson started talking about fatherhood, and it hit Brady that, by the time he'd spend any meaningful amount of time with his son, Jack would be almost six months old.

One night in Miami during the 2007 season, Brady, Bündchen, and Stallworth went to dinner at Prime 112, a beachside steakhouse. They sat outside—the private room was reserved for a more famous guest: Bill Clinton—and laughed and talked and were in no rush. Bündchen's rise to stardom had been more improbable than Brady's: she had been spotted by a talent agent at a McDonald's. As Stallworth watched them, he noted how similar they were: both laid-back, both independent, not prone to thinking highly of themselves—at least relative to celebrities.

"Okay," Stallworth said when Bündchen left for the restroom. "You guys are perfect for each other. You guys are the same person."

Brady both agreed and didn't. He and Gisele had each grown up with sisters. "Very sensitive households," Brady recalled with a laugh. She loved glitzy galas and fashion parties; he liked them, but always gravitated toward talking with the spouses of luminaries, not the luminaries themselves. She had an inner strength that he admired. He drove himself to the brink in football. Their relationship had been fast-tracked, due to his son. She would know "every single thing about me—good, bad, and indifferent," he said. She had handled a weird situation with kindness and compassion, loving Brady as a spouse and Jack as a son. They would marry in 2009, but in many ways, they were already life partners before it was official.

"I'm very, very grateful that I found her," Brady replied to Stallworth that night in Miami.

Belichick sometimes groused to friends around the league about the Hollywood turn Brady's life had taken, envying opponents whose quarterbacks—such as Philip Rivers of the Chargers, whom Belichick once coached at the Pro Bowl—he perceived as being all football. Of course, Brady was all football. And even though his notoriety had reached another level, he wasn't unapproachable, and his teammates seized on any opening to give him a hard time. One day in 2007, Brady walked into Brad Seely's office with a Louis Vuitton bag. Seely could see something furry sticking out from the bag.

"What the hell is that?" Seely said.

"That's Gisele's dog," Brady replied sheepishly. Her name was Vida, a Yorkie. She was peeking out from the bag. Bündchen often referred to her as her best friend.

"I gotta watch it," Brady said.

Seely sat back, amused. Brady needed to ask a favor: Could he leave Vida in Seely's office, just for a little while?

Sure, Seely offered.

"Don't tell anybody," Brady said.

Word spread in the locker room within an hour. The guys let Brady have it, and he went along with the jokes. He could still laugh at himself. But his new, more famous life had forced him to change in subtle ways. He was no longer everyone's All-American, but he was perhaps more of an American than ever before, unafraid to be an asshole. A few months after the season ended, Brady agreed to a cover story in *Esquire* magazine. The interview was scheduled to take place in a limo on the LA freeways on his way to Trump National Golf Club, on one condition: that Brady's son and his current and former girlfriends were off-limits. Steve Dubin, one of Brady's agents, told writer Tom Chiarella, "They will not appear in the story. If you ask about his son, they'll stop the car and drop you on the fucking 405."

Chiarella, a gifted journalist, ended up addressing the topic anyway, letting Brady's silence speak for itself. But what if Chiarella had asked about his son right to open the interview? Would Brady really have pitched Chiarella out on the 405? The threat was not reflective of the Brady so many knew—or thought they knew—but it was a reality of Brady's new world.

22

BURN THAT GAME

Tom Brady's first throw of Super Bowl XLII should have been a touchdown. That's what he thought. That's what haunted him years later, when he considered what could have been. It was a screen pass, a complicated Patriots version that they usually ran with ease, and they had it perfectly teed up, down 3–0, on February 3, 2008, at University of Phoenix Stadium. The Giants had just gone 63 yards on 16 plays to open the game—a long drive, with four third-down conversions, exactly the way New York wanted to play. It was a reprise of the Giants' win over the Buffalo Bills in Super Bowl XXV and the Patriots' win over the Rams in Super Bowl XXXVI—the Giants were controlling the clock and trying to "shorten the game," as Bill Parcells liked to say. But Brady knew: if the Patriots could score—and even better, score quickly—the Giants' entire game plan would work against them. Nobody was better than Bill Belichick at undoing an opponent's game plan and forcing them to adjust, rendering weeks of preparation useless, manufacturing doubt on the other sideline.

But the Patriots were navigating some doubt of their own. After the AFC Championship Game, Belichick practiced his team in full pads for three straight days. It backfired—especially along the offensive line, which wore down. The following week, New England's Wednesday and Thursday practices at Sun Devil Stadium at Arizona State University—the two vital practices leading up to the Super Bowl—were defined by dropped passes and missed blocks. "We went backwards," tight end Kyle Brady, whom the Patriots had signed from Jacksonville, recalled. "We had put out so much energy to get to that point. Maybe we had peaked too early and maybe we were physically and emotionally drained."

After one practice, Belichick told the team, "Fellas, the Giants got ahead of you."

Belichick might have felt differently if he had seen the Giants practice. On the Friday before the game, Eli Manning targeted a veteran backup receiver named David Tyree eight times. Tyree dropped seven of the passes; one bounced off his helmet. Manning knew that the Patriots would try to take away star receiver Plaxico Burress, making the Giants play left-handed, which would leave Tyree in favorable matchups. Manning not only needed Tyree to come through, but he needed to believe that Tyree would come through. He decided to "misremember" Tyree's practice, he later joked. When Eli spoke to his brother Peyton on Friday afternoon—they always spoke on the Friday before games—he said, "Guess what? David Tyree had the *best* practice of his life."

Belichick was relaxed all week in front of the media, chatting more than usual, deflecting Spygate questions. And as Sunday neared, Brady was loose. During a light practice, Brady and Matt Cassel competed over who could throw a more perfect deep pass to Moss in the back corner of the end zone. The quarterbacks stood at midfield and had to drop the ball into his arms, with mere inches to spare, like a half-court shot. Cassel went first and overthrew him. Brady went next and hit Moss so perfectly that the receiver barely had to extend his arms. Moss turned to the other receivers. "That motherfucker is gonna be in the Hall of Fame one day. Those are some Hall of Fame throws!"

But a difficult night before the game capped off a draining year. The *Boston Herald* published a bombshell by writer John Tomase, seemingly confirming the long-standing rumor that the Patriots had videotaped the St. Louis Rams walk-through before their first Super Bowl win. The Patriots and the NFL denied the story, but the damage was done. An Eagles fan and United States senator from Pennsylvania named Arlen Specter had announced an investigation into Roger Goodell's decision to have the Spygate evidence destroyed, threatening to do away with the league's cherished antitrust exemption if it refused to cooperate. Shortly before the Super Bowl, Specter had bumped into Carl Hulse, the congressional reporter for the *New York Times*. Hulse asked him which team he liked on Super Sunday.

"It all depends if there is cheating involved," Specter said.

Specter was 77 years old and the ranking Republican on the Senate Judiciary Committee. Twice during the season, Specter's office had written Goodell, seeking additional information about Spygate. Twice, the commissioner had failed to reply. At his pre–Super Bowl press conference, Goodell was asked about Spygate six times and insisted that the taping was "quite limited" and "not something done on a widespread basis," which contradicted what Belichick had told him in September, when he confessed that the Patriots had done it for "some time." Specter watched the press conference and rolled his eyes at Goodell's explanation that he had destroyed the tapes so as not to create an uneven playing field.

"You couldn't sell that in kindergarten," Specter said.

Making matters worse for the league and the Patriots was a profile of Matt Walsh, by dogged ESPN investigative reporter Mike Fish, that cast further doubt on the thoroughness of the Spygate investigation. Seeking immunity in exchange for what he had to share, Walsh told Fish that nobody in the league had called him during its investigation and that he possessed eight previously undisclosed tapes—as well as information indicating the Patriots' rule breaking went deeper than anyone knew. He was hinting at the taping of the walk-through. On Super Bowl Sunday, with an undefeated season at stake, potentially one of the most notable achievements in the history of the sport, the main storyline was New England's cheating.

Game time arrived, and Brady took the field deadeyed. The kid who grabbed Drew Bledsoe in the tunnel before the Rams Super Bowl in February 2002, shouting an undecipherable pep talk, was now a hardened veteran. When Manning jogged past Brady during warm-ups, the Giants quarterback gestured to say hi. Brady blew past him without so much as an acknowledgement.

Still, though: New England was down only 3–0, and on Brady's first play, he saw a chance to knock down the Giants right on his first drive, demoralizing them, reminding them that they had no business sharing a field with the Patriots. He faked a handoff to running back Laurence Maroney, then spun left to tease a reverse to Wes Welker. But the fake to

Welker was a beat slow, and when Brady pivoted to throw to Maroney, who had drifted out of the backfield, two Giants defensive linemen had closed in. It was only a ten-yard pass, but Brady was off balance and could barely see Maroney, and his ball was low, hitting the running back in the shoes, incomplete, and before Maroney could turn up field and see that he had a wall of three blockers and nothing but open pasture.

Brady knew he'd blown it. The Patriots scored on the drive, but it took 13 plays, a sign that the Giants could slow them. The highest-scoring offense in NFL history wouldn't score again until late in the fourth quarter, when it was too late to send any messages.

"WE JUST NEED ONE STOP," Tedy Bruschi said on the sideline. "Let's get it."

The Patriots were up 14–10 with 2:45 left in the fourth quarter. Bruschi wrapped fellow linebacker Junior Seau in a bear hug, cheeks touching, each speaking in the other's ear from an inch away as they prepared to go back onto the field. Brady had just pulled off one of the most impressive drives of his career. The Giants had punished him all game, exploiting his lack of mobility due to his ankle—limiting what was already limited—and dominating an offensive line that was confused and overmatched. Giants defensive coordinator Steve Spagnuolo had disguised his hand signals since Spygate. He had been the linebackers coach for the Eagles when they lost to New England in the Super Bowl, with some questioning whether the Patriots knew the Eagles' signals. Now he had disguised an array of looks from his front seven, dusting off an old Belichick philosophy: when facing an offense without weaknesses, make the quarterback the weakness. Yet Brady had picked himself up and led a 12-play drive, the final throw a short touchdown pass to Moss.

Eli Manning had the ball with 87 yards to go. He had a genius for coming up big—not in all critical moments, but in the *most* critical ones—something that was evident in him from a young age. When he was a boy, Eli was shooting baskets in his backyard in New Orleans with Peyton. Archie Manning filmed his sons and narrated. Eli missed every shot possible: short, long, off the top of the rim, off the bottom, off air.

He looked overmatched. But then he saw Peyton hit a shot from the far-thest location in the driveway, right on the edge of a step to the house. It was beyond his range, but he decided to match his brother, walking his ball to that spot, stepping up, letting go—and draining it. "Nice shot, E," Archie said, unaware that he had just documented his son's essential quality: he didn't make every shot, and often missed badly, but he always hit the most important one.

And so it went on the drive of Manning's life, on which he had *five* near turnovers. On one play, he was pressured and the ball sailed to Asante Samuel, who leapt to catch it. Time seemed to slow. This was it for New England: the ball game and 19–0. But Manning's pass came out of his hand so awkwardly that Samuel misjudged his jump and the ball grazed off his fingertips. "I didn't jump high enough," Samuel recalled. "Maybe, if I'd jumped a little higher . . ."

Manning had all but given away the game, but the Patriots wouldn't take it—an ideal prologue to one of the most unlikely and important plays in NFL history. On third and five with 1:15 left, Tyree lined up on the far right side, ready to run a post route. He exploded into the Patri-ots' quarters coverage—four defensive backs deep—and was open, but Manning couldn't see him. The pocket had collapsed. Patriots defen-sive tackle Jarvis Green held on to Manning's jersey by a fingernail, but Manning, under duress, saw an open white jersey nearby and consid-ered pitching him the ball, yet it was not an eligible receiver; instead, it was guard Chris Snee, who was somehow not blocking anyone on the biggest down of his career, which later made him the target of endless ribbing from Manning, and so, for a split second, everybody seemed to stop—not just time—with Manning in Green's hands, as if waiting for a whistle, but Manning snapped the entire game back into action, spin-ning right, where he collected himself and saw Tyree alone downfield. With three Patriots closing in, Manning took a shot, a wobbly line drive that Tyree leapt for with Rodney Harrison draped on his back like a cape, and . . . Tyree somehow wedged the ball against the right side of his helmet with one hand—showboating unnecessarily, Manning later joked, arguing that if Tyree had caught it cleanly, he wouldn't have *had* to use his helmet—and when Harrison and Tyree hit the ground, the receiver had two hands on the ball, and nobody in the stadium could exhale, and with Harrison punching in desperation to jar the ball free, Coughlin ran onto the field, screaming for a time-out, stopping the clock with 59 seconds.

"Did you catch it?" Manning asked Tyree.

"Yeah, yeah, I caught it."

"Don't lie to me," Manning said. Receivers had fooled him before, and, as he watched the replay, he thought the ball bounced off the ground.

"David, you're a Christian man," Manning said. "Did you catch it?"

"I promise you," Tyree said. The play was reviewed, and the replay proved him right.

New York still needed a touchdown. On first down from the 24-yard line, Manning, as if on cue, nearly fumbled. On second down, he nearly threw another interception. Then, he finally locked in, hitting receiver Steve Smith for a first down. With 39 seconds left and the ball at the 14-yard line, the Patriots called one of the worst plays of Bill Belichick's career: a blitz, sending Seau and Harrison and leaving the secondary in zero coverage—man-to-man across the board with no safety help. It isolated 5-foot-9 Ellis Hobbs on 6-foot-5 Plaxico Burress, a fatal mismatch, even though the height difference didn't matter in the end. Harrison recognized the problem and tried to call off the blitz. "What are we doing?" he yelled to Seau before pleading with him to audible to a better pass defense. "Check two! Cover two!" Seau waved him off. Harrison later said it was the "biggest regret" of his career that he allowed Seau to overrule him. Manning lofted a high and gentle throw into the back corner of the end zone, and Burress beat Hobbs by the length of a small subdivision for a touchdown. Thirty-five seconds left: 17–14, Giants. Center Shaun O'Hara hugged Manning and said, "I've got a shit ton of cold-ass beer at the hotel we are going to crush after this!"

Tom Brady still had one throw left in him to save the season. With 19 seconds remaining and from his own 16-yard line, Brady rolled right, stopped, and threw deep left across the field to Moss, who had a step on two defenders. Belichick had once said of Brady, "We're not talking about John Elway here." But this was an Elway throw: long and diagonal. All of Brady's hard work over years—on his release, his strength, his footwork—was manifest before the world, and there was a shudder in every football fan who watched the ball soar, knowing who was on the other end of it. Brady launched the pass from the Patriots' 13-yard line, and it descended to Moss at the Giants' 20. If Moss had caught it, the Patriots would not only have been in field goal range for the tie, but would have had enough time for a shot at the end zone for the win. But Moss either couldn't or didn't adjust to snare it before Giants cornerback Corey Webster managed to get his fingertips on the ball. Instead of the greatest play in football history, surpassing Tyree just minutes before, it was the greatest incomplete pass.

Belichick ran onto the field a play later and hugged Coughlin, congratulating his former colleague, then trudged straight to the locker room with a few players behind him, a stark, sour image to cap the season. In a stadium elevator, Marty Meehan, the former Massachusetts congressman who had accompanied Brady to the State of the Union, was on the phone with his son, who had recorded the game for him. With the phone speaker loud enough for everyone to hear, his son asked if his father wanted him to keep or erase the tape.

"Burn that game!" said a voice from the back of the elevator.

Meehan turned around.

It was Tom Brady Sr.

OF ALL THE LOSSES during the New England Patriots dynasty, none damaged Tom Brady and Bill Belichick like Super Bowl XLII. It was never far from their minds. In the locker room after the game, Belichick blamed himself, speaking for less than a minute, his voice low and shaky. "We were outcoached. I'm sorry we couldn't win the game for you guys." He seemed alone, broken. For 22 weeks, he had chased wins with a vengeance, but now it was over, history lost, with no Monday film session to serve as a correction and refuge, no Friday afternoon practice to fine-tune, the 2007 season both finished and unresolved. The room was quiet. Brady sat at his locker, staring at the floor. Few Patriots knew what it meant to lose a Super Bowl, from the emotion to the logistics. Was there a postgame party for the loser? Should anyone go? Months later, Belichick told the team after a practice to pick up its AFC championship rings on the way out of the building. He said it as a scheduling item, and as though he couldn't wait to dispose of them.

23

COVER-UP

A T 3 P.M. ON WEDNESDAY, FEBRUARY 13, TEN DAYS after the Super Bowl, Roger Goodell, Jeff Pash, and a few of the league's lawyers arrived at Arlen Specter's office, Room 711 of the Hart Senate Office Building on Capitol Hill.

Specter's staff had spent much of the previous weeks investigating Spygate, woefully overmatched in a foreign and secretive world. Danny Fisher, a counsel on the Judiciary Committee and member of Specter's staff, served as the lead investigator for the inquiry and had a list of 25 names of NFL people to call. Most hung up on him. The Patriots lawyered up quickly and refused to cooperate. So did Eric Mangini. Mike Martz returned a call and then disappeared. Specter made a few calls personally. One was to Woody Johnson, a major Republican donor who talked to him, but Specter didn't take notes. Another was to Damon Huard, the former Patriots backup who didn't believe a United States senator was actually on the line and got off the phone. Drew Bledsoe was "helpful and chatty," according to Fisher's notes. Matt Russell, a former Patriots scout, told Fisher to "keep digging." Fisher called the New York Jets switchboard and asked for general manager Mike Tannenbaum; he was connected straight to Tannenbaum's office and they spoke. Kurt Warner also took Fisher's call; the quarterback was curious about the investigation's findings, especially on the potential matter of a certain taped walk-through, but offered little insight himself. Tom Brady was listed in Specter's notes as a "critical witness," but the office wanted to hold off on calling him until it had more information—a fanciful strategy.

Specter aimed to appoint an independent counsel, as the Senate had done with Major League Baseball's steroids scandal. First, he needed to land two interviews. One was with Goodell; the other with Matt Walsh. The problem was that neither the league nor the Patriots would provide Walsh with a sufficient immunity agreement. Walsh's lawyer, Michael Levy, had received a letter from the Patriots that Specter had deemed "threatening." Specter had been a lawyer on the Warren Commission. He knew an attempt to silence witnesses when he saw it.

After months of exchanging contentious letters, Goodell and Pash agreed to a meeting—though only after Specter threatened to pursue legislation to cancel the NFL's antitrust exemption, backing up an earlier threat. The conversation was odd from the start. At one point, Vermont senator Patrick Leahy dipped his head in to say hello to Goodell. Specter welcomed Leahy to stay, but Leahy declined. It undermined the seriousness of the issue.

Goodell repeated what he had proclaimed publicly, assuring Specter that the destroyed tapes went back only to the 2006 season. Goodell was so relaxed and confident—"cool as a cucumber" and a "perfect witness," Fisher wrote in his notes—that it caught Specter's staff off guard. They had expected Goodell to be contrite, to admit he had erred in destroying the tapes and pledge to do better next time, as many did when hauled into a senator's office. But no. Goodell was adamant that the league had handled the investigation properly. Goodell did, though, disclose something new: the Patriots began their taping operation in 2000, and the destroyed notes were for games as early as 2002—"overwhelmingly for AFC East rivals," he said, contradicting an assertion he had made just two weeks earlier at the Super Bowl press conference. He admitted that among the shredded notes were the detailed diagrams of the Steelers' defensive signals from several games, including the 2002 AFC Championship Game. He repeated his assertion that the taping had a "limited effect. I don't believe it affected games. It had little competitive advantage."

"Then why did you destroy them?" Specter asked.

"We didn't want there to be any question of whether the tapes existed," Goodell said. "If something came out"—if new evidence emerged—"it would be outside of our investigation."

"Why did you impose a penalty before officials had examined the tapes?" Specter asked.

"If there were more tapes, I'd be able to impose more penalties," Goodell said.

Specter jotted in his notes, *No valid reason to destroy.*

As Specter pressed Goodell on the speed of the investigation, the commissioner became "defensive" and had "the overtone of something to hide," Fisher wrote. Specter asked whether the spying might have tipped the Patriots' Super Bowl win over the Eagles. Goodell said that both Jeffrey Lurie and Andy Reid believed the outcome of the game to be "legitimate," a statement at odds with the private feelings of many senior members of the Eagles organization, including defensive coordinator Jim Johnson, who had relayed his suspicion to his staff during the game that New England was stealing signals.

Specter asked what Goodell was imposing the fine on if he hadn't seen the evidence.

"Well, they already admitted their guilt," Goodell replied. The commissioner seemed irritable. Pash was squirming in his chair and kept taking bathroom breaks.

Specter turned to the issue of Walsh. Specter's office had learned that, in February, Dick Farley, one of the NFL's investigators, had started digging around on Walsh, asking his previous employers about his work ethic and character. Specter considered it a brazen attempt to silence Walsh and scare other potential whistleblowers.

"Yeah, he works for us," Goodell said of Farley, adding that he was "surprised" to learn that the league he ran was looking into Walsh.

Specter and his staff then raised the biggest accusation: the reportedly taped walk-through. Goodell acknowledged that he first "got wind" of the widespread rumor of the taped walk-through the previous September. The league interviewed the video staffs of both the Patriots and the Rams and found no evidence that New England had filmed St. Louis. If the walk-through had been taped, Goodell insisted, the Rams staff would have reported it.

Specter sat there, seething. The Rams couldn't have reported it if they didn't know it had occurred. After almost two hours, the meeting ended. Goodell met with reporters and insisted that he had "nothing to hide," but Specter believed he was on the verge of uncovering a massive scandal and wanted to put everyone—owners, executives, coaches, players, and Goodell—under oath.

AS THE SPYGATE INQUIRY was heating up, a mutual friend of Robert Kraft and Arlen Specter believed he could help make it go away.

Donald Trump had become close to each man over the decades. In early 2008, he was a businessman and reality show host with no apparent political ambitions beyond writing checks and appearing in the vicinity of power. He went back with Specter to the 1980s. He had donated a total of $11,300 over the years to Specter's campaigns, and even hosted fundraisers. In 2004, at an event for Specter at Trump Tower, the two men stood for photographs with a total of more than 100 donors. "Arlen is quite simply a friend of mine," Trump said that day. "He's just someone I like." Trump then glanced at Specter, adding with a laugh, "I don't know if that helps you or hurts you."

Trump's friendship with Kraft was helpful before it later became hurtful. It had started shortly after Trump got to know Specter, when Robert and Myra bought a place in Palm Beach. He and Trump played a few rounds of golf, and their relationship grew from there. Trump considered himself a winner and liked to be around winners—and the Patriots loved having him around. He was pals with Belichick. Before one game, Trump boasted that Belichick had hugged and kissed him. He brought Brady to the Miss USA pageant—Brady called him "Mr. Trump"—and at one point, Trump tried to sell him to his daughter, Ivanka. "You have to meet him!" he said. She wasn't interested, and she married Jared Kushner in 2009, leaving Trump to grouse over the years that he could have had Tom Brady as a son-in-law.

On March 18, 2008, Trump served as a cohost for a party in Philadelphia for Specter's book, *Never Give In*. The Spygate investigation was making news. Trump hated the NFL—hated Pete Rozelle, hated Paul Tagliabue, hated Roger Goodell. He had once tried to buy the Buffalo Bills, but the league suspected he didn't have the money. Trump insisted that George Steinbrenner would back him, which went nowhere. It was embarrassing for Trump, and nothing burned at him like public humiliation. Trump thought the Spygate investigation was ridiculous, and he decided to try to do something about it.

One day, Specter took a call from Trump. Spygate came up, and Trump said something stunning.

"If you laid off the Patriots, there'd be a lot of money in Palm Beach."

Specter was floored—and "pissed," his son, Shanin Specter, later told ESPN's Don Van Natta, Jr. Trump claimed to be acting as a messenger for Kraft—which Kraft later denied—but it didn't matter. Specter felt Trump had essentially offered him a bribe. He later researched the question and concluded that it was not—in Washington, there are bribes, and there are *bribes*—so he didn't report Trump to law enforcement or Senate ethics officials. He liked Trump, who later denied that he tried to influence Specter's investigation. But in the moment, Trump's words hung in the air. Deeply offended, Specter had to respond.

"I couldn't care less," he replied.

The only thing Specter cared about was investigating the league's investigation. He wanted Matt Walsh.

ROGER GOODELL CONVENED an emergency meeting. It was April 1, and the league was holding its annual spring gathering at the Breakers hotel in Palm Beach. Usually, league meetings are relaxed and an excuse for coaches and owners to play golf and drink and run up massive dinner tabs on the company card. Nights at the hotel bar, with Jerry Jones holding court and often whipping out thousands of dollars to keep the bar open for just one more Johnnie Walker Blue, are famous in the small circles that would know. The emergency meeting was tense. Owners and coaches were furious with the Patriots and Goodell, who seemed to act like partners, complicit in trying to sweep the scandal's details under the rug, forcing the rest of the league to defend their actions, all without answers as to how many wins, and even championships, the Patriots' cheating had cost their teams. The league's lone concrete response, besides the penalties for the Patriots and Jeff Pash stomping tapes, was to change the rule that Bill Belichick had so feverishly opposed for years, allowing headsets to be installed in the helmets of defensive players for sideline-to-field communication, rendering hand signals obsolete.

Goodell stood to address what he called the "elephant in the room." He turned the floor over to Kraft, who apologized for the embarrassment his team had brought the league and for the undermining of public faith in the integrity of the sport. He seemed contrite and sincere, appearing to tear up.

Belichick spoke next and conveyed the opposite tone, seemingly offended that he had to take part in a charade. He had lost his patience with the league, and the league had lost patience with him. One night during the meetings, there was a dinner for all of the head coaches and their wives. Afterward, people mingled. At one point, Julie Mangini, Eric's wife, looked up and found herself next to Belichick—the man who had spoken at her wedding and whom she had honored by giving her secondborn son the middle name William.

"Hi," she said, trying to ease the awkwardness.

Belichick glared at her, saying nothing, shaking his head, and then blew her off, as if galled that she would talk to him after all that had transpired. Julie told Eric what happened. Mangini hit the roof, and he charged at Belichick.

"Hey Bill, fuck you!" Mangini yelled.

The room quieted. Everyone stared. A few coaches grabbed Mangini and held him back, averting a fistfight.

Now Belichick stood before his peers, needing to say something after his boss had just spoken frankly. The rule and the violation were clear, but Belichick repeated the explanation he had given to Goodell and his players in September and in off-season interviews with the *Boston Globe* and CBS: that he had made a mistake—"my mistake"—and had merely misinterpreted league rules. It was a stunning display of arrogance. Even Kraft was disappointed in Belichick and was unsure how deep the cheating went. Two months before the league meeting, New England had announced a curious addition to the coaching staff: Dom Capers, whom Kraft would have hired in 2000 if Parcells hadn't decided to trade Belichick, joined as assistant head coach and as secondary coach. Kraft reportedly wanted Capers on staff in case Goodell found proof that the video crew taped the Rams' walk-through and suspended Belichick.

Goodell closed the discussion by reiterating that he had ordered the tapes and notes to be destroyed to prevent them from being exploited by another team. Nobody was satisfied. Before the meeting adjourned, Goodell made a final point: he pledged to treat cheating teams with the same forceful vengeance with which he had treated players who had broken league rules. It felt less like a warning to the rest of the league than to the two men alongside him at the front of the room.

ON THE MORNING OF May 13, after months of power plays on letter-head over the matter of an indemnification agreement, Matt Walsh and his attorney arrived at league headquarters in New York to meet with Goodell, Pash, Gregg Levy, Patriots lawyer Dan Goldberg, and NFL security director Milt Ahlerich. It was yet another Spygate media spec-tacle; reporters crowded outside on Park Avenue, as though awaiting a court decision. The meeting lasted just over three hours. Ahlerich asked the majority of the questions; Goodell was mostly silent. Walsh denied taping the walk-through and insisted that he didn't know if anyone had indeed taped it. Afterward, Goodell told reporters that he considered the league's interest in Spygate closed. Walsh exited the league office to cameras in his face and shouted questions. He couldn't talk—he had to catch a flight to Washington to meet with Arlen Specter.

SPECTER SAT IN HIS OFFICE, outlining his thoughts and ques-tions on Senate Judiciary Committee stationery. *Taping 2000–2007 . . . Change of story . . . Punishment B4 viewing.*

He began the meeting by asking Walsh about NFL security's inves-tigation of him. Like Specter, Walsh considered it a way to dissuade more whistleblowers from coming forward. Walsh then took the room through some of the facets of his former job. It involved not only produc-ing video contrary to league rules, but one instance of erasing evidence of the Patriots breaking other league rules: the Patriots had practiced a player who was on injured reserve, and Jimmy Dee asked Walsh to erase the video footage from that practice. Walsh also scalped tickets for play-ers on occasion, including for Tom Brady.

Specter said, "You're quoted in the press saying that if the public knew what you know, 'Some would be forced to answer for things they haven't taken responsibility for.' What were you referring to?"

"It was not yet public that Bill Belichick had been cheating since 2000," Walsh replied.

"Were you surprised that Belichick said he had misinterpreted the rules?" Specter asked.

"Yes," Walsh said. "I was surprised that Belichick would think that because of the culture of sneakiness."

Specter asked why other former Patriots videographers refused to cooperate.

"It's understandable," Walsh replied. "They've seen what's happened and don't want to be a part of it."

Specter noted that every team tried to steal signals by sending an advance scout who took notes at games. "What's the value of filming them?" he asked.

"It's much harder to translate signals by memory," Walsh explained. "Video is much easier."

The conversation then turned to the alleged taped walk-through of the Rams. Walsh's recollection was stunningly accurate at first. It was the Saturday before the game at the Louisiana Superdome. The Patriots had just taken team pictures, and the video staff stayed behind to set up camera and electronic equipment for the game. Soon, the Rams showed up and started to practice. The Patriots crew lingered and watched, still in their team gear for the photo. The walk-through lasted about 30 minutes, maybe longer. Walsh saw Marshall Faulk returning kickoffs and saw the Rams' tight ends featured in new ways, split wide and motioning out of the backfield. The Patriots videographers were everywhere, in the stands and on the field, and Walsh later told a confidant that they would have taped the walk-through if fewer stadium staff were around. That night, Walsh told Brian Daboll, one of the young assistants, what he had witnessed on the field. Daboll had an array of questions and drew some diagrams, asking if what Walsh saw matched what he drew.

Specter's staff asked how Walsh had replied: yes or no. Walsh gave a meandering answer, mentioning that perhaps other Patriots video staffers talked to the coaches, too. Specter found him suspiciously vague.

"Were there any live electronics during the walk-through?" he asked.

"It's certainly possible," Walsh said. "But I have no evidence."

Walsh's memory was sharp on most of the questions and almost purposefully unclear on key ones. Specter's staff suspected that Walsh had received some sort of severance for his silence, even though they lacked proof. In his notes, beneath Walsh's name, Specter jotted the phrase *Cover-up*.

LATER THAT DAY, Mike Martz was on the practice field in Santa Clara, California, as the offensive coordinator for the San Francisco 49ers when he returned a call from Roger Goodell. The loss to the Patriots had derailed his career—his Rams never reached another Super Bowl, and he was fired after the 2005 season—and reports of the taped walkthrough had sent him down a dark rabbit hole, replaying the game on his computer, especially plays in the red zone, which had been practiced at the walk-through. Since news broke of the alleged filming of his team, Martz had had a few conversations with league officials. "They know a lot," he told a confidant. Martz believed the Rams had lost due to their three turnovers, but the notion that the Patriots might have taped the walk-through—or even some of the Rams' practices during the week—infuriated him. "I'd like to hang Belichick by the nuts," he told the same confidant.

Martz connected with Goodell. The commissioner sounded panicked about Specter's call for a larger investigation and asked Martz to release a statement saying the league had done its due diligence.

"If it ever got to an investigation," Goodell continued, "it would be terrible for the league."

It would *kill* the league, Martz thought.

"You have to take me at my word," Goodell said.

Martz was under pressure. The Eagles and Steelers had released statements exonerating the Patriots, even though members of both teams still felt cheated. Martz later said that it was "hard to swallow because I always felt something happened" in the Super Bowl—a Patriots coach on the 2001 team told friends around the league that "a little birdie" had detailed some of the Rams' red zone plays—but he got in line. That evening, he wrote a statement saying that he was "very confident that there was no impropriety" and that it was "time to put this situation behind us." He sent it to the league the next morning. The league added a few lines—including disparaging remarks about Matt Walsh—and released it.

Martz later bumped into Jerry Jones.

"This was a big favor that we won't forget," Jones said.

THE LEAGUE'S STALLING moves and the public statements from the aggrieved parties worked. Specter's investigation was losing steam, especially after the *Herald* retracted its report of the taped walk-through in May. With the wars in Iraq and Afghanistan ongoing, it seemed like a waste of taxpayer money to investigate a football team that had not committed an actual crime. With a lengthy speech on the Senate floor, Specter backed off. The league later introduced a mandatory compliance policy, which included prohibited acts that read like a list of Spygate-era offenses and accusations, from "unauthorized videotaping on game day or of practices, meetings, and other organized team activities" to "unauthorized entry into locker rooms, coaches booths, meeting rooms or other private areas." The league also relaxed its investigative standard of proof to the "preponderance of evidence," making findings of guilt easier.

Over the following years, the policies were rarely invoked—until almost a decade later, when the league received a tip from the Indianapolis Colts about something few people had ever had reason to contemplate: deflated footballs.

24

ONE THING I'M NOT
IS SCARED

I T WAS TIME FOR STRONG A. THERE WAS 7:38 LEFT IN the first quarter of the first game of the season on September 7, 2008, Kansas City against New England, and Chiefs defensive coordinator Gunther Cunningham dialed up a blitz designed to trap Tom Brady. Kansas City's defensive ends would pinch the pocket, forcing Brady to step up and into strong safety Bernard Pollard, who would blitz up the middle—known in football parlance as the A Gap. Before the snap, Pollard lined up deep, disguising his intent, then rushed the line of scrimmage. Patriots running back Sammy Morris met Pollard head-on, but Pollard went low and landed on the turf. Brady slid up in the pocket and planted his feet to throw deep to Randy Moss. From all fours, Pollard saw Brady's white-and-blue cleats dancing toward him and lunged—directly into his left knee.

Brady bent back and twisted to the side. Pollard heard sounds he would never forget, of ligaments snapping and muscles overextended. "It was loud," Pollard recalled. "And it was the nastiest thing I've ever heard."

Brady screamed, a primal cry not only of pain but of fear. The force was so intense that he grabbed his knee with his left hand before he hit the ground. He sat on the field, shifting nervously, before rolling over in a heap familiar to any fan. Three trainers knelt before him. Pollard's hit had torn two ligaments in Brady's knee, his anterior cruciate and his medial collateral. His season was over.

Brady had surgery on October 6 in Los Angeles. He had never missed a game due to injury in his life, and he was eager to prove that he was ahead of schedule before a rehab schedule even had been created. He ignored orders to stay off the leg and carried Jack on his shoulders around the hospital room. It was a mistake. Brady developed a hematoma and staph infection, requiring two more operations.

Before his injury, Brady had sometimes wondered what the world had to offer outside of football. What would he do when football ended for him? Acting? Architecture? He was always happiest with a plan. But now, he was forced to contemplate these questions more seriously. Rehab for a major injury can be almost as devastating as the injury itself. You are alone. You have no idea if you will return to form. The team—the game—moves on without you. The limits of what you can control are clarified once again, and in the most discouraging way possible. The Patriots moved on without Brady, who stayed in Los Angeles, on Belichick's recommendation, neither of them wanting the specter of cameras cutting to Brady, up in a suite, watching games. It was as if he was in a different world. He spent days pondering life without football. Then he stopped.

Why would I even think of doing anything else?

Nothing else brought him as much joy. Pollard had apologized for the hit, explaining it as "just football." Brady accepted the apology, but he refused to accept that it was just football. He had failed to train his knee to absorb such hits. Brady rehabbed with the help of a trainer named Alex Guerrero, who had been a quiet presence around the Patriots the previous few years. Willie McGinest had introduced them in 2004, when he noticed that Brady was in constant arm pain. "Dude, you can't practice," McGinest told Brady. "You can't even move your elbow." McGinest referred to Guerrero as his "body coach." He suggested Brady allow Guerrero to give him a massage on the six or so days a month Guerrero visited Boston. One night at McGinest's house, they met up.

Working with the league's most important young quarterback was the chance of a lifetime for Guerrero. Since 1996, he had operated his own training facility in Southern California, and his clients included a range of professional athletes, superstar running back LaDainian Tomlinson among them. He had faced a slew of legal issues that nearly ended his career. He kept those private. His philosophy was different than that of the Patriots' doctors—and of all of Western medicine. It was a holistic approach based on massage and hydration and diet, and it appealed to the fragility deep inside Brady that he always found a way to transmute into confidence. That night at McGinest's house, Guerrero spent an hour on Brady's elbow, lengthening the inflamed elbow tendons by using what the quarterback later termed "deep-force muscle work." After two weeks, Brady's pain significantly lessened. He asked Guerrero to work on all his joints. Guerrero set a goal of eliminating pain completely. Football, with limited pain? It was impossible, but the notion appealed to Brady in terms both practical and philosophical. Why was it accepted that pain was a part of football? It was the exact type of assumption that Brady loved to challenge.

Now the two of them were alone in Los Angeles with Brady's knee to heal. They communicated with New England's medical staff, but implemented their own regime, both out of conviction and to accelerate Brady's recovery. Rather than a generic rehab plan, they focused on strengthening Brady's knee for what he needed it to do: withstand dropping back, pivoting in the pocket, stepping into throws, and absorbing hits. They practiced taking sacks. They used resistance training with rubber bands. It worked—or Brady *believed* it worked. To him, it felt like the two of them were inventing something, a new approach to surviving football. Brady had become a great quarterback by testing the limits of what his mind could control. He was now attempting to do the same with his body.

MATT CASSEL HELD a unique distinction in the NFL that went beyond the fact that he had been the backup to perhaps the best quarterback in the game for three years. He was a veteran professional quarterback who had not started a game at that position since he was a senior at Chatsworth Charter High School outside of Northridge, California— another example of the mystery surrounding the most difficult job in American sports. Cassel had committed to USC before his senior year of high school, but when he arrived on campus, he was buried, first behind Carson Palmer and then Matt Leinart, a pair of future Heisman Trophy winners and first-round draft picks. He threw a total of 33 passes in four years. A professional career was unlikely, but a former USC coach encouraged Cassel to participate at the team's pro day. USC was an NFL factory; every team in the league sent a scout. Cassel not only participated in pro day, but performed well, and Trojans head coach Pete Carroll—who years after being fired by Kraft had won at least a share of two straight national championships at USC—recommended Cassel to Belichick. With little to lose, Belichick drafted him in the seventh round of 2005.

During Cassel's first few years, New England's coaches viewed him as a goof-off, a caddy to Brady whose most notable contributions were his prank wars with the team's best player. He once poured a protein shake into Brady's shoes, and Brady retaliated by relieving himself on Cassel's practice jersey. Nobody knew what to make of him as a quarterback. Once, in a preseason game against the Giants, Cassel was blindsided by a corner blitz. In a quarterbacks meeting before another Giants preseason game the next year, Belichick said, "Okay, Cassel, what front do they like to bring the corner blitz from?"

There were only two possible answers: an "over front" or an "under front." He had a fifty-fifty chance of making a correct guess. Cassel had studied the night before, anticipating this exact question. "Coach, it's an over."

Belichick's eyes went blank. "Brady?" he said.

"An under," Brady said.

"Brady's right," Belichick said.

Belichick leveled with Cassel. "I don't want to have to send your mother another note that says, 'Dear Mrs. Cassel, we regret to inform you that your son got killed being a dumbass.'"

With Brady out, the suspected dumbass was now New England's starting quarterback—and a working theory on the competing legacies at the heart of the Patriots dynasty. For years, fans and other observers had wondered what was more responsible for New England's success: Bill Belichick's system or Tom Brady's brilliance. Belichick had mostly lost as a head coach prior to Brady's unexpected emergence as a second-year player, and had whiffed on every other quarterback he had ever drafted, dating back to his days in Cleveland. Belichick had once taken me through how he evaluated college quarterbacks. All of the tests were mostly mental, not physical. The coaches would inundate the prospect

with football information, from terminology to play design. An hour
after the quarterback left the building, New England's coaches would
call and quiz him, testing his recall. "It's very subjective," Belichick said,
and he eventually whittled it down to two factors: decision-making and
accuracy. The process sounded easy, but predicting how quarterbacks
would adjust coming out of college was still impossible, due in part
to the wider hash marks on the college field, which creates an almost
entirely different game than the sport played in the NFL. Both of the
quarterbacks New England drafted between Tom Brady in 2000 and
Matt Cassel in 2005—Rohan Davey out of Louisiana State and Kliff
Kingsbury out of Texas Tech—were busts.

The 2008 season was a chance for Belichick to counter the notion
that Brady had single-handedly transformed his career. He dusted off
his 2001 playbook, inspiring a locker room reeling from the loss of its
franchise player by refusing to concede an inch. What followed were
perhaps the most remarkable performances in the careers of both Bill
Belichick and Josh McDaniels. Cassel had a Pro Bowl–worthy season,
completing 63.4 percent of his passes, with 21 touchdown passes and 11
interceptions. In a mid-December game against the Oakland Raiders—
days after his father, Greg, had died unexpectedly—Cassel threw four
touchdown passes in a 49–26 win. Afterward, Belichick presented him
with a game ball, and Cassel cried. The Patriots finished 11–5, tied
for first place in the AFC East, but out of the playoffs due to a lost tiebreaker. As a consolation prize, Belichick's Patriots, with Cassel under
center, finished with a better record than Eric Mangini's Jets with Brett
Favre, who had been acquired in a trade shortly before the season. After
a promising first year in 2006—the New York press dubbed Mangini
"The Mangenius," and he and Julie had a cameo in the penultimate episode of *The Sopranos*—Mangini's Jets missed the playoffs in 2007. With
Favre in 2008, New York raced to an 8–3 start before finishing 9–7, costing Mangini his job, despite two winning seasons in three years and
some strong drafts, including star cornerback Darrelle Revis and center
Nick Mangold.

What Belichick did with Cassel after the 2008 season might have
been even more impressive than what he did with him during it. In late
February 2009, Scott Pioli, who had left New England to become gen-

eral manager of the Chiefs, offered Belichick the 34th-overall pick in the upcoming draft for Cassel and Mike Vrabel. Belichick took the deal. It was an epic return on investment—a seventh-round pick and a fading defensive veteran had together fetched an early second—and with the pick, Belichick drafted Oregon safety Patrick Chung, who would be a regular starter for the next decade.

The 2008 season was a weird blip in New England's two decades of dominance, but it also brought a subtle and vital philosophical break between the two leaders of the franchise. Belichick later spoke of the Cassel season with a fondness normally reserved for a championship year. "I'm proud of the fact that, without Tom Brady, we still won 11 games in 2008. We have a good program here. It's bigger than any of us individually. Collectively, we are competitive." On the other coast, Tom Brady had started to formulate new theories regarding performance and longevity, theories that stood in opposition to the practices of the New England team doctors—which is to say, in opposition of Belichick.

BY 2009, Belichick had enough personal wars to rival his successes. His grudges—against the league office, against various current coaches around the league, and, most of all, against Mangini—were destructive, and there was no living in their wake. They reflected his pettiness as much as his power and added to the perception that he had no use for people and relationships beyond football. His reputation had taken some hits. He and Debby had divorced, and over the summer of 2006, he was accused in a New Jersey divorce case of having an affair with a former New York Giants receptionist named Sharon Shenocca. And after the 2006 season ended, former Patriots linebacker Ted Johnson told the *Boston Globe* that he believed Belichick had, in 2002, overruled a trainer's recommendation and forced him to practice with a concussion—which had led to a second concussion. The horrific specter of head injuries was starting to shape views of the league, and the NFL's complicity in covering up their long-term effects from playing football would lead to a major crisis. Roger Goodell testified before Congress in 2009, and the league paid out nearly a billion dollars in settlements to former players. Johnson's story—and Belichick's alleged role in it—helped usher the issue into public consciousness.

Belichick would send some reporters handwritten notes or Christmas cards, but many of his relationships with the press were frayed. Even so, covering the New England Patriots became a launching pad for reporters over the entire two-decade dynasty. Michael Holley was a best-selling author and prominent radio host. Michael Smith and Mike Reiss would leave the *Boston Globe* and transition into stars at ESPN, as did Wendi Nix of WHDH-TV in Boston and ESPN Boston's Field Yates. Shalise Manza Young left the *Globe* for Yahoo! Sports. Albert Breer and Greg A. Bedard would go from the *Globe* and become top football writers at *Sports Illustrated*, and Bedard eventually founded the *Boston Sports Journal*. Years later, Nora Princiotti started covering the Patriots for the *Globe* at age 21 and was eventually plucked by the *Ringer*. Ian Rapoport of the *Boston Herald* and Mike Giardi of NBC Sports Boston jumped to the NFL Network. Kathryn Tappen of the New England Sports Network and Carolyn Manno of Comcast SportsNet New England both eventually ended up at NBC. Tom E. Curran went from the *Providence Journal* to NBC Sports in 2006 before returning to the beat in 2009. Many other daily writers, like Karen Guregian, Jeff Howe, Ben Volin, Phil Perry, Michael Felger, and Christopher Gasper became local sports institutions, some with their own radio shows and podcasts. And Kay Adams of NBC Sports Boston would go on to cohost the popular *Good Morning Football* show and become the face of the NFL Network. The message from the sports media industry was clear: if you could cover Belichick—"the Kremlin," as opposing coaching staffs called him—you could cover anyone.

Belichick liked to test reporters, to see if they would comply with his will. If you asked to speak with him, you would be given a day when he would call—not a time, or even an hour, but a *day*. He often called around midnight, with his work complete. But once on the phone, or if you were in his office, he was relaxed and expansive and friendly. In 2009, writer Jason Cole from Yahoo! was told to be at the stadium at 11 a.m., and that Belichick would speak with him for about 15 minutes before or after his noon press conference. But the interview kept getting pushed back, into the afternoon, and then early evening, and at one point, Cole realized what was at work and decided to stick it out. Belichick finally met with him around 10 p.m.—and, as always, removed his shoes and kicked up his bare feet on the desk, getting comfortable for an hour-long chat.

There was a belief among the Patriots beat writers that if you asked Belichick a thoughtful question, rooted in research and in fact, he would deviate from his standard brevity and give an expansive answer. This was only partly true. He deflected many great questions if the answers didn't serve his larger purposes. What he seemed to appreciate was *depth*. I once sat alone with Belichick to discuss how he assembled his draft board. Our conversation got off to a horrible start. My questions were missing right and left. He mostly stared at the ground and breathed hard out of his nose. Anyone who's interviewed Belichick has been there: you've lost him, he's barely masking his irritation, and you're digging yourself a deeper hole with every passing syllable. After about 15 minutes, I thanked him for his time and got up to leave. But then, he just started talking, as if he knew what I was looking for, even if my questions were off. He went on for five more minutes, telling draft stories, grinning, and, most of all, helping me. He was eager to give glimpses of the staggering knowledge and willpower that had both propelled and sustained his career. He might not want to reveal which player had pulled a hamstring in practice, but he wanted people to know how he worked, how he planned, how he thought, and so, for the 2009 season, he agreed to something his friends had once considered unthinkable: he allowed cameras to follow him around for the year.

"You CAN SAY a lot of things about me as a coach," Belichick told his players in a team meeting in September of 2009. "And I'm sure you do, and so do a lot of other people. But I'm just telling you guys something: one thing I'm not is scared."

He was on film, in the documentary titled *Bill Belichick: A Football Life*. Belichick was addressing his team in a dark auditorium lit only by a projector playing game film on a screen. It was one of the most autobiographical statements of his life, delivered clearly and directly and *loudly.* A man accustomed to mumbling for the cameras kicked it up a level, explaining himself and defending himself at once. It would have made his father proud. Steve Belichick had once spoken of the "cover-your-ass theory of coaching." Coaches talked tough about possessing thick skins and ignoring fallout from media and fans, but in the end, most of them couldn't stomach blowback. It was as if they'd rather lose and be blameless than win and be blamed.

Bill Belichick was truly unafraid. He had learned from Bill Parcells to be aggressive—Super Bowl XXI in 1987, against the Denver Broncos, had turned on a fake punt in the third quarter—and Steve Belichick had been impressed with his son's willingness to withstand the criticism, if not incredulity, when he chose Tom Brady over Drew Bledsoe. And now, the Belichick on camera was the version Belichick wanted people to see: on his fishing boat, chatting with his sons, game-planning with Tom Brady, talking trash with Baltimore Ravens wide receiver Derrick Mason, complimenting Ed Reed, and attending a team Halloween party dressed as a pirate, fearless and resourceful—and most of all, grinding. Spygate was never mentioned, but it hovered over the entire film, which seemed to serve as both a counterargument to it and an explanation for it. Belichick showed himself working long hours, as well as grieving after losses, as if he had been personally humiliated and might do anything not to suffer that feeling again.

The documentary's most revealing moments were unintentional. Robert Kraft sat in Belichick's office in the hours before the Patriots beat the Titans, 59–0, in the snow. Belichick leaned back in his chair with hands so tightly clasped against his chest, it was as though his arms were strapping him into it, like the restraints on a roller coaster or perhaps a straitjacket. It was the body language of someone who wanted to be alone.

"How are ya?" Kraft said.

"All right," Belichick said.

There was dead air between one man who was gifted in small talk and another who hated it.

"So, this, this weather," Kraft said, "is more of an equalizer?"

Belichick shrugged. All the snow in Foxborough over the years, and Kraft was still asking about it.

"Don't know," he mumbled. "Might affect our kicking game a little bit. Should affect the passing game."

"It *won't?*" Kraft said, like a grandfather struggling to understand a grandchild.

Belichick seemed to be losing patience. "It . . . will . . . affect . . . the . . . kicking . . . game," he said in a more enunciated mumble. "And . . . might . . . affect . . . the . . . passing . . . game."

Almost a decade had passed since Kraft had hired Belichick, and the owner was accustomed to his coach's moods. Known for passing his colleagues in the hallway without acknowledging them, Belichick sometimes did the same with his boss. Kraft had told people that, during the early years, Belichick kissed his ass from time to time, but that after the Patriots started winning multiple Super Bowls, all of that ended. An owner once asked Kraft, "When are you going to fire that asshole?" When he goes 8–8, Kraft replied. David Halberstam noted in his book that Belichick's outgoing voicemail message—"Sorry to have missed your call . . ."—was in the flat tone of a man who "seemed not at all sorry to have missed your call, and might in fact be delighted to miss it once again." Nearly everyone who'd had an interaction with Belichick over the years had experienced a moment when the coach seemed to lose his tolerance for the current conversation, his face subtly transforming from mildly attentive to blank, like a frozen computer screen. If *A Football Life* revealed anything, it was that the only place he seemed truly at peace was on a sideline or in his office, ideally alone.

One of the most controversial fourth-down calls in NFL history defined both New England's 2009 season and the film. On November 15, the 6–2 Patriots faced the 8–0 Colts in Indianapolis, the type of game that usually determined home-field advantage in the playoffs. "If we don't win, we have no chance to catch them," Belichick told the team the night before the game. "If we win, we're right on their ass." The Patriots led, 34–28, with just over two minutes left. On third and two from New England's 28-yard line, Brady threw incomplete. The offense started to jog off the field and the punt team started to jog on. Belichick shook his head.

"Go!" he yelled. "Go!"

Belichick decided to go for it on fourth down with 2:08 left, deep in his own territory. It was so unusual, and even reckless—the exact opposite of covering your ass—that it shocked his own players as much as the millions watching on television. It was also the ultimate sign of respect for Peyton Manning. The singular dominance New England had once exercised over Manning was long gone. One year, at the Pro Bowl, Manning and Belichick sat poolside, drinking beer and discussing football by moving salt and pepper shakers around a table. Belichick drank Corona, Manning downed Budweiser. One of Manning's favorite tricks was to feed drinks to superstar players and mine them for trade secrets, after the alcohol had dropped their defenses. Belichick was harder to crack. Each asked questions that the other didn't want to answer. Alcohol seemed to strengthen their hardwired urge to obfuscate and lie rather than weakening it. At the end of four hours, they gave up. "I didn't really get anything out of it," Belichick later said. "I hope he didn't, either."

With both his punt team and offense on the field against the Colts, Belichick called time-out. "I was thinking, *One play to win the game*," he recalled. Belichick huddled with Brady and new offensive coordinator Bill O'Brien.

"Look," Belichick told Brady, "if it's a shitty look . . ."

"Delay of game?" Brady said.

"Delay of game," Belichick said.

The look ended up being inviting. Patriots running back Kevin Faulk was matched up in man coverage with a safety named Melvin Bullitt. Brady liked Faulk's odds. But then Faulk went in motion—and it tipped off Bullitt. Colts coaches had told Bullitt that when Faulk went in motion, he almost always ran a quick out route. "It was one of their go-to's that season," Bullitt later said. Sure enough, Faulk cut outside at the sticks. Brady's pass was slightly behind him, forcing him to twist as he caught it and allowing Bullitt to close in and knock him down inches short of a first down. It was the Colts' ball—it was Manning's ball—and, four plays later, Reggie Wayne caught a game-winning one-yard touchdown pass.

The gamble unleashed a controversy that lasted for days. Football purists chastised Belichick for not trusting his defense. The analytics crowd—football's bastard children of *Moneyball*—unleashed an avalanche of data that mostly supported Belichick's call. If nothing else, the episode was proof that nobody could dominate a football news cycle like Belichick. He had not relied on advanced analytics, but on simple deduction: he didn't want to give Manning another possession, because it was the best way to ensure that the Colts wouldn't score. He also couldn't believe the Patriots had completed what appeared to be a two-yard pass and failed to gain two yards. As usual, he deployed the failure as a chance to galvanize his team, the moment captured by the documentary crew. The day after the game, the team auditorium was quiet. The only sounds were of people shifting positions in their seats. Belichick stood in front of the room, his hands forming a steeple against his blue hoodie, his words unequivocal and direct. "My decision there at the end was based on what I felt was best for the football team and our best chance to win. Okay? Whether you agree with it or disagree with it—I'm sure everybody's got an opinion—but I'm just telling you, I did what I thought was best. And it didn't work out. And I'm not apologizing to anybody for being aggressive and trying to win. That's what we're here for."

He reminded the players of an eye-level sign on the door that everyone saw when exiting the facility.

WHEN YOU LEAVE HERE . . .
Don't believe or fuel the hype
Manage expectations
Ignore the noise
Speak for yourself

"That's the most important thing about this week, right here," Belichick told the team. "Ignore the noise."

It was Belichick in his element, defiant and resolute. A man who had once been ridiculed by executives and owners for his poor communication skills now commanded a room better than anyone in the NFL.

The 2009 season, and the film, ended hard and fast with a 33–14 home loss to the Baltimore Ravens in the opening round of the playoffs. After the game, Belichick walked through the locker room with his eyes down, blowing past Kraft. The next morning, Belichick drove to work in his silver Volvo in the frigid predawn darkness, his misery so profound it was atmospheric. He spoke of all of the events he had missed during the season, missed during all of his seasons: moments with his children, their games and school and sporting events. "The world passes you by," he said. But here he was, on his way to work, like a train on its tracks. Whatever flicker of a classic family man existed inside him, home in time for dinner every night, was either long dead or never existed in the first place. He needed to coach; he had no other outlet for his energy and focus and talent. Jimmy Johnson used to trade stocks. Not Belichick. He got all the adrenaline he could handle from football. As he pulled up to the stadium, Belichick was not making a choice. He had made the choice long ago. Today, he would wrap up the season. Tomorrow, he would plan for the next one. So it went, and so it would always go.

"I have a hard time picturing not coaching football, at this point. I won't be like Marv Levy"—the Hall of Fame Buffalo Bills coach whom Belichick loved to mock—"and coaching in my 70s."

He looked at the road.

"You don't have to worry about that."

25

I'M NOT
BILL BELICHICK

FAMILIAR GHOST HOVERED OVER ERIC MANGINI AS he sat at an L-shaped desk in June of 2010, watching film. It was just past 7 a.m. A lawn mower hummed outside. He was entering his second season as head coach of the Cleveland Browns. His office was vast but empty, bereft of personality except for a few photos of his three boys, boxing gloves that once belonged to Muhammad Ali, and a Darth Vader mask. His bottom lip jutted out, stuffed with dip. He typed notes for a team speech that morning. He spat and groaned and breathed heavily through his nose. The Browns were a bad team, and Mangini was fighting both the perception and reality that had lingered since he had left New England in 2006: that he was trying to be Bill Belichick. He had emulated his mentor a little too often, from his stonewalling press conferences to his authoritarian approach to running a team. Learning to coach within his own personality was almost as hard for Mangini as winning games.

He rose from his desk, scooping out his chew with his index finger and whipping it into the trash in a single motion, and walked down the hall to the team auditorium. The players were seated. Idle chatter quieted when he entered.

"Good morning," he said.

Mangini dove into work right away. A screen behind him showed practice footage from the team's two-minute drill.

"Why do we practice two minutes?" Mangini asked the room.

"Uh, for conditioning?" a player responded.

"Yes," Mangini said. "But there are several other reasons. Offensively, we didn't have a good day."

He sifted through clips of practice, of an underperforming offense and sloppy play, pointing out a fraction of the mistakes on each snap, but just enough to make the meeting seem laborious, just as Belichick always did. Mangini then turned to defense. On one play, cornerback Sheldon Brown blew his pass-coverage assignment. "Sheldon," Mangini said, "what did I talk about?"

"Um, ball disruption?" Brown replied.

"Yes, but we also talked about something specific," Mangini said.

Moments passed.

"It has a *T* in it," Mangini said.

Quiet.

"And a *P*."

Nothing.

"T-R-A-P," Mangini said, referring to a defensive concept. "There's a way you have to trap."

There were former Patriots players on Cleveland's roster, and former Patriots coaches on its staff. They knew the trap concept—and, more importantly, recognized the tone and language of the meeting, down to when Mangini told the players, "We have to do our jobs." It was straight out of New England. Bill Belichick had such a presence in the lives of his coaches and in the culture that the Cleveland Browns knew where every word, every lesson, every philosophy—every *mannerism*—of their coach derived from.

In his office later that morning, Mangini explained what it was like to develop his own voice within Belichick's system. "Is this how I feel, or is this what I've been programmed to do? I'm coming from a place that won three Super Bowls. What's wrong with that program? Nothing. Why would I change anything? But then you realize that it's not you. So, you try to do things that are you."

The problem was, he said, "You haven't won shit."

Mangini felt trapped. He couldn't commit to being Belichick, but he couldn't commit to being himself, either. It was worth wondering whether he—whether everyone who left New England in an attempt to

forge a separate career and make their own name—was doomed to failure by half measure.

THE PUBLIC ECHO CHAMBER where Belichick's morals were debated
was divorced from the reality of professional football. Belichick's ethics had become *the* ethics of football, his system *the* system. In 2009,
eight of his protégés were head coaches in either college or the NFL, and
five were general managers. Mangini was in Cleveland. Josh McDaniels
departed New England after the 2008 season to replace Mike Shanahan
in Denver. Scott Pioli ran the Kansas City Chiefs, and his best friend,
Thomas Dimitroff—a former New England personnel executive—was
hired as GM of the Atlanta Falcons. All of them, and especially Mangini
and McDaniels, knew they had been hired to replicate how Belichick
operated, how he solved problems, how he *thought*. Belichick—the man
who dressed like a slob, who mumbled from the podium, who had been
busted for cheating, who turned the easiest part of the job, the postgame
handshake, into an event—had gone from being respected but disliked
in NFL circles to being admired and worth emulating.

Most of Belichick's charges emulated him a little too much. Something deeply psychological was at work. None of the coaches who had
grown out of Bill Walsh's tree had struggled to find themselves or to find
success away from San Francisco. The branches of Belichick's coaching tree seemed to grow toward the ground. His legacy was enhanced
not by the success of his acolytes, but by their failures—and because
New England continued to win regardless of who its coordinators and
assistant coaches were. Why was that? What was it about Belichick's
system—about Belichick himself—that simultaneously empowered and
limited those who had studied him so closely?

A year before I watched Mangini address the Browns, I was sitting
in McDaniels's office in the Broncos' building and witnessing a man
at war with himself. He spoke defensively and flatly from the podium
like Belichick, he twirled his whistle from his finger during practice
like Belichick, he coached all three phases of the game, just as Belichick did. He even wore a gray hoodie at times. McDaniels knew better.
He had watched Mangini leave New England for the Jets and had seen

what happened when you appeared to be a cover band. Few respected you. To the extent that Belichick gave blessings, McDaniels left New England with one. Belichick respected that McDaniels had declined all head-coaching interviews in January of 2008, with an undefeated season at stake. "I will help you in any way I can to get you ready for all the other things that go into the job," Belichick told him. "I'll help you learn more of the things you don't get to see as an assistant." When Belichick returned from vacation after the Super Bowl loss to the Giants, he gave McDaniels five pages of notes covering all the hidden aspects of being a head coach, about staff, roster designations, contract issues, stuff assistant coaches never considered. The document helped McDaniels land the Denver job; he asked 65 questions of owner Pat Bowlen based on Belichick's notes alone. The Broncos were blown away by his preparedness.

"It's been an effective system," McDaniels said in his office. "I know how it works, and we're trying like hell to make it work here."

Well, could it? Could Belichick's system exist without Belichick? McDaniels recalled one of his first meetings with his former boss. He had just been hired, young and impressionable. Belichick called him into his office for 20 or so minutes, a meeting the coach gave to most of his young staffers. Belichick showed McDaniels how to "pad" plays—Belichick jargon for diagramming them. You did it on a yellow legal pad, rather than inputting information into a computer. It took Belichick ten minutes to explain what he wanted from each play. He wanted each player's split and footwork and assignment. McDaniels was tasked with padding seven games. He did the arithmetic all Belichick assistants did early in their tenures: ten minutes minimum for each play, multiplied by 60 or so plays a game, multiplied by seven games equals . . . oh God, he would never sleep again.

It was not just a test of sorts, to see how "organized, disciplined, intelligent, and hard-working you're going to be," McDaniels said. Padding was sacred. It was the foundation of Belichick's life's work. It was how he had been taught football as a young man, and how he felt it should be taught as an older one. After McDaniels turned in his first padding assignment, Belichick sent it back with 75 sticky notes attached, highlighting every mistake. At first, the young coaches found it enlightening and thrilling to view the game through the eyes of a master. Then it became debilitating.

BILL BELICHICK DIDN'T HAVE a Bill Belichick. He had his dad, of course, but he never worked under Steve. His football education had taken place across the country, in different venues and with different men. To learn about him—to learn about the young coaches he taught and why he was such a dominant presence in their lives—I found myself in an office in Murfreesboro, Tennessee, across from a skinny 80-year-old man with fading blue eyes and a ski-jump nose. His name was Ken Shipp, and he had been a longtime NFL coach best known for his innovative passing offense in the 1970s. There were framed and signed pictures of Joe Namath and of Peyton and Eli Manning. Shipp pointed to a small off-white piece of stationery tacked to a wall, with three little Lombardi trophies and BILL BELICHICK in blue lettering.

> *March 24, 2005*
> *Dear Ken,*
> *I still have a lot of great memories from our time together in Detroit. I was fortunate to be introduced into your offensive system at such an early age. Thanks for your support + guidance.*
> *Best wishes always,*
> *Bill*

Shipp wasn't as influential on Belichick as Ted Marchibroda or Bill Parcells or his own father. But he was important enough that, when I returned from Tennessee, I put in a word to speak with Belichick about him and he called less than 24 hours later—late at night, of course. Belichick said of Shipp, "He was a slow-talking, pipe-smoking, Tennessee guy who was really smart and had a very good understanding of offensive football. He had an answer to everything."

I could feel Belichick smiling through the phone. In 1976, Lions head coach Rick Forzano informed Shipp that the team had hired an entry-level grunt named Billy Belichick, who had worked for the Baltimore

Colts for a year after graduating from Wesleyan. Forzano was friends with Steve Belichick and had known Billy since he was ten years old. Shipp had never heard of Wesleyan, and he hated legacy hires. When he met Belichick the next day, Shipp found him earnest and shy and eager to learn offense. Belichick knew a little from his playing days— single-wing in eighth grade, wing-T in high school, wishbone in college, the I formation from Navy, with his dad—and from his year with the Colts, when his job was to break down film of the upcoming opponent, padding plays before the term existed. Shipp handed Belichick his playbook, thick even by today's standards, and told him he would be quizzed in two weeks.

"I had a lot to learn," Belichick recalled.

Shipp wondered whether Belichick could handle the homework. But every night, he saw Belichick in an office, alone and unassuming, working hard and unobtrusively, with the playbook open and the projector on. Two weeks after giving him the playbook, Shipp gave Belichick a five-hour exam, as promised. Shipp graded it. Belichick not only passed, but Shipp later said, "He damn answered everything!"

Ken Shipp's playbook would be the least of what Bill Belichick learned in their year together. Belichick took two enduring football lessons from Shipp. One was to run few plays with many variations. The second was more vital, and helped determine not only the path of his own career and life, but of the careers and lives of all of the young men he later taught. It was to be a total head coach—fluent in offense, defense, and special teams—and not just a high-level coordinator of one unit. Shipp had learned that lesson through hard experience: he was passed over for head-coaching jobs, viewed only as a gifted play designer who lacked the broader expertise to run a team.

"You have to be balanced," Shipp told Belichick.

Belichick learned to look beyond calling plays, to the art of managing an entire game—to "think more like a basketball coach," in the words of Michael Lombardi. Offense and defense were not separate sides of the ball, but complementary weapons. It wasn't always a smooth education. In Belichick's time as the head coach in Cleveland, his quarterbacks coach, Gary Tranquill—who had worked with Steve Belichick, Nick Saban, and Woody Hayes—saw him as "a typical defensive coach who didn't know anything about offense and tried to be involved." Tom Brady believed that nobody could match Belichick's overall football knowledge, but likewise believed his offensive expertise was limited. Once, during a Saturday morning meeting, Belichick and Brady watched film of Jets quarterback Mark Sanchez. Belichick showed a play of Sanchez scrambling right, with a defender on his heels, and failing to throw a deep ball to an open receiver who was 60 yards down and across the field. It was an impossible throw, 70 or so yards, a throw only a handful of quarterbacks in history would attempt, much less complete.

"Just throw it," Belichick said. "You're not going to get any more open than this."

Brady sat in disbelief. *I can't throw it 85 yards!* he thought.

"Just let it go," Belichick said.

But Belichick had mastered all sides of the game more than any other coach, and that achievement did more than keep him immune from being "at the mercy of his coordinators," as Lombardi put it. It simplified the modern game to its essence: a coach and a quarterback. Little else was needed—at least in New England. Belichick had an army of young and talented men at work. He would cross-train them, moving them around from scouting to offense to defense. "Once they get the experience, they get how our system fits together," Belichick recalled. All the information they produced was funneled to him—flowing into his "steel trap" of a mind, as Jonathan Kraft often put it—and only he would decide how to use it. In New England, all of the young coaches felt they were essential contributors to a team that redefined what was possible in the salary-cap era of football. Once some were on their own, they realized the system was designed to make them disposable.

ONE DAY, Eric Mangini took out a pad of paper and tried to define all of the roles of his new job. There's always a learning curve when an assistant becomes a head coach, but to go from being a Bill Belichick assistant to attempting to run a Belichickian program was overwhelming. A head coach organized the staff, as many as 20 people, and the various football operations departments. He had to be the chief strategist. Primary motivator. Counselor. Salary-cap economist. Community leader. Team spokesman. He had to manage the players and coaches—and manage their families at times. "It's hard," Belichick once told me. "You're doing a lot of things, and it's hard to understand all of them, put them together, keep everything straight, and make things more efficient, not just a big mess."

Mangini struggled with organization and time management—and, like his mentor, drafting wide receivers. When he tried to deploy some of Belichick's most revered management practices, like green balls for underpaid and overperforming staff, it backfired on him. Mangini distributed around $100,000 out of his own pocket, but once word spread around the building that Mangini was doling out cash under the table, a team executive told him it posed a tax liability. Green balls now needed to be aboveboard. It defeated their entire purpose. Mangini followed the rules, figuring that some extra money was better than none. But one day, an assistant coach stormed into his office, seething because of the taxes. "Are you fucking kidding me?" Mangini replied. "Would you rather have no money?"

Late in the 2009 season, in which Mangini went 5–11, owner Randy Lerner installed former Packers and Seahawks coach Mike Holmgren over the coach as team president. Holmgren told Mangini that he needed to show more of his true self and fix his public perception as a Belichick clone. Holmgren understood why Belichick cast such a long shadow, but he couldn't relate to the challenges of learning to coach within your own personality.

"It's not hard," Holmgren said.

He had come from the supportive Walsh tree, and seven of Holmgren's Packers assistants had gone on to become head coaches. All of the Holmgren guys would convene at the combine or league meetings, reliving old memories and laughing over beers. They shared a bond that went beyond winning or losing games. It was a tribe—competitive, but success for one meant success for all.

The Belichick tree didn't work that way. "Our family is different than your family," Mangini said.

One night, at the combine in Indianapolis a year earlier, Mangini was at the bar at Shula's steakhouse for a few drinks. Belichick was less than ten feet away, at a high-top table, hovering over a pint. Neither man acknowledged the other. They radiated tension. They had emailed brief and curt notes over the years after Mangini's departure, enough to indicate a post-Spygate thaw, but not enough to ensure it. All the drama seemed unnecessary, and months later, when Belichick and I spoke again late at night, I asked him about the cost of the system he had created. "You put a lot of time and commitment in the relationship, but it's not easy because of the competitive part of it. You really do care about each other, after all you've been through, and for all of that to dissipate because you're in a competitive situation—you'd like to find a way to keep both going in the right balance, and it's not always the easiest thing to do."

MANGINI HAD NO CHOICE. He had to self-actualize, both in response to Holmgren's mandate and because his own internal drive was moving him in that direction. He began the process with a letter. He had always used New England's letter to the players explaining the off-season program, changing the letterhead and substituting "Jets" or "Browns" for "Patriots," and, most symbolically, "Mangini" for "Belichick." After the 2009 season, he decided to rewrite it in his voice. The delivery was different, even if the schedule was not. It was a small but liberating step.

The most obvious piece of the job where Mangini had to separate himself from Belichick was his press conferences. It was also the most frustrating. On a June morning, Neal Gulkis, the Browns' head of public relations, entered Mangini's office with a list of 14 bullet points, under the rubric "Potential Difficult Questions," for the day's press conference.

None of the former Slappies was prepared to handle the press. Belichick had continued the Parcells practice of barring them from speaking to the media. And as Belichick had done under Parcells, many had jerked at the end of the boss's leash, forming secret relationships and friendships with reporters. But it was one thing to chat with a reporter over drinks; it was another to stand behind a podium and field Potential Difficult Questions. Mangini was terrified before his introductory press conference in New York, in the same building where, a mere six years earlier, Belichick had stood and resigned as the "HC of the NYJ." He was the NFL's youngest head coach at the time, having just turned 35, but he looked younger. He gripped the edges of the podium like arm rests on an airplane going through severe turbulence. "It's nerve-wracking, because you've never done it before," Mangini later said.

There was a rationale behind the buzzkill that was the Belichick press conference. He used the press to reinforce his message to the team. He could not have cared less if he came off as standoffish or ungenerous, because everything was in the service of winning, and anyway, how he handled the press felt true to his own personality. Mangini was more of a pleaser. After his first year with the Jets, he tried to loosen up. He met with all of the team's beat writers individually, trying to forge personal relationships. He reached out if they were having a family problem, dissected film for them off the record, and even turned up to sign autographs at the Little League game of the son of a beat writer. But then the press conferences would roll around, and Mangini would speak in the familiar monotone of his mentor. "It didn't matter," Mangini later said. "No matter how much I said I'm not Bill Belichick, I was Bill Belichick."

It didn't only carry over to Cleveland. It carried over into the mock press conference now being staged in his office. Posing as a reporter, Gulkis asked Mangini about Peyton Hillis, the Browns' star running back, who was out with pneumonia.

"He's still in the hospital," Mangini said. "I don't want to talk about it."

Gulkis pivoted to asking about a newly created league-wide concussions seminar.

"Anything we can help learn about player safety is a positive," Mangini replied with zero affect.

The entire exercise was useless. Both men knew it. Mangini left to meet the media. After the press conference—strained both in its adherence to Belichick and in its departure from him—he inserted a dip and sat back in his chair, clearly frustrated. He spit into a cup and breathed deeply and opened film of the day's practice on his computer, hunting for ways to help his team improve, eager for something he could control. This much was clear: You don't want to be part of a coaching tree. You want to be the guy who has a tree.

THE 2010 SEASON WAS another difficult one for Bill Belichick. New England lost its opening playoff game at home for the second straight year, this time to the hated New York Jets and head coach Rex Ryan. The year was also disastrous for Belichick's coaching tree. The trouble began in late October in London, the night before McDaniels's Broncos played the San Francisco 49ers. McDaniels was on the phone in his hotel room when he heard a knock. It was Steve Scarnecchia, the Broncos' director of video operations, who would have been known only as Dante Scarnecchia's son if he hadn't been one of the Patriots' video guys who had illegally filmed signals. Scarnecchia held his laptop in the doorway, quietly asking McDaniels if he wanted to see what was on it.

A few hours earlier, Scarnecchia had been setting up camera equipment at Wembley Stadium when the 49ers took the field for their walk-through. The Patriots had always told video guys to linger at neutral-site fields, where security was lax. You never knew what you might see. Scarnecchia decided to film it. The 49ers spotted Scarnecchia and his camera—sometimes, the league-wide paranoia about the Patriot Way was justified—and only ran vanilla plays. Scarnecchia recorded six minutes of the walk-through, and then uploaded the footage to his laptop.

He had come to McDaniels's room to show him those six minutes. After a 6–0 start in 2009—including an overtime win over his mentor— McDaniels had lost 13 of his next 17 games and, alongside some strong personnel moves, had made a few blunders, most notably in trading up in the first round to draft Heisman Trophy–winning quarterback Tim Tebow, a talented athlete whose fame far eclipsed his skill set. McDaniels was in danger of losing his job, and he knew it.

Scarnecchia explained what was on his laptop.

"No, I'm not doing that," McDaniels replied.

McDaniels had done the right thing, but it didn't matter. Pat Bowlen and Broncos COO Joe Ellis were furious when they learned about the taped walk-through weeks later. It was not just a cheating scandal; it was a Patriots-like cheating scandal, centered on clandestine filming. The league fined the Broncos and McDaniels each $50,000. For the sizable chunk of the league that believed the Patriots had taped the Rams' walk-through, regardless of the denials and lack of evidence, this served as something closer to proof. Never in modern NFL history had the *idea* of taping a walk-through entered public discussion; now it had done so twice in three years, involving New England and Belichick's most accomplished pupil. Explaining Denver's fines to reporters on a conference call, Jeff Pash went out of his way to emphasize that the Broncos' "moral compass" was "pointed in the right direction," drawing an implicit contrast with New England and Spygate. "Here, you had a single incident as opposed to years of activity." It was a shot that didn't go unnoticed by Patriots ownership.

On Friday, November 26, McDaniels explained the incident to his staff, demanding that the conversation stay in the room. "If this gets out, there are jobs on the line," he warned. He then tried to differentiate Spygate from what was now being called Spygate II in the press. The incident in London, he explained, was a one-off thing from a rogue video operator. Spygate, he said, was something "that was practiced, that was coached, that was *worked* on."

His remarks were leaked almost immediately to Fox's Jay Glazer. There was no *omertà*, of the sort Belichick had long enjoyed in New England. Bowlen fired McDaniels a few weeks later, with four games to go and after less than two years on the job.

McDaniels's ouster seemed to trigger Belichick's trauma from his days in Cleveland. He called McDaniels, advising him to pay extra attention to his family, especially his parents, and later rehired him as offensive coordinator. In 1995, after Modell announced that the Browns were moving to Baltimore, he promised the team that Belichick would remain coach. But the Browns lost six of their final seven games that season, and a bad relationship between coach and owner cratered. Neither man trusted each other. On Valentine's Day 1996, Modell called Belichick and fired him, with two years left on his contract. The experience left scars, not only on Belichick, but on his sons as well. Stephen and Brian were young boys, with a poster of their father on the wall of the bedroom they shared. "Valentine's Day," Stephen later said. "How many coaches get fired on Valentine's Day?"

Three weeks after the Broncos fired McDaniels, on what coaches call Black Monday—the day after the regular season ends—Holmgren gave Mangini his walking papers. Mangini's career as an NFL head coach was over; he had plateaued at age 39. In Mangini's last season, the Browns won only five games for the second consecutive year, but a two-week midseason span had brought a pair of bright spots: they beat the defending Super Bowl champion Saints in New Orleans, and a week later, they hosted the Patriots. Using an array of trick plays on offense and varying looks on defense, Cleveland won, 34–14. Mangini strolled slowly to midfield as the final seconds ticked away for the postgame handshake, surrounded by cameras. When Mangini arrived, Belichick moved in. They spoke for a moment—what seemed to be a real moment—and then broke away.

Reporters asked Mangini what words were exchanged. "'Good game,'" he said with a smile. "We were making plans for the summer."

The room laughed. Mangini felt good. He had won a game against Belichick by taking the best of what he had learned and leaving the worst—put another way, he won a game as Eric Mangini. It was a crowning—and fleeting—achievement. Belichick never called after Mangini was fired. By 2010, all four head coaches hired so far from Belichick's tree in college and pro football—Weis, Crennel, Mangini, and McDaniels—had been dismissed. Eight years would pass before an NFL team hired another head coach straight from New England.

26

THAT'S A LOT
OF F—K YOUS!

A HANDFUL OF LEAGUE AND TEAM EXECUTIVES CIR-
cled around Jerry Jones. It was March 11, 2011, at the Federal
Mediation and Conciliation Service Building in Washington,
DC. The NFL was hours away from its first work stoppage since 1987.
Owners had set a mid-March deadline for a new collective bargaining
agreement and threatened to lock the players out if a deal couldn't be
reached. Management had presented a final offer, but union executives
and player representatives immediately rejected it, ensuring a lockout. A few minutes later, a small group of executives asked Jones what
had happened.

"Look," Jones said, "my daddy grew up on a farm in southwest Missouri. Every so often in the spring, the wind would come from a different part of the country, and the moon would set in a different way, and
the owls would start fucking the chickens."

Nobody knew where this story was headed.

"The owls are fucking the chickens. It makes no sense that they
turned this down, but it's a great thing for us."

IN JONES'S STORY, the head chicken was DeMaurice Smith, the executive director of the NFL Players Association. He had been on the job
two years, and almost from the start, he and Goodell rubbed each other
the wrong way. Smith was a litigator who knew how to push buttons;
Goodell had a hot temper and viewed Smith as just another annoying
lawyer. They argued so often during CBA negotiations that owners and

players eventually sidelined them, taking the lead themselves. The talks with less input from Smith and Goodell didn't go much better. At one point, Carolina Panthers owner Jerry Richardson tried to bully players by threatening to expand the regular season from 16 games to 17, which the league technically could do without union approval, per the terms of the existing CBA.

"We're not playing 17 games, Jerry," said union executive committee member Domonique Foxworth, a cornerback for the Baltimore Ravens.

"We can *make* you," Richardson said. "We don't have to ask you. We're being nice by not saying, 'Fuck you, you have to do it.'"

"We're being nice by not telling you, 'Fuck you, we're not playing,'" Foxworth replied.

"We're being nice by not telling you, 'Fuck you, we'll play with replacement players,'" Richardson said.

"We're being nice by not telling you, 'Fuck you, good luck filling up stadiums with Ryan Leaf at quarterback,'" Foxworth said.

Smith jumped in before it got uglier.

"That's a lot of fuck yous!"

With the 2011 season looming, Smith needed help to get talks back on track. He did something unthinkable: he reached out to the enemy. He approached Robert Kraft. The two men didn't know each other well, but Smith thought Kraft was the only owner with enough perspective and gravitas to break the impasse. In response, Kraft decided to take on a larger and more personal role in the negotiations. He would grab breakfast or dinner with player representatives and union brass. He bonded with executive committee member Jeff Saturday, a center for the Colts. Saturday felt Kraft was tough but sincere, and unafraid to laugh at himself. At one mediation session in Chicago, Kraft went on an extended tangent about how much he disliked various elements of the federal government. When he finished, it was quiet.

"I work for the government," the mediator said.

"I guess he's not leaning my way today," Kraft replied. Everyone laughed.

As the chair of the broadcast committee, Kraft had an insider's knowledge of how the next round of rights negotiations with the networks would proceed. The league would have enormous leverage over its broadcast partners if it could guarantee extended labor peace. Higher revenues would not only increase franchise values for owners, but also raise the salary cap. Smith agreed to give management a higher percentage of the overall revenue pie in exchange for more days off and fewer padded practices during the season. Although most league executives assumed they had taken Smith to the woodshed—the league, hypersensitive to the optics surrounding the head injury crisis, would have likely given up more days off—some owners were uncomfortable with the deal. At one point, John Mara said he feared that head coaches would be angry. Kraft turned to Mara and said, "We're not going to lose a deal over this. Thirty-two owners aren't going to turn this down because some GM or coach is pissed about practice."

It was a seminal moment for the players. Kraft had taken their side on a key issue. "He made sure everyone understood to not kill the golden goose," Saturday recalled.

Kraft's mere presence made clear how important he thought the new CBA was. Myra Kraft was in the final stages of battling ovarian cancer, and her husband was sacrificing precious time with her by attending the negotiations. On July 20, 2011, surrounded by family, Myra died at home at age 68. Most of the other owners and most league executives attended her funeral. Smith did, too. At various moments during the services, several owners independently approached Smith like sharks and attempted to talk about the CBA.

"I wanted to throw up," Smith told a confidant.

Talks continued over the next week. On July 25, both sides agreed to a new ten-year CBA. At a press conference, Saturday teared up when describing Kraft's impact. The two men hugged. It was a massive win for the NFL, and for Kraft. Some owners and executives felt the storyline that emerged from the CBA negotiations—that Kraft had saved the deal—not only overstated his role, but was on brand for a man overly worried about reputation. In any case, the CBA gave the league enormous leverage in negotiations with its broadcast partners. Kraft oversaw the striking of agreements on a rights package worth $27 billion across three networks over the coming nine years, a fees increase of approximately 60 percent—and that was in addition to a prior eight-year *Monday Night Football* deal with ESPN, worth $1.9 billion a year.

The relationships Kraft formed during the negotiations were not just for show. Peyton Manning sent Kraft a card, thanking him for his "crucial" work during a "difficult time." Kraft also became close with Smith—and got closer in 2015, when Roger Goodell became a shared enemy.

A LITTLE MORE THAN six months later, on February 5, 2012, Kraft was in Indianapolis to watch the Patriots' rematch with the New York Giants in Super Bowl XLVI. With 3:46 left in the game, the Giants had the ball at their own 12-yard line, trailing 17–15. Eli Manning ran onto the field. Every football fan knew, as did the Patriots, that his last-minute drive against New England four years earlier had been tinged by luck, enabled by two dropped interceptions and the Helmet Catch. By now, nobody doubted Manning's credentials as a late-game magician. Six times that year, he had led the Giants on fourth-quarter game-winning drives, including a midseason win against the Patriots in Foxborough. As he stepped into the huddle with another Super Bowl on the line, "it felt familiar," Manning later said.

The Super Bowl was an unlikely endpoint for each team, the Giants in particular. They had finished with a 9–7 record and were actually outscored by their opponents, 400–394, during the regular season. The Patriots were 13–3, but did not beat a team that finished with a winning record until knocking off the Baltimore Ravens in the AFC Championship Game. Between the Manning family, Tom and Gisele, and Madonna as the halftime performer, one of the NFL's smallest cities got a lot smaller. On the Monday before the game, Brady and Manning both booked private rooms at St. Elmo Steak House in downtown Indianapolis, treating their teammates to the legendary shrimp cocktail. A few days later, Peyton called Eli and asked how the preparation had gone. "Good week, good week," Eli replied. Peyton knew Eli was especially confident—he wouldn't have said "good week" twice otherwise.

The Patriots had dedicated the season to Myra Kraft and had her initials, MHK, patched on their jerseys. As Brady warmed up, a win felt preordained.

"I feel so good, man," Brady told Wes Welker.

"So do I," Welker said.

Shortly before kickoff, Brady hugged Kraft.

"I see the look in your eye," Kraft said.

"I got it today," Brady replied.

But when the game started, Brady looked lost. On New England's first offensive play, he dropped back into his own end zone, scanned his options—and flinched, launching a deep pass nowhere near a receiver. He was flagged for intentional grounding, resulting in a safety, handing the Giants a 2–0 lead. Manning was cruising—he threw a touchdown pass on the next possession to put New York up 9–0—but Brady was struggling to see downfield. New York's lanky and relentless defensive line swatted away two of his passes at the line of scrimmage.

"It's like throwing in a forest, dude," Brady said on the sideline.

In the second and third quarters, the game shifted. New England's defense suffocated Manning. Brady caught fire, hitting a Super Bowl-record 16 consecutive passes, two of them for touchdowns. But with New England up 17–9, something weird happened: the quarterback who always finished strong started to fade. Brady threw an interception on the second play of the fourth quarter on a badly thrown deep pass to tight end Rob Gronkowski. With 4:06 left, and up 17–15, New England faced a second and 11 at the Giants' 44-yard line. Brady dropped back to pass. Welker had exploded off the line, seen a gap in the secondary, and run to the empty space. He was wide open near the Giants' 20-yard line. Brady lofted a pass down the left side. It looked like it would be the game's signature, clinching moment involving two players who had connected on 122 passes in the regular season, with Welker leading the league in receptions.

But the ball drifted outside and behind Welker. He jumped and twisted and got two sets of fingertips on the ball, but couldn't make the catch. He fell to the turf face-first and lay there. Brady grabbed his head. Fans and media later blamed Welker, but Bill O'Brien said that the Patriots coaches didn't mark the play as a drop. It was a misfire—and Brady misfired again on the next play, to Deion Branch, throwing behind him over the middle. New England punted and pinned the Giants at their own 12-yard line.

On came Manning.

In the huddle, Manning called Otter W Go. The primary options on the play were receivers Victor Cruz and Hakeem Nicks, both of whom lined up on the right side. But as he came to the line of scrimmage, Manning suspected that New England linebacker Jerod Mayo and safety Patrick Chung would rotate over to bracket Cruz and Nicks with a total of four defenders—an old Belichick trick. "This is still a Cruz and Nicks game," Belichick told his players on the sideline before New York's final drive. "Those are still the guys. Make 'em go to Manningham."

That was Mario Manningham, a fourth-year receiver who had caught only 39 out of 77 passes thrown his way in 2011. He was assigned the "go" on Otter W Go, a streak up the left sideline. At the snap, Manning looked at Nicks. He was covered. Manning looked at Cruz. He was covered, too. Manning pivoted to Manningham. Patriots defensive tackle Vince Wilfork crumpled the inside of the pocket, forcing Manning to throw quickly and with a short stride. "Essentially, it was a no-look pass," Cruz recalled. The ball carried a controlled trajectory out of his hand: the gentle arc of a touch pass, but with the zip of a heater. Chung was closing in on Manningham. If the ball had been thrown inches inside, Chung would have broken it up. If it had arrived inches outside, it would have sailed out of bounds. But Manning fit it between Manningham's left shoulder and the sideline. Manningham caught it and planted his feet like a skier on a hard turn for a 38-yard gain—one of the greatest throws in NFL history.

Eight plays later, the Giants had a second and goal at the Patriots' six-yard line with 1:04 left. New England called time-out. The game was in New York's hands: all Manning had to do was run a few more plays, bleed the clock, and allow kicker Lawrence Tynes to trot on for the game-winning field goal, leaving Brady no time to answer.

"We're gonna have, like, 10 seconds," Brady said on the sideline.

Belichick decided to let New York score a touchdown, hoping to give Brady as much time as possible. The Giants called an inside run to running back Ahmad Bradshaw. As Manning approached the line of scrimmage, it occurred to him that Belichick might let Bradshaw walk in. Manning turned around to tell Bradshaw to *not* score—but then decided against it, not wanting to confuse his running back. Manning handed off to Bradshaw. The Patriots cleared out. Manning put his arms in the air, not in celebration, but out of fear.

"Don't go in!" he yelled.

Bradshaw pulled up at the goal line, crouching and twirling and trying not to break the plane. But his momentum carried him, backside-first, into the end zone. New York led, 21–17, with 57 seconds left.

A few plays later, Brady moved the ball to the Giants' 49-yard line. Five seconds remained. He called a Hail Mary. "Run to the goalpost and catch it," he told tight end Aaron Hernandez.

And catch it. Brady was nothing if not a believer. But his desperation pass fell incomplete. The Giants had won their second Super Bowl in four years, and the Patriots had lost their second. A camera caught Bündchen complaining about New England's receivers. "My husband cannot fucking throw the ball and catch the ball at the same time," she said, a lament that would trigger an avalanche of media coverage over the following days. But more than an hour after the game, in a locker room that had mostly cleared out, one man remained. It was Brady, staring at the ground, with a towel over his head.

SUPER BOWL XLVI appeared to mark a power shift in the NFL. Since New England's most recent championship, after the 2004 season, four quarterbacks had been named Super Bowl MVP: Peyton and Eli Manning, who won it twice; Drew Brees of the New Orleans Saints; and Aaron Rodgers of the Green Bay Packers. Joe Flacco of the Baltimore Ravens took the award the next year. Ben Roethlisberger of the Pittsburgh Steelers, Matthew Stafford of the Detroit Lions, and Matt Ryan of the Atlanta Falcons were emerging as stars, while Tom Brady—and Peyton Manning, who missed all of 2011 with a neck injury—looked mortal. The Patriots came up short again a year later, during the 2012 playoffs. A 12–4 year ended with a home loss in the AFC Championship Game to the Baltimore Ravens. Brady threw two interceptions. Belichick's defense gave up 21 points in the second half.

Tom Brady and Bill Belichick were in professional and cultural thin air. But a plateau at the highest elevation was a plateau nonetheless. Dynasties are fleeting for a reason. There are strong forces set in motion to destroy them, immutable laws of the sporting universe, and especially in the NFL, where careers are short and parity is almost mandated. For most of New England's run, both men had sought immunity from those laws by returning to a shared belief system. Now, there were fewer answers. It left Bill Belichick more resolute in his own methodologies— and Tom Brady focused on ideas beyond the Patriot Way.

27

ALEJANDRO!

T HERE WAS NO DOOR TO TOM BRADY'S BACK BAY apartment. There was just an elevator at the building's main entrance on Beacon Street, where a security guy named Brian waved you in. When you reached the third floor, the elevator opened into Brady's living room. There was no hallway or foyer. On a clear and icy morning in March of 2013, I exited the elevator, stepped inside, and looked around. Nobody was there. It was quiet. I was not only in Tom Brady's living room, I was *alone* in Tom Brady's living room. I wondered if his wife or one of his kids would enter the room to the sight of a stranger, until a familiar voice shouted from downstairs.

"Hey, make yourself comfortable! I'll be right up."

So, I did. I walked to the right, past Brady's kitchen, to a bookshelf with family photos on it. Perusing them felt oddly familiar: the picture of his wife—on the beach in a two-piece—was essentially the same shot that had landed in the mailboxes of anyone who received the Victoria's Secret catalog. A few minutes later, Brady emerged from downstairs, in a navy sweater and blue jeans. He was congested, wrestling one of those parental colds that last weeks. He mentioned that he'd purchased the place years ago, when he owned a few homes around Boston, "back when I thought I was a real estate mogul." We went upstairs to the fourth floor, past a small exercise room with scattered weights and rubber bands, and then up again to the roof of the building, a vast space with deck chairs and toys and a grill, overlooking the Charles River. There was a playground below, where he would take his kids—and where paparazzi had shot his *parents* taking the kids. He lived here during football season and LA in the off-season. On most days, he would leave before the sun rose and return after it set. He was in a tunnel, from the field to his bedroom, somewhat oblivious to current events and his surroundings. He had no idea that the domed building across the river was the centerpiece of the Massachusetts Institute of Technology campus.

Back inside, we strolled along a small hallway with a flat-screen television on one wall and memorabilia everywhere else. Tom Brady didn't have a Tom Brady Room in his apartment; he had a Tom Brady Passage, where I saw his two Super Bowl MVP trophies, a few game balls, a scrapbook from his Michigan days, and a photo with Bono from the One Campaign trip to Africa—mementos from an unprecedented rise that had stalled. Brady pointed to a photo on the shelf of himself with Joe Montana at Montana's Napa home. Brady looked young, maybe 24 or 25, when he had in abundance the magic that he was now trying to recapture. Brady would be 36 years old at the start of the next season, two years younger than Montana was when he retired, and even though Brady had eclipsed Montana in every major statistical category except Super Bowl wins, he lingered on that photo for a bit, as if he still saw it as a thrill to be alongside his idol—and as if he still saw himself as unworthy of being mentioned in the same class.

"Pretty cool," Brady said.

We moved to the couches in a family room. We talked about what all young fathers talk about: kids. By then, he had two boys, Jack and Benny, and a newborn girl, Vivian. His boys loved the Tom Brady Passage, not because of their father's memorabilia, but because it was dark—better for movies. A life that was once expansive now seemed constrained. Gone were the days of jetting down to New York to hit the bars after a win. Gone were the days of hitting the bars in *Boston* after a win. Sleep was too valuable.

Brady had been thinking about his boys through the prism of his own life. He felt lucky to have been raised by three older sisters, because otherwise he would have had no understanding of women, after attending all-boys Serra High. "Not that any of us can ever figure out girls, because we can't. But at least you have some of an *idea* that you can't figure them out." Between his wife, his ex, his wife's five sisters, and his own three sisters, Brady's boys were surrounded by a sufficient number of strong and confident women. It got him thinking: a place like Serra might be good for them one day. "I was talking to my wife, and I'm like, 'I would love for our boys to go to an all-boys school.' She's like, 'Certainly not!' "

Just then, someone walked into the apartment. Brady's eyes lit up.

"Alejandro!" Brady said.

"How are ya?" Alex Guerrero said from near the elevator.

"Welcome to Beantown, baby!" Brady said.

"I know, man," Guerrero said.

Brady rose from his couch and hugged Guerrero, who was thin and gray at the temples; he was friendly, but never held eye contact for long. They chatted for a few minutes, then Guerrero disappeared downstairs. Guerrero was something of a mystery, even to those close to Brady. Brady called him "my best friend."

"Is he a trainer?" I asked.

"Um, it's really hard to explain his role."

TOM BRADY WAS searching for something. What it was, he didn't know. That morning, he had stood alone in front of a mirror and practiced a new throwing technique, part of a plan to search within himself, and beyond, for new ideas. He had reached a point in his career where his drive had not waned—if anything, it had increased—but coming up short in Super Bowls and the playoffs forced him to question all of his methods, looking for flaws invisible to even the trained eye. He essentially admitted that he needed to step away from activities and patterns and belief systems that had worked well for him to this point and that had already made him perhaps better at his position than just about everyone else in NFL history. He didn't know if he needed to sharpen his philosophy or reimagine it, but he wanted to find out.

He was in his first months of working on his throwing mechanics with a new tutor, Tom House, a former major league pitcher. Tom Martinez had died a few weeks earlier from a heart attack on February 22, his 66th birthday, after years of declining health. House looked part New Age guru, part scientist, with big glasses and a thick, full mustache. On April 8, 1974, he was in the bullpen in left-center field at Atlanta-Fulton County Stadium, when he heard a ball hit hard his way. He stood under it and caught Hank Aaron's record-breaking 715th home run. Based in Southern California, House had become a pitching coach in retirement, helping the likes of Nolan Ryan and Randy Johnson. In the early 2000s, Cam Cameron, at the time the offensive coordinator of the San Diego Chargers, learned about House's work and told Drew Brees that it might be worth meeting him.

House saw more than a chance to help a talented quarterback. He saw a market inefficiency. For decades, quarterbacks had been taught that throwing a football was different than throwing a baseball. House saw them as similar skills. Quarterbacks needed to throw faster than pitchers, but the architecture of the throw was the same for all "rotational athletes," as House called them. In their first meeting, House diagnosed Brees's problems, from the biomechanics of his release to his diet. House's methods were based on science and data and computer simulations. More than he helped Brees with his arm, he helped him with his mind. With so few opportunities, quarterbacks tended to beat themselves up over mistakes, demanding and expecting perfection on each throw. The mindset was crippling. House's baseball background helped him embrace progress over perfection. In baseball, players fail most of the time. Brees was not yet a future Hall of Famer. It was unclear whether he was even an NFL starter. He lacked confidence. House helped, with a mantra he had given to pitchers: Fail Fast Forward.

Quarterback gurus were fashionable and numerous in the mid-2000s, working out of camps ranging from Elite 11 to the Manning Passing Academy, all promising a specific version of the American dream: the chance to be a quarterback at an elite level. House was different. He didn't consider himself a quarterback coach, but a throwing specialist. He launched a new business, 3DQB. Matt Cassel became a client, then introduced Brady to House.

In February of 2013, Brady asked House to visit his mansion in the Brentwood hills. House put Brady through an array of exercises, including one called the Fogel Drill, a torture mechanism that calls for the athlete to step and shuffle as quickly as possible while simulating throws for 30 seconds. Pitchers do four sets; House wanted Brady to try one. After 30 seconds, Brady looked like he might faint. But he kept going, impressing House, who wondered if an athlete as accomplished as Brady might have too much pride to endure such punishment. Brady, of course, relished punishment, as long as it helped him improve as a quarterback. His days of measuring improvement by how much he could bench press were long over. Every exercise, every moment, every technique, every breath needed to be in service of helping him improve on the 600-some times he threw a football in a season. That was the standard.

Breathing hard and heavy after the Fogel Drill, Brady looked up at House and said, "How long will it take before I can do what the pitchers do?"

House watched Brady throw. He believed that Brady didn't need a major mechanical overhaul. He needed to improve by a few percentage points, the inches that would turn the Super Bowl miss to Wes Welker into a completion. It started with balance. Most quarterbacks transfer weight from back to forward as they throw; House wanted Brady to remain sturdy and straight. Then House worked with Brady on his release, instructing him to keep his left arm tight and almost touching his right shoulder, crossing his arms as he followed through. Brady saw immediate results. His spiral was slightly tighter, his passes slightly more accurate. House liked that about great quarterbacks. They needed to be given instruction only once. Pitchers needed it 15, maybe 20 times.

Brady had practiced that new motion in the mirror the morning I visited. He didn't want to discuss it much—"Well done is better than well said," he said, smiling, quoting his dad. But he was excited. You could feel it. He knew he needed to be better, but he couldn't do it alone. He needed help, and he had found help. For him, it was an addictive and rejuvenating rush. "There is no off button," Brady said. "I love golf, but if I never played another day of golf in my life, it would never bother me."

On a flight a few months earlier, he had watched *Jiro Dreams of Sushi*, a documentary about an 85-year-old sushi master who woke up each day trying to improve at his craft. "It smacked me in the face as reaffirmation," Brady said. "Just be in the moment. What's better than what you're doing?" He had always been asked what he would do after football, as though he were as eager to talk about that question as the general public might have been. But he wasn't eager at all. He wanted to play football, fully aware that he needed the game more than it needed him. Tom Sr. had once told me that his son would be "a modern-day

George Blanda," the Raiders quarterback who had played into his 40s as a kicker.

"There's really nothing that will be able to replace" football, Brady said in his living room. "Hopefully, it gets to a point where there is when I retire in nine, ten years."

He said it so quickly and casually that I almost missed it, but there it was: a declaration to play until he was 45. He wasn't going to stop. He *couldn't* stop. He would have to be dragged off the football field. Brady often thought about his childhood friend Kevin Brady. They used to play baseball together and dream of being pros, but Kevin was a realist and always had a backup plan. Brady had one moment, late in the 2000 draft, when he thought he would need to dust off his résumé and plan for a career in business. But he had survived, barely—and wanted to keep surviving. "For me, I've never said, 'Well, if that doesn't work, I'm going to do this.' It's like, 'No, this is what I'm going to do,'" he said.

"Do you have a backup plan now?" I asked.

"No. Certainly not."

BRADY WAS AT his sister's wedding in Hawaii, which not only gave him a semblance of a vacation—he never truly took time off—but also a chance to take stock of life. Who was he? What had he become? He had spent much of the prior 13 years growing accustomed to fame. He would ask his friends or family if they wanted to get dinner, and when they'd come over, expecting to go out, he would have the meal ready inside the house. He could feel their disappointment, but he knew he couldn't actually have a conversation in public. It took so much effort for him to focus that it was all but impossible. People were always watching, approaching, photographing. "It's a nervous feeling," Galynn said. "It's not enjoyable." And even when people let him eat in peace, Brady felt their presence anyway, an energy field closing in. "You're your own secret service agent," he said. "Even if no one's paying attention, you're still paying attention to them, and that's part of the problem."

It was a strange time in America to be a celebrity. Social media had turned anyone with a camera phone into a news crew. In some ways, it was worse than old-school paparazzi, who followed celebrities on the street, but not into a restaurant. Brady was the type of celebrity people wanted to meet as much as photograph. He seemed like such a nice guy, fans always said, and Brady tried hard not to be an asshole. He remembered how much it meant when Dwight Clark or Roger Craig or Will Clark signed for him as a kid. But it was tricky. Every time he ventured out of his house or condo, he needed to be ready to be Tom Brady, with all of the opportunities and headaches that entailed. He ate at certain restaurants with back entrances or side doors, but he knew word would get out and that, before he left, he'd have to shake hands with 25 people. He wasn't asking for anyone to feel sorry for him; he didn't feel sorry for himself. It was a binary problem that he was constantly trying to solve. "I really don't want a little boy from Framingham, Massachusetts, to go, 'God, I met Tom Brady and he was like, 'Buzz off, kid.' I'm really conscious of that. But there are also times where I really don't feel like saying, 'Hey, good to meet you!' So, what I do is I just don't go out, and I don't really put myself in a position to be Tom Brady, the quarterback. I want to be Tom Brady, the dad, with my kids, and that's a balance. It's really a balance."

Brady wasn't trying to elicit empathy. He knew that he had lived a charmed life compared to just about everyone else on the planet, and also compared to many professional athletes, raised as he was in a two-parent household with enough money to support his dreams. He was also a father, and fame had rendered his parenting template—his own childhood—all but useless. Something essential had been lost in the life he had created for himself. Brady didn't want to raise entitled kids, and he would ask his famous friends about their parenting techniques, but not much was transferrable. His fame was on the level of his friend Ben Affleck's, but their daily lives were different. Brady had to parent within his own reality. When he would take Jack and Benny to a baseball game, up high in a luxury box with platters of free food, he would remember how much he loved roaming the bleachers in Candlestick Park. That felt like a long time ago. He hoped to raise grounded kids because that's how he was raised, and he knew that so much, if not all, of what he achieved was tied directly to his childhood.

What could be passed down? What could not? Those questions circled in his head. Brady wanted his kids to appreciate their life—the private planes, the estates, the exclusive opportunities—but this was the only life his kids knew, and as Brady often said, "This is not the way the rest of the world is."

He understood that, as he put it, "my parenting experience is going to be different than the way I was parented." The demands of his job and the demands he put on himself were extreme. He idolized his father, but his father's work ended when he left the office. "My dad was always available," Brady said. But for him, there was no off switch. Some days, he never saw his kids. The responsibilities of his support staff would expand to include tasks nobody ever thought would fall to them. His assistant sometimes gave the kids baths. And football continued in the off-season, just without the games. To be great, Brady had to be selfish. He also had to be aware that he was being selfish, and as a condition of his presence, everyone around him had to accept it—especially his wife. Galynn Brady thought that having children "kind of balances every-thing out" for her son, because "kids have a way to make you forget what happened at work." Tom Sr. believed that parenthood had given his son a "release" that he had lacked before. They were right and wrong. If Brady happened to zone out during family time, thinking about foot-ball or typing on his phone, Bündchen would say, "Is this a Tommy day or a family day?"

Every mistake on the field haunted Brady, his perfectionist tendencies worsening with age. He had always stayed up all night after a season-ending loss; now he struggled to sleep if he had thrown a few inter-ceptions in a midseason win. He was unforgiving of himself, and the more that people around him pleaded with him to ease up, the harder he drilled down. When the Patriots lost the AFC Championship Game to the Ravens in January 2013, Brady lay awake, replaying his miscues—like the botched clock management at the end of the first half—and text-ing with Kurt Warner, who was long retired and now a friend. "Being the best doesn't mean you always win," Warner messaged him. "It just means you win more than anybody else." Come morning, Brady's kids wanted to play. It was hard to focus on them. No—"impossible," Brady recalled. "But I try."

Jack and Benny were good boys. They loved to watch *Toy Story*, which meant that Brady had "You've Got a Friend in Me" looping in his head.

He was a loving father, kissing his kids often, extending the tradition of Brady men kissing each other. Sometimes, his sons didn't want to give him a kiss, and so he would say, "No kisses for Daddy," and—voilà!—they would give him a kiss. "Reverse psychology," he explained.

Discipline came harder. When his boys would have meltdowns, crying on the ground, Brady didn't exactly know what to do. He longed for them to be a little older, when he could pick them up and say, "Get your butt off the floor! We're not doing that!" But he would learn that he was in no more control of them than his father had been of him when he would throw fits at the golf course. Like anyone else, his sons were their own people with their own personalities from the moment they were born. Brady could help shape and mold them, but this wasn't football, where he could yell at a receiver and the receiver would listen as if a higher power had spoken.

Vivian was born in December of 2012, right at the end of the season, when Brady was preparing for the playoffs and in his own personal tunnel. The imbalances of life kicked in. He was a heavy sleeper when not agonizing over in-game mistakes. Not even an infant woke him. He would spring out of bed in the morning and jump in the shower, ready to attack the day, ready to practice his motion or get a workout in, and Gisele would say, "Hey, can you help me out?" He was in trouble before the day had even started and would think, *What did I do?*

By February, with an infant and another championshipless season, it was time for a vacation. But in Hawaii for his Brady's sister's wedding, it was hard to relax. Photographers hid inside and outside the hotel, clamoring to get the first photo of Vivian. Shots of post-baby Gisele poolside sprang up online. She always told Tom that "you raise your children for the world," but this was too much. Gisele refused to allow the paparazzi to be the first to publish a picture of her baby, so she took a photo of Vivian herself and posted it to Facebook with the caption, "Love is everything!!!"

The wedding itself wasn't much of a respite. The groomsmen and bridesmaids decided to hold a dance competition. An email had gone out to all of the groomsmen proposing a dance beginning with the hukilau and then breaking into something else, with faces and chests painted. Brady replied immediately, "I'm out!" He worried it would be taped and leaked, and as soon as the season started, people would mock him for how he spent his off-season. Then he felt bad. He emailed the group: "Awww man. I can't be the only one. . . . I'm in. This better not show up anywhere."

They worked on the routine. The guys downed a few cocktails before-hand. But they did it, and Brady was out there, dancing with his face painted and chest bare, hoping nobody outside the wedding would ever see it.

Tom Brady had become so famous that no matter how well his parents knew him, no matter how often they spoke, no matter how many photos of his children popped up on their iPhones—Gisele tended to send most of the pictures of the kids—his life was unrecognizable and unknowable. Tom Sr. and Galynn would joke that when they wanted to know what their son was up to on any given day, they would go to Inside Track or TMZ. Brady would sleep in his old bed in his old room in his old home when he was in San Mateo, but each visit served as a reminder that life had irrevocably changed. One day, Tom Sr. was playing golf and he bumped into a friend, who was playing with his son, their weekend ritual. Tom Sr. had grown accustomed to adulation and envy, as though other parents wanted his life, but watching a father and son play golf in anonymity made him wistful. They tried to replicate those moments on an altogether different scale. Brady would book a private plane for Dad and tell him to show up at the airport, and they would meet in Palm Springs or Augusta, and enjoy a weekend at a world-class course, living a life nobody could have predicted.

Fame had trickled down to the entire family. People treated Brady's parents, sisters, and inner circle like celebrities. When Tom Sr. and Galynn boarded the flight to Hawaii for the wedding, word leaked to the press that Tom Brady was on the plane. Photographers were wait-ing when it landed. Tom Sr. and Galynn relished these moments, when they'd enter the lens frames and watch the photographer's faces sink.

"They were so disappointed," Galynn said with a laugh.

On the flight home, an attendant approached Tom Sr. and asked if he would be willing to sign a ball and helmet. He gave a look that he had grown accustomed to using in those situations. You sure you want *my* autograph? It became clear that the flight attendant had no idea who Tom Sr. was; she was relaying a request from a gate agent who was a Patriots fan and had a helmet and ball at the ready. Tom Sr. asked if she wanted him to sign it like he signs his name, or like his son signs his name. He signed "Tom Brady," because as he often joked, "I'm really Tom Brady. I'm really not senior. He's junior."

The Bradys often looked at one another in disbelief over their lives. After all these years, it was still surreal. Reporters frequently called Tom Sr., and he had embraced his role as his son's spokesman, not only because he was proud, but because he enjoyed the conversation. One of Brady's sisters had nicknamed him "Loose Lips" in 1999, when Tom Sr. accidentally told a reporter about the quarterback rotation with Drew Henson at Michigan. But in 2013, Tom told him, "Dad, I never want to see your name in print again." Brady had been in enough situations to see how all of the attention veered to him, even when he was with his team-mates. "There could be 52 Patriots in the room," Brady said, "and I come into the room? It's all about me. It's not fair to the other 52 Patriots." He would intentionally show up late to team functions to avoid drawing attention, but sometimes it only built anticipation, the headline band making an entrance. Brady told his father that if he refused to cooperate with stories, it would be harder for reporters to write about him.

"I don't want the attention," Brady said. "I don't want anything."

Tom Sr. promised to abide by his son's request—mostly. "I control myself as much as I can," he told me with a wink.

Tom Sr. genuinely wanted to explain his son to the masses. Other-wise, as he saw it, people would treat Tom Brady as an empty vessel to fill as they pleased. One day, he saw Tom and Gisele ranked on a magazine's list of celebrity "power couples," alongside Jay Z and Beyoncé, Kim Kar-dashian and Kanye West, Brangelina, even Barack and Michelle Obama. "It sells magazines," Tom Sr. said, "but it doesn't speak to who they are."

But every step Tom Brady had taken away from his parents, begin-ning with his move to Ann Arbor in 1995, was a step into an unmapped territory—a wilderness with no guides, no comfort stations or trail shacks for rest, no way to see where your next footstep would land. Tom Sr. certainly believed his own words about his son's marriage and life.

Maybe he needed to believe them, because the version of his son that had emerged on the national stage—the Tom Brady who had pined for an outsized life; who was in the process of moving out of a custom-built, 14,000-square-foot Brentwood mansion and into a custom-built, 9,700-square-foot Chestnut Hill mansion; who was ruthlessly focused, supremely confident, surprisingly petty—was real, too. Tom Sr. wanted to believe that the sweet and temperamental boy he raised was still inside the wealthy, famous person who visited his home and slept in that boy's old room. The truth didn't lie in the chasm between two extremes. The truth was in the extremes themselves, as always with Tom Brady— and with the New England Patriots.

ALL PARENTS WATCH their children grow and change, and seeing them through the prism of the child they used to be is to not see them at all. The Bradys saw their son as he was and knew that it came with conditions. "We don't have the same relationship that we do with our daughters," Galynn told me. "I mean, I don't call him every day. I don't bother. I know all that he has on his plate. He's different." From the time he was a teenager, Tom Brady wanted to be different—and had grown so accustomed to sacrificing for the game that it wasn't a matter of deciding to sacrifice again; it was simply his life. His parents knew he loved football, but how much he loved it, how deeply he loved it, would continue to be redefined in the direction of *more* that it was worth wondering if he was using football to quiet something else, a part of his mind that never turned off. Football wouldn't last forever. Tony Gonzalez, the future Hall of Fame tight end for the Chiefs and Falcons, had so much trouble walking away from football that he preemptively hired a therapist. Brady knew that would be him one day. "I know how much he loves this game," Galynn said. "I worry about him finding—when they don't want him anymore, how will he find his next passion?"

Her son didn't want to know. He wanted to keep this thing going for as long as he could. He wanted more control over his fate in a sport that was brutal and random. And so, as hard as it was to explain Alex Guerrero's role, it was also easy: his job was to help Brady make it happen.

Guerrero had studied traditional Chinese medicine at Samra University in Los Angeles. He owned a company called 6 Degree Nutrition, which sold numerous supplements, including a sports drink called NeuroSafe, marketed as a "seat belt for the brain" that could expedite recovery from concussions. Tom Brady and Wes Welker publicly endorsed it. "Neuro-Safe makes me feel comfortable that if I get a concusion," Brady wrote in an ad, misspelling the key word, "I can recover faster and more fully." In 2011, the Federal Trade Commission got wind of NeuroSafe—not the first time it had investigated Guerrero—and concluded that the "extraordinary" claims about the product were not rooted in science. Guerrero stopped marketing the drink, but his influence with the game's premier quarterback continued to grow. Guerrero was no longer just a masseur or physical trainer. He was one of the few people in Brady's life—maybe the only person—who reacted to the quarterback's grand vision without a hint of doubt.

"What's your purpose?" Guerrero often asked Brady.

All professional athletes need some sort of religion. The stakes are too high, the games too unpredictable. Some depend on God, some on booze, women, gambling, drugs, Twitter. In 2013, Brady was vulnerable. He hadn't finished well in the playoffs for eight years. His opponent was not only every other NFL team, it was the inevitability of an ending.

Guerrero often reminded Brady that, in some cultures, the word *retirement* doesn't exist. You did what made you happy. Guerrero saw the game as a spiritual experience. "We're a physical body, emotional body, and spiritual body," he often said. His job was to keep all of Brady's bodies in balance. By 2013, Brady had accumulated a lot of celebrity capital. If he chose to throw his weight behind a business, it would be a statement. He kept working with Guerrero despite transgressions that had landed the trainer in trouble with the federal government, an attitude that wouldn't change when more transgressions came out in the future. Brady truly believed in Guerrero and his methods and wanted to spread the gospel.

In March 2013, in his living room, Brady spelled out this next step. "Alex has taught me so many things that, really, I want to be able to share with other athletes at some point."

Later, Guerrero emerged from downstairs. The two of them stood together near the elevator door, ready to begin their day. "Got some business at the stadium," Brady said.

Six months later, in September of 2013, a new gym opened near Gillette Stadium. It was called TB12 Sports Therapy Center.

28

LOVE IN THE TIME
OF BELICHICK

J UST AFTER 8 A.M. ON A CLOUDY AND COOL SATURDAY
morning in December 2012, Scott Pioli got out of his car in the
parking lot of Arrowhead Stadium and saw one of his players holding a gun.

It was Jovan Belcher, a linebacker. Less than an hour earlier, he had
fired ten shots into Kasandra Perkins, his girlfriend and the mother of
their three-month-old child, after an argument about her coming home
late from a concert. Now Belcher was distraught and panicked, reckon-
ing with what he had done. Pioli stood a few yards away. Even though
Belcher was armed, the Chiefs' general manager felt safe. Belcher wasn't
pointing the gun; he was just holding it.

"I came here to thank you," Belcher told Pioli cryptically. "Thank you
for my chance."

Minutes later, Romeo Crennel, then the Chiefs' head coach, and linebackers coach Gary Gibbs arrived. Both pleaded with Belcher to surrender his weapon. From down the road, there came the sound of a
police siren.

"You know that I'm having some major problems at home with my
girlfriend," Belcher said. The siren grew louder. "I've hurt my girlfriend
already, and I can't go back now."

With that, Belcher decided it was over. He knelt behind his black
2007 Bentley Continental GT, traced a cross on his chest, and pointed
the gun at his head.

NOBODY ON THE CHIEFS knew how to handle the shock that a teammate—a brother in arms—had revealed himself to be a murderer before committing suicide in front of team officials. That night, the team gathered in an auditorium for consoling words, not from Pioli or Crennel, but from the team chaplain, a man named Jack Easterby. He was a lanky and balding former college basketball player and golfer with a thick Southern accent. He had interned for the Jacksonville Jaguars and worked in the University of South Carolina athletic department. He had been with the Chiefs for two years. What started with a weekly bible study had expanded organically. Easterby had demonstrated such an innate ability to connect with players and coaches—listening rather than talking, investing more in lives than in games, always hugging as a greeting and goodbye—that Pioli started to personally pay for his flights from South Carolina to Kansas City. Easterby had a rare gift in a football facility: he made others feel better about themselves.

"There is hope beyond these moments," Easterby said to the team that night. "There's something bigger going on."

He told the men in front of him that if they prepared for death and for the life that continued after it, the devastation of the day's tragedies might linger less. He gave everyone notes from his speech and urged them to call him whenever they felt moved to or needed to. "Men left encouraged," linebacker Andy Studebaker recalled. "And they left in tears."

A month later, Chiefs owner Clark Hunt fired Pioli and Crennel, leaving Easterby without a job. Right before the 2013 season started, he got a call from Foxborough. It was Bill Belichick—whose team was reeling from a murderous player of its own.

"We heard you're the best in the league at what you do," Belichick said. "And we want to bring you up here."

TWO DAYS BEFORE training camp, Bill Belichick stood behind a podium and attempted to explain the inexplicable. On June 26, 2013, Aaron Hernandez—a talented tight end Belichick had drafted in 2010 and, two years later, awarded a five-year contract worth $39.58 million—had been arrested and charged with the first-degree murder of an associate named Odin Lloyd. He was later convicted and given a life sentence, and in April of 2017 was found hanging in his prison cell. In the coming years, books and documentaries and newspaper investigations would mine Hernandez's life—from an abusive childhood in Bristol, Connecticut, to his drug use, to his alleged bisexuality—to attempt to explain how an emerging star for the league's marquee franchise had turned out to be a murderer. But as Belichick spoke into the microphone, the only thing clear was that Hernandez was irrevocably broken. Questions turned to the New England Patriots, and what signs Belichick might or might not have missed.

In a navy Patriots pullover, Belichick was somber and sincere and spoke for over seven minutes straight, expressing sympathy for the victims before talking about his team. "Having someone in your organization who's involved in a murder investigation is a terrible thing." He added, "We'll all learn from this terrible experience."

Nobody accused the Patriots of knowingly harboring a murderer. But a breakdown of some sort had occurred. Many inside and outside the organization wondered whether its leadership had made compromises it shouldn't have. The post-Spygate years had seen New England lose two Super Bowls, which gave license to some to question the validity of the three they had won. As the championship drought continued, Belichick took more risks on players of suspect character. More than a few of these decisions had poor results, though nothing like what had happened with Hernandez. Although Hernandez had lied to both Robert Kraft and Belichick about his involvement in Lloyd's murder—"We were duped," Kraft later said—all of it was hugely embarrassing to the Kraft family. The owner felt Belichick hadn't been very forthcoming about Hernandez's troubled history, dating back to the tight end's college years at Florida, where he had a myriad of drug and behavioral problems. In 1996, Myra Kraft believed so strongly that the Patriots should field a team of upstanding men that she had wanted Nebraska defensive tackle Christian Peter, the team's fifth-round pick, who had been charged and convicted of sexual assault, to be cut shortly after he was drafted. He was.

Something more than a season was in peril. Morale was low, and it was never that high in New England to begin with. Players privately struggled with the ruthlessness of life under Belichick. Each year without a Super Bowl was more crushing, given the expectations and the history. Players and assistants needed an outlet, a presence in the building who would "offer love with no strings attached," special-teams star Matt Slater later said.

Scott Pioli called Belichick and suggested that he hire Jack Easterby.

IT WAS HARD TO earn trust from a team that trafficked in fear. Easterby was eventually awarded an unusual title—character coach—and his responsibility was both straightforward and daunting: he was the team therapist. His job was to make sure that every player and coach entered practices and games with a clear head. It wasn't easy; in fact, it was overwhelming, not only because of the hundreds of conversations he had each week, but because he was an outsider entering an insular world. On Easterby's second day, he met Tom Brady. They talked for a few hours. Brady was polite but cautious. At first, players and coaches were scared to confide in Easterby. He was not only management, he was *Belichick's* management. What if Easterby was a spy for Belichick, who would then leverage a personal issue against a player in contract negotiations?

But Easterby was persistent, an ambitious man among ambitious men. He wrote notes to every single player and coach before games, recapping their personal goals and reminding them of how thankful he was to know them. In one, he quoted a famous Teddy Roosevelt speech and signed it, *Aiming to be the man in the arena, Jack*. Players related to Easterby's own deep-seated desire to be great in his work. He ran Bible study but didn't push religion on anyone. He sometimes counseled players and their wives, couples' therapy without anyone calling it that. He threw passes to defensive backs in practice and even jumped in on scout-team drills. Belichick always told players that nobody was ever going to feel sorry for them—Ben Watson, a former tight end, had been so "miserable" in New England that he saw a psychiatrist to cope with the pressure and anxiety—but Easterby did, even though he was a special Belichick hire. "As macho as we are in this locker room, we all want to be loved," Slater recalled. "As men, sometimes we don't know how to deal with emotions or ups and downs. We don't grieve the way we should, experience sadness the way we should, or express joy the way we should because we're so focused on the job. Jack has been there to say, 'It's okay to be down. It's okay to have heartache.'"

Players who at first were fearful of opening up to Easterby suddenly couldn't stop. "You feel a special connection with him and with his genuine caring for all the people in his life," Brady later said. Kraft called him a "wonderful individual." Safety Devin McCourty said he was a "godsend to this team." When Easterby would talk to players, he pulled them in for an embrace—he was a "big hugger, a loud hugger," Pioli said—and raised their handshake to his heart. He fixed his eyes to theirs for so long that it felt both awkward and somehow liberating for the player on the receiving end. He would remind them that he was a quick judge of character and that he could tell they were men of integrity. It was not something Patriots players and coaches had heard in the wake of Aaron Hernandez—or, for that matter, since before Spygate.

When Belichick first arrived in New England, he had vowed to do a better job of staying attuned to players' lives than he did in Cleveland. He had improved, but it still wasn't his strong suit. The hiring of Easterby not only showed that Belichick was willing to adapt to a system straining under its own weight. It also was a concession. It was easier for him to hire someone to show love than it was for him to show love himself.

PATRIOTS FANS STARTED TO bail on Tom Brady, having seen enough. It was October 13, 2013, and New England trailed the New Orleans Saints, 27–23, with 1:13 left. Brady jogged onto the field with no timeouts and Gillette Stadium emptying. Twice in the past two minutes of game time, he had a chance to drive New England to a game-winning score, and twice he had come up short. His previous pass had been intercepted, and every errant throw was now the subject of a weeklong sports-radio debate. Was Brady starting to lose it? The questions were not only being asked loudly outside the team, but also quietly within it, with coaches wondering how much he had left.

Brady and Josh McDaniels, in his second year back with the Patriots as offensive coordinator after his Broncos debacle, huddled on the sideline. McDaniels didn't have much of a plan: throw over the middle, spike the ball to stop the clock, complete one more, and then "try to hit something in the end zone," he told Brady.

"Just gotta gain 10, 15 a play," Brady said.

On first down, Brady completed a pass to wide receiver Julian Edelman over the middle for 23 yards, moving New England to midfield. Two plays later, Brady hit another receiver, Austin Collie, for 15 more. The clock was running. Under center, Brady got the ball and motioned to spike it, but then pivoted and fired outside to receiver Aaron Dobson, an echo of a classic fake Dan Marino had used successfully against the Jets in 1994. It was a huge risk. If Dobson failed to get out of bounds, the clock would run and New England would only have a play or two left. Dobson ran upfield and collided with cornerback Keenan Lewis, who threw Dobson over the sideline rather than keeping him inbounds—the type of play Belichick would often refer to as a "stupid mistake" that "ruins it for everybody."

With ten seconds left, Brady lofted an arcing pass to rookie receiver Kenbrell Thompkins. The ball looked high, seemingly destined to sail out of bounds, and Thompkins was blanketed by a Saints defensive back. But Brady had thrown him open, dropping the ball outside and inches over the outstretched arms of cornerback Jabari Greer for a touchdown with five seconds left.

The remaining fans screamed. After the game, an elated Belichick said, "That took about five years off my life."

Later that night, a friend told Brady, "Still got it."

"Never lost it," he replied.

THAT WAS MOSTLY TRUE. But the 2013 season ended with the Patriots coaches wondering whether Brady's skills were in a subtle but irrevocable decline at age 36. New England finished with a 12–4 record. The team whipped the Indianapolis Colts in the divisional round, and met the Broncos in Denver for the AFC championship. Denver was now led by the Patriots' first major rival, Peyton Manning, who responded to the Colts' moving on from him after multiple neck operations with the greatest statistical season ever for a quarterback. He set records with

5,477 yards and 55 touchdown passes. Perhaps more interesting was that he had done so with methods that reduced the game to pure intellect. His neck injury had sapped his arm strength and left some fingers on his right hand permanently numb. He couldn't throw long, and the ball often wobbled out of his release, but Manning had carved up the league with a dizzying array of short passes, improvising based not only on what the defense showed him, but on what his body, on any given snap, allowed him to do.

Brady was superior physically to Manning, but that season he was not the better quarterback. Trailing 3–0 in the first quarter, Brady dropped back and threw deep to Edelman, who had slipped free on a crossing route for what might have been a touchdown. But Brady missed him over the top. New England fell behind, 23–3, and lost, 26–16. Denver went on to be throttled by Pete Carroll's Seattle Seahawks in Super Bowl XLVIII by a score of 43–8. With a ferocious defense and a young superstar quarterback in Russell Wilson—who had been a third-round draft pick, in part because he was just under six feet tall—the Seahawks had the dynastic look of the early-century Patriots.

Brady's misfire to Edelman was not only yet another instance of his recent habit of missing open receivers in big games, dating back to the Welker miss against the Giants. It was indicative of a problem that both Patriots coaches and opposing defenses had noticed: trepidation and inaccuracy when throwing deep. Brady had always believed that accuracy was as much about decisiveness as it was about technique. Now he had moments of indecision—or, rather, he was decisive in throwing to the nearest receiver and not the farther one. Belichick had tried to encourage him—"Tom, keep throwing deep, keep working on it"—but the smarter defensive coaches had started to challenge Brady by clogging the middle of the field, taking away the short crossing routes that he loved, and daring him to throw outside and downfield. No coaching staff in the league was more hyper-aware of their own players' weaknesses than New England. The coaches—and Ernie Adams—had spent hours with Brady in the off-season, pointing out his flaws, coaching him to be his best self. But in 2013, Brady's yards per attempt fell to 6.92, his lowest since 2006, and he completed only 17 of 68 throws beyond 20 yards.

In the off-season, Belichick issued a challenge to the coaches. "We gotta be able to throw downfield."

Complicating matters was that Brady was spending most of his off-seasons in Los Angeles, not Foxborough. For most of his career, Brady had won a coveted parking spot at Gillette Stadium, awarded each year to the Patriot or Patriots with sterling attendance at the team off-season program. Brady had lost it for the first time in 2010—to *ten* other Patriots. And when Brady was in Foxborough, he was now often separate from the team, in a private room on a massage table with Alex Guerrero, cruising through the cafeteria only to grab a snack. Brady was still a model teammate and leader, but even he considered himself "more coach than player." Belichick finally asked him to spend more time around the team, but it was as though Brady were the team dad. He implored the younger Patriots to skip late nights at the bars and focus on sleep and recovery. One day, Brady asked the teenage son of a personal friend what music younger people liked.

"Gucci Mane? A$AP Rocky? Something like that?" Brady later said, trying to remember the artists' names.

Belichick was asking more of Brady at a time when he felt unappreciated. For years, Brady had endured brutal coaching, risen above and elevated pedestrian surrounding talent, backed Belichick unequivocally during rough periods—above all, Spygate and its lingering aftermath—and been an ideal face of the franchise. Unlike Peyton Manning, who signed massive contracts as if he felt a duty to maximize quarterback pay for future generations, Brady had always agreed to team-friendly deals that allowed New England uncommon salary-cap flexibility for a team with one of the best quarterbacks in history. The negotiations had been labored and strained in recent years, with Brady wanting higher compensation and shorter contracts, leaving some in New England to wonder if he wanted to remain a Patriot. Robert Kraft had promised Brady that, if Belichick ever decided to move on from him, he would allow Brady to have a say in his fate. Some people close to Brady believed that if there were an NFL franchise in Los Angeles in those championshipless years between 2010 and 2013, he might have attempted to force a trade. In 2010, negotiations dragged on for seven months before both sides agreed to a deal that paid Brady an average of $18 million annually, highest in the league. In 2013, New England restructured Brady's deal, lowering his base salary in exchange for $57 million in guarantees. The tacit agreement was that Belichick would use the resulting cap space to give Brady more weapons, but Belichick spent as he saw fit, infuriating Brady by letting Wes Welker sign with Denver in 2013.

Belichick was at least able to use Brady's salary as leverage, with beneficial results for the team overall. In 2014, New England wanted to sign future Hall of Fame cornerback Darrelle Revis. Revis demanded a minimum of $16 million annually. Tom makes 14, Belichick replied. The message was clear: if you come here, it's at a discount. Revis signed what was essentially a one-year deal for $12 million. But even though the move helped the Patriots, Revis wasn't going to be catching passes from Brady.

At the 2014 Kentucky Derby, Brady was hanging out with Vince Wilfork, New England's all-pro defensive tackle, when the conversation turned to the team's lack of offensive weapons and getting the quarterback "some help."

"Some help?" Brady said. "About damn time."

"About damn time!" Wilfork said. "About damn time! About damn time!"

Belichick appreciated Brady and his contributions to both the franchise and to his own career, but there was a gap between how he felt and what he was willing to say. He simply wouldn't express the love or gratitude that Brady sought. That task fell to Kraft. So, Brady would complain directly to ownership, bypassing the coach. Brady and Belichick were forever linked, spent hours each week during the season in meetings, two of the most disciplined and driven people in sports history in the same room, one of them the youngest child in a family who was raised having to compete for attention—collegial and compliant by nature—and the other an only child, singular and distrustful of others. Neither man was confrontational, at least beyond the football field. Brady, in his heart, knew he was an employee, even if he had a direct line to the owner. Belichick's pride, his interpersonal awkwardness, his utter lack of sentimentality, his system based on personal sacrifice for the greater good—all of it conspired to keep his quarterback at an emotional distance.

By 2014, Belichick had started to imagine life beyond Brady. He hired his old friend and the man who had been his general manager in Cleveland, Michael Lombardi, as an assistant to the coaching staff and asked him to scout college quarterbacks. Ahead of the 2014 draft, Belichick, Josh McDaniels, and Lombardi had narrowed the list to two. One was famous: Johnny Manziel out of Texas A&M, who in 2012 had been the first freshman to win the Heisman Trophy. The other was lesser known: Jimmy Garoppolo, a four-year starter from Eastern Illinois. Both were dual-option players, gifted as both throwers and runners. McDaniels liked quarterbacks who could keep plays alive with their feet. "We need someone who can do more than just throw the ball," he said in one draft meeting.

New England studied both quarterbacks and quickly settled on Garoppolo. He was a hard worker who had walked each morning to the Eastern Illinois facility—he didn't own a car in college—and was often the first player there. He had a compact and quick release and the perfect mix of confidence and earnestness required to back up, and perhaps challenge, a legend. On May 9, 2014, with the 62nd pick overall pick, Belichick called Garoppolo to welcome him to New England as Kraft sat nearby, trying to mask his unease. On the other end of the line, Garoppolo's family was cheering so loudly that the quarterback couldn't hear Belichick. He just said, "Yes, sir. Yes, sir. Yes, sir."

Belichick justified the pick to the press in uncustomarily blunt terms. "We know what Tom's age and contract situation is." For his part, Brady knew ahead of the draft that New England would likely draft a quarterback, and he knew, as his dad had once told me, that as soon as Belichick got "a quarterback who is better for a dollar less, he'll be gone." But it was another reminder that Belichick would never allow nostalgia to gain an inch on him or his process. It was also a public declaration that Bill Belichick was personally invested in a future beyond Tom Brady.

29

FIGHT SONG

A RUNNING BACK FOR THE BALTIMORE RAVENS NAMED Justin Forsett knelt in the end zone and opened his arms toward the sky, the celebration of not just a touchdown, but a knockout blow. It was January 10, 2015, an AFC divisional playoff game at Gillette Stadium. Forsett had slipped out of the backfield and caught a pass from Joe Flacco and scored easily, giving Baltimore a 28–14 lead with 10:22 remaining in the third quarter. The team that had ended New England's season in Foxborough twice in the past five years appeared on track to do it again. A loss would extend the Patriots' championship drought to a decade.

No one could have foreseen it at that moment, but New England was at a turning point, not just in the game, but in its dynastic run. The strain of coming up so short for so long had started to show during the regular season. Tom Brady played so poorly—he had looked creaky, even—early in the year that fans, and Brady himself, wondered if Bill Belichick would bench him. After Brady threw a pick-six late in what would be a 41–14 week 4 loss to the Kansas City Chiefs on *Monday Night Football*, Belichick inserted Jimmy Garoppolo, who promptly threw a garbage-time touchdown. On the sideline, Brady congratulated almost every offensive teammate—except the one who had thrown the touchdown pass—and then sat on the bench alone, arms folded. In the days after the game, Belichick not only backed Brady, but authored his most famous press conference performance, to that point or since, swatting away questions about the quarterback's status as the starter and about the quality of his surrounding cast by repeating, "We're on to Cincinnati," the next week's opponent, three times.

But Brady was under attack, outside the building and within. At a meeting the week after the Chiefs loss, the team's running backs coach, Ivan Fears, addressed the offensive players and looked Brady in the eye.

"Your body language reeks of fear," he said.

Brady rebounded the following game, as always, throwing two touchdowns and eclipsing 50,000 career yards in a blowout over the Bengals. But years of living on edge—with a nagging part of him constantly worried that one bad practice could cost him his job—was taking its toll. Rage bubbled under the surface, manifesting itself in novel ways. Two weeks after the Bengals game, against the New York Jets on October 16, Brady exploded on the sideline over the air pressure of the game balls. The grip of a football was primal to Brady. Over the years, he had asked the team's equipment managers to rub footballs with sandpaper, dirt, leather conditioner—they once put footballs in a sauna—so that they were soft enough and slightly deflated, his preferences, feeling perfect in his hand.

Against the Jets, though, the balls were hard and fat. "Like bricks," Brady said on the sidelines. He blew up, letting loose on equipment assistant John Jastremski, telling him the balls "fucking suck."

Brady had trusted Jastremski against his better judgment. On the Friday before the game, Jastremski convinced Brady to use old footballs from training camp, which were soft and would absorb rain without the use of Lexol, a leather conditioner that left the balls oily when wet. Brady usually preferred new footballs, but he went along with the suggestion. Now, Brady was reduced to a bundle of exposed nerve endings, suspecting that someone had tampered with the footballs. Jastremski thought Brady was acting crazy. He found Jim McNally, a Patriots seasonal employee whose primary job was to prepare the footballs.

Brady is angry, Jastremski told McNally.

"Fuck Tom," McNally said.

Both Jastremski and McNally had tried for months to please Brady on the air pressure of footballs—maybe too much. McNally referred to himself as "The Deflator" and indicated to Jastremski that he drained the balls after the refs had approved them—a rules violation. Were the two men sitting on a scandal? In May of 2014, McNally texted Jastremski, "im not going to espn. . . . . . . yet."

The morning after the Jets game, McNally texted Jastremski again: "Tom sucks . . . im going to make that next ball a fuckin balloon."

Jastremski replied that he had spoken with Brady, who felt guilty about his blowup. "He actually brought you up and said you must have a lot of stress trying to get them done . . . I checked some of the balls this morn . . . The refs fucked us . . . A few of [sic] then were at almost 16" psi, or pounds per square inch.

"Fuck tom," McNally replied. "16 is nothing . . . wait till next Sunday."

"Omg!" Jastremski texted. "Spaz."

A week later, Jastremski texted, "I have a big needle for u this week."

"Better be surrounded by cash and new kicks. . . . or it's a rugby Sunday," McNally replied.

"Fuck tom," Jastremski texted.

Brady asked Dave Schoenfeld, the Patriots' head equipment manager, "What does it say in the rule book as to how the balls should be inflated?" Schoenfeld highlighted the rule on a piece of paper, showing that it called for balls to be inflated in a range between 12.5 and 13.5 pounds per square inch. It turned out that Brady had a right to be furious: the balls against the Jets were at 16 psi. Brady asked Jastremski to give the highlighted sheet to refs before games to make sure the footballs were never again so overinflated.

But a bigger question remained: What did this say about Tom Brady? By the standards of American superstar athletes, Brady was relatively unentitled. He had always tried to be polite and respectful—"Awkwardly nice," in Edelman's words—and success had hardened his work ethic rather than softened it. But fans knew little about his demons and insecurities, and the fact that low-rung staffers—invisible servants— seemed to hold a level of contempt for Brady not only revealed him as a perfectionist who couldn't handle mistakes, but also as a man keenly aware of the discrepancy in stature. He was Tom Effing Brady. And for the first time in his career, Brady was starting to exploit his name and reputation. In December of 2014, Greg Bishop of *Sports Illustrated* profiled Brady and Alex Guerrero, giving a glimpse into the TB12 methodology and business. Brady reiterated his desire to play forever and revealed a few secrets: he ate avocado ice cream for dessert, a concoction Guerrero had created.

Teammates had noticed Brady's peculiarities around food for years. He'd pick sausage out of an omelet. Or eat one chip. Or one bite of a cheeseburger. If anyone asked Brady about it, he'd reply, "Why put it on if I have to take it off?" But the *SI* story created national news and angered the coaches, who were incredulous that, in the middle of a season, Brady was pushing his personal business. It was very un-Patriotlike, and it would have been unimaginable for a younger Brady to do anything like it. While Brady lauded Guerrero's massages for helping his muscles stretch "like rubber bands," keeping them soft and durable—they called it "pliability"—the coaches saw a more basic element at play: he wasn't getting hit as much. New England had redesigned its offense to allow Brady to throw quickly and avoid contact, and Brady wasn't too proud to fire the ball in the dirt at the first sign of danger.

But, as New England recovered from a slow start and finished 12–4, it was inarguable that Brady was playing beyond the expectations of anyone but himself. He finished 2014 with a 64.1 completion percentage, four points higher than 2013, and 33 touchdown passes, up eight from the year before. His nine interceptions were lower than 2013 as well, meeting his annual goal of keeping that number in single digits. After spending his life without "one cell in my body that ever tells me to run," Brady had somehow gotten quicker and more elusive, and tried more often to find ways to extend plays. When New England trailed Baltimore, 14–0, in the first quarter of the playoff game, Brady scrambled for a four-yard touchdown, capping it off with a spike reminiscent of his famous one in the snow in the Tuck Game.

But two quarters later, Forsett scored, extending the Ravens' lead to 14 points. New England was desperate. The game, and maybe the most successful coach–quarterback partnership in NFL history, were on the line. But the Patriots had an idea. Belichick found Josh McDaniels on the sideline.

"This is it. Let's go with 'Baltimore.'"

THE FORMATION AND PLAY that reignited the Patriots dynasty was derived from a play called Fight Song. When Lane Kiffin—son of Monte Kiffin, considered one of the top defensive coordinators in history—was the head coach at USC from 2010 to 2013, he had a clever idea for a pass out of a funky alignment. The left tackle would split out as a receiver, but would remain an ineligible pass-catcher. The left tackle's replacement along the line of scrimmage would actually be a tight end who would run a pass route. It was a legal formation—as long as an offense has seven players on the line of scrimmage, it doesn't matter where they line up if the eligible or ineglible receivers are declared—but confusing to defend.

Kiffin called the play "Fight Song." "When we run it," he said, "we're gonna score."

He never ran it at USC, but he did at his next stop, as Alabama's offensive coordinator under Belichick's longtime friend and former Browns colleague, Nick Saban. In a November 2014 overtime game against Louisiana State, Tide left tackle Cam Robinson lined up in the right slot. Offensive lineman Brandon Greene lined up as a tight end in the left tackle position. LSU was lost. Uncovered, Greene ran a short seam route and gained 24 yards, leading to the game-winning touchdown. Bill Belichick had watched it live, catching the final moments of the game when he got home from work. He loved the play—the notion of a displaced receiver was so devious—and called the offensive coaches into his office the next morning. "It's a tough look," Belichick said. He wanted them to work on a version of it to use as a jump-starter in the playoffs, in case the team needed it after nearly a decade of failure in crucial moments.

McDaniels showed Fight Song to the players, then tinkered with it. In New England's modification, tight end Michael Hoomanawanui lined up as the faux left tackle. Rather than splitting out the tackle as an ineligible receiver, McDaniels used running back Shane Vereen. Belichick suspected that, in the chaos of a game, the defense couldn't help but cover Vereen, even if he had declared himself ineligible.

New England called the play "Baltimore." The week before the playoff game, Brady and Belichick cooked up yet another iteration of it called "Raven," in which Hoomanawanui would line up in Vereen's spot as an ineligible receiver. Belichick cleared the formation with the league office and with the game officials. In a staff meeting, Belichick instructed McDaniels to not call "Baltimore" until the second half so that the Ravens couldn't study it at halftime. "I don't want them to have time to adjust," he said. He suspected that the play might cause Ravens head coach John Harbaugh—a great coach with a great temper—to blow a fuse during the game, revealing his worst self under Belichickian pressure. It was diabolically brilliant.

Now down two touchdowns in the third quarter, New England needed a spark. Brady jogged onto the field and signaled that "Baltimore" was coming. On the third play of the drive, Vereen reported as ineligible to referee Bill Vinovich, who announced it to the stadium, per the rules. But then, something curious happened: Vinovich never announced that Hoomanawanui, lined up as the left tackle, was an *eligible* receiver, as he would normally do. Brady hustled into his cadence. The Ravens were confused and shifted coverage to Vereen, leaving Hoomanawanui uncovered—exactly as Belichick planned, and exactly as LSU had done against Alabama. Brady connected with Hoomanawanui on a seam route for 16 yards, then hit him again, five plays later, out of the same formation. Brady capped the drive with a five-yard touchdown pass to Rob Gronkowski, cutting the lead to 28–21.

Just as Belichick had predicted, Harbaugh was livid. His defense was supposed to be notified and have time to cover eligible receivers. The refs were allowing Brady to snap the ball so quickly that the Ravens couldn't adjust. Baltimore linebacker Terrell Suggs complained that the play was illegal. Trying to plead his case to the officials, Harbaugh ran onto the field and was flagged for unsportsmanlike conduct. Belichick had forced his opponent into a tailspin. The Patriots thought it was funny. During a time-out, Julian Edelman said to Vinovich, "You guys getting your money's worth with them formations." Vinovich rolled his eyes and smiled in agreement.

On New England's next possession, knowing the Ravens were still trying to decipher "Baltimore," Belichick and McDaniels moved in for the kill. They called a double pass in which Edelman would catch a backward pass from Brady, and then throw deep to receiver Danny Amendola.

Edelman had been a quarterback at Kent State, but at 5-foot-10 was seen as too short to play that position in the NFL. A respected football writer named Rick Gosselin—a man who would walk around the annual NFL scouting combine with binders full of information on prospects, better prepared than some scouts—liked Edelman's versatility and toughness and suggested him to Belichick. During the seventh round of the 2009 draft, Belichick called Edelman and said, "Eeeeeeeedelman, I don't know what we're going to do with you, but you're a hell of a football player." Belichick converted him to receiver. Edelman worked his way into the starting lineup as a rookie, determined to outwork everyone on a team of legendary workers. Sometimes, he would stare at his helmet, in case he got cut the next day. At 11 p.m. one night in the team facility, Edelman went to the hot tub—and as soon as he did, he noticed that Belichick was in there. Belichick got out, and as he did, Edelman saw that he was naked. "Free ball," he recalled. It was awkward; Edelman had nowhere to escape. They passed each other in silence. Half an hour later, when he was leaving, Edelman saw Belichick again on the way out the door. The two men walked near each other down the hallway in silence. Finally, Edelman worked up the nerve to say something. "Coach, it's pretty amazing that you're here this late."

"It beats being a plumber," Belichick said. "See you tomorrow."

Edelman developed into one of the team's best and most dependable players. Now, in the playoffs, Belichick was about to call his number. Edelman had practiced the play in the lead-up to the game and arrived at meetings with ice wrapped around his shoulder, laughing that he had to care for his arm like a quarterback. Before kickoff, he warmed up with the quarterbacks. "I gotta throw," he joked.

McDaniels radioed in Double Pass X Slant. Brady threw back and to his left to Edelman, who then hit Amendola in stride down the sideline for a 51-yard touchdown. "Just like the backyard!" Edelman said to Amendola as they came off the field.

In less than three minutes, New England had tied the game, reignited the crowd, and caused a Ravens meltdown. Still, Baltimore was a veteran team. The Ravens regained their composure, and in the fourth quarter, kicked a field goal to go up 31–28 with 10:19 left.

Brady completed seven consecutive passes on the next drive, moving New England to the Ravens' 23-yard line. As he approached the line of scrimmage, he saw Baltimore in man-to-man coverage, with only one safety deep. He liked it, and was thinking touchdown. All he had to do was shift the protection.

"Gold 62 Alabama!" he said at the line of scrimmage.

"Gold" was what the Patriots called a "live" color. It indicated an audible. If Brady had said "white," for instance, it would have been a dummy call. "Sixty-two" was the new protection, with running back Brandon Bolden responsible for blitz pickup. "Alabama" was the type of snap count. The Patriots had an ever-changing family of snap counts. This time, a word with the letter A—the first letter in the alphabet— meant the ball would be snapped after the first "hut!"

From the shotgun, and now with the ball in his hands, Brady looked down the left sideline for receiver Brandon LaFell. Brady and LaFell had gone through some difficult moments during the season, but the quarterback chose to trust all of his receivers on this night. He launched a deep pass—the exact type of throw he had missed too often in previous years. It turned on its axis and landed so perfectly that LaFell didn't so much catch it as get under it, like a human basket. The play put New England up 35–31. The score held.

The win meant more than just advancing to the AFC Championship Game. New England became the first team in NFL history to win a playoff game after rallying from two separate 14-point deficits—and had done so by putting almost the entire offense on Tom Brady's shoulders. The Patriots rushed for just 14 yards on 13 carries, an astonishingly abysmal performance on the ground. Brady threw 50 passes, completing 33 of them for 367 yards. He accounted for three total touchdowns, despite getting poked in the eye by a Raven at one point, and despite absorbing brutal hits, including one in the first half that left him doubled over. Suggs had for years talked trash with Brady—he had once asked him how to bag a model, to which Brady replied, "Punk-ass bitch"—but after the game, he approached Brady and congratulated him.

"You're a great player," Brady replied.

Harbaugh seethed after the game. He believed the refs had lost control in a critical moment, overwhelmed by Belichick's stature. He declined to comment on whether the alignments were dirty, but he did say that what the Patriots had done was "clearly deception." When told of Harbaugh's comments, Brady was in no mood to ignore them. "Maybe those guys gotta study the rule book and figure it out," he said. It was mild, as far as trash talk in the NFL goes, but it brought out Harbaugh's rage all over again. Belichick personally apologized to Harbaugh for Brady's comments. Harbaugh accepted it, but some of his friends around the league were outraged on his behalf and wanted more than to abolish New England's baffling formation, which the competition committee would do in the coming months. They wanted revenge.

30

THE MAKEUP CALL

BOUT THREE HOURS BEFORE THE PATRIOTS KICKED
off in the AFC Championship Game against the Indianapolis Colts, Tom Brady and John Jastremski met in the Gillette Stadium equipment room to approve game balls. On Friday, Brady had learned that it might rain during the game. Not wanting a repeat of the Jets debacle, he and Jastremski devised a new protocol: Jastremski would break in 24 brand new footballs in 36 hours—again without the use of Lexol. For days, Jastremski threw the balls and caught them and rubbed them with leather gloves, a bizarre but effective method. Now Brady gripped the balls. He liked them, and left to prepare for the game.

Soon after, Jim McNally stood with head referee Walt Anderson in the officials' locker room as Anderson approved the footballs. McNally told Anderson that Brady wanted the balls inflated to 12.5 psi, the lowest pressure allowed. Anderson found that two of the footballs were illegally low, and so he inflated them to 12.5 psi and certified the footballs. Game-day protocol stated that no one was to remove the footballs from the locker room without permission from the officials, but when Anderson left the room, McNally took the bag of footballs and went to another room in the stadium to watch the Seattle Seahawks play the Green Bay Packers in the NFC Championship Game. After the Seahawks clinched a second consecutive trip to the Super Bowl on a Russell Wilson 35-yard touchdown pass in overtime, one of the referees said, "We're back on again." McNally took the footballs—without an official's consent. Anderson later said he had never seen a ball boy remove the footballs before. McNally ducked into a bathroom near the field with the foot-

balls, locked the door, and remained there for approximately one minute and 40 seconds.

Almost from the moment the AFC Championship Game started,
there was no question that the Patriots would win. But with New
England up 14–0, Brady underthrew a post route to Gronkowski near
the goal line. Colts linebacker D'Qwell Jackson picked it off—an irrelevant turnover in the course of the game, but one of the most consequen-
tial of Brady's career. Jackson saved the ball as a memento. He handed it
to a Colts staffer, who passed it on to Brian Seabrooks, the team's assistant equipment manager. Seabrooks thought the ball seemed soft—and
suspiciously similar to one that Brady had thrown to Colts safety Mike
Adams earlier in the season. After the Adams interception, Seabrooks
asked a Colts equipment intern to measure the ball's air pressure. It was
11 psi—illegally low. At the time, the two men had not raised an alarm.
But now Seabrooks gave Jackson's ball to head equipment manager Sean
Sullivan, who squeezed it and agreed that it was suspiciously soft and
spongy. The Colts alerted NFL representatives on site. Word made its
way to Colts general manager Ryan Grigson in the press box.

The news didn't surprise Grigson. In fact, he had suspected that
Brady was using deflated balls. The day before the AFC Championship
Game, Grigson had emailed NFL executives Dave Gardi and Mike Kensil with an attached note from Sullivan that seemed to echo suspicions
from the Spygate era: "As far as the gameballs are concerned, it is well
known around the league that after the Patriots gameballs are checked
by the officials . . . the ballboys for the Patriots will let out some air with
a ball needle because their quarterback likes a small football so he can
grip it better." The Colts had asked the league to test the footballs during
the game so that New England didn't have an "illegal advantage." The
email was forwarded to various league officials.

Grigson now rushed to the suite where Kensil and NFL executive vice
president Troy Vincent were sitting, and knocked on the door.

"We are playing with a small ball," Grigson said.

Vincent and Kensil went downstairs at halftime to test both teams'
footballs. Three times, league executives tested the pressure of the intercepted ball, and every time, it measured below 12 psi: 11.45, 11.35, and
11.75. Kensil saw McNally carrying a bag of footballs onto the field for

the second half and confiscated it. Officials tested some of New England's footballs and four of the Colts', using two different gauges. Eleven of the Patriots' footballs measured below 12 psi; none of the Colts' balls did.

The league believed it had caught New England red-needled. Kensil found Dave Schoenfeld on the sideline and said, "We weighed the balls. You are in big fucking trouble."

WITH THE EXCEPTION OF Eli Manning and the possible exception of his older brother, the biggest threat to the greatness of the New England Patriots was their own behavior. The morning after the 45–7 win over the Colts that sent Tom Brady and Bill Belichick to their sixth Super Bowl, Brady was halfway into his weekly radio interview on Boston sports-radio station WEEI when host Kirk Minihane asked about an overnight tweet by Bob Kravitz of WTHR-TV in Indianapolis. Kravitz had said that the NFL was investigating New England's possible use of deflated footballs.

"I think I've heard it all at this point," Brady replied, forcing a nervous laugh.

He was about to hear more. Within days, Deflategate had been named and had exploded into an international story.

Two forces were at work. One was the dark potency of the feel and air pressure of footballs to shape Brady's psyche. Nothing—not frenzied crowds, not elaborate blitzes, not mediocre surrounding casts—seemed to affect Brady's confidence like the basic grip of a football. He wasn't alone. The controversy brought to light the eccentric craft and subculture of game-ball preparation. Eli Manning preferred his footballs brushed for 45 minutes, waterlogged, brushed again, scrubbed against a spinning mechanical wheel—the entire process repeated *three times* before each game—and stored in a separate trunk so that nobody could touch them. NFL quarterbacks Matt Leinart and Jeff Blake stated publicly that "every team" tampers with footballs, with Blake adding that the balls are often deflated. Aaron Rodgers admitted within days of the AFC Championship Game that he preferred *overinflated* footballs and often filled them up past the permissible 13.5 psi, just to see if he could get away with it.

But the other force was so powerful that it was beyond the control of the league's most powerful team: payback. The widespread perception that Roger Goodell had given the Patriots a break on Spygate, followed by the league's stonewalling of Arlen Specter's investigation, shaped owners' expectations of how this new matter, though laughable on its face, needed to be handled. The day after the AFC Championship Game, an influential owner called Goodell, demanding that the league outsource the investigation, a sentiment shared by many colleagues. The sins of Spygate—the expediency of the investigation and the destruction of evidence—would not be tolerated this time around. Four days after the story broke, the league announced that Ted Wells, a veteran white-collar lawyer in New York whom the league had dispatched years earlier in a Miami Dolphins bullying investigation, would join Jeff Pash in leading the Deflategate inquiry.

It was, one owner later said, time for "a makeup call."

IF SPYGATE SERVED AS a unifying mechanism for the franchise, with the Patriots—especially Tom Brady—unequivocally backing Bill Belichick, then Deflategate widened small but preexisting divides. That inexorable process began the morning after the Colts game, when Robert Kraft spoke with Brady and Belichick. Both men professed to have no knowledge of a scheme to deflate footballs. Kraft made clear to Brady that if he had done something wrong, he should just admit it. Brady was adamant that nobody deflated footballs under his orders.

"I have nothing to hide," he told people in the building.

Belichick was angry, not only because he doubted the quarterback's denials, and not only because it was a massive distraction before the Super Bowl, but because his legacy was at risk. He knew that some Hall of Fame voters planned to raise Spygate, effectively as an asterisk, on the inevitable day when his name came up. Coaches of other teams often pointed out privately that the Patriots hadn't won a Super Bowl since being caught illegally taping signals. To be remembered as he deserved—as one of the game's greatest coaches, at the very least—Belichick couldn't afford another cheating scandal, no matter how small. Moles throughout the building kept Belichick informed of the behavior of coaches and staff. If any act suggested or came close to a violation, he smothered it, even shutting down NCAA tournament pools among the staff.

Ten days before the Super Bowl, Belichick addressed Deflategate publicly, proclaiming himself eager to distance his name from all allegations. He pledged to cooperate with the investigation and vowed that all Patriots footballs now would be inflated past 12.5 psi to account for deflation that might occur over the course of the game—a hint that he thought New England's footballs had shrunk due to the weather during the game and not McNally's discreet needle. This could have been received as a partial defense of Brady, if Belichick hadn't then made it resoundingly clear that Brady owed everyone an explanation. "Tom's personal preference on his footballs are something he can talk about in much better detail and information than I could possibly provide."

Brady's family and friends were furious. Although Brady had privately complained about Belichick over the years—his merciless personnel decisions, his hard coaching, his unaccountable moodiness—he had never cracked publicly. Not even close. He had responded to Spygate by serving as Belichick's chief defender, calling him the greatest coach in history. After Belichick's press conference, Brady's friend and former de facto manager, Will McDonough, emailed Brady and said, "Belichick has really dropped this in your lap just now. Don't take this lightly."

Later that day, in sweats and a Patriots pom-pom stocking hat, Brady strode to the podium. His right eye was still bloodshot from the poke during the Ravens game. "Hey guys, how ya doing?" he said. Fielding 61 questions, Brady's made an unconvincing effort to clear his name on live television. The second question cut to the heart of the matter: "So, can you answer right now," a reporter asked, "is Tom Brady a cheater?"

"I don't believe so," Brady said.

It was the enduring sound bite of the press conference, used against him as the response of a guilty man. Brady later told friends that what tripped him up in answering wasn't the alleged cheating with footballs, but some of the proven cheating over the years run by Bill Belichick. Brady had unrepentantly benefited from Spygate and some of New England's other illicit activities. He had once bragged to a former Jets assistant coach that the Patriots "may or may not have had possession" of a few Jets playbooks. But the damage was done. A few days after Brady's press conference, *Saturday Night Live* mocked it. On the Monday before the Super Bowl, Belichick forcefully defended himself, his program—

and, this time, his quarterback. He had administered an in-house study that indicated that any loss of air pressure in footballs was likely due to weather, backing up his suggestion from the previous week. "I'm embarrassed to talk about the amount of time that I put into this relative to the other important challenges in front of us," Belichick said.

Two days later, when New England landed in Phoenix, Robert Kraft tried to take the burden off his team and place it onto himself, declaring that he expected an apology from the NFL if the Wells investigation cleared his team. Between Kraft, Belichick, and Brady, New England's holy trinity of victimhood galled some league executives and team owners, to say nothing of coaches who believed that the Patriots were serial cheaters. Goodell and Kraft were so close—and Kraft so influential—that some owners called him the "assistant commissioner," a nickname that embarrassed Kraft because it wasn't how he wanted to be perceived. Kraft had stood by Goodell during the roughest patch of his tenure earlier that fall, when the commissioner mishandled the punishment of Ray Rice, a star running back for the Baltimore Ravens, for domestic violence. After Rice had knocked his future wife, Janay, unconscious in the elevator of an Atlantic City hotel, Goodell initially suspended him for a mere two games. He increased it to an indefinite suspension only after TMZ obtained and published video of the incident. Goodell insisted that Rice had been ambiguous as to whether he had hit Janay, but an ESPN report from Don Van Natta and Kevin Van Valkenburg cast severe doubt on that claim, making it clear that Rice was honest with Goodell about striking her. Fans and protesters called for Goodell to resign. It was a disaster for the league, externally and internally. One woman who worked for the NFL told friends she worked at a nonprofit—which was technically true, given the league's tax status at the time—out of embarrassment.

Kraft publicly supported Goodell, saying he had been "excellent" on Rice, though he confided in friends that Goodell was "on very thin ice." He was irate at some of the league staff, especially Pash. "Roger's people don't have a fucking clue as to what they are doing," Kraft told a friend.

Those people were now after Kraft's fifth son. Brady spent the days before the team left for Arizona angry and surprised at how the story had taken on a life of its own, remarking to a friend, "This is the stupidest thing." For years, Brady had tried to maintain a casual and unbothered veneer when it came to what people said about him. He had read a self-help book called *The Four Agreements*, and one of its tenets was to not take anything personally. He certainly made an effort; Brady referenced that phrase so often, it felt like a survival mechanism. With Deflate-gate, he relied on his usual array of family and friends, as well as Greg Harden and a more recent addition to his inner circle: Jack Easterby, who believed that blind rage at the world—the clichéd us-against-them mentality—could only take a person so far. It was a negative emotion Belichick not only fostered, but occasionally manufactured. Easterby felt it was dangerous to constantly live in reaction to others. That idea appealed to Brady, who always preferred to look inward first—and was also starting to grow tired of waiting for Belichick to give him more than a cursory compliment. Easterby's words jump-started Brady's instinct to turn negatives into positives. "Everyone will say, 'God, it's been a tough week for you,'" Brady said in a radio interview before the Super Bowl. "But it's been a great week for me, to really be able to recali-brate the things that are important in my life and understand the people that support me and love me and care about me."

His mind clear, or at least clearer, Brady returned to work. He watched the NFC Championship Game between the Seahawks and Packers three times, New England's 2012 loss to Seattle three times, and a Seahawks–Cowboys game from the 2014 season a few times. Seattle's defense, led by its Legion of Boom secondary and talented pass rusher Michael Ben-nett, was already historically dominant. In the regular season, it allowed the fewest points, fewest yards, and second-fewest touchdown passes in the NFL. If the Seahawks could knock off Peyton Manning and Tom Brady in consecutive years, they would not only flirt with dynastyhood but would have a claim to possessing the greatest defense ever.

The day of the game, Brady arrived at University of Phoenix Stadium in Glendale and set up his locker. He texted his old friend and teammate Rodney Harrison, who had retired after the 2008 season: "I'm ready to play the biggest game of my life." Brady held handwritten reminders. *More on toes . . . Stay behind the ball . . . Loose torso.* Finally, he hung pictures of his wife and children at the beach and a handwritten sign, with three painted handprints from each of his kids: *Go Patriots, We Love You, Daddy.*

31

MALCOLM, GO!

T OM BRADY FIDGETED IN THE POCKET. IT WAS THIRD and six from the Seattle 10-yard line, late in the first quarter of a scoreless Super Bowl on February 1, 2015. So far, Brady had diced up the Seahawks with short and quick passes. He was fourth in the league in 2014 in the unofficial statistic of getting rid of the ball fast, at an average of 2.3 seconds between snap and throw, and in the week leading up to the game, Seahawks coaches blew practice plays dead if the pass rush failed to reach the quarterback within that time. But on this play, Brady got the ball and danced nervously in the pocket. Michael Bennett closed in on him. Brady spotted Julian Edelman in the back of the end zone, open by the length of a brick, and thought, *Yes, yes, yes.* But as he threw, he saw Jeremy Lane, Seattle's nickel cornerback, stationed at the goal line. *No!* The ball sailed off Brady's fingertips, and Lane intercepted it in the end zone. Lane decided to run it out—a decision that changed the game. Edelman knocked him out of bounds, and Lane landed on his wrist, shattering his arm.

Seattle players cheered—and then stopped, realizing that Lane was down. Brady was raging at himself. For the second straight Super Bowl, he had made an early mistake that cost his team points. But Josh McDaniels was expert at jarring Brady out of a spiraling frustration, getting him back to firing "no-fear throws," as he often said. This time, it was easy.

"Lane is out of the game," McDaniels told Brady.

Brady perked up. Tharold Simon, a second-year backup, was now Seattle's nickelback, and in New England's crosshairs. "We tried to take advantage of it as much as we could," McDaniels recalled. Brady burned Simon twice on the next drive, including an 11-yard touchdown pass to Brandon LaFell to put New England up 7–0. The Patriots were in control of the game throughout the first half, but the Seahawks were too talented to contain. Seattle took the lead, 17–14, in the third quarter. Brady soon needed another reset. All-Pro Seahawks linebacker Bobby Wagner read his eyes on a short throw over the middle to Rob Gronkowski and snared the ball. Six plays later, Russell Wilson threw a touchdown pass to put Seattle up 24–14 with just more than a quarter left.

From the start of his career, Brady had displayed a gift exclusive to the truly great quarterbacks: he had a way of single-handedly shifting momentum, bending a game to his will when everything was going against him and his team. New England had planned to keep Seattle's defense off balance by running the ball 30 to 35 times in the game. That goal was now out the window: it was all on Brady. Bill Belichick huddled in front of his quarterback, trying to remind him that, even though Seattle had scored 17 straight points, football was a simple game and Seattle was a simple team. "The chances of them playing three good defensive plays in a row aren't very good," he said. Nobody in NFL history refused to concede the future like Belichick and Brady, a shared belief in the limitless possibilities of their preparation, their talents, and the next play.

Brady walked down the sideline and clapped at his teammates. "It's our time! Hey, we've been through worse situations than this!"

But soon, it was third and 14. Brady dropped back to pass and climbed the pocket with a clean view downfield. Nobody was open. Edelman crossed the middle with Simon trailing, Brady's last and only option. It was a dangerous throw. Kam Chancellor, Seattle's hulking safety, was patrolling the middle of the field and tracking Brady's eyes. Brady looked at Edelman, glanced at Chancellor to force a split second of hesitation and buy six inches of space, and hit Edelman in an opening the size of a mailbox. Chancellor launched himself at Edelman, leveling the receiver high and hard, helmet to helmet, a collision that seemed destined to bring a stop to the game and each team to bended knee as Edelman lay motionless before leaving the game immobilized on a board . . .

But Edelman not only hung on to the ball, not only kept his feet—

disoriented and wobbly, as if he had just gotten off a cheap amusement park ride—but he had enough presence and determination to scurry upfield before falling down like an unwinding top.

Edelman tried to stand up and nearly tipped over. The NFL was in the head-injury era, an age that may not end until the NFL itself does. As writer Tom Junod put it, the moment was "ushered in by a combination of athleticism unfolding at the edge of human capability, the expanding authority of neuroscience, and the horror stories of middle-aged football heroes descending into depression, dementia, and derangement." In 2013, the league had settled a lawsuit brought by more than 4,500 former players for $765 million. Vowing to make the game safer, it instituted a series of in-game protocols to test for head injuries. Seattle had lost one of its leaders, linebacker Cliff Avril, to a concussion earlier in the game. Now it seemed New England would, too. But Edelman not only stayed in the game, he converted another third down later in the drive. After the game, the Associated Press reported that he had gone through the concussion protocol and passed, which prompted an eye roll from many in the media and beyond.

Six plays later, Brady threw a short touchdown pass to Danny Amendola, cutting the lead to 24–21. Seattle then went three-and-out. For the past decade, Belichick's defense had struggled to get the vital stop in the key moment. Now it had succeeded. Brady had another chance.

"We need a big championship drive!" Brady told the team.

New England took over with 6:52 left. Brady hit three short passes. On second and 11, Gronkowski lined up opposite Chancellor and caught a pass for 20 yards. Now in his fifth year, the 6-foot-6, 265-pound tight end had not only become the game's biggest pass-catching mismatch since Randy Moss and the second-greatest offensive draft pick of Belichick's career, but he was a walking body shot, a welcome antidote to New England's patented dehumanization and standardization of its players. Every week in the off-season, it seemed, there was a viral clip of Gronk dancing shirtless on South Beach. During his visit with the Patriots before the 2010 draft, Gronk had fallen asleep on the floor of the meeting room. "He didn't make a very good impression," Belichick recalled. But what Gronk lacked in curiosity and reflection, he made up for in testosterone and brute force and raw likability. Gronk once called up Brady and asked him to throw a day before the tight end was due for a *GQ* cover shoot. He was worried he didn't look sufficiently muscled. Brady met him the next day, and they played catch for an hour in the rain on a baseball field. Brady threw 60 passes; none hit the ground. "Dude," Gronk said afterward, "that was great, that was perfect, that was just what I needed. I feel ripped now!"

Seattle couldn't cover Gronk—or anyone else, all of a sudden. Brady was picking the Seahawks apart with short and sharp throws, accumulating yards and reshaping the game. At one point, Bobby Wagner turned to safety Earl Thomas and said, "We'll be considered the best D, bro. We got to stop them now." But Seattle couldn't stop them. From Seattle's three-yard line, Brady threw an out route to Edelman, who had darted inside, pivoted outside, gotten away with pushing off Simon, and caught a touchdown. It was 28–24 New England with 2:06 left. On his last two drives, Brady had connected on 13 of 15 passes for two touchdowns. It was the greatest quarter of his life. And for the third time in a row in the Super Bowl, Brady walked off the field late in the fourth quarter having provided his defense with a lead to protect.

RUSSELL WILSON WAS a young quarterback ready to take over the league, his rise nearly as unlikely as Tom Brady's. He was only 5-foot-11, normally a deal killer for a quarterback with NFL aspirations. Seattle general manager John Schneider preferred tall quarterbacks, but in 2012, after Wilson had led Wisconsin to a Rose Bowl win, something about Wilson's rigorous self-belief intrigued him. "Obviously we are really interested in passers with better height, but this guy may just be the exception to the rule," Schneider's scouting report read. "He has the 'it' factor." Schneider drafted Wilson in the third round in 2012, and by the season opener, Wilson had won the starting job. He led the Seahawks to the playoffs in his first year, a championship in his second, and now, with 11 career fourth quarter or overtime game-winning drives in only 48 starts, he seemed destined to establish a dynasty.

With 80 yards to go and 2:02 left, Wilson began Seattle's drive by completing a pass to superstar running back Marshawn Lynch, irrepressible in the second half, out of the backfield for 31 yards. Four plays later, Wilson launched a deep pass down the right sideline for wide receiver Jermaine Kearse, who was covered by an undrafted rookie out of West Alabama named Malcolm Butler. The two had battled in the third quarter, when Butler broke up a fade route in Kearse's arms—an overlooked key play, in the eyes of New England's coaches. If Kearse had caught it, Seattle would have been in field goal range already up ten, with a chance to build an insurmountable lead.

Butler and Kearse went vertical for Wilson's vertical ball. Falling backward, Butler tipped the pass, taking Kearse down with him. Kearse landed on his back—and looked up to see that the ball had miraculously landed on him, bouncing off his leg and into his lap. It was a catch. Kearse rolled over to get to his feet, thinking touchdown. Butler recovered just in time to push him out of bounds at the New England five-yard line.

Even by the standards of New England's Super Bowl opposition— David Tyree and Mario Manningham—this was breathtaking. Nobody could believe it.

"Did he catch it?" Belichick asked from across the field.

Brady stared at the replay screen, hands on his hips and shaking his head, as if to say, *You kidding me?* Up in the owner's suite, Robert Kraft blurted, "We have no fucking luck." Butler sulked to the bench, unhooking his chinstrap in anger, thinking he had cost his team a championship.

Brady sat next to McDaniels, looking lost. "Man. . . ."

On the next play, Wilson handed off to Lynch, who ran left through a gaping hole. New England's coaches in the box upstairs, with their clear view of the action, thought Lynch was going to score, but linebacker Dont'a Hightower slipped his block and dove at Lynch, clipping the running back's ankles with his shoulder. Lynch landed at the one-yard line. The clock showed 55 seconds left and was running, a dire situation that set up the defining decision and play call of Bill Belichick's career.

A LIFETIME OF thinking and work and study had led Belichick to this moment. Matt Patricia, New England's defensive coordinator, looked at Belichick, expecting him to call time-out, to stop the clock and give the Patriots some kind of chance to respond if Seattle scored. But Belichick didn't call time-out. He didn't even talk to his coaches. He was staring across the field at Pete Carroll and the Seattle Seahawks' sideline, watching what they would do next.

Seconds passed. The Patriots coaches were starting to panic. Patricia said to Belichick, "Do you want the time-out?"

Belichick said nothing, his focus resolute.

"Bill," said linebackers coach Patrick Graham over the headset, "they're wondering about a time-out."

"Yeah," Belichick said calmly, tugging on the collar of his navy hoodie. "I got it."

The other sideline was even more confused. Belichick's patience—his gift for allowing situations to play out—had undone Seattle. Carroll expected Belichick to call a time-out, but when he didn't, Seattle's players and coaches were left to scramble. Belichick watched the chaos unfold on the other side and felt New England now had an edge. If he had been considering a time-out before, he definitely was not going to call one now. "I wasn't going to let them off the hook," he later said. An entire subgenre of football strategy and debate—when and why to use time-outs—was playing out on international television. Seattle had one left, and if Carroll used it, his options would be limited. The Seahawks could no longer run the ball, because if they failed to reach the end zone, the clock would continue to tick down and there might not be time to call two more plays. Carroll wanted to maximize his scoring chances, his play options, and preserve the time-out. So, he sent out three receivers. Belichick saw the personnel group running out onto the field, and, after seconds of quiet, finally gave a command.

"Goal line," he said.

"Goal line" meant Goal Line 3, with three cornerbacks to match up against Seattle's three receivers. Belichick had spent the entire off-season prior to the 2014 season designing a goal-line defense with three cornerbacks and no safeties, matching speed with speed. New England hadn't called it once in the regular season or playoffs until now.

On the headset, Patriots cornerbacks coach Josh Boyer told safeties coach Brian Flores, "Flo, send Malcolm!"

Flores turned to Butler. "Malcolm, go!"

Butler sprinted onto the field, praying for another chance. Seattle sent two receivers to the right, side by side: Kearse inside and Ricardo Lockette offset outside. Kearse was Butler's man. But Patriots cornerback Brandon Browner, a former Seahawk, read the alignment and knew what was coming: it was a pick play, where one receiver screens a defender, creating just enough space for the second receiver to get open. New England had practiced against this exact route combination on the Friday before the game, working off a play card that Ernie Adams had prepared called 14 Raffle Utah. In practice, Butler had screwed up, following the receiver rather than racing to where the ball would be thrown. The teaching point from the coaches was clear: Butler had no time to think. Just go.

Seconds before the play, Browner switched assignments, taking Kearse and giving Lockette to Butler. Browner, a bruiser, figured he could better jam Kearse, allowing Butler to blow up the play. It was a staggering level of preparation and trust and confidence, all coming together in a matter of seconds in the most important moment in the careers of the players and many of the coaches involved.

Twenty-six seconds remained. Both Belichick and Carroll crouched over, hands at their knees. Wilson got the ball in the shotgun and quickly fired right to Lockette, who appeared open. *Touchdown, second ring, here we go*, Wilson thought. But Browner drilled Kearse, stopping him in his tracks. If Kearse had done his job, Lockette would have walked into the end zone. Instead, Butler jumped the route like nobody had done in Super Bowl history. "My instincts were really on that night," he later said. He collided with Lockette at the goal line and caught the ball, so fast that it was hard to process.

Carroll dropped his head and screamed. "Oh no!"

Belichick raised his right arm and yelled, "Yes!"

New England's bench erupted. Brady leapt up and down, knees at his chest, screaming and hugging McDaniels. "We did it, Josh!"

Wilson walked to the sidelines in shock. "I thought it was a touchdown," he said to offensive coordinator Darrell Bevell. "He had him. I don't know. I don't know. I don't know what happened. It was there."

Brady took two more snaps and knelt each time, running out the clock. He had won his fourth Super Bowl and his third MVP award, both matching Joe Montana. Moments before he took the stage to accept the trophy, Brady found Butler.

"Malcolm!" he yelled, wrapping him in a hug. "Are you kidding me?"

TWENTY YARDS AWAY, Brady's parents and sisters arrived on the field, covered in confetti. Tom Sr. wore a navy hat that read Team Brady and leaned against a red Chevy Colorado that his son had won as MVP—Brady would give it to Butler—and seemed on the verge of tears, his pent-up Deflategate anger palpable. "He is all class," Brady Sr. said. "For people to question his integrity . . ."

There is no rage like that of a parent who believes their child has been wronged. Tom Sr. stood on the field after a championship ten years in the making, and looked more eager to lash out against every real and perceived critic of his son than to celebrate. It had been a long two weeks, defined by accusations about deflated footballs and commentary suggesting that his namesake, his only son, was a cheater, and now Tom Sr. was ready to pop. Who knew what he was about to say? Just then, his son appeared on stage to accept the Lombardi Trophy. The family wanted to watch. Tom Sr. bit his lip, saved by his own silence.

IT WAS ALMOST 2 A.M. when Tom Brady made the final rounds at his private postgame party. The crowd had thinned out. Bündchen had left, her first party with her husband as a champion. So had Brady's parents. So had Guerrero. Only a dozen or so people remained, mostly former teammates. Brady was at the center of what was called the Buzzard Room of the team hotel, with the larger party raging across the hall to the music of Darius Rucker. It was quiet and the light was low. It felt like cocktail hour. Brady was in a gray sweater and white championship hat, standing next to Robert Kraft, circled by Troy Brown, Deion Branch, Donté Stallworth, and other longtime friends.

They didn't want the night to end. Kraft and Brady had traveled this road before and knew how the next morning would start to whittle away at the joy, even in normal times. But the sun would rise in a few hours, and with it not only a new literal day, but a new kind of day, a new kind of future, where the architects of America's greatest sports dynasty would battle against the NFL—and each other. The Lombardi Trophy stood on a nearby table, dulled by fingerprints. Brady ambled about, posing for pictures, holding up four fingers for four Super Bowls, holding his smile an extra beat when the flash failed. He saw Jay Feely, a former NFL kicker who had played with Brady at Michigan.

"Your ego," Feely said, raising his hand above his head, "is going to be back up here now."

"Awesome," Brady said. "It's awesome."

A few minutes later, Brady ducked out a back door and walked through a dimly lit courtyard, checking his phone. He kept going until all you could see of him was a silhouette lit by the touch screen, and then he faded into darkness, trying to keep tomorrow at bay just a little bit longer.

PART III

FEARED AGAIN

2015–2020

32

I HAD TO DO IT
FOR THE FANS

THE MAKEUP CALL BRIEFLY FADED FROM PUBLIC CON-sciousness. In the months after the Super Bowl victory over the Seahawks, Tom Brady skied in Montana, cliff-dived in Costa Rica, and played three-on-three basketball in the Bahamas on the same team as Michael Jordan. Both men were at Baker's Bay Golf and Ocean Club for a wedding. A crowd gathered to watch the two legends. Jordan and Brady had been friends for years. In 2004, they attended the same Kentucky Derby party. Jordan was sitting on a couch. Celebrities approached to shake his hand, but he stayed seated, giving the distinct impression that he preferred to be alone with his friends. But when Brady walked by, Jordan rose, eager to chat. Jordan seemed to recognize an element of himself in Brady. Jordan had played basketball off and on until age 40—and if not for his body breaking down, he would have kept going. In retirement, he traveled the world and increased his fortune and bought the Charlotte Bobcats, but life was empty without being able to do what he loved most. Golf was no fix. Neither were card games with friends, nor lavish vacations. The fire inside wouldn't go out. Few understood. It wasn't *meant* to be understood. Months before his 50th birthday, Jordan told Wright Thompson of *ESPN The Magazine*, "Man, I wish I was playing right now. I would give up everything now to go back and play the game of basketball."

"How do you replace it?" Thompson asked.

"You don't. You learn to live with it."

"How?"

"It's a process."

Brady wanted to stave off that process for as long as possible. He kept pushing the endpoint out. First, it was playing until age 40. Then into his 40s. Now it was 45, and he was leaving the door open to play longer. Aside from brief trips—even *during* brief trips—there was no off-season anymore. Within hours of the Super Bowl, Brady was grinding with Alex Guerrero, needing the rush of daily improvement. It was starting to put additional strain on his family. As Bündchen sacrificed for him—retiring from the runway in April 2015 and moving to Boston full time during the season, a global icon in a big-little city—Brady sacrificed even more for *himself.* It had been a running joke for years that Guerrero had his hands on Brady's body more than Bündchen did. It seemed less funny now. Brady was aware of the toll of his job, but he had watched Jordan and Joe Montana and John Elway and Steve Young and Dan Marino walk away from the game not because they lost their drive, but because their bodies proved mortal. For Brady, the ambition was simple: if he took care of himself, if he committed to the daily discipline, he could avoid their fate. He had just won a Super Bowl at age 37, and he felt like he was just getting started.

One day in the Bahamas, during a round of golf, Brady talked junk to Jordan, who was more competitive on the course than anyone, including even him.

"Come back to me when you've got six championships," Jordan said.

ON MAY 6, 2015, more than a hundred days after his inquiry began and at a cost of at least $2.5 million, Ted Wells released a 243-page report about the New England Patriots' use of deflated footballs. Applying the league's relaxed evidentiary standards after Spygate, Wells found that it was "more probable than not" that Tom Brady was "at least generally aware" of a scheme to illegally deflate footballs. Wells interviewed 66 people, obtained the salty text messages between John Jastremski and Jim "The Deflator" McNally, and watched surveillance footage of McNally disappearing into the bathroom for 100 seconds. Unlike Spygate, Roger Goodell waited until after the investigation was completed to decide on a punishment. Although Bill Belichick was cleared in the Wells investigation, New England—as a repeat offender—was fined $1 million and docked two draft picks. Tom Brady was suspended for the first four games of the 2015 season without pay. For the second time in less than a decade, the league had dropped the hammer on the New England Patriots.

Robert and Jonathan Kraft knew the verdict was shaped by Spygate, but still viewed the Wells investigation as a witch hunt fueled by resentful owners and coaches who whined about supposed cheating to justify their own mediocrity. Ever the power broker, Kraft arrived at the annual league spring meeting in San Francisco two weeks after the report was issued and tried to walk a fine line. Privately, he visited with Goodell, laughing with and hugging the commissioner—while publicly threatening legal action against the league. Kraft wondered if, after all of Goodell's public debacles, from the Saints' Bountygate to Ray Rice, there might be momentum among owners to challenge his unilateral authority to impose discipline. It went nowhere. John Mara, Jerry Jones, and Stephen Ross of the Miami Dolphins, among others, stood in solidarity with the commissioner.

"We're not there with you on this," Mara told Kraft. "Something has to happen. The commissioner has to do his job."

Those words "rocked" Kraft, a friend of his later said. But he got the message. On May 19, as the meetings drew to a close, Kraft gave a press conference broadcast live on ESPN and said he would "accept, reluctantly" the punishment. "We won't appeal," Kraft said.

Tom Brady watched the press conference at home. He was now alone against the NFL—and he knew it. He dialed DeMaurice Smith's number. "What the fuck?" Brady yelled. "Why am I not getting the support I deserve on this thing?"

In truth, the Patriots had attacked an unprecedented investigation with unprecedented ferocity. Belichick, after initially dropping the crisis into Brady's lap, had backed him in every venue since, even after the Super Bowl, when he was asked to do a few NFL-related apparences and replied, "Fuck the league," and on *The Late Show with David Letterman*. He privately thanked a few journalists whose coverage sided with Brady. Days after the Wells Report was released, the Patriots published a massive rebuttal titled *The Wells Report in Context*, an ill-advised brief in an already ridiculous scandal. Some high-level Patriots employees warned Kraft against making it public, believing it was an easy target for mockery—the document claimed that McNally was nicknamed "The Deflator" due to weight loss—and would undermine Brady's attempts to clear his name. But that was the fundamental problem: several people in the organization believed there was merit to the allegations, regardless of the absurdity of the case. Years earlier, in a WEEI interview, Brady had stated preference for a "deflated ball." Few inside the building felt that Brady had explicitly ordered the equipment managers to illegally lower the air pressure of footballs. But then, Brady also didn't need to. Jastremski and McNally might do whatever it took to please an icon. And, while the Patriots had pledged to cooperate fully with Wells, Robyn Glaser, New England's club counsel, had prepped both Jastremski and McNally for their meetings with the investigator—and the team declined to make McNally available for a follow-up interview. After the Wells Report was released, the team suspended the two ball boys, and, within the next year, quietly parted ways with them. Belichick reorganized the equipment department to ensure ethical compliance.

Brady still felt burned. His family started to refer to the owner as "Benedict Kraft." But Brady did what he always did: he compartmentalized, no matter how complicated it got. At the Patriots' ring ceremony a few weeks after Kraft had accepted the punishment, Kraft and Brady found a quiet moment as if the entire mess had never existed.

"We're lucky," Kraft said.

"I know, we sure are," Brady replied.

"And I'm lucky to have you in my life."

"I feel the same way. I love you so much."

Kraft hoped that accepting the penalties would encourage Goodell to settle with Brady, as that was the way business was often done in the NFL. Like the Patriots' rebuttal, although to a lesser degree, the Wells Report had become an embarrassment for the league, picked apart for its use of flawed science, lack of basic understanding of the ideal gas law, and criticized for its author's questionable independence. Tom Brady Sr. called it "Framegate." Goodell wanted to find a way out. He didn't look forward to a prolonged public fight with the game's biggest star over deflated footballs. But Brady had no intention of settling. Backed by the NFLPA, he had scheduled an appeal hearing at the league office, where he had agreed to testify under oath. The hashtag #FreeBrady went viral, but the entire spectacle was more evidence that the New England Patriots were willing to win something cosmically small in exchange for losing something cosmically big. Nobody would have cared about Deflategate in ten years. Tom Brady wanted to fight, all but ensuring that nobody would win.

THE CEILINGS WERE LOW. That's what stood out. When Brady and his legal team arrived at the NFL's Park Avenue offices on June 23, 2015, they were ushered to the basement, into a cramped and windowless conference room. Brady was hunched over, as if standing on an airplane. It felt like an intimidation tactic by the league. The NFL had recently renovated its posh sixth floor, which had a beautiful conference room furnished with a giant football-shaped table and windows looking out on the city. Why not hold the meeting there? The league saw it as a practical matter. Its basement conference room was its biggest—and most private. Goodell opened the meeting with a short speech, then a renowned sports litigator named Jeffrey Kessler launched into a defense of Brady. Kessler had battled the NFL many times over the years, with moderate success. He had represented Bill Belichick during his failed attempt to break his Jets contract in 2000.

Kessler introduced his client by asking him how many Super Bowls he'd won.

"Four," Brady said.

"Okay. Has anybody won any more?"

"Same, Montana."

It was the peak of the hearing for Brady. For the third time—the first during his January press conference, and the second during a discussion in May at Salem State University with his friend, famed broadcaster Jim Gray, when his only reaction to the Wells Report was that he had "not had much time to digest it"—Brady revealed himself to be an ineffective defendant, at least in the eyes of the commissioner. Brady insisted he had never thought about air pressure in footballs during his career, but then Goodell noticed how the quarterback discussed in detail how he made sure the refs saw a sheet of paper with the rules highlighted after the Jets game. Brady denied any knowledge of a scheme to tamper with footballs, but admitted that neither Jastremski nor McNally would have altered them without his approval. He claimed to have not known McNally's name prior to all of the allegations. The frequency of Brady's communication with both Jastremski and McNally had skyrocketed in the hours and days after Deflategate broke, but he stated that he couldn't remember what specifically was discussed, aside from ball preparation for the Super Bowl. Goodell found that especially suspicious. Brady had no answer for their "fuck Tom" text exchanges, declining to try to explain other people's words. Topping it off, he had failed to provide phone records to Wells's team—an early decision, made by Brady's longtime agent, Don Yee, with which the union disagreed—and a new piece of information was revealed at the hearing: Brady had ordered his assistant to destroy his cell phone shortly before his interview with Wells. Goodell believed that Brady had both lied during the appeal and not cooperated with the investigation, and he didn't buy Brady's excuse that the quarterback periodically cycled through phones. In a 20-page letter a month after the hearing, Goodell upheld the four-game suspension.

Smith immediately filed a petition in federal court to vacate the suspension. But now, the union was playing on the league's turf. From a legal standpoint, Brady's guilt or innocence didn't matter. The only thing that mattered was whether Goodell had adhered to the CBA. Goodell had wide authority under Article 46 to levy punishment—an authority Smith had collectively bargained. The union won the first round: in a decision that overturned the suspension and allowed Brady to play in 2015, judge Richard M. Berman concluded that Goodell had "dispensed his own brand of industrial justice." But the union was destined to fail. "We always lose in the first court, because those people are politicians," Pash told league executives about the Berman decision. "We always win on appeal, because those judges aren't."

A toxic situation got worse. Kraft held a press conference before training camp, apologizing to the team and to fans for accepting the punishment in the hope of a settlement. "I was wrong to put my faith in the league," he said, adding that it was "incomprehensible to me that the league continues to take steps to disparage one of its all-time great players." The league-wide blowback was fierce. Several owners and league executives told Kraft he had gone too far. "I had to do it for the fans," Kraft replied. But for one of the most powerful owners to launch a prolonged war against the league was bad for business, executives and owners felt. One day at the league offices, Kraft was standing outside of Goodell's office when Pash walked by. Kraft didn't even acknowledge him. He spoke more often, and more frankly, with Smith than he did with many of his colleagues. One night, Kraft held a dinner in Boston with a few other owners, and began the night by thanking them for showing up. "I don't have many friends left," Kraft said.

Donald Trump, who in the summer of 2015 had launched his bid for the White House, told Kraft, "Bob, you should have never made the deal."

"I had a wink from the commissioner," Kraft replied.

"Bob, when you make a deal, you should have gotten it all wrapped up."

Goodell kept pushing to settle. So did Kraft. But now that Brady could play in 2015, he had no intention of backing down. It baffled league executives. Many of them had spent time around politicians, who shape-shifted and changed positions easily and without a second thought. Brady was so driven, so insulated, so praised and insecure, that the story of innocence he told himself—like the story of being unwanted out of high school—he now believed to his core, as league executives saw it. The mentality that sustained him on Sundays sustained him against his own employer. The league office was overmatched, regardless of evidence. Goodell was fighting with the league's best player over air pressure in footballs, the most farcical scandal in sports history. But like Brady, Goodell wouldn't back down—not after the quarterback had destroyed his cell phone. One day, a league executtive, worried about the long-term damage to the NFL's brand, stopped by the office of another executive who was one of Goodell's closest advisors. "You've gotta get him to stop," the executive said.

"You don't know the guy very well," the other executive replied.

33

HOW DID YOU GET
BLOOD ON THERE?

A S DEFLATEGATE WAS STILL ONGOING AND WITH
Brady's reputation tarnished, Bill Belichick participated in a
piece of legacy management. Shortly before the 2015 season,
on September 9, the NFL Network aired a documentary titled *Do Your
Job: Bill Belichick and the 2014 New England Patriots*. It was catnip for
Patriots fans and football obsessives, a fascinating examination of two
of the season's critical moments: the "Baltimore" formation and Malcolm Butler's interception. Once again, the specter of Spygate seemed to
hover over everything. Belichick detailed how he cleared the "Baltimore"
formation with the league office to ensure its legality—a discussion perhaps directed at John Harbaugh, the league's competition committee,
and every other football mind who thought he was underhanded. Ernie
Adams, who had rarely spoken publicly before or after his role in Spygate,
appeared and talked at length about all of the scouting and preparation
that went into Butler's interception. It was an hour-long victory lap for
the staff, and New England's players came off as they often felt: as faceless cogs in a grinding, militaristic machine whose primary attribute
was neither their superior ability nor intelligence, but blind obedience—
doing their job. The greatest quarter of football in Tom Brady's life was
barely mentioned. When Belichick insisted, at the end of the documentary, that the sport was a "player's game," it came off as perfunctory, even
though he meant it sincerely. A coach who wanted to be known in the
culture as indifferent to credit revealed himself as welcoming it.

On September 10, one night after it aired, New England's season
opener against the Pittsburgh Steelers began with the raising of a fourth

banner to the top of Gillette Stadium—and ended with another cheating controversy. Pittsburgh coach Mike Tomlin told the press after New England's 28–3 win that the Steelers' headsets had malfunctioned for most of the first quarter. His coach-to-coach dialogue had been replaced with audio from the Patriots Radio Network. "That's always the case" at Gillette Stadium, Tomlin said, visibly angry. The next morning, Belichick shot back that the Patriots' headsets often glitched out, too. The league backed up Belichick, explaining that the headset issue had occurred due to rain during the game. But the league and the Patriots had another challenge to address. Days before the game, Don Van Natta Jr. and I had published an 11,000-word story for ESPN titled "From Spygate to Deflategate: Inside What Split the NFL and Patriots Apart." We revealed that New England's illegal filming and cheating was far more extensive than previously known—and the league far more likely than previously thought to be complicit in a cover-up. On the same day, *Sports Illustrated* issued its own report on New England's cheating, which including revelations that ranged from the minor, but revealing (that Gillette Stadium often served opposing teams warm Gatorade during games) to the more serious (before the Super Bowl, multiple officials from other teams implored the Seattle Seahawks to hire extra security to guard their practices).

Perception is reality in the NFL, as in many—if not most—other fields of endeavor, and Belichick found himself between dueling narratives: one said he was football's smartest and most prepared coach; the other held that he would cross any line to win. Both were beyond Belichick's control and had been so for a long time. Neither needed his participation to exist or to persist. Belichick and Brady were fighting for the legitimacy of their accomplishments, against public headwinds and unforced errors. All they could do was prepare for the next game, and the redemptive power of another win.

BACK IN NOVEMBER of 2014, the day before the Patriots beat the Broncos, 43–21, in Foxborough, Tom Brady's friend Kevin Brady emailed him a *Grantland* story about how Peyton Manning and Brady had defied time and only improved with age.

"Thanks popa," Brady replied. "I've got another 7 or 8 years. He has 2. That's the final chapter. Game on."

For once, Brady overestimated Manning. The final chapter took place the following season, in the AFC Championship Game on January 24, 2016, in Denver. In 2015, Brady led the league with 36 touchdown passes. Only seven of his 624 attempts were intercepted—a 1.1 percent rate, the best in the league and second lowest of his career. Defenses were so scared of Rob Gronkowski downfield—he averaged 16.3 yards per catch in 2015, which would rise to an impossible-for-a-tight-end 21.6 in 2016—that they all but conceded the short passing game to Brady, which played right into his strengths, namely reading, reacting, and throwing quickly, stacking short passes that added up to devastation for the opponent. Working with Tom House and Alex Guerrero, Brady had quickened his release and improved his arm strength. He had perfected House's technique of rotating his shoulders 20 degrees past his hips, farther back than most quarterbacks. He now cocked his torso, turning his arm into a slingshot. It helped to increase his velocity by approximately four to six miles per hour, which allowed him to hold the ball an estimated seven-tenths of a second longer in the pocket.

Brady's brilliance on the field in 2015 was all the more remarkable given how taxing the year was, with Deflategate hovering over him and his patience for dealing with it—and the many aspects of his job outside of Sunday afternoons—running thin. In August, 40,000 pages of documents were unsealed as part of the ongoing litigation, allowing the public to feast on details of his private life, everything from how often he emailed Josh McDaniels to what color of pool cover he preferred. In September, he was asked to address tabloid reports of marital struggles. In November, *GQ* published a story in which Brady ended an interview with writer Chuck Klosterman after repeated Deflategate questions. Football, normally a respite, now felt "like brain surgery at times," he said. After Brady led a comeback to beat the Giants, a reporter asked if, during the game, his mind had flashed to the Super Bowl losses to New York. Brady stared away for ten seconds and flexed his jaw, as though trying to contain his irritation. "Nope," he finally said.

There were a few laughs along the way. On October 19, New England visited Indianapolis, seeking revenge against the instigators of Deflategate. Late in the third quarter, with the Patriots up 27–21, the Colts decided to unveil a new fake punt. They came out in a formation that featured backup receiver Griff Whalen over the ball as a center and punter Pat McAfee deep, as though for a normal punt. Backup safety Colt Anderson lined up under Waylen, like a quarterback, ready to take the snap—and the rest of the Colts players on the field, all eight of them, flanked to the right, near the sideline. It left Anderson with no one beyond Whalen to block for him once he got the ball. It was such a bizarre formation that, at first, the Patriots seemed confused by it, unprepared to handle something that made no logical sense. Five Patriots players lined up near Whalen and Anderson, and when the ball was snapped, dropped the latter for a loss. The Colts later blamed a miscommunication, but it came to be known as the dumbest play in modern NFL history. Colts coach Chuck Pagano had momentarily unraveled against Belichick, as had so many others over the years, and Belichick later hung a blowup photo of the Patriots defending that play in the facility as one of the year's highlights and for the occasional laugh.

The Patriots finished 12–4, an excellent record, but routine for them. In a long year, Brady seemed happiest after a 27–20 divisional-round win over the Kansas City Chiefs. He sat at his locker, shedding his game-day armor, as Jack and Benny—who were now eight and six; time had flown—played in front of him. The young man who once vowed to put off parenthood so that his rise to greatness would remain unimpeded now enjoyed having his kids at work with him. Brady and Guerrero often discussed how important that was, for the boys to have a template for finding and chasing a passion.

Jack saw a red gash on his father's ankle. "Dad, how did you get that blood on there?" he asked.

"Just from playing football, bud," Brady said.

Playing football continued the following week in Denver. By now, Peyton Manning was 39 years old, his mind sharp but his arm in decline. The 2015 season was easily his worst as a pro, with nine touchdown passes and 17 interceptions. Before the season, Manning had engaged in a contentious contract standoff with John Elway, who had been hired as the Broncos' general manager in 2011 and who had signed him in 2012. Elway wanted Manning to take a pay cut from $19 million to $10 million and thereby create salary-cap room to improve the team. Manning refused. It got ugly—Elway considered releasing him. During one meeting, Elway cut to Manning's core. "Do you want to be considered better than Brady?" he said. "Championships will be the tiebreaker." That helped resolve the matter. Manning agreed to a $14 million deal.

Belichick spent much of the week before the AFC Championship Game showing clips of Manning's limited throwing range to his team, while reminding them the quarterback could still trick them into mistakes. Which is exactly what the quarterback did. Manning played well in his final game against Brady and Belichick, throwing two first-half touchdown passes. Brady was under duress all afternoon from Broncos linebackers Von Miller and DeMarcus Ware. He threw two interceptions and took several hard hits, one of which led Denver players to believe he was concussed. Still, as always, Brady rallied. Down 20–12 late in the fourth quarter, Brady converted two fourth downs with astonishing passes to Gronkowski, who caught each ball between two defenders, the second in the end zone with 12 seconds left. It was now 20–18. On the two-point conversion, Brady rolled right—and had Gronkowski open toward the corner of the end zone. But Brady failed to see him, and he threw back across his body and the field to Edelman—late over the middle, the one throw quarterbacks are taught to never make. The ball was tipped and intercepted, sealing Denver's win.

On the field, Belichick fought through a mass of photographers to find Manning. They hugged, but before Belichick could go, Manning pulled him in.

"Hey, listen, this might be my last rodeo," Manning said. "So, it sure has been a pleasure."

Belichick leaned in to Manning's ear. "You are a great competitor," he responded.

A special era of football was over. The relationship between the Patriots and Manning was both competitive and symbiotic. During the 2011 lockout, Brady visited Manning for a few days of throwing sessions, where Manning detailed one of his favorite plays: a quick strike over the middle off a play-action fake. What made the play tough to defend was that the offensive line blocked for the run rather than the pass—a Counter Hot protection. The quarterback had no choice but to get rid of the ball quickly, but for Manning or Brady, that was an advantage, not an obstacle. When the season started, Brady told the coaches to insert the play for Rob Gronkowski. Brady later estimated that half of Gronk's Hall of Fame–level production derived from that one design.

Years after the lockout, in March of 2015, Peyton and Eli were at Augusta National Golf Club for two days, a chance to play a legendary course with a few friends. The Mannings decided to squeeze in an early morning workout before their round. At 6:30 a.m. they covertly hustled to the small gym off the par-3 course—each in a T-shirt and shorts, which isn't allowed at Augusta, even at the gym, where a golf shirt and long pants are required—and when they arrived in the tiny workout room, they saw a familiar face: Tom Brady.

Peyton and Eli knew that Brady was at Augusta. They'd seen him at dinner the night before. They didn't know that he'd be at the gym that morning—and that he would beat them by fifteen minutes. "Hey guys, what's going on?" Brady said.

Rory McIlroy was there, too, and he couldn't believe what he was witnessing. Three American sports legends, three members of a small and select quarterbacking fraternity, three rivals and friends, with seven total championships and counting, all mere feet from each other in this tight space. McIlroy had won four majors and was a future Hall of Famer in his own sport, but this felt too exclusive for him—he felt that he didn't belong—so he left. It was now just the three of them.

Brady's greeting was the only chatter. It was work, after all. There wasn't a lot of equipment to choose from: one treadmill, one elliptical, and a few dumbbells. "You had to be creative," Eli later said. The Mannings went straight to the treadmill and elliptical to work up a sweat, then did some step-ups with the barbells—all the while, they watched Brady out of the corners of their eyes, wondering what another elite athlete was up to, scouting the TB12 Method up close. Brady never touched the weights. He focused only on core workouts, using resistance bands. After about 30 minutes of silence except for the sounds of three superstars grunting in close proximity—"Almost on top of each other," Eli recalled—Brady left, waving on the way out. "See you guys on the course."

Out on the course, Peyton and Eli didn't discuss the half hour in the gym alongside Brady. Only years later did they think about how rare and precious it was that they were at the same property, over the same two-day span, and in the same weight room on the same morning. "What are the odds?" Eli later said. On the fairway, the Mannings hit the ball and played well. But they kept hearing a loud and sharp crash echoing through the trees, the sound a dumpster makes when a truck's lift places it on concrete after emptying it. The noise was unnerving in one of America's quaintest settings. "What if it's construction?" they wondered. The sound turned out to be McIlroy's driver—so powerful that it could be heard, and felt, hundreds of yards away. The quarterbacks were now on *his* turf, where *he* was a member of a small and select fraternity, and his club delivered that point home.

TWO WEEKS AFTER beating the Patriots, on February 7, 2016, Denver dominated the Carolina Panthers in Super Bowl L at Levi's Stadium in Santa Clara, California, sending Manning off with nearly every meaningful passing record—and as a champion for the second time.

Brady was on hand for the pregame festivities. He was roundly booed during a ceremony for past Super Bowl MVPs—the only living legend who received that treatment. When he returned to Boston, he installed a digital clock in his home workout room that would count down the time until the next Super Bowl. It was as if he'd put a piece of his psyche on the wall. Brady's suspension for Deflategate had been overturned by the initial court decision, but the NFL had appealed, and so it still loomed, due largely to Brady's own intransigence. He and DeMaurice Smith tried to negotiate a settlement with the league that would reverse the suspension, with Kraft in the middle. It was hard for the league to figure out what Brady wanted. He offered to pay a $1 million fine, but the league wanted more. Then, the league offered to waive Brady's suspension and absolve him of wrongdoing if he would state publicly that the two ball boys had illegally deflated the footballs without his knowledge. He refused, hating the optics of it all. In March, the Patriots and Brady announced a two-year contract extension, which the league believed was an attention-getting way to ease the pain of a fine and show defiance.

In April, a federal appeals court upheld the Deflategate suspension. In July, the US Court of Appeals for the Second Circuit denied Brady's petition for a rehearing. He faced a choice: he could appeal to the Supreme Court for both a stay on his suspension and a hearing—the highest court took only one percent of cases annually—or back down, accepting a suspension for the first four games of 2016. He chose the latter, announcing in a Facebook post that Deflategate was mercifully over after 544 days. He placed his suspension letter from Roger Goodell in a binder, both as an artifact and a reminder, and attacked the off-season as the clock on the wall ticked down to Super Bowl LI on February 5, 2017, at Houston's NRG Stadium.

34

DEFINITELY HUMAN

D URING QUIET MOMENTS, BILL BELICHICK TOLD associates about his vision of how, after more than four decades in the NFL, he wanted to walk away. He wanted his sons, Brian and Steve, now both Patriots assistants, to be established in their football careers—and for New England to be fixed at quarterback over the long term. He wanted the winning to continue without him, so that he would be remembered for always keeping the best interests of the franchise in mind. It was a rare mindset for a great coach, and Belichick probably knew that. When Bill Walsh retired after his third Super Bowl following the 1988 season, burned out from the grind, he handed a talented roster to George Seifert, who was elevated into the top job after serving as the team's defensive coordinator. Walsh secretly hoped that Seifert would flop. Instead, Seifert went 14–2 in 1989 and won another Super Bowl, leaving Walsh distraught and depressed. Eventually, he reemerged from retirement to coach at Stanford, in a bid to rewrite an unfinished legacy. Belichick had too much pride in his work to turn over a bad situation to his successor.

Belichick was deeply invested in Jimmy Garoppolo. Everyone, Belichick included, knew he had gotten lucky with Tom Brady. Garoppolo, though, was *his* project—and now, for the first month of the 2016 season, he was the starter. The team rallied around Garoppolo, sensing a chance to prove that their franchise quarterback wasn't the only good player on the roster. Josh McDaniels was beginning to resurface as a head-coaching candidate, and he knew that the two biggest raps against him were the Denver disaster and the widely held notion that Brady's greatness rendered the offense coach-proof.

Nobody was more aware of the coaches' curiosity about life without Brady than Brady himself. It seemed as though he was fighting external and internal opponents for the first time since Michigan. After Garoppolo was drafted—after Belichick's blunt assessment of Brady's age and contract—Brady saw him as a nice guy, but also as a threat, as Joe Montana had Steve Young and Brett Favre had Aaron Rodgers. They were friends—Tom and Gisele once set up Jimmy on a blind double date with a model—but fierce competitors. Brady didn't see it as his job to groom his own replacement, and sometimes refused to talk to Garoppolo if the youngster beat him at an accuracy drill. Garoppolo admired and emulated Brady, from his throwing motion to the avocado ice cream, but wasn't intimidated by him.

Some of New England's coaches predicted the team would go 2–2 without Brady. Which would have been fine. The Patriots often started slow, using September as an extended training camp to find their identity and relying on Brady to cover up holes. The biggest challenge was to give the team, and Garoppolo in particular, confidence. Before the season opener against the Arizona Cardinals in Glendale on September 11, 2016, Belichick showed players highlights from the win over the Seahawks in the Super Bowl, invoking the positive memories from the last New England visit to University of Phoenix Stadium. McDaniels reminded the offensive staff that they had won without Brady before, a reference to the Matt Cassel season, and asked receivers to refrain from talking to Garoppolo a lot on the sidelines. McDaniels didn't want to overwhelm him.

"It's a simple game," McDaniels told Garoppolo. "And I'll help you through it."

Garoppolo's family attended his debut, and he played well, throwing a touchdown pass in a win. The next week, against Miami on September 18, Garoppolo threw three touchdown passes the first 17 minutes before injuring his shoulder. Days after the game, Garoppolo booked an appointment for treatment at the TB12 center adjacent to Gillette Stadium. When Garoppolo arrived, he later told people in the Patriots' building—and denied after the account was made public—the door was locked. Nobody was there. It was odd. He ended up getting treatment that night from a team trainer, grousing about what had happened. A few high-level Patriots wondered if TB12 had refused to see him out of loyalty to Brady, something Guerrero later denied. Garoppolo eventually was treated by TB12—after a high-ranking football operations employee called to ask why Garoppolo hadn't been allowed in. The temperature was slowly rising in New England.

BRADY DEALT WITH his first September without football since he was a preteen by seeking solace in the people in his life who mattered most to him. He went home to San Mateo for four days, playing golf with Tom Sr.—and spending time with Galynn, who had been diagnosed with breast cancer. He attended a movie premiere with his wife in New York, and because they had never taken a honeymoon, the two of them flew to Italy for a quick vacation, dining at Aurora, believed to be the oldest restaurant in Capri, and sunbathing naked, which ended up on TMZ.

If Brady ever wondered who truly valued him, his forced time away from the Patriots was clarifying. On the second weekend of his suspension, the weekend of September 17, Brady attended a Michigan football game in Ann Arbor. He had been a rare presence in Michigan since graduating. He delivered a pep talk to the team in 2013, but the relationship was "estranged," in the words of Wolverines booster Todd Anson. Deep scars hadn't fully healed. But on this trip, time washed everything clean. Michigan head coach Jim Harbaugh—a former Wolverines quarterback who had played 14 years in the NFL—wanted to honor Brady, bringing him forever into the Michigan family. "We had to recognize that there was some bitterness and communicate that things would be different under Jim Harbaugh," Anson recalled. "We had to identify that there was an issue and address it. It was basic stuff." Harbaugh saw an opening, at one of the low points of Brady's career, maybe the lowest since he rotated with Drew Henson. He asked if Brady would be an honorary captain for Michigan against Colorado.

Brady arrived in Ann Arbor on the Friday before the game, not as a famous alum eager to lord over the place, but as a father indulging in nostalgia with his son alongside him. Brady brought Jack—a boys' weekend—and as soon as they touched down, they went to Michigan Stadium. Pat Kratus, one of Brady's college roommates, joined them. They walked the field, an empty cathedral. Brady loved roaming empty stadiums, gaining a measure of peace in the still moments before a game. Jack couldn't possibly understand the pain and joy his father had endured in this venue. Before they left, Brady wanted to throw Jack a touchdown. They lined up outside the five-yard line, and Brady told his son to run a fade route. Jack did, and Brady sent up a soft pass, perfectly executing his follow-through retooled by House—every throw mattered—and Jack caught it. Brady raised his hands and trotted to the end zone, where Jack leapt into his dad's arms. It was so fun that Jack asked to keep playing, and so they threw the ball around for the next half hour. A few friends later asked Jack if he wanted to attempt to follow his dad's path, like Bronny James, LeBron James's son.

"I think I want to be a soccer player," Jack said.

On Saturday, a red Chevy Suburban picked up Brady and Jack from their hotel and took them back to Michigan Stadium. They stood on the field during pregame warm-ups as the stands slowly filled. Brady posed for selfies, and then a trainer handed him a ball and Harbaugh stood ten or so yards away. It was time for two quarterbacks to throw. A crowd formed. People filmed on their phones. Harbaugh backed up to 20 yards, which exposed the coach's 50-something-year-old arm as much as it showcased Brady's. "I wish I wouldn't have given him the wind," Harbaugh later said.

The moment arrived. Brady stood on the sideline at midfield as the scoreboard played his highlights, legendary throws only in retrospect. As the final play ran—Brady's last throw as a Wolverine was an overtime touchdown pass in the Orange Bowl—the crowd of just over 110,000 started to swell into a warm ovation that Brady had heard before, but which felt different this time. An announcer read Brady's honors, the cheers growing with each one until they drowned out the disembodied voice as it said, "Please welcome back number 10, Tom Brady."

Brady's mouth trembled. His eyes were shielded behind sunglasses—

out of pride, a friend later said, in case he teared up. Tom Brady was in a strange moment in life, universally respected, but also utterly alone, football royalty in exile. He was less alone now. The Michigan he had always wanted—the Michigan that wanted *him*—had finally appeared.

WITH GAROPPOLO INJURED, the Patriots were now down to their third-string quarterback, a rookie third-rounder out of North Carolina State named Jacoby Brissett. In week 3, played on September 22 against the Houston Texans, Brissett became the first Black quarterback to start for the Patriots in the team's history, and led New England to a 27–0 win. New England lost, 19–0, to the Bills the following week, but it had weathered Brady's suspension, emerging 3–1—and giving Belichick 14 wins in 20 games without Brady since 2008.

Brady returned to the team feeling like he had to earn his job all over again from a coaching staff a little too enamored with his backup. When asked what it was like to have Brady back, Belichick said flatly, "It was good to have Tom back." The players were more effusive. At Brady's first meeting, Julian Edelman led a "Bra-dy!" chant. Some hugged him. Brady's face turned red. And he went out and played like a man possessed, throwing 12 touchdowns and no interceptions over his first four starts, all wins. In week 10, the Patriots faced the Seattle Seahawks in a Super Bowl rematch. Yet that week, they learned that their biggest obstacle in the 2016 regular season would not be a football problem, but a political one.

ON WEDNESDAY, November 9, the day after Donald Trump surprisingly defeated Hillary Clinton to become the nation's 45th president, Bill Belichick stood in a team meeting needing to explain himself. Or, specifically, several players needed him to explain himself.

Two days earlier, an election eve Trump rally in Manchester, New Hampshire, had taken an unexpected turn. "I was in the plane and they handed me a letter," Trump told the crowd. "And it was from . . . Coach Belichick."

The audience cheered. Trump stretched out his arms, as if on a victory lap, and then shuffled papers at the podium, looking for the note. "The most beautiful letter," he said.

"We called back," Trump continued, "and we said, 'Do you think that Mr. Trump could read that letter to the people of New Hampshire?' And he said, 'Absolutely, if you'd like. But do me a favor and don't read that letter. Let me send one that's a little bit different.' I figured he was going to take all the good things out, like most gutless people do. Gutless. But he's the opposite. He's a champ. So he sent me the new letter, and it was much better! It was stronger!"

Trump read the letter:

> *Congratulations on a tremendous campaign. You have dealt with an unbelievable slanted and negative media and have come out beautifully. You've proved to be the ultimate competitor and fighter. Your leadership is amazing. I have always had tremendous respect for you, but the toughness and perseverance you've displayed over the past year is remarkable. Hopefully, tomorrow's election results will give the opportunity to make America great again.*
> *Best wishes for great results tomorrow, Bill Belichick.*

"So, Tom Brady and Bill Belichick," Trump said, "I want to thank you both!"

Great American sports teams usually reflect something essential about the nation. After 9/11, the Patriots seemed not only to stand for love of country—"Today we are all Patriots," in Robert Kraft's indelible post–Super Bowl remarks—but also to exist as a regime built on surveillance, suspicion, and paranoia. The Patriots were so good, for so long, that they managed to straddle multiple eras. If the friendship between John F. Kennedy and Vince Lombardi represented a sort of idealism, then Trump and the New England Patriots now embodied a ruthless cynicism. It was a shame, because the Patriots were a true team, relatively unselfish and supportive of one another, a rarity in sports. But by the time Trump read the letter from Belichick, it was already clear that the Patriots were also *his* team. In the fall of 2015, Robert Kraft gave Brady a red hat embroidered with Trump's slogan: "Make America

Great Again." Brady put it in his locker, thinking it was cool and joking to reporters that it would be "great" if Trump were elected because he'd install a putting green at the White House.

Over the course of 2016, as Trump's unlikely campaign became a mainstream one—with violent rallies, the race-baiting comments, the insistence that his political opponents be jailed, the taped comments about grabbing women "by the pussy"—Brady's explanations were less funny, inside the locker room and beyond. Professional athletes had started to kneel during the national anthem, a movement started by San Francisco 49ers quarterback Colin Kaepernick—not only a protest of systemic racism and police brutality, but also a challenge to the NFL's power structure. From Jerry Jones of the Dallas Cowboys to Bob McNair of the Houston Texans, many NFL team owners supported Trump. But no franchise was publicly linked to him as frequently or as closely as the Patriots. Trump later said that Brady called him to congratulate him before his inauguration, and White House advisor Kellyanne Conway added that the president was grateful for friends like Kraft and Brady, who "are loyal and can ignore the shrapnel."

Now Belichick was in front of the team, the usual dynamic in meetings turned on its head. His letter had angered a lot of Patriots players, and not just Black players. Many had raised concerns with assistant coaches, surprised that Belichick was close with a man they felt had deemed the lives and dreams of many American citizens expendable. At a staff meeting, Brian Flores addressed it with Belichick.

Coach, I think you need to know this isn't okay, Flores explained. You need to say something.

Belichick seemed surprised. But it was now an issue, whether he agreed that it should be or not. He told the team: "It's my fault. I wrote a letter to a friend, not knowing it would be shared publicly, but in support of a friend."

Few bought it. After all, Trump said at the rally that he had not only asked Belichick if he could read the letter, but that Belichick had offered to write an even more laudatory one. Belichick was digging himself a deeper hole. "It was hypocritical and out of character," a Patriots player recalled. "I don't think he's an intolerant coach. He isn't a bad guy. Bill just fucked up and justified it in a way that he would never accept from a player."

A small group of Patriots discussed kneeling or even boycotting practice. But those idealistic notions evaporated as the Patriot Way reasserted itself. In New England, fear of the head coach always surpassed anger at him.

In addition to addressing the team, Belichick explained the letter at a press conference, resolved to move forward—and to look a little classier in doing so. He had slowly started to dress more professionally for press conferences, in a buttoned-up shirt and slacks. Some thought it was of his own volition; most thought it was the influence of his longtime girlfriend, Linda Holliday. He was often in business casual when with her, when he was photographed on Nantucket or mentioned on gossip sites or at a charity event, smiling much more often than anyone gave him credit for, not pretentious but distinguished. He still indulged his inner slob with his array of hoodies—by 2016, the selection had broadened from severed-sleeved gray to include severed-sleeved navy and severed-sleeved red—as well as pullovers, mock turtlenecks, and sweatshirts with the sleeves now awkwardly cut at the biceps, looking a little like his friend Jon Bon Jovi. And he still stiffed the press: every time he was asked a follow-up about Trump, he replied, "Seattle. Seattle. Seattle." But at least he looked like something more than just a coach.

The issue wasn't over internally. In the captains' meeting before the Seahawks game, safety Devin McCourty—one of the most respected players on the team—raised it with Belichick. What's going on here? he wanted to know.

Belichick unhelpfully repeated his refrain from the team meeting. Brady was also in the captains' meeting, and although Gisele Bündchen had responded to a social media question asking if she and her husband supported Trump with a loud "NO!" the quarterback was still aligned with Trump in the eyes of many teammates. There was a divide in the meeting and in the locker room. Hard feelings lingered.

On Sunday night, November 13, a game between New England and Seattle once again came down to a last-second goal-line stand. This time, it was Seahawks safety Kam Chancellor who made the game-winning play, breaking up a pass intended for Gronkowski. There was a feeling in the locker room that the Patriots had not only lost due to a flawed defensive game plan that allowed Russell Wilson to throw three touchdowns, but because of the internal and external distraction created by the head coach. New England lost only two games in 2016, a coach later pointed out. One with the third-string quarterback, the other after the letter.

TOM BRADY FOLLOWED UP one of his greatest regular seasons—11 wins in 12 starts; a 67.4 percent completion rate, his highest since 2007; 28 touchdowns and *two* interceptions—with one of his worst playoff games, against the Houston Texans, completing only 18 of 38 passes with two touchdowns and two interceptions. Again and again, Romeo Crennel, now the Texans' defensive coordinator, rushed defensive end Jadeveon Clowney up the middle, forcing Brady to throw off balance. "We didn't want him to step up," Crennel later said. In New England's film session after the Patriots' 34–16 win, Belichick lit into Brady in front of the entire team like few had ever seen, ripping him for carelessness with the ball. "This will get us beat," Belichick said. "We were lucky to get away with a win."

In a staff meeting, the coaches were even more critical of Brady. Word got back to him about it. He was furious that after one of his best seasons, the coaches were so eager to bury him.

The bigger issue was that, after almost 15 years as a starting NFL quarterback—as one of the best in history, if not *the* best—and as a player who continued to improve with age instead of tailing off, Brady found that Belichick's negativity was getting old. There was an inherent tension between the quarterback's steadfast desire to be a positive thinker and the often miserable environment the coach intentionally created. Brady likened New England's culture to being "brainwashed." So many lies flew around that it was hard to tell what was true. Belichick frequently complimented Brady before the team and in private—he would regularly say publicly that there was no quarterback he'd rather have than Brady, which Belichick considered ultimate and unequivocal praise—but there was also a strange emotional block when it came to the quarterback who had altered his life and legacy. When asked about

Brady's astounding durability—except for most of the 2008 season, Brady hadn't missed a single game due to injury—Belichick managed to pivot to praise for Jimmy Garoppolo. "Jimmy could go out there and run everything that Tom can run. We've seen that. . . . And he does a great job of it. And when we put Jimmy in there, it's really seamless."

Seamless.

Deflategate had helped Brady sort his relationships. His family was so resolutely in his corner—at one point, Tom Sr. called in to a radio show and yelled at the host at such a decibel level and strain that it sounded dangerous for the health of a man in his 70s—that Brady had less patience for anyone or anything fake. He cut off a few friendly reporters who had been critical of him during Deflategate. He refused to comment when asked if he was comfortable with the way Kraft handled the scandal, which revealed plenty.

"I'm human," he said at one point. "There's no doubt. I'm definitely human."

Brady rebounded after the Texans game, throwing three touchdown passes to help whip the Pittsburgh Steelers in the AFC Championship Game on January 22, 2017. *ESPN The Magazine* put a gaunt and shadowy Brady on the cover of its Super Bowl preview issue under the banner "Brady's Revenge." It was the type of storyline that a quarterback who had vowed to remain above the fray, refusing to dignify media storylines, might have ignored.

Brady loved the cover.

35

FOR YOUR MOM, BRO

Trump's team was in the Super Bowl at NRG Stadium in Houston, playing against the Atlanta Falcons and quarterback Matt Ryan, a friend of Brady's and the reigning league MVP. It was the first major sporting event since the inauguration. The league was concerned that the president would attend, which posed more of a logistical nightmare than a political one. The White House had reached out to the NFL and asked what the president's "role" was for the game. The league didn't have one for him. George and Barbara Bush, Texas residents and frequent Trump critics, were due to take part in the ceremonial coin toss. If Trump was in the building, too, it had the potential to be awkward, if not worse, before an international audience.

Vice President Mike Pence attended instead of Trump, and he watched from Bob McNair's suite. League staff wanted Roger Goodell to welcome Pence, but the commissioner was tied up with pregame festivities and unable to make it to the box until the second half. Joe Lockhart, the league's PR chief, saw Pence and decided to greet the vice president himself. They had met years earlier. Lockhart was a veteran of Washington, having served as President Bill Clinton's press secretary in the 1990s and as an advisor to Senator John Kerry during his presidential campaign in 2004. Lockhart lingered around Pence, not wanting to interrupt what appeared to be an in-depth conversation with Texas governor Greg Abbott. Finally, he moved in. Pence quickly turned to Lockhart, turning his shoulder to Abbott and making small talk until the governor had moved beyond earshot.

"Oh, thank you," Pence joked. "That guy wouldn't shut up."

TOM BRADY WAS QUIET. Uncharacteristically quiet, given the circumstance. He had just been baited into throwing a pass to the wrong man, and suddenly he stood exposed on the field. Midway through the second quarter, New England was trailing, 14–0, but deep in Atlanta territory. On third and six, Brady dropped back to pass. Falcons defensive end Dwight Freeney, one of Brady's old headaches from his time on the Colts, flew off the edge, leading to a quick Brady throw to Danny Amendola. Falcons cornerback Robert Alford saw New England's twin receivers on the left, Julian Edelman and Amendola, cut inside, one after the other—what the Falcons called a "follow route"—and jumped it as cleanly as Malcolm Butler had jumped the pick play two years earlier, intercepting the pass. Brady dove in an attempt to tackle him, but he landed in a rolling heap, lifting his head just in time to see the back of Alford's cleats headed 82 yards for a touchdown, giving the Falcons a 21–0 lead.

"Trouble now," Belichick said over the headset.

Brady returned to the sideline, quietly studying the play on an iPad.

"What happened there?" Josh McDaniels said.

The bigger question was what was happening to the Patriots. The game was a rout. Down 21–3 at halftime, players tried to believe. Edelman paced around the locker room, yelling, "We're better than this!" Safety Duron Harmon rode a stationary bike to stay loose and hollered, "Just keep fighting, because this is going to be the greatest comeback ever!"

Brady was unshaken. If it were any other game, he would have thrown his helmet and screamed after the play. But he knew that the Super Bowl was a long game. It tended to go haywire late, when defenses were exhausted. Belichick stopped to chat with Brady, to make sure that they conserved time-outs. Both had a similar feeling about the game: The Patriots had controlled it, but they couldn't get out of their own way.

"We're stopping ourselves," Belichick said. "It's going to take more than 21 points to beat us."

The Falcons understood as much. Atlanta scored another touchdown, Matt Ryan's second scoring pass of the day, with 8:31 left in the third quarter to take a 28–3 lead. It was stunning. New England had lost Super Bowls before, but it had never failed to show up. The game looked over.

There were only a few people who thought that New England might make a run, though they were not limited to the Krafts, who tried to keep each other's spirits up, and the Bradys, who reminded one another on a family text chat to find faith. Roger Goodell had walked the field before the game with his wife and twin daughters to such sustained boos that, for once, it bothered him. Up in a suite, a league executive now prepared Goodell's remarks for the trophy presentation. Goodell, the Patriots' and Tom Brady's sworn enemy, scanned the notes for a speech celebrating a Falcons win.

"This is good," he said, "but where's the other one?"

The other one was useless. It was drafted for a Patriots win. But if New England came back now, from *this*, it would have to be completely rewritten, the executive said.

"Do it," Goodell said.

AT THAT MOMENT, it seemed beyond impossible that New England could not just get back into the game, but actually win it. The Falcons had a 99.6 percent win probability, according to ESPN's calculations. Years later, whenever the game was replayed on television, it still warped the mind to see how the remaining 22 minutes, after the Falcons' fourth touchdown, unfolded. New England cobbled together a touchdown— though it missed the extra point—to end the third quarter and a second field goal to begin the fourth. It was 28–12. *Man*, Brady thought, *we're back in the game.*

"We're gonna need two more drives anyway," Belichick said to Brady. "Let's go."

On the next series, with 8:31 left, the Falcons faced a third and one at their own 36-yard line. Ryan was in the shotgun. Dont'a Hightower lined up on the left side of the defense, so wide as to be in pass coverage. New England's scouting reports had detailed that running back Devonta Freeman, lined up to Ryan's right side, struggled with pass blocking. This defense was designed to exploit him. Linebacker Kyle Van Noy faked a blitz up the middle, holding Freeman's eyes for a split second. Hightower rushed hard from the outside. By the time Freeman saw him, it was too late. Freeman whiffed, giving Hightower a clean shot at Ryan.

Ryan had drifted left, anticipating pressure, eyes locked downfield. He had receiver Aldrick Robinson on a deep corner route for what might have been a touchdown. But Ryan hitched for a split second, failing to pull the trigger, a brief delay that was as costly as Freeman's missed block, in the eyes of the Falcons coaches. Hightower attacked Ryan, who lost the ball like a waiter slipping with a tray in his hands. Patriots defensive tackle Alan Branch recovered, the break the team desperately needed.

"Our ball!" Brady yelled, staring at the replay screen.

Five plays later, Brady hit Amendola for a six-yard touchdown and running back James White rushed up the middle to convert a two-point try. It was 28–20 Falcons, with 5:56 left.

Atlanta wasn't finished. On the first play of their next drive, from their own ten-yard line, Ryan completed a pass to Freeman on a flare out of the backfield for 39 yards. Patriots linebacker Elandon Roberts had fallen down in traffic, gotten back up, and hustled downfield to bring Freeman down from behind, preventing a touchdown. Two plays later, Ryan rolled right and threw to superstar receiver Julio Jones, who extended himself to make a fingertip catch on the sideline and touched both feet down at the Patriots' 22-yard line, a feat of athleticism and control so spectacular that later, whenever Belichick watched it, he shook his head in disbelief, unsure of how New England could have defended it better. "We made the play to win the Super Bowl," Ryan later said.

Atlanta was in field goal range with 4:40 left, roughly when leading teams turn to what NFL coaches refer to as the four-minute offense, calling plays designed to bleed the clock and protect a lead. New England practiced it weekly during the season, and Josh McDaniels selected certain plays to choose from—and, just as important, certain plays he would avoid altogether.

In game-planning sessions in the lead-up to the Super Bowl, Belichick seemed more nervous about Atlanta offensive coordinator Kyle Shanahan than he did about any of the Falcons' players, marveling at how the assistant coach had adapted his father's offensive system and elevated it, adding his own touches and theories. But on this series, as so often in the past 15 years, New England used its opponent's self-conception—in this case, Shanahan's aggressiveness—against him. On first down, Ryan pitched outside to Freeman. It violated one of the Patriots' rules of the four-minute offense: don't pitch, only hand off. A pitch not only increases the chances of a fumble, but it's a slow-developing play. New England stuffed Freeman for a loss of a yard. On second down, Shanahan called a pass out of the shotgun, with Ryan dropping deep, another play New England never would have called. A sack would take them out of field goal range. Sure enough, defensive end Trey Flowers corralled Ryan for a loss of 12 yards.

It was now third and 23. Atlanta needed yards, and it also needed the clock to run. In these situations, New England often called screen passes—always to the weak side of the defense, away from the majority of the defenders—to both move the chains and drain the clock. Ryan completed an out route to receiver Mohamed Sanu, who was knocked out of bounds after gaining nine yards. It stopped the clock, but moved Atlanta into better field goal range. Falcons head coach Dan Quinn—who had been victimized by a Brady comeback as Seattle's defensive coordinator in the Super Bowl two years earlier—sent out kicker Matt Bryant, believing he had a chance to ice the game. Then everyone froze.

There was a flag. Holding on Atlanta, a ten-yard penalty. It was now third and 33 from the Patriots' 45-yard line.

"What the fuck, guys," Ryan said.

Ryan threw incomplete, not only ensuring a punt, but stopping the clock with 3:44 left. Edelman leapt off the bench and looked at Brady.

"Let's go score and win this thing, baby!" Edelman said.

"Let's go win it all," Brady replied.

"For your mom," Edelman said. "For your mom, bro." Brady looked him in the eye.

The Super Bowl was the first game that Galynn Brady had attended all year. Brady's suspension had given him the gift of time with his parents in September for the first time since high school, but had also worn on all of them in untold ways. In dark moments, some in Brady's family wondered if two years of Deflategate stress had rendered Galynn more susceptible to disease. There was a general belief that Brady worked harder in 2016, looking to avenge every wrong visited upon him, but Belichick later dismissed it. Brady was a consummate professional who *always* worked his ass off. But he did have a deeper motivation, a starker one, which he hid until he couldn't. Brady's first home game in October was during the NFL's breast cancer awareness month, where players wore pink decals on their uniforms. In the locker room before the game, Brady asked an equipment staffer to fetch him something pink to wear. The staffer returned with an armband. Brady slid it on his left arm, tucked against his wristband play sheet. He started to tear up, right there at his locker, in full view of staff and teammates.

Galynn's illness was an open secret in the Patriots' building and even among some members of the media. Days before the Super Bowl, at media night, Brady was asked by a kid reporter to name his hero. "My dad," Brady replied, his lip quivering and his eyes wet. Later that week, Tom E. Curran of NBC Sports Boston broke the news of Galynn's cancer. Brady was famously private when it came to his family—if anything, he was more tight-lipped than his family—but during a week when most expected him to put up his guard in response to Deflategate, he allowed himself to be vulnerable, processing private pain on the sport's most public stage, and injecting it into the game itself.

Brady didn't react outwardly to Edelman's words, but they affected him. That Edelman remembered Brady's mom with a Super Bowl on the line was pretty cool, he thought.

For decades, Brady's entire life had been geared around this exact kind of moment, but when he took the field, with 91 yards to go, needing a touchdown and a two-point conversion to tie, the drive almost immediately ended in disaster. On the first play, Falcons defensive tackle Grady Jarrett hit Brady low and another defender hit him high as he threw. Brady was slow to get up, touching the side of his head. But he shook it off and completed two passes for a total of 27 yards to move New England to its own 36-yard line.

On first down, Brady fired over the middle to Edelman on a chute route, a diagonal cross with Robert Alford shadowing him. The ball came out of Brady's hand low at a moment when it needed to come out high. It headed straight for Alford. *Oh shit*, Edelman thought. Alford leapt and the ball caromed off his fingertips, in the air in a negative parabola. The ball went up, and as it came down, three men—two Falcons and Edelman—dove for it.

This is the game, Brady thought.

Everyone landed on Alford, splayed on the ground. Edelman grabbed the ball between a thicket of arms and legs, getting his hands underneath it by a slimming inch.

Not that Edelman knew it at the time. He *thought* he caught it, but either way, he sold it hard.

"I caught it," Edelman yelled to the refs. "I caught it. I caught it."

It was ruled a catch. Twenty-three yards, a huge chunk. The Falcons challenged the play, but the replay confirmed the call on the field. For once, a miracle catch in the Super Bowl had gone in New England's favor. Brady hit three more passes for a total of 40 yards, and on second and goal from the one-yard line, James White scored. A two-point conversion tied the game. New England had undone a 25-point lead in 16 minutes: 28–28.

The game was headed to the first overtime in Super Bowl history. Captains for both teams met at midfield for the coin toss. New England got to call it, and Matthew Slater, the Patriots' special-teams star, called heads. He always called heads, because that's what his father, Jackie, a Hall of Fame offensive tackle for the Los Angeles Rams, had always called.

It was heads.

Brady started overtime with a short flare to White, who, with 20 total touches for 139 yards and three touchdowns, would have been named MVP of the game any other year. But this was a night when an already immortal quarterback entered a previously untouched realm of his craft. He threw consecutive timing passes to Amendola and Chris Hogan into windows that few quarterbacks would be able to see, much less exploit. It felt like an out-of-body experience, Brady later said, leaving him to try to explain what transpired in manageable terms, a series of decisions and learned behaviors and an accumulation of knowledge, in high-leverage moment after high-leverage moment. But quarterbacking is meant to be understood only to a point. Nobody else could try to describe what Brady was experiencing that night, because no other quarterback had ever felt it. That space was reserved for Michael Jordan, Wayne Gretzky, Ted Williams, Reggie Jackson, LeBron James. And now Tom Brady.

Six plays later, White powered into the end zone from two yards out, ending the game, New England 34, Atlanta 28. The Patriots rushed the field. Brady removed his helmet and raised his arms. Roger Goodell soon found Brady in the chaos behind the makeshift presentation stage that had just been assembled. Cameras were trained on them. Both were relieved that the game, and Deflategate, were over. Goodell admired Brady—even in his suspension letter, Goodell praised the quarterback's accomplishments and character—and the disclosure that Galynn was suffering from breast cancer provided a sense of kinship between the two men. Cancer had claimed the life of Goodell's mother, Jean, in 1984. In her final few months, Roger had combined caretaker hours with entry-level league-office hours. He spoke of her infrequently, but called her the most "influential person" in his life. "She taught me how to live," Goodell once said, almost crying. "And she taught me how to die."

Goodell extended his hand to Brady and congratulated him. "That was incredible. What a comeback."

"Thank you," Brady replied.

Goodell turned away, almost at the precise moment Brady's family arrived. Brady found his kids. He found his wife. He found his dad. "Oh my God," Tom Sr. said through tears. And when Brady found his mom, wearing a blue wrap around her head and a white T-shirt with her son's number and "Brady's Ladies" on the back, she leaned into his arms.

THE NEXT MORNING, before the Super Bowl MVP press conference at Houston's convention center, Roger Goodell entered a huge and mostly empty waiting room. Tom Brady and Bill Belichick were already there. Brady stood to the side, signing footballs and helmets. Belichick was in the middle of the room, and when he wheeled around, when he saw Goodell, he smiled and gave the commissioner a bear hug—nearly lifting the larger man's feet off the ground. Few knew that Goodell and Belichick, for all the infractions and punishments over the years, and despite the public war between the commissioner and Belichick's most important player, had become friends. At one point, Belichick called

Goodell and asked to talk about league rules. Belichick had strong opinions on certain changes, and Goodell was eager to hear them—and to align himself with the game's greatest coach rather than fight him. Goodell flew from New York to a private airport near Foxborough, and he and Belichick met on the second floor of a shacklike airplane hangar to ensure privacy. They talked shop for more than three hours, and then Goodell flew home.

Goodell and Belichick now laughed and told inside jokes. Brady watched out of the corner of his eye as his coach cozied up to a man who had tried to strip him of the credit and legitimacy he'd craved and achieved since he first arrived on campus at Michigan—and maybe as far back as those golf outings with his father. Finally, Brady started to walk over. The few staff in the room felt like voyeurs, trying to watch without getting caught. Goodell, Belichick, and Brady all stood there, within feet of each other, three of the most important football men in the world, who at the same time needed one other and didn't fully trust one other, whose shifting alliances laid bare the naked politics of fame, wealth, and legacy. Brady greeted Goodell with a one-armed hug and joined the conversation, as if none of it had ever happened.

36

THE PLIABILITY
MOVEMENT

I F THE HARDEST THING IN FOOTBALL IS WINNING A
Super Bowl, and the second-hardest thing is managing the celebrity and entitlement that attend a Super Bowl victory, the next-hardest thing is forgetting a catastrophic Super Bowl loss. New England had done more than rally in the fourth quarter twice to win two championships in three years; it had broken proud teams. The Seattle Seahawks never recovered emotionally from Malcolm Butler's interception. A lot of players, especially Richard Sherman, lost faith in Pete Carroll, and it started to spill into public view. After Russell Wilson was almost intercepted at the one-yard line in a 2016 game against the Los Angeles Rams, Sherman exploded on Carroll on the sideline. "We've already seen how that goes," he later told reporters. In the spring of 2017, Seattle dangled Sherman for a trade. He wanted out, and fantasized about landing in New England. But nobody was willing to meet Seattle's price. Sherman returned for a final season, which ended early due to a midseason injury. The Legion of Boom, already diminished, was later dismantled, a potential dynasty undone.

The Falcons hung together. Navy SEALs spoke to the players in the months after the Super Bowl, relaying the importance of teamwork. A banner was painted on a hallway in the facility, reading, "Brotherhood Is an Unwavering Kinship." But after all the speeches and slogans, a precocious team was never the same. Over the next few years, blowing a big lead became the Falcons' *identity*.

Tom Brady and Bill Belichick were so great that they had become their own center of power in the NFL, forcing the most cloistered halls of the league to reckon with the damage. Owners who had all but ordered Goodell to go to war over the football equivalent of a parking ticket were now privately lamenting that the commissioner had gone too far with Deflategate. Something needed to be done. In summer of 2017, Goodell suggested that he attend a preseason game in Foxborough—his first visit to Gillette Stadium since the AFC Championship Game against the Colts after the 2014 season. He had an idea of how he wanted it to go: he would walk the field before the game, taking medicine from fans. That way, Goodell said, he could be at the season opener a few weeks later against the Kansas City Chiefs, when the Patriots would raise their fifth Super Bowl banner, and not be the focal point. "Let's just take this off the table of me going up," Goodell told staff.

It was a rare preemptive measure by a commissioner and a league that far more often found themselves reacting, not in control when they should have been. Goodell had allowed himself to be managed so much by aides and owners, sacrificing his reputation for them, that he had lost his own personality—or, more specifically, never showed it to begin with. Those who worked at the league offices learned that there were unwritten Roger's Rules, based both on expectations from owners and from Goodell himself, ever the politican's son, aware that he was front-facing and that the cameras were always on. He couldn't drink a beer during a game, even though beer companies were among the league's top sponsors. He loved Chick-fil-A, but couldn't be seen eating it, because the company had donated to charities with anti-LGBTQ stances. He needed to wear a suit and tie to games and never jeans, rules that would be relaxed over the years. Staffers were advised not to share bad news with Goodell on the league's plane because the commissioner might not be able to let it go for hours, and nobody could escape. There was once an entire series of staff meetings to determine how to handle fans booing him as he announced the first pick of the draft. Should he play along, have fun, maybe even return fire—or just announce the pick? The last, and safest, option won.

The preseason Foxborough trip was a mess before it began. The league's plane broke down at Westchester County Airport, with Goodell and other executives on board. The league finally secured another plane, but by the time they took off, landed, and were navigating Gillette

Stadium traffic, kickoff against the Jacksonville Jaguars was imminent, preventing Goodell from walking the field and getting booed, negating the point of the trip. Nobody knew what to do. The only thing worse than the optics of Goodell at Gillette Stadium were the optics of Goodell attending in secret, as if he were sneaking around to avoid the wrath of fans.

League executives had an idea: leak the news of Goodell's visit. That way, fans would know that he attended, and he could still return in a few weeks for the opener and it wouldn't be a shock.

A public relations executive called Ben Volin of the *Boston Globe*. Soon after, Volin tweeted a grainy picture of Goodell and Kraft chatting in the back of Robert Kraft's luxury box, almost out of sight. When word of the picture boomeranged to Kraft, he fumed.

"You're killing me with the fans," he told the executives. "Why would I want to be seen here with Roger with all this stuff going on with Brady?"

A few weeks later, Goodell was back in Foxborough for the season opener. This time, he arrived early. He walked the field with Chiefs owner Clark Hunt and a mass of security and staff, smiling as fans chanted derisively, "Ro-ger! Ro-ger!" Just then, a flood of boos warmed all the way to cheers. Brady had run out of the tunnel and down the field to the corner of the end zone where Goodell stood with Hunt, screaming and pumping his arms. Goodell took the cue. He ducked away, into the bowels of the stadium, as the crowd screamed, "Bra-dy! Bra-dy!"

As the 2017 regular season arrived, the dull creep of entitlement had finally started to intensify in the Patriots' building. The story of Brady's 2016 season, from suspension to 28–3 to 34–28, was so potent that it had overshadowed the team, opening pathways for resentment from coaches. For his part, Brady discouraged the increased attention on him, praising teammates and coaches and family. But he had run out of football measuring sticks. There were no more Joe Montanas. Determined not to become one of those legends left chasing his own ghost, Brady started to become fascinated with undefeated boxer Floyd Mayweather. *How did he never lose?* Brady wondered. He FaceTimed with Mayweather on a few occasions, picking his brain about training and eating habits, but little translated. Brady stood alone, with the same person he has had his entire life: himself. No other sport was the same, and no other quarterback had five.

Brady was also more comfortable taking steps to establish himself beyond the game and, more significantly, beyond the Patriots. He agreed to allow unprecedented access—for him, anyway—for a Facebook documentary called *Tom vs. Time*, of which the Patriots, according to the *New York Times*, were only nominally aware. And right before the season, Brady promoted the release of his own lifestyle book, *The TB12 Method: How to Achieve a Lifetime of Peak Performance*. If *Tom vs. Time* showed Brady to be something of a team parent, making smoothies for Julian Edelman and Danny Amendola and searching for joy under his head coach—author Mark Leibovich, who was close to Brady, called the film a "subversion campaign against the colorless code" of Belichick—then *The TB12 Method* was an exercise in self-disclosure, revealing how Brady not only viewed himself as an aging athlete, but how he viewed aging itself. Hoping to "decelerate the aging process as most people experience it," Brady was launching a global crusade: the "pliability movement."

Brady's 2008 knee injury, and his vow to never make the mistake, as he saw it, of getting injured again, hovered over it all. "When athletes get injured, they shouldn't blame the sport—or their age," *The TB12 Method* argues. The idea that actually playing football was not a cause of injuries—that if a player were to suffer a concussion, it was his fault for not training and treating his body properly—was so absurd that Brady backed away from it in interviews. People close to him wondered if it was really Alex Guerrero's book under Brady's byline. But *The TB12 Method* depicted a human being so fiercely focused, so disciplined, so evangelical about his own beliefs—he drank up to 300 ounces of water daily, which he said prevented sunburns—and so unforgiving of those who failed to follow his lead, that it felt like a guide for removing joy from your life. Did Brady have fun, or did he just hydrate and piss and throw and eat plants and lie under the "50 newtons of force in a single finger" generated by Guerrero's hands and hit the sack early?

Shortly after the book's release, Tom Junod and I wrote a story about the inherent catch of the TB12 Method: that in order to transcend football, Brady had to keep playing it, a dangerous game within a dangerous game. Yes, that meant head injuries—about which, whenever Brady was asked about them, he provided a standard reply that his body was none of our business, even as he was building a business around his body. As it turned out, he wanted to do a job he loved and to stay whole, wanted to be able to ski and surf and carry his kids without arthritic joints and splitting headaches and loss of memory. It was too much to ask for many professional football players. For Brady, maybe not.

In an interview with Brady for the piece, though, we began with a question designed to see if he could laugh at himself. We asked about the conflict at the heart of the twin TB12 laws of long and uninterrupted rest and unyielding hydration: How do you get the sleep you need without constantly having to go to the bathroom?

Brady didn't laugh, either at the question or himself. Peyton Manning would have hit it out of the park, perhaps joking about how he was a faucet, able to turn himself on or off on command. Brady just couldn't do it. He answered with the earnestness of someone well aware that people were laughing at him and his methods, and of someone who had lived in a particular orbit for so long that our question was like insulting the orbit itself. "If you start drinking more water all of the sudden, there's definitely a chance you'll find yourself probably making more trips to the bathroom. But ultimately, I think your body gets used to the extra water consumption quickly."

The TB12 Method was a *New York Times* best seller, but the science community roundly dismissed it. Stuart Phillips, an expert in muscle physiology, called it "balderdash." The book also put Guerrero, and his suspect past, under the spotlight. In 2015, *Boston* magazine reported that Guerrero had paid a fine to the Federal Trade Commission to settle charges that he claimed dietary supplements could help cure cancer. And the FTC had investigated him for other potential offenses. Brady's support of his friend and business partner remained unwavering. He had gone on the attack, disavowing a large portion of Western medicine and calling Coca-Cola "poison." Some close to Brady were beginning to worry about Guerrero's influence. When an updated edition of *The*

TB12 Method was later released, some of the most ridiculous and ridiculed claims—such as water as a sunburn preventative—had been quietly removed.

Collectively, *Tom vs. Time* and *The TB12 Method* betrayed a man so in love with the art of quarterbacking, so eager to redefine his capabilities and possibilities, so terrified of life without the game, that he was willing to risk almost anything if it meant his career would never end. In the film, Tom and Gisele sat on a couch in Costa Rica, where she disclosed a truth that had always, on some level, been obvious. "Football, as far as I'm concerned, is his first love." He watched her, laughing uncomfortably. Brady, of course, is one of the least ironic celebrities—and there was no irony on either face.

Nobody in the league was like Alex Guerrero, a team consultant but not on staff, paid by the owner to run a shadow business that was at odds with the philosophies of the head coach. For a few years, Belichick had welcomed Guerrero into the fold, granting him sideline access during games and even allowing him to attend confidential medical meetings where players' health was discussed. In the secretive world of the New England Patriots, it was like being invited into the Situation Room at the White House. But in 2014, after Guerrero too many times blamed the Patriots for what he saw as antiquated training techniques while offering few insights of his own, Belichick stopped inviting him. Kraft had made Guerrero a business partner by that point, paying TB12 a consulting fee—which raised the question of whether the arrangement was an illegal salary-cap workaround, compensating for Brady's below-market deals. The league office, perhaps wary of yet another fight with the Patriots, insisted that the deal was legal. The entire situation was bound to cause problems.

By 2017, Belichick was making it resoundingly clear that Guerrero had no role on the staff. When asked if he planned to read *The TB12 Method*, he replied, "I see Tom every day. I don't really feel like I need to read a book."

Brady was angry over the doubts surrounding TB12 and Guerrero, but as the 2017 season began—as Brady was hawking his book—Patriots players started to go down, all of them members of the pliability movement. It began against the Detroit Lions in the preseason, when Julian Edelman blew out his knee, ending his year. Brady told friends that he believed Edelman had lifted weights too frequently in the off-season in preparation for a photo shoot for *ESPN The Magazine*'s Body Issue, putting enormous strain on his muscles. As the season went on, Dont'a Hightower suffered a knee issue and a pectoral tear; Danny Amendola, a concussion; Rob Gronkowski, a groin injury.

With Edelman out, Brady was down one of his favorite targets for the season, and there was a derby among receivers to replace him. Players came to believe that the surest way to align themselves with Brady was to join guys like Gronkowski—whose body and psyche were so beaten down by football and by Belichick's culture that he sometimes cried before practice—and seek treatment at the TB12 clinic, not from team doctors.

It created a no-win situation for some players: alienate the game's most powerful coach, or its most powerful quarterback?

One player visited TB12 under what he perceived as pressure, but declined to allow Guerrero to work on his injured legs, out of fear that one of Guerrero's famous deep-force massages would hamper his recovery. Instead, he asked that the treatment be limited to his arm. The *Boston Sports Journal* reported that another player had been told by Patriots trainers to do squats, but was later instructed by Guerrero to not do them. Brady would often tell teammates that "Bill's answer to everything is to lift more weights," a claim the Patriots staff felt was unfair, given the team's dedication to soft-tissue and diet science. Many Patriots coaches thought the staff, especially head strength and conditioning coach Moses Cabrera, were the hidden heroes of the team's comeback against the Falcons, helping the players reach peak physical condition late in the season.

Sensing a locker-room divide, Belichick discussed all of these issues with Brady in September. Brady claimed not to know anything about players feeling pressured to go to TB12. The problem remained unresolved, so Belichick resolved it himself—by permanently clarifying

Guerrero's role. Belichick wrote Guerrero an email revoking his access to the sideline and the team plane, and banning him from treating players other than Brady at the stadium.

An email designed to end a problem only created more of them.

BRADY WANTED CLARITY. The two-year, $41 million contract extension he had signed in 2016 set up 2017 as a key year. Both Brady and management understood the stakes: if Brady failed to perform, Belichick could look at the 41-year-old and his $22 million salary-cap hit and argue to ownership that it was time to transition to Jimmy Garoppolo in 2018. Belichick seemed to already prefer that route. Kraft cringed at it. After Deflategate and after all the stress it put on relationships, Kraft was more resolute than ever that Brady must retire a Patriot. He believed Brady had earned the right to walk away on his terms. And if the Patriots had signed Brady to a five-year deal right after the Super Bowl against the Falcons, much of the turmoil and anger and drama of the subsequent few years would likely have been avoided. Brady would have ended his career a Patriot.

Brady playing football until age 45 was no longer just a personal goal. It was a business plan, a test case and the best advertisement for the TB12 Method. Brady preferred to do it in New England, but he was prepared to do it elsewhere. And if the team wanted to move on to Garoppolo, somebody needed to own the decision. Belichick was a master at allowing situations to play out, on the field and off, and always found it far easier to keep his plans to himself than to confide in anyone. But his actions spoke for him. He had turned down major trade offers for Garoppolo after the Super Bowl win over Atlanta—reportedly, at least one first-round pick—and had traded Jacoby Brissett to the Indianapolis Colts in the preseason. These were clear signs that Garoppolo was very much part of New England's present and future in the view of the team's coach, who seemed to have the power to make it so.

As the 2017 season went on, Brady played well, but absorbed an atypical amount of punishment that led to shoulder and Achilles injuries. He missed more practice than usual. And the only contract for a quarterback Belichick seemed to want to discuss was one for Garoppolo. New

England offered Garoppolo a two-year bridge deal, until the Brady sit-uation sorted itself out. Belichick knew that Garoppolo wanted to play, but hoped that an investment in him by the game's greatest coach would be enough to keep him around. It wasn't. Through his agent, Don Yee—who also represented Brady—Garoppolo passed on the offer, setting himself up to become a free agent, unless Belichick elected to apply the franchise tag on him, paying him like a starter and perhaps taking the first step toward trading Brady.

In October, Brady and Belichick met to discuss his future. Belichick was respectful but skeptical about a long-term contract extension. The meeting ended in "a little blowup," a senior Patriots official later said. Between Belichick's clear faith in Garoppolo, his tensions with Guer-rero, and his refusal to commit to Brady, the coach and quarterback were at an impasse. Outside of regular game-planning meetings, they barely spoke the rest of the year. Brady took his case directly to the top.

37

YOU THINK
BOB KRAFT CAME
AFTER YOU HARD

OGER GOODELL'S PHONE RANG AT 5:30 IN THE MORN-
ing on September 23, 2017. He was in Aspen. Joe Lockhart was
on the line, with news of a major problem.

At a rally in Alabama the night before, President Trump had veered
from politics to the NFL. Trump often took shots at the league, and
on this night, after mocking efforts to make football safer, he turned
his attention to the handful of players who knelt during the national
anthem. "Wouldn't you love to see one of these NFL owners, when
somebody disrespects our flag, to say, 'Get that son of a bitch off the
field right now. Out! He's fired! He's fired!'"

The crowd ate it up. A small protest, started by Colin Kaepernick in
2016 during Barack Obama's final year in office, was about to become a
league-wide, nationally polarizing crisis at the hands of Trump.

"We've got to say something," Lockhart told Goodell.

The commissioner agreed. The league released a statement that
morning, defending its players, but Goodell wanted every owner to put
out one of their own in a show of solidarity. It was all hands on deck.
On a conference call, Goodell, Lockhart, Jeff Pash, and other league
executives ran down a list of owners, assigning them into groups for
each executive to call. They reached Robert Kraft and Jerry Jones—two
stress-inducing names, both big personalities, not to mention friends of
Trump and inauguration donors.

The line went quiet.

"Roger?" someone finally said.

Everyone laughed. Those two were Goodell's.

TRUMP WAS ALREADY a volatile issue in New England's locker room, and Kraft's statement in reaction to the president's remarks—that he was "deeply disappointed" by Trump's "tone"—only made it worse. The president of the United States had called peaceful protesters against racism "sons of bitches"—and Kraft was disappointed by his *tone*?

Kraft had been attempting the impossible for almost two years, supporting the friend who had called him weekly at the darkest moments of his life after Myra died, while distancing himself from almost everything that came out of the president's mouth. It wasn't working. At one point, Atlanta Falcons owner Arthur Blank told Kraft, "You fucker, you've given him a lot of money." After the Super Bowl win over Atlanta, the team was scheduled for the ceremonial visit to the White House. Many players skipped it, including Brady, who was said to be tending to family matters, and Hightower and McCourty, who spoke for many on the team when he said, "I don't feel accepted at the White House." Hoping to avoid a lackluster turnout, Kraft showed players a photo of himself in the Lincoln Bedroom, promising the team would get a special tour of the White House residence. Thirty-four players ended up going. It was awkward throughout. Trump riffed for a minute about how much he appreciated Belichick's "beautiful" letter, reopening a wound. Robert Kraft rubbed his face. Jonathan Kraft looked at the ground. Belichick stared straight ahead, determined to not display any reaction on camera, easy enough for him. During the tour, and after Kraft had given him a Super Bowl ring to go along with the customary gifts of a jersey and helmet, Trump said before a group of players and coaches, "Let's go to the Lincoln Bedroom!"

An aide told the president that visitors don't go up there. "We take the Patriots!" Trump said.

Months after the White House visit, before the 2017 season, Belichick had both tried to heal the team and get ahead of the anthem issue, as if he knew it might blow up. He hosted a meeting about the anthem and its history. The players watched films on Francis Scott Key. Belichick played the anthem for the players, encouraging them to analyze it, some of them hearing it in a new way—before the meeting adjourned.

Now Belichick's premonition was proving accurate. Nobody within the league offices knew how to handle Trump. After Kraft released his statement, he spoke with Goodell. They discussed changing the timing of the anthem, to play it before teams left the locker rooms. But as the season neared, the anthem went on as planned and each team decided how to handle it on its own. The Steelers, Seahawks, and Titans defied league rules by remaining in the locker room as it played. Twenty or so Patriots knelt—and were booed by a swath of fans. It was only the beginning. A league known for trying to control everything now grappled with how to deal with losing control altogether, with the president of the United States steadfast in his determination to keep the corrosive issue in the national conversation.

Two days later, the owners convened in the sixth-floor conference room of the league's headquarters, a mass of spooked billionaires. Kraft and Jones expressed concerns that the sight of hundreds of players kneeling, sitting, or remaining in the locker room during the national anthem would alienate many fans at a perilous moment for the league. Television ratings had continued a slide that began in 2016. Some league sponsors were skittish about the backlash against the anthem protests as well. Most surveys showed that a majority of NFL fans were turned off by the politicization of the game, meaning by Kaepernick and his cause and actions. Women's jersey sales were down. The NFL was losing some portion of its casual fans. A few league executives got voicemails from fans ordering them to "fire criminals" who had violated the "morals clause" in their contracts.

The meeting was typical for the league: nobody seemed to be running it, owners sat behind poker faces as they wondered whether to express an opinion, and finally, Jones filled the void. He mentioned that he had spoken with Trump within the past 24 hours and that the president had no intention of letting the matter go. Trump believed it was a winning issue for him: He had tweeted nearly two dozen times about the NFL and its players since he first made the comments, thinking it galvanized his base.

The owners found the response by the league office so far, from its communications to its strategy, to be underwhelming. One league executive presented an idea for all players to wear a patch on their jerseys reading "Team America." What seemed like a joke was not. Nobody knew what to say. Finally one owner spoke: "We need to do better than that."

The meeting ended without resolution or optimism. In the days that followed, the lack of a uniform strategy showed. Goodell and Kraft wanted the protests to end, but were at least somewhat empathetic toward the players. Jones threatened to bench any player who knelt and advocated a league mandate that players had to stand. The players themselves refused to acquiesce; hundreds of them knelt before games the following weekend. The league was in crisis, in a war it couldn't win.

THE NEXT SEVERAL WEEKS witnessed fights in boardrooms and on social media and in stadiums. During a meeting with a select group of players and owners on October 17, there were several well-intentioned but cringeworthy moments. Buffalo Bills owner Terry Pegula suggested that the league needed to find a lead spokesman for social justice— preferably "someone who's Black"—and accidentally referred to Anquan Boldin, a former wide receiver and now an activist, as "Antwan." Players pointed out that most of the owners, including Kraft, were "aligned" with the president. The meeting ended with a joint statement from the league and the union—a rare instance of cooperation—and some levity. After the discussion passed the 90-minute mark, Kraft whispered to the Jets players seated on either side of him, "Can we just shut the fuck up and end this?" Everyone on his side of the table laughed.

Any unity gained was undone the next day, during an owners-only meeting with league executives at the Conrad Hotel in downtown Manhattan. The league presented confidential slides illustrating the ratings drop. Local market viewership was down year over year for all but six teams. The Patriots were down 8 percent, while 11 teams had double-digit declines. Owners were anxious. Jones stood and left no question that he thought it was his floor—if not *his* league.

"I'm the ranking owner here," he said.

Jones told the room that owners had to take the business impact of the kneeling seriously. He was trying to build momentum for a mandate to stand. He was already at odds with the league office, specifically with Goodell. In August of 2017, shortly after Jones was inducted into the Hall of Fame—an honor that, so far, had eluded Kraft—he was on a conference call with Goodell and Jeff Pash, who informed him that the Cowboys' star running back Ezekiel Elliott would be suspended for a domestic violence incident. Jones believed that there was "absolutely nothing" to the allegations against Elliott, who was never charged in connection with these allegations.. But after a yearlong investigation, Goodell and other league executives disagreed—and the commissioner was facing pressure to act. Kraft had spoken with Goodell over the summer of 2017, when the investigation was dragging on, and said, "My guy got four games for footballs and there's still nothing on this?" On the conference call, Jones was enraged. Don Van Natta and I later reported that Jones yelled, "I'm gonna come after you with everything I have." Then he mentioned Deflategate. "If you think Bob Kraft came after you hard, Bob Kraft is a pussy compared to what I'm going to do."

Now Jones was angry again, this time in front of his peers. The support for the mandate wasn't there, and its opponents included Kraft. Jones wasn't getting his way, and he knew it.

Washington's Dan Snyder spoke up in support of a mandate. "See—Jones gets it," he said, persuading nobody. Bob McNair then gave a speech that hurt the league and caused him anguish until he died of cancer a year later. He supported a mandate to stand, and then emphasized that the owners needed to take control of the issue. "We can't have the inmates running the prison," he said.

The comment stunned many in the room. Anger between league executives trying to navigate a complicated issue and a small group of hardline owners boiled over. Executive vice president Troy Vincent was deeply offended by McNair's remark. He said that, in all his years of playing in the NFL—during which, he said, he had been called every name in the book, including the N-word—he never felt like an "inmate."

Jones spoke up and backed McNair, reminding Vincent that the league became a $15 billion-a-year business due to visionary owners, not league-office suits. Two white, Southern, Trump-donating billionaires were attacking one of the league's few executives of color. Kraft tried to step in, advocating continued dialogue rather than new rules surrounding the anthem. This was the most popular position. But the room was tired, the entire league on edge. McNair felt horrible and later apologized to Vincent, saying that he misspoke. But when Van Natta and I reported on the exchange a few weeks later, it became a huge controversy. Richard Sherman said, "I think there are some conservative owners who have Confederate flags at their homes," and Texans players threatened to stage a walkout. "We've never seen anything like this," ESPN's Adam Schefter said on air. "The league is on fire." Jay-Z addressed McNair's comments at a concert. "That's how they look at you. That's exactly how they feel about you." LeBron James later said that NFL owners were "old white men" with a "slave mentality" toward players.

McNair released a statement insisting that he was referring to league executives, not players, as inmates. No one believed him. McNair asked Goodell to publicly back him. Goodell declined.

In the following weeks, the anthem chaos seemed to fade as Trump moved on to other targets—and the league, as if on cue, turned to the next crisis. In November, Jones threatened to sue the NFL and the six owners on the compensation committee to block the commissioner's pending contract extension. It was unheard of: the league's most famous and powerful owner trying to take out a commissioner. Since Goodell's reign began, the league had been drifting from scandal to scandal: Michael Vick; Spygate; Bountygate; head injuries; wars with the union; Ray Rice; Deflategate; the anthem and McNair's "inmates" comment. And now Jones's assault. It was always something, an unending loop of often-self-inflicted wounds. The NFL liked to call itself America's Game, united and glorious—united in its glory—but the league was more like Washington, DC, just with more sides: a massive circular firing squad.

The Patriots' dynasty coincided with and helped drive a period of endless controversy at the league level. But even as the league seemed to be coming apart at various points, the game's preeminent franchise largely had other concerns. Its unprecedented accomplishments had raised expectations and possibilities so high as to be incomprehensible. Only Robert Kraft, Bill Belichick, and Tom Brady knew what the view was like from the top of their particular mountain. They weren't only pushing past the limits of team success in the salary-cap era. They were also challenging basic understandings of how a group of high achievers escape the inevitable pulls of ego and pride. No other NFL dynasty had lasted this long, and the three men had managed to stay together because all of them knew it—their only true opponent was history. But, after nearly two decades of dominance, they were finally starting to unravel in the only way possible: from within.

38

I DON'T WANT TO
PLAY FOR BILL
ANYMORE

THE TWO RECENT SUPER BOWL VICTORIES HAD
changed the three heads of state in New England, none more
than Robert Kraft. He felt the press of time running out more
than Bill Belichick or even Tom Brady, and he was both more sentimental and more active than ever. He was no longer the widely despised
man who had threatened to move the team to Hartford. He was a local
icon who had changed Boston sports forever, routinely named by various outlets as the best owner in sports. Unlike after the first three
championships, Kraft was now single—more specifically, he dated a
few "gals"—and he globe-trotted with a younger crowd, most notably
Philadelphia 76ers co-owner and Fanatics executive chairman Michael
Rubin. He was a TMZ draw. His hair, once cropped tight, was now longer
and wavy. His trademark blue buttoned-up shirt with a white collar—
the look of a salesman—was seen less. He now wore suits without ties
and modified Nike Air Force 1 sneakers from his own shoe line with
the company. But as he aged, as he thought about his life and legacy, as
he watched Jerry Jones reach the Hall of Fame—*Jerry Jones*, whose ego
had run Jimmy Johnson off and who hadn't sniffed a Super Bowl since
1996, who said all kinds of weird things, laughed off as "Jerryisms," like
wanting to return the Cowboys to the "gloryhole days" and discussing
masturbating into his shoes—as he sat for interviews over the years
with writers working on books about Tom Brady and Bill Belichick and
wondered why nobody had looked at the big picture, that a homegrown
Patriots fan had saved the franchise and pulled off the greatest trade in

NFL history and managed all of these massive egos and negotiated all of these billion-dollar broadcast contracts that made rich men richer and sent the league to unrivaled popularity, he wanted a little recognition.

A Hall of Fame nod would certainly work. But that was out of his hands. Kraft met with author Mark Leibovich a few times for the book *Big Game: The NFL in Dangerous Times.* When Leibovich asked Kraft if he felt overlooked due to the focus on Brady and Belichick, the owner danced around the question. "Sweethaht"—a word Kraft used when he was irritated, Leibovich observed—"when you own the team, at some point someone figures out that ownership can mess it up. And maybe if you look around the league, you'll see maybe that has happened. I'll tell you, they'll be no team in the NFL that will win consistently without having good ownership, so I don't worry."

Leibovich didn't buy it, and in his book referred to Kraft as a "whiny star-fucker" and "sniveling in victory."

But now, with his two most vital employees barely talking, Kraft wanted to be more involved with the team itself. He started speaking to players and coaches and staff alone, often without Belichick's knowledge, quietly taking the pulse of the building, offering to host them at his summer home in Cape Cod, making clear that Belichick wasn't going to be there forever and implying that their ultimate loyalty should be to the owner, lest they forget. Coaches came to hate it when he drifted into their offices and closed the door, knowing what would come next: nitpicking over decisions, with no end in sight. They felt pinched between the owner and the boss. But it was Kraft's team. He could run it whatever way he wanted, and on the list of meddling owners, he was still near the bottom. Washington coaches told horror stories about Dan Snyder, for example. Before the draft, Washington's football operations department spent months assembling, considering, debating, and finally, deciding on which players to select. But in the first round, former head coach Jay Gruden said, Snyder would "come in off his yacht and make the pick."

Still, Kraft was threatening the siloed world that Belichick had created. Belichick groused to the staff at times that the autonomy with which he had run the team to that point was starting to erode. Kraft often reminded Belichick how he had saved his career after Cleveland. "Bill was an idiot savant," Kraft told a confidant. "I gave him this opportunity."

As the 2017 season reached its midway point, Jimmy Garoppolo—or, rather, the Garoppolo *situation*, as people inside New England called it, as if he were more pawn than passer—hovered over the team. Brady was worried Belichick would ship him out. Trying to finesse a delicate relationship and keep the band together, Kraft listened to Brady, maybe too closely. Some coaches thought that Kraft's undying loyalty to Brady—his love for him—further strained the quarterback's relationship with the head coach. Kraft's willingness to make himself available to Brady—to hear him out, to appease him, to let him in on company secrets, to make it resoundingly clear that the owner had his back—painted Belichick as even more of the bad guy, for Brady and for others in the building. After Belichick banned Guerrero from the team plane, Kraft let him fly at least once on his own jet. Brady's stature had grown so large that new players referred to him as "sir," which embarrassed him. After 17 seasons and five rings and many years of covering up for Belichick's struggle to develop receivers, Brady was as much Kraft's employee as Belichick's, and he wanted more influence over personnel, something few quarterbacks in history—Elway and Manning, to name a couple—had enjoyed.

Belichick wanted to keep Garoppolo. If Garoppolo refused a new contract, Belichick had the option to apply the franchise tag to him, paying the backup like a starter and perhaps signaling that a Brady trade was inevitable. But, for once, Belichick wasn't working from a position of ultimate leverage. Keeping both Brady and Garoppolo would be expensive. Quarterbacks had never accounted for more than 14 percent of the salary cap during Belichick's tenure. And Kraft believed that Brady had earned the right to walk away on his own volition, giving him at least some input over his fate.

I later reported on a meeting between Kraft and Belichick that ended with a mandate that Brady was both the team's quarterback of the present and future—and that the team would move on from Garoppolo because he wasn't in New England's long-term plans, which Kraft denied after the piece ran. Greg A. Bedard of the *Boston Sports Journal* cited three sources as saying that Kraft "made it known to Belichick that he was to trade Garoppolo." In the book *12: The Inside Story of Tom Brady's Fight for Redemption*, with which both Kraft and Brady cooperated, authors Casey Sherman and Dave Wedge described a meeting between Belichick and Kraft in which the head coach broached the idea of trading Brady—claiming to have a deal in place—and the owner vetoed it, setting the stage for Garoppolo to be traded. It was abundantly, and understandably, clear that Kraft's loyalties were to Brady, who in 2017 continued to play at a high level, injuries and all.

His options narrowing, Belichick did something rare: he looked out for the player. Early in the morning of October 30, he texted Kyle Shanahan, who was then in his first year as the San Francisco 49ers' head coach. A lot had changed since Belichick and Mike Shanahan booted Kyle from the room after the playoff game in 2006. Shanahan had suffered a blowout loss to the Eagles the previous day and wondered if Belichick was offering a pick-me-up. They had become friendly. Weeks after New England's Super Bowl win over Atlanta, Belichick reached out to Shanahan and asked to meet at the combine. Kyle was flattered. "It's the biggest compliment for a guy like Belichick to want to talk football with you," his dad told him. Belichick spent hours with Shanahan, dissecting the Super Bowl and passing down wisdom on how to be a head coach, helping a rival more than he had helped some of his own.

When Shanahan returned the latest call, Belichick presented a trade: Garoppolo in exchange for a second-round pick. And he did need an answer quickly. Belichick saw himself as doing a favor for two people he liked, giving Garoppolo a brilliant young coach and giving the brilliant young coach, running a team in the other conference and across the country, a franchise player he had personally developed.

Shanahan was surprised. At first, nobody in the 49ers brain trust believed Belichick was serious. You never knew with Belichick. Sometimes, he was direct; at other times, he would probe, seeing what he could get away with. In the off-season, general manager John Lynch had been one of many who inquired about Garoppolo. It had gone nowhere. Now it was very real, with the clock ticking.

The 49ers were in. Word of the trade reached New England's coaches, many of whom were at a Celtics game, that night. They were surprised and confused. The game's shrewdest long-term strategist had traded two backup quarterbacks in a two-month span, even though his starter was 40 years old and banged-up—and had practically given away a quarterback they saw as a potential top-ten player in the league. Without Garoppolo, one coach later said, "We're the Cleveland Browns, with no succession plan." Michael Lombardi argued it was the worst trade of Belichick's career, and he later wrote in a book—to which Belichick contributed the foreword—that "word is, it was not" Belichick's call alone. New England's coaching staff understood this was a special case, but felt Belichick had earned the right to make all football decisions. And while there was a line of thinking among Patriots executives that Belichick tried to save face by telling people that Kraft forced the trade, he had also always subscribed to the philosophy that it's time to go once an owner gets too involved—and left the impression with some friends that the current dynamic was unsustainable.

At a post-trade press conference, Belichick made clear that he had wanted to keep Garoppolo and spoke glowingly about him for more than a minute, in a manner that he rarely did about any player—especially Brady. After each ensuing 49ers game—Garoppolo won all five of his starts in 2017—Belichick texted his former quarterback, congratulating him. Kraft later confessed to people in the building that the trade might have been a mistake. Brady, though, seemed liberated. Kraft hugged Brady when he saw him days after the deal, in full view of teammates. At practice, some players and staffers noticed that Brady seemed especially invigorated, hollering and cajoling. And why wouldn't he? Tom Brady had won.

THE HIGH WORE OFF as the season wore on. One play in particular that occurred before the Garoppolo trade—a fourth-quarter throw against the Chargers—bothered the coaches. Brady had a clean pocket and Rob Gronkowski open deep, possibly for a touchdown. But Brady—tailoring his game to his injuries, in the eyes of the coaches—went quick and short to receiver Chris Hogan in traffic. Hogan was hit hard, suffering an injured shoulder, and missed all but one game the rest of the season, further depleting an already thin receiver corps. The reporter and author Ian O'Connor later reported on a devastating internal evaluation of Brady. "If you gave us any of the top 15, we could do it," an assistant coach said. "I don't think the coaches view Tom as special as everyone else in football does. Mr. Kraft thinks Tom is the greatest gift ever, but the coaches don't."

Defenses of Brady in staff meetings often came from Belichick. "He's still pretty good," he told a few coaches, purposefully understated.

But Brady was on edge, months of silent anger starting to seep out. On December 3 against the Buffalo Bills, he walked to the sideline after throwing late and behind receiver Brandin Cooks on third down, ending a drive. As he started to remove his helmet, Brady passed Josh McDaniels.

"He was wide open," McDaniels said, referring to Cooks.

Brady kept walking, glaring at McDaniels.

"We had him open," McDaniels repeated.

Brady blew up. "I got it!" he said. Then he unloaded, yelling so loudly that everyone within earshot, including Belichick, turned to watch. Sitting a few seats behind the bench was McDaniels's father, Thom. A Patriots staffer roped his arms around Brady, holding him back, but he kept going at McDaniels.

"Fuck you!" Brady yelled.

Video of the exchange went viral. McDaniels let it roll off his back, and Brady later apologized. They were like brothers, finding it easy to irritate each other but hard to stay mad. But Brady seemed to be searching. "The last couple years, a lot of parts about football weren't enjoyable when they should have been," he later said. The pinnacle of his profession was more fleeting than rewarding.

NICK CASERIO WAS New England's top personnel executive, a trusted aide to Bill Belichick who had risen from a lowly job in the organization. He was also one of Robert Kraft's most valued employees, someone the owner seemed to consider a vital part of the team's post-Belichick plans. Kraft often called Caserio for insight into the team, a chance to learn what was going on without having to call Belichick—or because when he did talk with Belichick, the coach would simply withhold information. Sometimes, Caserio had no answers for Kraft; Belichick withheld information from him, too. Caserio was mentioned across the league as a candidate for general manager jobs, but as with many New England guys, nobody knew if he would actually leave. Kraft might have been planning to make Caserio the GM of the Patriots. Kraft had been asking him for years to keep an eye out for overlooked coaching talent around the league—the kind Belichick was in 2000.

"Who's the next guy?" Kraft often asked Caserio.

That moment seemed to be looming. Brady, Belichick, and Kraft were supposed to meet in December to try to clear the air, but that meeting never happened. Nobody was budging. With the regular season nearing its end, Belichick spoke with various owners and executives about potential openings, which wasn't in itself a new development. Belichick was a quiet kingmaker in the NFL, a role he had earned and enjoyed. While Kraft at times treated Belichick like a management hurdle, other owners valued his word as gold. After Belichick suggested to Jacksonville Jaguars ownership that they should consider giving interim head coach Doug Marrone the full-time job in 2017, they hired him weeks later. But Belichick had told people close to him that an executive job—the chance to build an organization from upstairs rather than the sideline, as Mike Holmgren, Tom Coughlin, and Bill Parcells had done after finishing their coaching careers—seemed appealing, under the right circumstances. He had always looked at clubs not only as teams but as businesses, and he knew that if he ever left New England, it would be for a select few owners or locations that made business sense. Certain coaches were fits in only certain regions of the country, he often told associates. When Massachusetts native Bill O'Brien was hired as head coach of the Houston Texans in 2014, Belichick told him, "You don't own one pair of cowboy boots. They're going to run you out." Belichick knew himself well: he was an East Coast guy. He occasionally had mentioned Miami as a possible next spot, and NBC Sports Boston later reported that, after the Garoppolo trade, Belichick "inquired" about working for the New York Giants and Washington. Belichick had great reverence for the Giants organization; Washington was near Annapolis, where his mom still lived. Those who spoke to Belichick later said that it was hard to gauge whether he was serious or flirting.

Kraft sometimes groaned to confidants that Belichick didn't show him the respect he deserved, but he was in no rush for life after him. Brady, though, seemed ready for it. In 2017, with his coaches critiquing him as a good but not great performer, Brady led the league in yards and threw 32 touchdowns and only eight interceptions. But he noted a few times to coaches that he hadn't won Patriot of the Week all year, an award given to the player who best demonstrated the team's ethos of selflessness and sacrifice. It wasn't the award that Brady craved, but an acknowledgement from Belichick, a sign of appreciation. "He's so negative," Brady told people in the building. Brady always viewed football as a means of self-actualization. He wanted to keep growing, as a player and person, but as the 2017 season wore on, he hit an emotional plateau in New England.

"I don't want to play for Bill anymore," he told people close to him.

That was new. Even on his worst days with Belichick, Brady was able to separate the coach's personality from his talent. He had told friends that he thought Belichick was a "genius" and that he hoped never to play for anyone else. All of that had now changed. During one meeting between Kraft and Brady and a few others, they discussed scenarios, including: If Belichick should happen to retire, after this year or next, who would replace him? They spitballed a creative solution. If McDaniels left after the season to be a head coach elsewhere, New England could hire O'Brien, who, as Belichick had predicted, now seemed to be on his way out of Houston, to replace him—and, soon enough, to succeed Belichick. Brady loved working with O'Brien during the latter's years in New England, and O'Brien was a promising coach who would lead the Texans to the playoffs four times. Unlike Belichick, O'Brien might welcome Brady's suggestions on roster decisions.

The plan was fanciful, but O'Brien heard about it. He was in a power struggle of his own in Houston, fighting with general manager Rick Smith, a "dysfunctional" and "toxic" situation, according to the *Houston Chronicle*. The leaks from O'Brien's camp, claiming he wanted out, were so aggressive as to be suspicious, as if he knew he had a golden parachute. In the end, though, the McNair family chose O'Brien over Smith, giving the coach more control over football operations. O'Brien later joked to a confidant that it was a somewhat empty victory. "I was *trying* to get fired," he said.

ON NEW YEAR'S EVE, after the Patriots beat the Jets decisively in the season finale—New England had not only survived the regular season, it had excelled, finishing 13–3 and as the AFC's first seed—Brady and Bündchen drove home from the stadium in his black Ford pickup. The sun was low. It had been a long year, and, as usual for the Patriots, it was just beginning, with the playoffs impending. Sitting next to each other, their minds were in different places.

"Look at the moon," Bündchen said. "The moon is incredible."

"I think we're supposed to play on Saturday night," Brady replied.

She had a plan for New Year's Eve. After the kids were asleep, she wanted to start a fire and write a list of all the aspects of their 2017 lives to "let go" of, and "offer it to the fire."

Brady quietly stared at the road.

"And then we meditate for an hour," she said.

"We meditate for an hour?"

"Yeah."

"All right. We'll see how I do."

She leaned into his ear. "You can meditate less if you like."

It had been an eventful year even by Brady and Patriots standards, beginning with a historic comeback and ending with meditation and more winning. That night, a mass email went out to all members of the Patriots organization, outlining "3 Keys to a Great 2018," with the tension between the faces of the franchise a clear subtext:

Stay connected—to your family and team. You are more powerful together than alone.

THE PUBLIC HAD LEARNED of New England's internal struggles during the season. On October 31, I reported that "a collision" was coming between the quarterback and the head coach over Guerrero. Later that day, reporter Ryan Burr tweeted that the Garoppolo trade was "a

Kraft decision" and that the relationship between Brady and Belichick was "not great." In November, the *Boston Globe* issued its report that Belichick had curtailed Guerrero's access, causing "some friction." In late December, Tom E. Curran of NBC Sports Boston wrote that the season had an "end of party scent to it. Like people are gathering up their coats and saying their goodbyes." In early January, I wrote a story on the divide, highlighting the disagreements over Guerrero and Garoppolo and the palpable sense within the team that this might be the end. The Patriots issued a statement denying "multiple media reports that have speculated theories that are unsubstantiated, highly exaggerated or flat out inaccurate." It ended with an affirmation that Kraft, Belichick, and Brady "stand united."

The statement didn't hold up well. When asked if Kraft had pushed the Garoppolo trade, Belichick initially refused to defuse the situation with an easy no, saying he had already spoken at length about it. Brady was asked about problems in the building on his radio show. He never wanted to wade into public fights, seeing little point in exerting energy on something unwinnable, so he responded with an existential riff about the ineffable nature of truth. And after an easy win in the divisional round over the Tennessee Titans and before the AFC Championship Game against the Jacksonville Jaguars, Kraft contradicted his own statement and admitted to the NFL Network that there was "tension." He put a positive spin on it. "A certain amount of tension makes great things happen."

"The fact that Tommy and Bill Belichick and my family have been together for 18 years—that's unheard of," he continued. "There's a lot of strong-minded people, but when you have something good going, everyone has to get their egos checked in and try and hold it together."

Get their egos checked. Many Patriots coaches thought Kraft had taken a brazen shot at Belichick—in the middle of the playoffs, no less. The wall between what went on behind the scenes in New England and what the public knew was breaking down for good. For the rest of the time that Robert Kraft, Tom Brady, and Bill Belichick spent together, the perception of how the team operated in private would be as much of a presence in the room as their magnificent accomplishments.

39

IT'S NOT
BRAIN SURGERY

JUST AS THE SEASON WAS APPROACHING THE MOMENT Tom Brady had worked for all year, it looked like it might be over. On January 18, 2018, a frigid Wednesday afternoon, days before the AFC Championship Game against Jacksonville, Brady collided in practice with running back Rex Burkhead on a routine handoff. The thumb on his passing hand bent back so far that it nearly detached, splitting skin to the bone. It was horrific. He looked at his thumb, with blood streaking from its joint and down his palm, and thought, *This is it. This is the way the season ends.*

The Patriots trainers called Dr. Matthew Leibman, who served as a hand and wrist surgeon for most of the Boston professional sports teams. Leibman reviewed the X-ray and came back with good news—no, great news: the thumb wasn't fractured or dislocated. It was just hyperextended, painful but not catastrophic. Brady dressed for practice the next day, but didn't participate. The thumb felt better, but not close to right. By Friday, he believed he could go on game day. Guerrero massaged the thumb and hand at Brady's house, trying to reduce swelling, poking pins into it as Brady gasped and winced and released a primal groan.

Sunday arrived, and Brady was worried that he wouldn't be effective on the field. He was offered a painkilling injection but passed, preferring to feel pain rather than feeling nothing. Only quarterbacks understand the singular threat of thumb injuries. The thumb is the anchor of their grip. If you don't have a thumb, you don't have a release—and you become Kurt Warner, whose career was nearly derailed due to a thumb injury. Brady would wear a black strip of tape alongside the inside of his palm, covering the laceration. Before kickoff, he ran onto the field in his usual manner: screaming, "Let's goooo!"

Nothing went right. New England moved the ball, but couldn't score. Gronkowski was knocked out of the game after taking a shot to the head, leaving Brady with only his tiny receivers and a 20–10 deficit in the fourth quarter.

Many times throughout the 2017 season, Brady had wondered, *Why am I doing this?* Why deal with Belichick's weirdness and the moodiness of the other coaches? Why eat shit from the press and scientists for trying to persuade people to be healthier? Why watch the rage on his wife's iconic face on his behalf for the way Belichick treated him—*fucking Johnny Foxborough*—and the dull panic in her eyes after another hit to his head? Why continue to test her patience with his uncompromising year-round work schedule? Why subject himself to the talking heads who were waiting for him to fall on his face? Why live in the cold—it was a particularly bad winter in the Northeast—and why constantly have to reread *The Four Agreements* to remind himself what really mattered?

Maybe *this* was why.

Brady always found that the football field was the only place he could be his true self—a mix of natural talent with rage and focus. So, fuck the score, the thumb, the talk shows, the excuses. "Whatever it takes!" Brady yelled in the huddle. He completed five passes on the second drive of the fourth quarter and three passes on the next-to-last, ending both series with touchdown throws to Danny Amendola. New England won, 24–20, and would face the Philadelphia Eagles in Minneapolis in Super Bowl LII, the eighth trip for Brady and Belichick in 16 glorious, stressful years together.

After the game, Brady stood in a hallway outside the locker room, in a gray "AFC Conference Champions" T-shirt, surrounded by friends both new and old. His buddy Kevin Brady—everyone now called him KB12—was there, in his third decade as witness to Brady's rise. Brady threw up his arms, fully aware that the team had pulled off yet another miracle, but a miracle all the same. He wrapped his left arm around his wife and kissed her forehead, above the bridge of her nose and under the brim of her stocking hat, which read, "TEAM BRADY." *Her* allegiances, at least, were clear.

A few doors down, Belichick stood in the auditorium. A reporter asked about Brady's toughness. "I mean, look—Tom did a great job and he's a tough guy. All right?" Belichick said. His eyes shot around, as if calculating whether he should *go there,* say how he really felt, knowing it might create a stir . . .

"But we're not talking about open-heart surgery here," Belichick said.

Those words were, author Ian O'Connor later wrote, "a swift kick in the ass" directed at Brady. The next day, Kraft sat in his office, pondering with an associate the fractured relationship between his two most important employees. He thought it didn't matter if they liked each other. "It's how you deal with it. Do you stay cool or do you act? You just deal. It's not"—choosing words carefully and for maximum effect—"*brain* surgery."

WHILE KRAFT TRIED to hold on to what was, and Brady considered what could be, the coach was navigating a staff in transition. Defensive coordinator Matt Patricia, who had whiffed on all of his head-coaching interviews a year earlier—Belichick helped him prepare this time around, both a courtesy and maybe as a nudge—was now due to become the head coach of the Detroit Lions. Brian Flores was promoted, New England–style, receiving most of Patricia's responsibility, but without the title. As always, Belichick made him earn it first.

Josh McDaniels was also set to leave. After years of both coordinating an outstanding offense and working on his image and leadership—he participated in a long piece for *Bleacher Report*—McDaniels agreed in principle to be the head coach of the Indianapolis Colts. Belichick blessed the move, believing it was a good job. The Colts had a superstar quarterback in Andrew Luck and a precocious general manager named Chris Ballard. McDaniels was polished in his interviews, owning his mistakes, treading a fine line between respect for Brady and describing how his offense would excel without him. But, to his confidants, he still seemed nervous, as if he understood that this was a prized landing spot, but was wary of making the jump. Had the Denver experience wrecked his ambition as much as his reputation? Friends wondered if he truly wanted to be a head coach again, or if he simply wanted to be wanted. He had indicated to the Browns that he would take their head-coaching job in 2014, only to decide against it. In January 2017, he danced with the 49ers for weeks—discussions were granular, down to details of the IT staff—but then pulled out, the job going to Kyle Shanahan.

Replacing McDaniels was tricky for Belichick. If he promoted from within, someone like receivers coach Chad O'Shea, Brady might run all over him. By now, Brady knew more about offensive football than most head coaches around the league. And McDaniels had coordinated the offense so well that he had earned trust and autonomy. Belichick told associates he wanted more control over the offense. He considered splitting up the duties between himself and special teams coach Joe Judge, another promising staffer. But if Belichick became the de facto offensive coordinator, would Brady ask to be released? Their relationship barely sustained twice-weekly quarterback meetings; how could they meet for long hours on a daily basis—especially with Brady wanting more influence over personnel and scheme?

But then, Josh McDaniels started to solve the Josh McDaniels problem. NBC's Mike Florio reported that there was "increasing chatter" that McDaniels might have some doubts about Indianapolis. McDaniels trusted Ballard to draft players, but the two had never discussed other elements of the organization, such as the medical and video staffs. Those close to him felt that was a thin reason—perhaps a rationale for someone who was looking for reasons to not leave New England.

ON SUPER BOWL EVE, February 3, Robert Kraft threw a party at a downtown Minneapolis hotel—part celebration of the dynasty, part unintentional wake. He had been wistful and proud and reflective and grateful in the days leading up to the game, tearing up as he thought about how all of this came to be. Myra spending Sundays doing the *Times* crossword puzzle as he and the boys went to Patriots games, dreaming of owning the team one day . . . the $56 million of blue steel that he personally signed for to build the stadium . . . the Super Bowl that launched it all, in the shadow of 9/11, a team with red, white, and blue colors holding the trophy . . . the mementos in his office: Jon Gruden inscribing a photo of Charles Woodson colliding with Brady in the snow with *It was a fumble*; a chair from Jon Bon Jovi; a red guitar from Bono; photos of himself alongside Barack Obama and Bill Clinton and Joe Biden and dancing with Jackie O. Kraft had celebrated the win over the Jaguars with a glass of Johnnie Walker Blue and snuck in a cigar with a few of the coaches. He was now 76 years old and on his way to his ninth Super Bowl.

Kraft arrived for the party in a blue blazer, gray sneakers, and black shirt, with his cloudy hair tucked behind his ears. In the hotel, security guards ushered him to the fifth floor, where the elevator doors opened and a crowd surged. His movement was measured by handshakes: CBS chairman Les Moonves, Donnie and Mark Wahlberg, Melissa McCarthy, ESPN's Chris Berman, DeMaurice Smith. Kenny Chesney—"my good-luck charm," Kraft called him. No Goodell, no other jealous owners—they were all at league events. Five minutes passed, and Kraft was only a few feet from the elevator.

In a ballroom across the hall, waiters carried trays of sparking water and wine, framed by two 40-foot projection screens behind them, flashing the Super Bowl emblem and the Patriots logo. As soon as most of the 298 attendees were seated, Kraft took the stage.

"Hi, everyone," he said.

Kraft seemed humbled by the turnout. He told the crowd that, after the first time his team went to the Super Bowl, after the 1996 season, he realized how special it was—and vowed to plan each time as though it would never happen again. The night-before gatherings began in 2002 and had continued ever since. It wasn't a party *for* Kraft, but it was a Kraft party. He worked the room, visiting each table, like a groom.

After dinner, Jonathan Kraft got up to introduce Kevin Hart, a noted Eagles fan. Hart asked everyone to put away their phones and delivered a condensed version of his live act before chastising the audience for being too white and too old. Then the huge screens lit up with a sizzle reel from the season, well-produced and soundtracked, covering key wins, Gronk spikes, Brady touchdown passes, Slater pep talks, Garoppolo's trade, Kraft congratulating Belichick for passing Tom Landry for third all-time in wins, behind only Don Shula and George Halas, and finally, the comeback against the Jaguars. It ended with Brady holding the AFC championship trophy, his passing hand bandaged. The subtext was clear: it had been a tough year—and yet, here they were again, playing in the Super Bowl.

After the film finished, the night flipped from cocktail hour to party. Lionel Richie sang "Dancing on the Ceiling." Mark Wahlberg danced. So did Kraft, near Melissa McCarthy, singing along and waving his hands in the air.

"Welcome to the show," Richie said. "This is rock and roll. You get wild, you get crazy, you get out of control!" He took a sip of cranberry juice and said, "Is Diddy here?"

Sean Combs joined him on stage, draped in mink.

"I want a coat like that," Richie said.

"It's cold!" Diddy said.

As midnight neared, the party started to thin. Richie said that Kraft wanted one more number—the "love thing"—and launched into "All Night Long." Everyone was on their feet, clapping, rushing Kraft for a selfie before the night ended, and the old man was having a blast, bobbing his head at Diddy's side. Richie howled for the last time, "All night!" Diddy hugged Kraft, who held tight for an extra beat. The moment felt vaguely melancholic to some attendees, as if Kraft was starting to reckon with the end, not just of the night—*his* night—but of something bigger. If the Patriots won, Kraft might be able to hold the team together. If they lost, nobody knew.

40

LIGHTS OUT

THE PATRIOTS WERE SHARP IN PRACTICE LEADING UP to the Super Bowl, except for one key player: Malcolm Butler. He had been sick after the AFC Championship Game, hospitalized for a night. When he returned to the team, he learned that, after playing 97.83 percent of the team's snaps during the regular season and 100 percent during the playoffs, he had been replaced in the starting lineup by cornerback Eric Rowe. Butler was a local hero. Signed photographs of his Super Bowl interception against Seattle hung in restaurants. But life with the team had been strained since his famous, history-altering play. He was late for the first organized team activity after it, in May of 2015, leading to a prolonged staredown with Belichick. The NFLPA had to intervene. Some coaches felt Butler had gotten too big. Butler wasn't a standout in the Super Bowl win over the Falcons—he had been burned deep in the third quarter—and in the off-season, the Patriots and Butler had engaged in a tense contract negotiation, Belichick's semiannual ritual with players.

Butler's greatest attribute was his unwillingness to back down—his nickname was "Scrap." But now he was finally broken by Belichick. He checked out and half-assed it in practice, the coaches felt. He later suspected that the staff believed that he wasn't as "locked in" as he should have been.

New England's coaches overlooked many sins, but pouting in the run-up to a Super Bowl was unforgivable. Later that week, Butler and Patricia traded words at practice, and the defensive coordinator seemed to give up on Butler even more than the head coach. The Patriots used backup safety Jordan Richards as its nickel corner and cornerback Johnson Bademosi as Richards's replacement on the depth chart. Butler was demoted. He was effectively done as a Patriot.

On February 4, 2018 at US Bank Stadium, Butler started to cry during the national anthem. At the team hotel after the game ended, with his benching the dominant storyline in New England, Butler was both in a good mood, relieved that it was over—the game *and* his time with the team—and deeply hurt, cursing as players asked him what the hell had happened and saying that they were sorry for him. "These dudes," Butler said, shaking his head, not referring to his teammates. "These motherfuckers."

TWO VERSIONS OF the same play defined the Super Bowl. The Patriots deployed it first, early in the second quarter and trailing, 9–3. So far, it was a typically aberrant New England Super Bowl, with the defense unable to stop Eagles quarterback Nick Foles and the offense both in rhythm and clumsy. On its first two drives, New England drove to the Eagles' eight-yard line before having to settle for short field goal attempts. Stephen Gostkowski's first 26-yard attempt was good; his second missed off the upright after a botched hold. Now New England was driving again, facing a third and five at the Philadelphia 35-yard line.

Josh McDaniels dialed up a play called Clemson. Like Fight Song, the Lane Kiffin formation they had modified to beat the Ravens two years before, New England had lifted it from the college game—from high school, actually, in this case. In late summer of 2012, Chad Morris, the offensive coordinator for Clemson, spoke with a high school coach named Hunter Spivey at a coaches convention. Spivey had a play that called for the quarterback to drift down the line of scrimmage to the right, faking an audible, then for the running back to receive a direct snap, run left, and pitch to a receiver on a reverse. The receiver would then throw to the quarterback, who had slipped out into a pass pattern. Spivey drew it on a napkin for Morris. It was called Detroit—or *Dee*-troit, to a pair of southern coaches. Morris loved the concept. A few months later, in the fourth quarter of a close game against Georgia Tech,

Morris called Detroit for a two-point conversion. It worked. Highlight shows ran it on an endless loop.

Detroit found its way to New England, where McDaniels called it Clemson. He saw potential in it as more than a two-point conversion play. He first gave it a shot during a 2015 home loss to none other than the Eagles. It gained 36 yards. It was perfect for the Super Bowl. Nobody would expect Brady to slip out for a pass—not at age 40, not with a sore thumb. Brady took the snap, handed off left to James White, and scooted out of the backfield and up the sideline. White pitched to Danny Amendola, who saw Brady alone downfield. He floated a soft pass, and Brady raised his arms, extending his sore ribs—he had been hit so hard earlier in the game that it had left him bent over—and the ball grazed off his fingertips. Eagles cornerback Malcolm Jenkins slapped Brady's ass.

"C'mon, Tom!" he said.

Later, with 38 seconds left in the first half, the Eagles were up 15–12 and facing a fourth and goal from the one-yard line. Eagles head coach Doug Pederson said, "We're going for it right here."

Foles asked, "You want Philly Philly?"

Pederson's eyes froze—and then darted to Foles, as if his mind had opened. Philly Special, their version of Clemson. "Yeah, let's do it," he said.

From the shotgun, Foles crouched down to his offensive lineman, yelling, "Easy, easy! Kill, kill!" The ball was snapped to running back Corey Clement, who ran left and tossed to tight end Trey Burton, a former college quarterback. Burton lofted an easy pass to Foles, who was uncovered, for a touchdown. The Eagles' bench was in a frenzy. NBC announcer Cris Collinsworth said that the play "has a chance to be remembered as one of the all-time greats."

On the other side of the field, Dion Lewis, a fellow running back, turned to James White on the sideline and said, "They hit us with our shit."

DOWN 22–12 AT HALFTIME, the lights went out on New England. Ernie Adams was in Belichick's face about how the defense needed to adjust—and suddenly, part of the locker room was dark. Nobody knew what to do. As Justin Timberlake's performance thumped through the walls, Adams kept speaking. While preparing the defensive game plan, the coaches had been unified behind the goal of trying to force Foles, a career off-and-on starter, to win the game. But Adams and Matt Patricia had disagreed about how to defend the Eagles' running game. Adams felt New England was vulnerable to power running back LeGarrette Blount, a former Patriot who had left for the Eagles after the 2016 season. Patricia had put speed on the field—light personnel—to stop the pass. Blount had gashed that look in the second quarter, setting up a touchdown with a 36-yard run and scoring one himself from 21 yards out.

"What are we doing in light personnel?" Adams said to Belichick. "What the hell are we doing?"

Some of the coaches used their phone lights in the locker room. After about ten minutes, all the lights came back on. Both teams went back and forth in the third quarter, and midway through the fourth, Brady threw a short touchdown to Gronkowski to give New England its first lead, 33–32. But Philadelphia drove down the field, converting a fourth and one along the way. The Patriots were used to being the team in superior physical shape in the Super Bowl. But, the week before the game, Pederson had stopped things halfway through practice and sent the players into the locker room, preparing them for the long halftime. Now they were fresh and aggressive with the game in the balance.

With 2:25 left and trailing, 33–32, Philadelphia had a third and seven at the Patriots' 11-yard line.

"We're gonna have to double 86," Patricia said over the headset. "Eighty-six" was tight end Zach Ertz. Pederson called Gun Trey Left, Open Buster Star Motion, 383 X Follow Y Slant. Ertz was the slant. New England came out bracketing him with Devin McCourty and Duron Harmon, but then motion by the Eagles left McCourty alone. It was too easy: Foles hit Ertz over the middle for a touchdown. Philadelphia led, 38–33, with 2:21 to go.

On came Brady, starting at New England's 25-yard line, so proficient as to be automatic. First play: eight yards to Gronkowski. There was now 2:16 left, second and two. Brady was supposed to throw short and quick to White outside, but when he dropped back, he locked in on Gronkowski downfield on what New England called an Otto route—a deep out by the tight end. White was open for a first down, but by the time Brady saw him, Eagles defensive end Brandon Graham had crashed through the pocket, knocking the ball out of Brady's hand. New England's coaches were furious that Brady had held the ball and not hit White earlier. The ball bounced off the leg of defensive lineman Derek Barnett, onto the ground, and up into his arms, like an errant dribble. Eagles ball. Brady sat on the field, elbows at his knees, the pain of inevitability visible on his frame.

The Eagles kicked a field goal to go up 41–33—the final score. It was Super Bowl loss number three for Brady and Belichick. Among quarterbacks, only Jim Kelly had lost more. Among coaches, only Dan Reeves, Bud Grant, and Marv Levy.

Brady entered the locker room, sullen, quiet, devastated, having skipped a handshake with Foles—it became a bit of a thing with Brady after certain losses, as if he was unchanged from the enraged kid on the golf course—knowing what was in store: another night spent staring into the void, replaying in his head the crucial little moments no one else had noticed or even seen, hoping that it was all a nightmare and he would wake up with another chance.

His kids were waiting for him. Benny and Vivian were in tears. "We don't like the Eagles," they said.

Brady had to say something in reply. "Guys, look: Daddy doesn't always win. That isn't the way life is. You try really hard—that's the most important thing. If you give it your best, you live with the outcome."

TWO DAYS LATER, at Gillette, Brady was furious. The Patriots had put up 613 yards on offense, not even punting a single time. How did they lose? Coaches privately pointed the finger at Patricia, who only a year earlier had made several critical play calls to help beat the Falcons. Maybe no coach—not Eric Mangini with his press conferences, or Josh McDaniels with his gray hoodie—emulated Belichick so shamelessly, or with so little self-awareness, as Patricia. He wore a pencil over his ear, including during games, looking studious, just like Belichick. But unlike Belichick, he never used the pencil to write. And anyway, Patricia carried a laminated play sheet—which, the staff noted, you couldn't write on with a pencil. A few coaches and players were happy to see Patricia on his way out. And a portion of the locker room was incensed with Belichick for benching Butler, as if it were an act of self-sabotage. At a year-end team meeting, Brady mostly kept his eyes down, barely glancing up as Belichick spoke. Brady separately told some of the coaches he wasn't coming back.

At a full staff meeting, the coaches said goodbye to McDaniels and Patricia.

Ballard and McDaniels connected on the phone. The general manager asked if they were good. Yes, McDaniels assured him. McDaniels went to his office. His wife, Laura, joined him. The Colts sent a plane to Foxborough and tweeted news of a press conference to announce McDaniels as their new head coach.

The day took a turn. A few coaches passed by, noticing that McDaniels hadn't packed his office. That was weird. Then they passed again and noticed that Laura had been sitting in there, alone, for hours. That was weirder.

McDaniels was upstairs in Kraft's office, hearing the owner's final pitch for him to stay. Kraft offered to pay McDaniels at a head coach's rate, eclipsing $4 million annually. Kraft didn't extend a guarantee that McDaniels would succeed Belichick, and McDaniels didn't want one. He had said privately for years that he didn't want to replace Belichick. He still wanted to be a head coach somewhere. Or, at least, he insisted that he did. Just not Indianapolis, not now.

At 7:15 that evening, McDaniels called Ballard. "I've got bad news," McDaniels said.

"I just need a yes-or-no answer," Ballard said. "Are you in or out?"

"I'm out."

Kraft had just made it more enticing for Brady to return—and humiliated the team that had launched Deflategate. "That's Kraft putting it to the Colts again," a league source told Adam Schefter. But it was another blow to McDaniels's reputation, maybe worse than his tenure in Denver, even though this was a non-event, something *not* happening. He had given his word, not only to the Colts, but to an entire coaching staff he had assembled. Some owners believed that McDaniels's skill set as a play caller and quarterback coach would keep him in demand. Others felt he was simply untrustworthy, permanently damaged, as if he had inherited the best and worst of Belichick's traits.

Two days after the Super Bowl, Kraft and Belichick dined in a corner booth at Davio's in Foxborough. Belichick was drained after a long year and facing what he called the "tidal wave" of tasks and requests and decisions that arrived after the season, things that people had not wanted to bother him with until now. This particular request, from his boss, he couldn't put off. Kraft asked Belichick to meet with Brady at the owner's house, an attempt to clear the air. Belichick agreed. Getting Brady to commit to playing in New England would be more difficult.

41

PLEADING
THE FIFTH

G ISELE WROTE TOM A LETTER. THIS LIFE, THEIR life—it wasn't working for her. She had hoped that his desire to play might wane as he aged, but it was only intensifying. During the fall, Brady was on Belichick Time, mostly gone during daylight hours. She held the house together. Now the season was over, and Brady was having Tommy Days, spending time with Guerrero, working on his quickness in the pocket and all of the ways he could improve, obvious to him but invisible to the rest of us. TB12 was growing—it now had around two dozen employees—and Brady wanted to expand beyond Foxborough and open a store in the Back Bay and maybe elsewhere, spreading pliability across the globe. His phone was constantly buzzing—he usually replied to texts and emails within an hour—and meanwhile, there was homework and housework. The kids still needed rides to school. Family vacations often included Guerrero and a host of wide receivers for early-morning throwing sessions. Brady never slept in. His wife's goals and dreams were squeezed to the margins of his own. There was no end in sight. He was *only* 41 at the start of next season. He still had years to play, things to accomplish. There's a reason so many of the greatest sports figures end up divorced. So, she put it on paper.

She felt unappreciated at a time when *he* felt unappreciated. A friend asked Brady how he was doing, and Brady sat on the couch, staring ahead. "I'm feeling, umm. . . . That's a loaded question." For 18 years, he had given everything to the team, helping his coach earn millions and his boss billions, in addition to all the glory. For what? So that his wife could be mad at him and his head coach could mock his toughness?

Bündchen needed him to be more present. Everyone in Brady's orbit could tell when his mind drifted off to third and six or the merits of a slight change of degree in release point. Brady thought of himself as a typical guy: it was just easy for him to focus on his own career. Whenever people asked if he thought that he missed out on life due to his job, he replied that no, he didn't, because he got to provide his family and friends with all these trips to the Super Bowl, all these cool experiences. But she wanted him to recognize—*he* needed to recognize—something essential that neither he nor his employer seemed capable of accepting: that there was such a thing as an off-season.

The letter hit Brady hard. He put in in a drawer, as a reminder and a warning. He needed to choose between a team that endlessly criticized him and a home that unconditionally loved him. It was an easy decision.

In 2018, for the first time in his career, Brady decided to skip all of the voluntary off-season program. It was the off-season of Tom. He flew to Monaco. He chugged a beer on *The Late Show with Stephen Colbert*, with impressive speed for someone who rarely drank. He flew to Qatar, and noticed that one of the American military jets stationed at the airport there had the decal of Michigan's main rival, Ohio State, on its tail. He visited Brazil. He went to the Met Gala. He worked out in Southern California with Guerrero and House. If it appeared both to the world beyond the team and within the team itself that he was no longer a member of the Patriots, so be it. Brady, Kraft, and Belichick met at the owner's house. But the issues went too deep to unpack in one night, much less fix. Brady wanted some of Guerrero's privileges restored, and saw that as a deal breaker. Belichick agreed to compromise, as long as Guerrero didn't interfere with the rest of the team. Still, a bigger question lingered: Was Brady's unhappiness beyond resolution?

He knew Belichick and Kraft all too well, each man's genius and his flaws. If he wanted to play in New England, he knew what awaited him, all of the benefits and headaches. But he was also running out of options. After Robert and Jonathan had given their word, both privately and publicly, that Brady could end his New England career on his terms, Robert started to take it back. Kraft told Brady that he was disinclined to let him out of the last two years of his contract, not after the team had traded Garoppolo.

This change angered Brady, but what could he do? He could demand his release. But he would risk insulting and losing a fan base that was overwhelmingly loyal to him, above anyone else. He certainly wasn't going to retire. He was trapped.

Still lacking the input that he craved, Brady at least wanted what he had wanted the previous fall: a longer contract and a public display of commitment. But Belichick was dug in, committed only to the two years remaining on his contract. Belichick and Brady were stuck with each other—and it was clear that Belichick would be the last man standing. During one of Tom Sr.'s business meetings in the Bay Area, an associate posed a theory to him that Bill and Tom might go out together.

"No," Tom Sr. replied. Tommy would go first, Bill would stay, and then the family would sit back and watch it all crumble.

Brady was left to deploy the tools of modern celebrity conflict: passive-aggressive posts on social media. When Malcolm Butler took to Instagram to thank the Patriots for his time in New England, Brady replied to the post, publicly writing, "Love you Malcolm. You are an incredible player and teammate and friend. Always!!!!!" After Danny Amendola left to sign with Miami—calling Belichick "an asshole sometimes" and criticizing the decision to sit Butler in the Super Bowl—Gronkowski posted on Instagram, in part, "Be FREE, Be Happy."

"Well said gronk!!!!" Brady replied, for the world to see.

Belichick was not much for social media. He had once mocked it as "Snapface" in a press conference, and he always tried to hammer a vital lesson into his players: "Who cares how many likes you get from 2,000 people you don't even know? There's 53 guys in the locker room. Those are the 53 that matter." But Belichick knew and was aware enough about social media to grasp that his two most famous players were taking shots at him.

At the league meetings in March in Orlando, Kraft tried to provide perspective on the quote-unquote tension in the building, even though, behind the scenes, he was desperate to solve it. In one meeting, the league proposed what it called the Josh McDaniels Rule, allowing teams to officially hire new head coaches while the coach's current team was still in the postseason, preventing another McDaniels–Colts fiasco.

Belichick spoke against it before his peers. First of all, he said, it should be illegal for a coach to be under contract to two teams at once. Second, he argued that it was a competitive disadvantage for the former team because the assistant would have exposure to proprietary information that he could take to his new post.

John Mara pushed back, as did Roger Goodell. "That happens anyway," Goodell said.

Belichick refused to let it go. One of his key personnel staffers, Bob Quinn, had left in 2016 to be the general manager of the Lions. McDaniels was expected to be in demand as long as he was in New England. Jack Easterby was considering other opportunities. Belichick started to block interviews, playing hardball with his own staff. In 2017, the 49ers had wanted to speak with Brian Flores about becoming their defensive coordinator, but Belichick was allowed to prevent the opportunity—a team was only required to permit interviews for head-coaching jobs— and did. In early 2018, the Texans had asked to interview Nick Caserio and Monti Ossenfort, New England's director of college scouting, for their opening at general manager. Belichick stopped both interviews from happening, on the grounds that Bill O'Brien was the de facto GM, regardless of title. Both Caserio and Ossenfort separately confronted Belichick about it. For Ossenfort, it was particularly crushing because it represented a major promotion from his position at the time. He eventually allowed his contract to expire and left New England.

In the league meeting, Belichick cut to the essence of his argument. He said it was patently unfair for a losing team to be able to distract a winning team during the playoffs. Some in the room took that as a direct attack on the Colts. Belichick didn't intend it that way, but it didn't matter. New England was at war, with itself and with everyone else.

THE DRAMA WITH BRADY and Gronkowski dragged into April. Brady refused to commit to a return to New England, so Gronkowski joined him in skipping the off-season program, brothers in protest. The week before the draft, Gronkowski delivered a bizarre press conference during a dirt bike rally at Gillette Stadium. He was asked about his status for the upcoming season.

"My status is doing really great," he replied. "I've been riding dirt bikes, I've been training really hard. *Vroom, vroom!*"

Was he was still contemplating retirement from football?

"Depends on how my racing skills go today."

Was he going to attend New England's optional off-season workouts?

"No. I've got my dirt biking skills to work on."

Belichick, who already doubted whether Gronkowski was "all in," according to ESPN's Jeff Darlington, had seen enough. Within days, he had an agreement to trade the tight end to the Lions. Gronkowski fought back, nixing the deal by threatening to retire. If he played football, it would be only with Tom Brady. Belichick backed off. The two men met and reached an accord. Gronkowski agreed to play for New England and to get in line; the Patriots sweetened his contract with incentives.

That left Brady as a lone dissenter. The draft was nearing, and the team needed an answer to a question no one had asked outright but that was implied by Brady's actions during the off-season: Would he play football that fall for the Patriots? New England liked some of the quarterbacks who had entered the draft, especially Lamar Jackson, the multitalented Heisman trophy winner out of Louisville. On April 18, Adam Schefter reported that Brady had still not committed to play. Brady's inner circle and the team were leaking against each other. Kraft went back to his prior position, telling Brady he was willing to let him out of his contract, if that's what he wanted. It wasn't what Brady wanted—not exactly. Brady seemed to prefer that the team release him, allowing him to win the battle over perception, according to people close to him. He asked to be allowed to sleep on it. The next morning, he told Kraft he was staying put—that he would "work it out on my end."

But Brady was still unsettled. In late April, he spoke at a conference in Los Angeles with Jim Gray, who asked him about a moment in *Tom vs. Time*. Bündchen had told the cameras that her husband often said, "I love it so much, and I just want to go work and feel appreciated and have fun."

Gray asked Brady if he felt appreciated by Belichick and Kraft. Brady turned to the audience, as if he had rehearsed his line. "I plead the Fifth. Man, that is a tough question."

Was he happy?

"I have my moments."

Brady had never spoken publicly like this before. News cycles were now in a sixth straight month of New England palace intrigue. A few weeks later, Brady skipped the Patriots' voluntary organized team activities, irritating the coaches. But when mandatory June minicamps arrived, Brady was there—with Guerrero, who received a big hug from Kraft in front of the entire team—and was on fire. After one beautiful throw, McDaniels started busting his old friend's chops. "Last one, Thomas," McDaniels said after Brady completed a pass. "Perfect, that's it. Good shot, Thomas!"

McDaniels pulled Brady and put in the backups. "Every third down, I get yanked," Brady said, jokingly whining.

"Hey, you know," McDaniels said.

"I'm hot right now."

"You are?"

"Can't take out the pitcher who's throwing a no-hitter. Especially when it's the fourth inning."

"I know," McDaniels said. "But you're old."

But outside of his interactions with McDaniels, Brady was professional but seemed disconnected, as though he wanted to keep the team at arm's length. During another run of voluntary workouts, Brady was gone again—the NFL's only starting quarterback not to show up with his team. He was 130 miles away from Foxborough, at Friar's Head golf course on Long Island's north shore, playing a round with Phil Mickelson and Rickie Fowler.

42

ONCE YOU STOP, YOU'RE DONE

THEY WERE POOLSIDE WHEN THE CALL CAME FROM A Pennsylvania prison. It was in early April 2018, and Kraft was in Turks and Caicos with Michael Rubin, nearing the end of a short vacation, when the 76ers co-owner's phone rang. It was Meek Mill, a rapper who had been in legal trouble since he was a teenager and was currently incarcerated for violating his probation for a crime he didn't commit. He had been convicted in 2008 for pointing a gun at a police officer, a charge Mill denied. Mill was jailed and served his time, got a record contract—and was then imprisoned for up to four years for multiple parole violations. The officer was later accused of lying under oath by a colleague, who said that Mill tried to discard his weapon. But the judge who heard his appeal refused to release him. It infuriated Rubin, who saw it as another terrible example of the treatment of Black Americans. A movement had arisen to fight for Mill's release. Rubin had become close friends with Mill, and when he received Mill's call in Turks and Caicos, he handed the phone to Kraft, hoping that he could offer encouragement.

Kraft had known Mill for years. Whenever Mill called Rubin in Kraft's presence, Rubin would put Kraft on the phone. Kraft had heard Mill's story before, but something about his current situation left him devastated. "Hey, you know what?" he told Rubin. "I need to go see him."

"I agree," Rubin said.

They left for Philadelphia the next day, moving up the departure so that they would arrive at the State Correctional Institution in Chester before visiting hours ended. They were ushered into a room that was usually packed with guests and inmates. This time, because Kraft was present—"I think they thought the president was coming," Rubin recalled—nobody else was allowed in. The three men spoke for two hours, Mill in an orange jumpsuit, Kraft and Rubin in flip-flops. Toward the end, Kraft said, "Meek, I've got a question for you. You've been sent to prison four different times for never committing a crime, but I'm sitting here with you and you're smiling ear to ear. If I were you, I'd be so mad at the world. Why are you so happy?"

Mill sat in silence. A minute passed. "You know, Robert, the last three times I went to prison for not committing a crime, nobody cared. Now the whole country is fighting for me. You're here to see me. How could I not be happy?"

They left shortly after and, on Rubin's advice, held a press conference outside the jail. Kraft spoke about Mill's case and about the larger need for criminal justice reform. "It's just sad," Kraft said. "This guy is a great guy and shouldn't be here." After it ended, Rubin returned to his home in the Philadelphia suburbs, while Kraft flew to Boston. That night, Kraft called Rubin repeatedly. It was normal for them to speak four or five times a day; it wasn't to speak four or five times a night. Kraft wanted to know why Rubin hadn't been able to speak with his high-up friends in government to get Mill released. "Why haven't you fixed this shit?" Kraft asked.

"Robert, I don't control the prisons," Rubin said sarcastically.

"What else can we do?" Kraft said.

Applying public pressure seemed to help. Two weeks after Kraft's press conference, Pennsylvania's Supreme Court granted Meek's bail request and he was released. Kraft kept it up days later, when he, Jonathan, Devin McCourty, and Duron Harmon spoke at a panel on criminal justice reform at Walpole High School outside of Boston. For months, they had thrown their weight behind a Massachusetts bill that had only recently passed, raising the age at which a child could be held criminally responsible and tried in juvenile court from seven years old to twelve.

The connection to protests against police violence by NFL players was unspoken but unmistakable. But eight months after Donald Trump had lit a fire, the anthem issue still loomed over the league. The owners still wanted players to stand. The league, meanwhile, had pledged more than $100 million to various social justice causes. At owners meetings in May, in an Atlanta luxury hotel off one of the many Peachtree Streets in the city, Goodell expressed the view that the league needed to do something about the anthem. What, exactly, he wasn't sure. Goodell wasn't pushing for a mandate to stand, but the league had to show sponsors that it was addressing their concerns. Executives presented owners with more data confirming what they knew: there was a negative reaction in the business community to the protests.

A new policy was on the table. It would require players to stand if they were on the field during the anthem, but gave them the option to remain in the locker room if they preferred. It subjected a team to a fine if it failed to show respect for the anthem, including any attempt to sit or kneel, which the club could then turn into fines for personnel. "Respect" went undefined beyond that. A rump group—Jeffrey Lurie of Philadelphia, Jed York of San Francisco, Zygi Wilf of Minnesota, Mark Davis of Oakland—thought the rule was the wrong approach and feared it would backfire. Continue dialogue with the players, they argued.

Debate was respectful, unlike in the meetings the past fall. Kraft was mostly silent. Still, something about it felt wrong, a few in the room believed—a group of mostly old white men discussing how mostly young Black men should protest. Goodell asked for an informal show of hands to see who supported the new policy. He didn't want to put up a doomed proposal for a vote. All owners raised hands, except two: York and Davis.

Goodell was irritated. "You're a no?" he asked.

They responded that they were abstaining, not voting no.

Goodell moved on to the next issue—and the league soon publicly announced the resolution and that it had passed. He had taken the show of hands as a formal vote. It stunned the owners. Not taking an official vote was atypical for a major resolution. Goodell told the press later in the day that the vote was "unanimous," which became another unforced error when news broke that two owners had abstained. Some players took to social media to criticize the new policy; Trump appeared on *Fox and Friends* and said the NFL had done "the right thing." A subsequent joint statement by the NFL and NFLPA said the policy wouldn't be enforced. In June of 2020, after Minneapolis police killed George

Floyd and a massive protest movement sprung up in response, Goodell released a video in which he admitted he was wrong for not listening enough and encouraged all players to "speak out and peacefully protest." That meant kneeling. Though many American corporations were making analogous statements, and though Goodell was reacting to the overwhelming sentiment and anger around the country—and listening to Kraft, who urged him to take a stand—it was still one of the finest and most genuine moments of his tenure as commissioner. After the NFL pledged another $250 million over ten years to try to combat systemic racism, the NBA—commonly viewed as more progressive than the NFL—found itself far behind and called league executives for help with the basics, like how to set up a foundation. Trump took to Twitter, trying to bait the league into another controversy, asking if Goodell was telling players that it was "O.K. for players to KNEEL, or not to stand, for the national anthem, thereby disrespecting our Country & our Flag?" This time, nobody at the league cared.

TRAINING CAMP FOR the 2018 season was nearing, and familiar urges started to be felt. One day, Brady was sitting in his home with a friend, his face tanned and fresh and showing no signs of the strain of the past year. The topic, as usual, was football, and how long Brady wanted to continue playing.

"Once you stop," Brady said, "you're done."

Brady had detached himself from his team in the off-season, but not from his craft. He had worked harder than ever, fine-tuning his release with House, practicing dropbacks with resistance bands around his legs on a beach in Southern California early in the morning, before the clouds burned away, asking friends to film it on their phones and reviewing the video right away for immediate analysis. You're either serious about it or you're not, Brady believed. It was simple. He knew that he had limited time left when he could be who he was right now, limited time with the immeasurable pleasure and privilege of running out in front of 80,000 screaming fans alongside so many of his dearest friends, with a chance to prove once again that he belonged. He was better now than he had been 10 years prior, but there were still no shortcuts. It was reps, reps,

reps. The other life—the life away from the team and with his family—
was fun, he didn't regret a minute of it, but he was still a quarterback. He
wasn't ready to let the dream go.

In his home, Brady raised his right hand and counted from thumb
to pinky, from his current age to his goal: "Forty-one, 42, 43, 44, 45. . . .
It's going to be very hard to do. But"—he patted the arm of the couch—
"but, I think I can do it."

NEW ENGLAND WAS slow out of the gate, almost tradition by this
point, using September as an extended training camp. The Patriots beat
the Texans at home in the opener, then lost a road game to the Jaguars.
Days later, the internal problems of the previous year were put under
the microscope again when Ian O'Connor's *New York Times* best-selling
book *Belichick* hit shelves. It reported that Brady had wanted a "divorce"
from the team in the off-season, setting off another wave of debate and
chatter and news coverage. Belichick ordered all of the televisions in
the facility turned off. The message was clear: what plagued last season
would not impact this one. There were new posters lining the walls of
the team facility. It wasn't just "Do Your Job" anymore.

DTRT: Do The Right Thing

Better Men
Better Fathers
Better Brothers
Better Friends
Better Citizens
Better Teammates
And Better Everything

What Comes Easy Won't Last Long
What Lasts Long Won't Come Easy

The Patriots' three principals were trying to be professionals, to set
aside any lingering grievances in the service of winning games. But

they all felt taken for granted, in their own ways. Brady was tired of taking team-friendly deals with no input into how the money saved was spent—and still wanted a long-term contractual commitment. Belichick told associates that every organizational decision now was in support of Brady, geared toward pleasing him and making him successful—and that Kraft meddled with the team, sometimes with opinions, sometimes with restrictive budgets. As for Kraft, in late September, he was in Aspen for a conference and bumped into a few friends in the hotel lobby early one morning. He told them he was leaving later for Detroit, where the Patriots were playing their next game. "I hate leaving here," Kraft said. "You leave here and you leave some of the most brilliant people you've ever met. You pick up so much knowledge from all these brilliant minds. And I have to go to Detroit to be with the biggest fucking asshole in my life—my head coach."

The next day, September 23, the Patriots lost to the Lions. With Julian Edelman out for the first four games of the season due to a suspension for performance-enhancing steroids and Rob Gronkowski grinding through injuries, the offense struggled. Brady and McDaniels were lobbying for more, and better, wideouts. Belichick was now 66 years old, and he still struggled to draft receivers successfully, even though he had found Hall of Fame–worthy pass catchers in Edelman and Gronkowski. Why, nobody knew, though there were some partial explanations. Even the best personnel minds in the NFL missed more often than they hit, for one, while New England's precise improvisational offense was particularly difficult for wide receivers to pick up, and the intensity of Brady and Belichick didn't work for everyone. "When my expectations are higher than . . . the individual player's, that's not going to work out," Belichick said. The Patriots had made 28 transactions at the wide receiver position since March of 2018, which ESPN noted was tied for most in the league.

And then, a potential opportunity appeared. Word leaked out of Cleveland that the Browns were planning to release Josh Gordon, an immensely talented receiver with a substance-abuse problem.

Belichick moved fast. He called Browns general manager John Dorsey and proposed a trade: New England's 2019 fifth-round pick for Gordon. The Patriots would receive a conditional seventh-rounder if Gordon wasn't active for New England for ten games. The terms seemed to confuse Dorsey; Belichick had to spell out how it would work over the phone. Kraft met with a handful of staff to discuss it. Gordon was 27 years old, but had little wear: he had missed most of the 2014, 2015, and 2016 seasons due to violations of the league's substance-abuse policy and because he chose to enter rehab, testing positive for alcohol and weed. He had played in only five games in 2017. His ability was clear. The question was whether he could stay clean and sober—and out of trouble.

"It's just like Moss," Kraft said.

Not really, the coaches thought. But Kraft signed off on the trade. Gordon was now a Patriot, giving Brady a vertical threat on the outside. New England built a support system for Gordon. The team, from Brady down, spoke of him in excited but measured terms, trying to keep the pressure manageable. Gordon moved into a condo a few doors down from Jack Easterby, who all but lived with him, spending time after hours discussing life and trying to help Gordon keep his dark currents at bay. Brady felt for Gordon: the receiver had been raised in chaos—his family moving from apartment to apartment in Houston, Gordon first trying drugs in seventh grade—and now the effects of an enormously difficult childhood were playing out before a national audience. "Kids come into this world pure," Brady told his father one night, "and we adults screw them up."

Gordon saw his first action in a September 30 win over Miami. He scored his first touchdown a week later in a win over the Colts. New England was on a four-game winning streak entering *Monday Night Football* against the Buffalo Bills on October 29. Hours before the game, Ian Rapoport of the NFL Network reported that Gordon had been late and would be benched for "several series" early in the game. Belichick generally didn't worry too much about leaks. He knew that many of his coaches were friendly with various reporters, as he had been when he was under Parcells's thumb. But this one gave away a competitive advantage. Belichick was so angry that he started Gordon, invalidating a correct report, sending a message to the staff more than the player.

STILL, THE FACT REMAINED: Josh Gordon was late for practice, after all the investment the team was putting in him, after all the assumptions made within the team and beyond that Gordon would get in line now that he was a part of the Patriot Way. For years, Belichick had struggled with a problem coaches in professional sports were used to dealing with: it was hard to get players to buy in. That even Belichick—after all his success, and despite his near-total authority in New England—faced the problem spoke to the difficulty it posed. Belichick had once tried to remedy it by spending hours sitting in the stands at the NFL combine with a former Green Beret named Brian Decker. Then 44, Decker was a retired lieutenant colonel who had fought in Iraq and revolutionized the selection process for Green Berets. He had developed a methodology, based on 1,200 data points, that measured internal drive and willingness to work within a team—the clichéd "intangibles." It was groundbreaking within the military, and Decker felt it could translate to football. Belichick was fascinated, both with Decker—he loved anything military—and with his techniques, and later brought him to New England to present before the coaches.

But getting players to buy in wasn't something that analytics could fix. Belichick thought there were a lot of things that analytics couldn't help with, despite how driven people within the NFL and outside of it were to find a *Moneyball* approach to football. There was a perception around the league that the Patriots were on the cutting edge of football data, that they had a proprietary system of advanced analytics, led by Ernie Adams crunching numbers. That was only partly true. Adams spent a lot of time analyzing statistics, but there were many teams—the Jaguars, the 49ers, the Browns—that were more invested in and sophisticated with data. On the plane after a loss, Belichick sometimes saw coaches buried in laptops, sifting through proprietary statistics. He'd shake his head. "You know, fellas, the reason why we got beat is because we can't tackle. We can't force the run. All the rest of this is a bunch of garbage. This isn't about a computer."

As the 2018 season wore on, Belichick found himself needing to be more resourceful than ever, to devise new ways to win each week, often utilizing different players than in the prior week. Two games within a month against two superstar quarterbacks provided a glimpse of a general formula the Patriots would ride until the end of the season. In a mid-October home game against the 5–0 Kansas City Chiefs, Belichick met head coach Andy Reid and quarterback Patrick Mahomes, who was in his first year as a starter and was on his way to throwing 50 touchdown passes. Nobody since Dan Marino had been so good so young. This contest had been billed not only as a matchup between two of the game's best coaches and quarterbacks, but also between two of the game's premier tight ends: Rob Gronkowski and Kansas City's Travis Kelce, who was the same age as Gronkowski, had a similar build, and also wore number 87—and who claimed he had eclipsed his counterpart. In the days before the game, Kelce told *The Dan Patrick Show*, "I feel like I'm the best tight end in the league."

But the Patriots showed a national audience why Gronkowski was perhaps the best tight end in history and why Travis Kelce was a mere Hall of Fame–caliber player. Gronkowski spent most of the game as a blocker, often drawing critical assignments. Late in the game, McDaniels finally unleashed him as a receiver. With the game on the line, Gronkowski slipped out of the backfield for a 42-yard catch. And on New England's final drive, Brady hit him for 39 yards, down to the Chiefs' nine-yard line with 17 seconds left. Stephen Gostkowski was good from 28 yards as time expired, the game-winning kick.

Afterward, writer Greg A. Bedard looked closely at the use of Gronkowski and Kelce by their teams, and discovered a statement by Belichick and McDaniels, delivered in the best way they knew: on the field. Kelce had five catches to Gronkowski's three, but Bedard noted that Gronkowski was asked to block on 63.5 percent of his snaps and was successful 93.6 percent of the time—and he still caught the crucial passes. As Bedard wrote, "it was basically Josh McDaniels and Bill Belichick giving the middle finger to anyone who dared compare Kelce to Gronkowski."

On another Sunday night three weeks later, November 4, New England faced the Green Bay Packers and its biggest test of the season, the task of trying to throttle Aaron Rodgers. A two-time league MVP, an elusive runner and enterprising passer, Rodgers threaded needles off balance and from unimaginable angles, considered by most—including Belichick and Brady—to be the game's best quarterback. Rodgers and Brady had met one off-season, swapping notes, Brady always eager to learn from those whom he admired, even younger men playing the same position he did.

Belichick knew that the key to stopping a great quarterback was not with tricks in the secondary—there were only so many coverages that could be called—but instead with the pass rush. Too many teams were undisciplined when it came to rushing Rodgers, so eager to reach him that it created gaps for him to exploit. Belichick pressured Rodgers the same way he had once pressured Peyton Manning: in his face, backed with man-to-man coverage. It seemed like a risk, considering the stricter rules protecting receivers and the passing game overall. On a third and four in the second quarter, New England rushed for four, and Green Bay kept six players in to block. Patriots defensive tackle Adam Butler used a spin move to set up a clear rush at Rodgers, crumpling the pocket and giving the Patriots an instant numbers advantage. All of a sudden, the six Green Bay blockers were rendered useless, and New England had seven defensive backs glued to four Packers receivers. Nobody was open. Rodgers danced to his right, but linebacker Kyle Van Noy ran him to the sideline, forcing an incompletion.

"The pass rush is what we want," Belichick told the defensive linemen on the sideline. "That's the idea right there. Some of those incompletions are because of the rush."

In the fourth quarter, Green Bay was down 24–17. On a critical third down, New England's rush got to Rodgers again. He lay on the turf after a sack, chinstrap at his lips, and rolled the ball away in frustration.

New England now had a chance to essentially end the game. On the third play of their drive, Brady threw down the left sideline. Edelman and Gordon were there, both streaking downfield. Edelman leapt for the ball, but it sailed over his head—and into Gordon's arms for a 55-yard touchdown.

On the sideline, Belichick asked Brady, "Who were you throwing that to?"

"That was to Josh," Brady said.

"All right," Belichick said.

The 31–17 score held. On the field after the game, Belichick found Rodgers.

"You're the best," Rodgers said.

"No, you are," Belichick replied. "You are."

Even after a tempestuous off-season, Edelman's suspension, and a

1–2 start—and even after 17 years and five Super Bowl victories, having apparently achieved everything there was to achieve—the Patriots were once again a force, with a 7–2 record and seemingly headed deep into the playoffs yet again. The pillars of two key wins in late October and early November—situational use of Gronkowski and a disciplined pass rush—became the latest template for January.

43

RIGHT, T?

Tom Brady was on the phone with his father, and it dawned on both men that the 2018 season had been weirdly easy. Not because New England was dispatching the competition with ease—on the contrary, the Patriots entered the playoffs looking vulnerable. On December 9, New England lost to the Dolphins on the final play of the game—a 69-yard kickoff return for a touchdown that featured two laterals. Then they lost in Pittsburgh the next week, Brady throwing a horrible interception with the game on the line. The Patriots were 9–5, and four days later, Josh Gordon left for a Florida treatment center—further evidence that addiction is both ruthless and patient—and was suspended indefinitely for violating the terms of his reinstatement. Losses in Foxborough were experienced like small deaths, but Belichick, of all people—Doom—provided perspective. "Look, it's the National Football League," he said. "Nobody died." New England won its final two games, finishing 11–5 and as the second seed in the AFC, behind the Chiefs. "Don't believe all the other shit out there, about how bad we are, how bad we suck, how old we are," Belichick told the team before the playoffs. "Just keep doing what we're doing."

But on the phone, father and son realized that so many of the struggles that had shadowed Tom's past few years were gone. No Deflategate. No worries about Galynn's health. Less drama with the head coach. No injuries, aside from a tweaked knee that had healed. No throwing issues that couldn't be solved by a midseason tune-up visit from Tom House. No problems on the home front, after an off-season more devoted to family. Most talking heads outside of Boston, and some in the city, were calling Brady old and pronouncing the Patriots dynasty over, but that was just chatter. The year was hard, as every year was, but relatively calm. Brady had entered the season determined to be a relentlessly positive thinker, and he and Belichick were "vibing" much better, according to a December report from ESPN's Jeff Darlington. Belichick eased up on the Johnny Foxborough routine and treated him more like a grown-up. Strain persisted under the surface, but neither man wanted to let the other down on the field. It was still a motivation, after all these years. People underestimated that aspect of their relationship—it seemed too basic to be true—but it was palpable to those around them.

During treatment one day, Alex Guerrero decided to mess with Brady.

You suck, he said. Can't play this game anymore.

Brady laughed. But Guerrero knew that, somewhere deep inside, Brady was still pick number 199. In the divisional round, the Patriots hosted and dismantled the Los Angeles Chargers, setting up a visit to the Chiefs. In the locker room after the game, Matt Slater addressed the team. "Don't forget what it felt like when they said you weren't good enough, you shouldn't be here, you're *old*."

Slater turned to Brady. "Right, T?"

"That's right," Brady said from the back. On most days, Brady looked young—or refused to look old—but on this afternoon, he was weathered and sallow, specks of gray near his temples and faint traces of eye black above his cheekbones. But he was content.

"Still here, baby," he said.

THE AFTERNOON OF January 19, the day before the AFC Championship Game against Kansas City, Robert Kraft was riding with a friend in a Bentley in Palm Beach County, when a police officer pulled them over. Kraft had visited a strip-mall massage parlor called Orchids of Asia at the suggestion of his friend, the dairy and plastics magnate Peter Bernon. Kraft had wanted to get a massage at a hotel, but no slots were available. Bernon had another option in mind, and drove Kraft 20 miles up the coast to the mall. Kraft entered—and his day changed. He later told a friend that he thought he was going to get a regular massage, but instead, the spa's co-owner, a woman named Lei Wang and another worker named Shen Mingbi, gave him a one of a different sort, cleaning up afterward with a white towel, according to police. Even though Kraft paid for the service—paid cash—"it wasn't like *that*," he told the same friend, according to *Vanity Fair*. He thought he and Wang had a connection.

Now, police officer Scott Kimbark was standing next to the Bentley, explaining that he had stopped the car for a minor traffic violation. Four days earlier, police forced all of the workers at the strip mall to evacuate due to what they claimed was a bomb threat. But the true purpose was to install surveillance cameras in the ceilings of the massage rooms. Police then staked out the spa, and over the next few days, Detective Andrew Sharp and his team watched on a live feed as more than 20 men received various forms of sex. To identify each patron, an officer pulled them over after they left the spa, under the guise of a traffic stop.

Kraft couldn't have been friendlier. He asked Kimbark if he was a Dolphins fan and then pulled out a Super Bowl ring, introducing himself as the owner of the Patriots. They chatted about the game against the Chiefs. Kimbark let them go with a warning, having collected a name— all he needed to pass on to investigators. The next morning, Kraft stopped at Orchids again, and saw Wang again. Kraft received similar treatment as the day before, paying cash, and left after 14 minutes to fly to Kansas City, unaware that he had been the target of a sting—and it was all on video.

"How you feeling?" Brady asked Edelman in warm-ups.

It was 19 degrees and windy. Arrowhead Stadium was loud, a howling bowl of red. "I feel great," Edelman said.

Before road playoff games, the Patriots' coaches—and Tom Brady— sometimes knew they didn't have the horses. Today, against the highest-scoring team in the league, New England was calm and eager. The Patriots usually came out throwing in playoff games—pass to get the lead, run to keep it, the old Bill Walsh tenet—but Josh McDaniels decided to beat up the Chiefs with an old-school drive on the Patriots' opening possession: 15 plays, 80 yards, a total of 8:05 that Patrick Mahomes and the NFL's most dangerous offense weren't on the field.

Ten of the plays were runs, the last a short touchdown by rookie Sony Michel. The crowd of 77,034 was silent.

"Keep the gas on it now!" Edelman said on the sideline.

New England was up 14–0 at halftime and 17–7 through three quarters—and the lead could have been larger if Brady hadn't thrown an end-zone interception. New England relied on much of its Aaron Rodgers game plan for Mahomes: man coverage, rushers in his face— the Patriots blitzed on nine of Mahomes's 12 first-half dropbacks—and defensive ends pinching the pocket so that when the similarly elusive quarterback tried to escape, there was nowhere to go. But, by the fourth quarter, the Chiefs had solved New England and led 28–24 with 2:03 left. Brady took over with 65 yards to go. On third and ten, he dropped back and looked past the sticks to the right, but the Chiefs had two receivers covered downfield, so he turned to Gronkowski as an outlet. Brady threw high and hard—quarterbacks sometimes get angry when downfield options are covered, and they take it out on the dump-off pass—and it grazed off Gronk's fingertips, redirected into the arms of Chiefs defensive back Charvarius Ward with 54 seconds left.

Arrowhead exploded. Drive over. Game over. Patriots dynasty, apparently ov—but wait: there was a flag.

"What happened?" Edelman asked Brady.

"Offside," Brady said.

Chiefs defensive end Dee Ford had lined up past the line of scrimmage, an epic screwup that cost him his job in the off-season. New England had a second chance, the Chiefs having violated the Iron Law of Tom Brady, with the punishment coming quickly. Brady lined up and saw Gronkowski in man coverage against safety Eric Berry on the left side and sent him on a go. Brady put the ball up high, allowing Gronkowski to twist under it, and he cradled it at the Chiefs' four-yard line. Rex Burkhead scored a play later to put New England up 31–28 with 39 seconds left.

But Mahomes was coming into his own in real time. He moved the Chiefs into field goal range, and they tied the game with eight seconds left, forcing overtime. Matthew Slater stood at midfield for the coin toss, and New England's good luck charm made his good luck call: heads. It was heads. New England took the ball. All of America, with the exception of the Northeast, groaned. New England drove down the field, converting three third and tens. Burkhead scored from two yards out for the win. Brady and Belichick hugged.

"Couldn't have done that any other way," Brady said.

"Nope," Belichick replied. "On the road. On the road."

An hour later, Brady and Gronkowski walked through the tunnels of a cold and quiet stadium to the bus. Brady held out his phone to take an Instagram video, tilting it to the perfect angle. He preened for the camera, smiling and trying not to laugh, shrugging his shoulders, with Gronk trotting behind him, wearing AFC championship gear and a grin. The short video, its soundtrack Diddy's "Bad Boys for Life," ended with the words "STILL HERE"—two lovable assholes rubbing it in America's face.

44

WE'RE CHAMPS,
MAN!

OLICE ESCORTS FLASHED THROUGH DOWNTOWN
Atlanta the night before Super Bowl LIII, lead blockers for a caravan of SUVs. The procession stopped in front of a hotel. Security guards with earbuds stood alert and mumbled into walkie-talkies. He was here—Robert Kraft, strolling out of his vehicle in a blue blazer, sneakers, and dress shirt.

A man, perhaps drunk, yelled, "Hey Bob—the Patriots are gonna lose! You're going down, Bob!"

Kraft ignored him and entered his annual party. Jon Bon Jovi was inside. So was Martha Stewart, in a red coat and red heels. Shari Redstone was talking with Rupert Murdoch. Meek Mill was there, toasting Kraft. So were David Spade, Jamie Foxx, and Jermaine Dupri. The ballroom was bigger than the one the previous year in Minnesota, with better lighting.

"Hello, everyone," Kraft told the room. "I'd like to be rude and ask everyone to take a seat for a moment. . . . We're living in a world that's splintered in so many ways. Not as empathetic as it should be." He asked for everyone to celebrate "like we're family" and added that "hopefully, we're kicking butt tomorrow."

Tomorrow was February 3, 2019, the Patriots against the Rams in Super Bowl LIII, a game with a circular quality to it. In the 17 years since that magical night in New Orleans, New England's foundation had remained intact. Belichick had cycled through countless supporting casts. Patriots legends including Troy Brown, Vince Wilfork, Richard Seymour, Tedy Bruschi, Mike Vrabel, Willie McGinest, Adam Vinatieri,

Wes Welker, Randy Moss, and Rodney Harrison were long gone. Stars for a day—such as running back Jonas Gray, an undrafted free-agent running back who had rushed for 201 yards and four touchdowns in his first start, against the Colts on November 16, 2014, earning the cover of *Sports Illustrated*, and then, the following week, was benched after being late to a meeting; "We just can't have it," Belichick told him—came and went. Coaches like Eric Mangini, Charlie Weis, and Romeo Crennel had all been fired multiple times since they left New England. The Patriots needed more than Tom Brady and Bill Belichick to win games— Devin McCourty and Matthew Slater were both cherished teammates and great players in their own rights, even if not known as stars by the general public; Rob Gronkowski had easily produced a Hall of Fame–worthy career by age 29; Dont'a Hightower had made two Super Bowl–changing plays; cornerback Stephon Gilmore was an All-Pro in 2018; and Julian Edelman was the league's most reliable clutch receiver—but not much more. The longevity of New England's greatness was already far beyond unprecedented when the latest iteration of the team arrived in Atlanta.

The Rams were on their seventh head coach since 2002, second first-overall draft pick quarterback—and weren't even from St. Louis anymore. In January of 2016, the league approved owner Stan Kroenke's request to move the team to Los Angeles, returning to its longtime home after 21 years in St. Louis. As always, Jerry Jones shoved the vote over the line, and Kraft was one of a handful of owners left to broker peace in the aftermath between Kroenke and the Raiders and Chargers, who had lost a joint competing bid to move to LA.

At his party, Kraft was thankful. Three Super Bowl appearances in a row; four of the last five; ten overall, dating back to 1997. The Packers, the Steelers, the 49ers, the . . . Patriots? It still sounded crazy, to anyone of a certain age, the league's hallowed teams easily surpassed in a relatively short period by a former laughingstock. The rest of the country, of course, was sick of New England. Brady's family even wondered if Super Bowl fatigue might reach its own fan base. At the prior year's game, a dozen California friends flew in, and the Bradys threw a party the night before the game on the second floor of a bowling alley in Edina, with many of Galynn's Minnesota Johnson relations in attendance. There would be no party this year—no Bradys lived in Atlanta—and it was strangely quiet for the immediate family, with few ticket requests. The family wondered if the game itself would feel like it had a few years ago in Arizona, where Seahawks fans swamped the stadium.

But then Super Bowl Sunday arrived, and Mercedes-Benz Stadium felt louder than Gillette ever was. The Patriots weren't America's Team, and Jerry Jones often reminded league executives, other owners, and even reporters off the record that the Cowboys were a bigger ratings draw. But the Patriots were something else: a relentless force on the field and in the culture that had absorbed the hardest shots from everyone—the league, opposing teams, journalists, fans— and still managed to exert their will. A team sign had been made to commemorate the game, set against the Super Bowl LIII logo: *We are not a team just because we work together. We have become a team because we respected each other, trusted each other, and deeply cared for each other.*

THE SECOND RAMS Super Bowl, like the first, was a Belichickian masterpiece, ugly and low-scoring. Brady started badly, throwing an interception on the first drive. New England could move the ball, but only put up a field goal. After 50 minutes, the score was tied, 3–3. *We need a drive*, Josh McDaniels thought. *A drive.* He was almost out of ideas. To that point, Los Angeles had assembled a novel game plan designed to avoid unfavorable matchups for its defense. If James White was in the game, the Rams answered with a nickel defense, matching speed with speed and refusing to allow the latest in New England's line of overlooked pass-catching backs—first Kevin Faulk, then Shane Vereen, now White—to sneak in a decisive performance in the Super Bowl. With 9:49 left, New England took over at its 31-yard line. What followed was McDaniels's finest moment as a coach, the years of learning from Belichick about how to adjust and tinker and *think* playing out on the biggest stage. He switched to a 22 personnel grouping—one receiver, two backs, two tight ends—but with a twist: he replaced Michel with Burkhead, a tough back with good hands, knowing the Rams would answer with bulk rather than speed. Sure enough, the Rams sent on fewer cornerbacks and more linebackers.

New England immediately exploited it, calling a route for Gronkowski called Y Shake. He faked a block, then caught a short pass from Brady and turned upfield. An 18-yard gain felt like 50 to the New England sideline. On the next play, Brady threw to Edelman over the middle. It was Edelman's tenth catch for a total of 141 yards, enough to win him the game's MVP award.

Edelman had spent the days leading up to the Super Bowl remembering how it all started for him. He always felt a kinship with Brady, both of them overlooked Bay Area guys. More than a decade earlier, he had watched the 2006 AFC Championship Game against the Colts in his room—he called it the Dungeon—and rooted for Brady over Peyton Manning. "I liked how he was a fucking underdog," Edelman later said. "He had to earn everything he got. He wasn't just given it. He wasn't ever the guy. He had to compete his balls off in college to be the guy. I appreciate that." At the College of San Mateo, Edelman had once told an English teacher that he was "going to the league," and the teacher replied by encouraging him to set more realistic career goals. Who could blame the teacher? Edelman was an undersized small-college quarterback. But Edelman always reveled in being an underdog—his Judaism had hardwired it into him, he often said—and when he got to New England in 2009, he studied Wes Welker, the little dynamo out of the slot: how Welker read Brady, how he tiptoed and almost jumped before breaking into routes, setting himself up to explode like a slingshot. In 2010, Edelman heard that Brady worked out with receivers in LA in the off-season, so "I packed my shit" and moved there, living in a Residence Inn in Manhattan Beach, waiting for Tom to call, too scared to reach out, asking their mutual agent to drop a reminder to Brady that he was in town. One Friday afternoon, at a barbecue, the call arrived. Edelman left immediately, and his life changed. He started arriving to the workouts an hour early—he never wanted Brady to wait—and they threw 45 routes a day, sometimes 75, no huddle, with Brady in helmet and shoulder pads and sipping water out of a massive canteen, audibling at the line of scrimmage, changing assignments. *You're the X receiver on this play. Now you're the F.* "You're fucking piss-tired," Edelman later told an associate, but Brady was so relentless—*Holding! Run it again!*—it was as if he wore a gray hoodie.

At first, Edelman was like Brady's kid brother, one of many tagalongs. Before his fourth season, Belichick pulled him into his office and said, "You need to either get really good at a lot of things or you need to be excellent at one thing." He decided to improve at everything, and became excellent along the way—not that he ever felt truly secure. He waited eight years to buy a house in Massachusetts, knowing Belichick could cut him at any time. After coming up big in Super Bowls, he carved out his own identity, becoming another hero to the fans. Edelman's father, Frank, thought of it this way: Brady was the king of Boston, Gronk was the jester, Jules was the prince. "I'm just an ordinary male," Edelman once said, "with exceptional hair."

On this play, Edelman gained 13 yards. Now, for the first time all day, New England had that familiar look. A team that knew how to close better than any other in modern NFL history closed out another ultimately helpless opponent. Brady stepped back and lofted a long and arching throw down the left sideline for Gronkowski—their most indefensible route all season—and Gronk extended inside the five, catching it between three defenders and landing at the two, setting up the lone touchdown in the game two plays later, giving the Patriots a 10–3 lead with seven minutes left. Nobody knew it at the time, but it was Brady's final iconic pass as a New England Patriot. New England tacked on a field goal with 1:16 left, the final dagger: 13–3.

"We're champs, man!" Belichick said, hugging McDaniels. "We're champs!"

Confetti dropped, and it was impossible to watch the Belichick and Brady families and not consider the passage of time. Once, Steve Belichick had patrolled the sidelines with his son by his side, and now both of Bill Belichick's boys, Brian and Steve, were on New England's staff, celebrating alongside him. Amanda Belichick, Bill's only daughter, ran onto the field and hugged her dad, just as she had done 17 years earlier after Adam Vinatieri's kick sailed true. Now she was the head coach of women's lacrosse at Holy Cross—and had just led the team to its first Patriot League playoff appearance since 2015. She had married a year earlier on the Rhode Island coast, and when her dad toasted the bride and groom, he did so as both father and coach. He recalled October of 1984, Giants against the 49ers on Monday night, when San Francisco crushed New York, Walsh embarrassing Belichick's defense. But, shortly after midnight, Amanda arrived, Bill and Debby's firstborn. "I was captured by her blue eyes, her smile," Belichick said with champagne in his right hand, handsome and tan in a blue suit, bursting with pride.

Now Belichick was soaked in Gatorade. He put his head down as his arms were around Amanda, exhaling for what seemed like the first time in hours. "Oh my God," he said. "What a night."

On stage, Edelman carried Belichick's toddler granddaughter and Steve's daughter, Blakely. "Wanna see Papa?" Edelman asked, turning toward Belichick. "Grampa—er, Coach!"

"Hi!" Belichick said, hugging her, his voice high and warm. "Hi!"

Behind the stage, Brady crouched down on the field as his kids huddled around him.

"Group hug," Bündchen said.

Brady carried Vivian, in a glittery white shirt that read "Brady's Little Ladies," up on the platform. Tom Sr. and Galynn circled around back, her hair full again. Vivian smiled as she tried to snare strips of paper out of the air, the wonder on her face not unlike her dad's when the Patriots first beat the Rams almost two decades earlier. She lunged toward Edelman, pulling her father into a hug. "Are you happy?" Vivian asked.

"I'm happy," he replied.

45

TALK TO MR. KRAFT

R EALITY REASSERTED ITSELF. TOM BRADY WAS SKIP-
ping the off-season program again, this time out of habit rather
than protest. He was also entering the last year of his contract,
the dominant storyline for the team. Brian Flores was gone, hired by
Miami as its head coach, one of the few Belichick charges who knew
how to be more than a mimic. Five other assistant coaches left, too. Josh
McDaniels wanted to be a head coach, but couldn't get out. Eight jobs
had opened up, but only the Packers interviewed him, and passed. Jack
Easterby, burned out from years of mediating internal disputes, had
refused to sign a new contract.

Kraft held a series of meetings with Easterby, trying to convince him
to stay. Easterby had shot up the ranks in New England, and his office
was now near Belichick's. He hosted college prospects during their official visits to Foxborough and conducted interviews with them. Players and ownership liked Easterby, but had grown slightly suspicious
of him. The players started to see him less as their friend and more as
management—Belichick's eyes and ears. But he still spent hours each
week listening to guys vent, helping them get their minds right, a walking release valve in a high-pressure building. Kraft seemed to want Easterby to join Nick Caserio as part of a post-Belichick succession plan, but
in the meantime, his situation would change. Kraft wanted Easterby to
report to both Belichick and to himself, no longer just the former. Easterby was concerned about being involved in even more internal politics. Belichick didn't want to lose Easterby—he appreciated him, had
learned from him, and knew he couldn't replace him with one person—

and thought the two of them should talk with Kraft together. A meeting was scheduled for Monday, February 25, 2019.

All hell broke loose the weekend before. The Vero Beach Police Department announced a massive sex-trafficking bust, spanning at least ten massage parlors. At least 173 people were charged—including Kraft—in a case police described as involving men preying on trapped women who were forced to sleep in Orchids of Asia. A dynasty that began with the near death of its franchise quarterback and that had endured Spygate, Aaron Hernandez, Deflategate, and Trump now added Orchids of Asia to its legacy. Kraft was charged with two counts of soliciting prostitution, backed by video evidence, police said.

America's new face of sex trafficking, Kraft was humiliated and defiant. He hired a guided missile of a defense team, including William A. Burck, who had represented a dozen current and former Trump administration witnesses against Robert Mueller in the Russia investigation. One of Kraft's lawyers told the *Wall Street Journal* that there was "zero evidence of human trafficking in this case," and that his team was prepared to do anything to keep the video from being released to the public. Kraft waived his arraignment, pleaded not guilty, and requested a jury trial. Other owners both laughed about it, texting each other Twitter jokes— *Fellategate!*—and clutched their rosaries. But with vital negotiations coming up with the union and with broadcast partners, billions of dollars at stake, there was a quiet question floating around the league as to whether they could trust Kraft's judgment. At the very least, Kraft would not get what he wanted most: a Hall of Fame induction on the next ballot. Not a chance the selection committee would ignore his recent behavior.

Against that backdrop, Kraft tried to convince Easterby to stay. Kraft made the decision hard for him, as he had with McDaniels. This time, it didn't work. Easterby stood up for Belichick in the meeting, stating his belief that the owner took the "greatest coach in history for granted." His time in New England was over. News broke of his departure, and even though Easterby didn't leave because of Orchids of Asia, the two events—the team's character coach resigning without having a new job lined up, in the wake of Kraft's prostitution charges—arrived in such quick succession that it looked like more than a coincidence. The *Boston Globe* wrote that Kraft's charges did "not sit well with" Easterby and cited it as a reason for his departure, making an already embarrassing situation worse.

ROGER GOODELL APPEARED as though he didn't want to touch this thing, vowing to let the legal proceedings play out before considering a punishment for Kraft. It was the inverse of how he handled player discipline, but that's how it went in the NFL: owners played by different rules. Kraft was silent for weeks, allowing his lawyers to speak for him. But ahead of the March league meetings at Phoenix's Biltmore resort, he issued a lawyer-vetted statement, saying that he was "truly sorry," while not stating what he was apologizing for due to the ongoing legal situation. Kraft kept a low profile at the meetings, saying nothing to the press and little in owners-only sessions, which mostly centered on fights over instant replay. After 100 years of professional football, it seemed nobody knew what constituted a catch.

Some owners wondered if Kraft would apologize to the room for the deluge of negative publicity. He didn't. Reporters trailed Kraft from meeting rooms to elevators, not hounding him, but drifting in his wake, hoping he might wheel around for the microphones. He never did.

Jonathan, though, was on edge. He was universally considered one of the smartest and most strategic team executives around the league, but he sometimes acted rashly. He once threw a bottle down a hallway after the Patriots team picture had been rescheduled, angry that nobody had notified him. And in 2016, he left a league meeting abruptly after a long argument with Jerry Jones over the NFL's social media policy, which he later explained as having to depart for a prior commitment. He took slights against his dad personally. At the entrance to the Biltmore, Jonathan and Tom E. Curran of NBC Sports Boston got into it—at the precise moment that Russell Wilson and his wife, pop star Ciara, arrived at the resort amid a cocoon of security and handlers. It was a striking scene: Jonathan shifted aside for the entourage, then stepped onto a stone ledge near the walkway, literally shouting down at Curran. When Jonathan returned to ground level, one of Ciara's bodyguards stood next to him. Jonathan seemed puzzled, as if the guard was for *him*. Already in a state of agita, Kraft asked the guard why he couldn't stand in the entryway.

The bodyguard nodded toward Ciara, as if to tell Jonathan that he was with her—and to chill out.

Jonathan returned to laying into Curran about coverage of his dad's visit to a strip-mall massage parlor, as billionaires ambled around and as Ciara and her people strolled past, with *Deadspin* on hand to chronicle it all. Just another day in the life of the Patriots and the NFL.

On May 6, 2019, Tom Brady boarded a helicopter, with a potentially awkward day ahead of him. He was flying from New York City to Mount Laurel, outside of Philadelphia—the home of NFL Films. The league's centennial anniversary was nearing, and hosts Rich Eisen and Cris Collinsworth were taping a series to air in the fall, counting down the top 100 players and coaches in history. Belichick had served as one of the list's contributors—a career highlight, as he saw it. NFL Films had asked Brady and Belichick to join the hosts on set for an episode in which Brady would be named among the ten greatest quarterbacks ever.

Brady told friends that he hoped it wouldn't be uncomfortable with Belichick, what with Brady's absence from most of the off-season and the contract impasse. But when Brady arrived on set—with a gray suit and a face too tan for May—it was natural and fun. He and Belichick spoke about certain moments in their shared past, from the joy of 2001 to the pain of 2007. Belichick took to the clicker to detail the greatness of many coaches and players, a performance that later earned him an Emmy. Brady flew back to New York feeling good about the day—and about his relationship with his head coach.

At the Patriots' ring ceremony a month later, Brady and Bündchen chatted and laughed with Belichick and Linda Holliday, with Brady and Belichick's suit pockets filled with some of their Super Bowl rings. That night, Belichick addressed the party with gratitude and more self-reflection than usual, fully aware of the near mutiny with Brady and Gronk before the season. "It's not easy to play for me," he said. "You know what? In the end, it's worth it."

But when training camp arrived, Belichick reverted easily to regular-season mode. At his first press conference, Belichick was asked about the possible extension for Brady that was being discussed. "I'm not going to talk about player contracts. Or any other contracts, for that matter." A few days later, Brady was asked if he believed he had earned a new deal. "I don't know—that's up for talk show debate. What do you guys think? Should we take a poll? Talk to Mr. Kraft, come on."

The reporters laughed, but Brady wasn't trying to be funny. Brady told a friend that Kraft had promised him he would take care of the contract, but now, it was Belichick setting the terms. Belichick thought Brady was close to done—and that the Patriots had gone for broke the past few years, wringing championships out of an aging roster. He was stubborn in his appraisal. Tom Curran later reported that Brady considered walking out of camp in protest. Belichick didn't seem to realize how angry Brady was, though coaches on the staff told him the situation with Brady was deteriorating. On August 4, a day after Brady's 42nd birthday, news broke that the two sides had agreed on a two-year, $70 million extension. But, like most NFL contracts, it was a mirage: it was essentially a one-year deal, with an $8 million salary bump, with two additional years that would automatically be voided on March 17, 2020—the first day of free agency after the upcoming season. Most important, Don Yee had muscled in a provision that prevented the team from slapping the franchise tag on Brady after the season. The most accomplished quarterback of all time was going to be an unrestricted free agent in 2020. Kraft believed Brady had earned not only a new deal, but the right, as a selfless icon, to decide his next move—and hoped that, in the end, he would return or retire.

Brady seemed to eliminate both options two days after news broke of the contract, when he and his wife answered with an act that made headlines:

FOR SALE:
TOM BRADY PUTS BROOKLINE HOME ON THE MARKET

IT WAS TIME. Brady knew it right then, in August of 2019. The team had moved on, even though he would lead the Patriots for another season, and so Brady needed to prepare to work elsewhere, something he had alternately feared and fantasized about for years. What about other football heroes who had preceded him and moved on, only to look foreign in another team's colors—Joe Montana as a Chief, Joe Namath as a Ram, Johnny Unitas as a Charger? Brady never once cared about legacy, except when parents named their children after him. That was cool, he thought—to have touched someone's life so deeply that they wanted to keep an element of him close forever. But legacy, at least the way many sports fans defined it? Brady said he "couldn't give a shit." Nobody could take away his accomplishments. Brady always played for himself—for the love of the game, for the opportunities of personal growth the sport provided, and for the rush that came with continually raising the stakes. He needed to be great, not to impress anyone else, but to satisfy his own innate needs, and perhaps out of a certain obsession that bordered on compulsion. "A little sickness in me that just wants to throw a frickin' spiral," Brady later said.

The new season was set to be a long one. New England was about to enter another September bereft of offensive weapons, leaving Brady to cover things up until the team found its identity. Gronkowski had retired in the off-season, as much due to Belichick's no-excuses program as injuries. "I was not in a good place. Football was bringing me down, and I didn't like it," he later said. The NFL Network's Mike Giardi reported that the Patriots felt that if Gronkowski had listened to team doctors rather than the TB12 method, the injuries might not have piled up. But no matter: he was now hawking pain treatments that contained cannabidiol. But on the Saturday before week 1, a new top target for Brady was found, eight inches shorter than his forerunner. Antonio Brown, perhaps the best wide receiver in the league in the 2010s, was released by the Oakland Raiders. His next team would be his third in six months.

In March, Brown had worn out his welcome in Pittsburgh after nine years, seven of them Pro Bowl seasons, and the Steelers traded him to the Raiders. It was a disaster from the start. Brown threatened to retire because the league wouldn't allow him to wear his preferred helmet. He missed practice because of severely frostbitten feet—he had used a cryotherapy machine while wearing improper footwear. As the season neared, he threatened to fight Raiders general manager Mike Mayock, cried for forgiveness in front of his teammates, secretly recorded a conversation with head coach Jon Gruden—"Please stop this shit and just play football," Gruden pleaded—and then posted the audio on social media. Though Brown was probably the best player on their roster, the Raiders had no choice but to cut him.

Brown seemed too erratic for the NFL, to say nothing of the Patriots and their overriding emphasis on team over player. But Belichick moved fast, asking Kraft for permission to sign Brown to a one-year, $15 million deal. Kraft then called Brady, knowing that Brown could provide a lift, for the quarterback's spirits as much as for the actual offense. Before the end of the day, Brown was a New England Patriot. A day after New England blew out Pittsburgh in the season opener, Barstool Sports posted a selfie of Brown smiling next to Brady.

But after Brown signed with the Patriots, a trainer who had been hired by him sued him for sexual assault, alleging that he had exposed himself on one occasion, ejaculated on her back on another, and raped her on a third. Brown denied every charge, and in April 2021, he and the trainer settled the suit. But shortly after the allegations by the trainer against Brown had been made, *Sports Illustrated* published a deeply reported account of Brown's life, which included more allegations of sexual misconduct and domestic violence. Brown met with local reporters in Foxborough, answering four questions in a minute—"I'm just here to focus on ball," he said—and in his first game, he caught four passes and scored a touchdown in a win over the Dolphins. But, within days, *Sports Illustrated* reported that Brown had sent threatening text messages to one of his accusers in the wake of its original story, including pictures of her children.

Kraft found it all unacceptable. The texts weren't something dug up from Brown's past; he had sent them as a member of the New England Patriots. Brady and Belichick wanted to stick with Brown, but New England released him 11 days after signing him, making sure word leaked that it was Kraft who "insisted" on the move.

Brady told a friend that he believed the entire episode was driven by optics, after the headlines the owner himself had generated in the off-season. But by now, the case involving Kraft looked a lot less like the bust of a massive sex ring and more like an illicit act between two consenting adults. Palm Beach prosecutor Greg Kridos had confessed in court in the spring that "there is no human trafficking that arises out of this investigation." Kraft's lawyers had successfully argued to keep the surveillance footage from being released to the public and as impermissible evidence. Without video, there was no case, and the prostitution charges were dropped. The court eventually ordered the video to be destroyed. Only Kraft's reputation was damaged. The two women he patronized were fined a combined $45,000 for soliciting *him*.

THE SEASON WENT ON and New England was winning, unlike prior Patriots teams early in September. Internal alliances and fractures were evident. After Brown apologized to the Patriots on social media, seemingly begging for another chance, Belichick made clear it was not his call. "You'd have to talk to Robert about that," he said.

And when New England faced Houston later in the season, a storyline leading up to the game was about Jack Easterby, who had landed with the Texans as executive vice president of team development. After Easterby was hired, the Texans had once again requested permission to interview Nick Caserio for their general manager position. The Patriots denied the request—and filed tampering charges, accusing Easterby of recruiting Caserio at New England's ring ceremony. It was a rare move—clubs often accuse one another of tampering with players, but rarely with front office personnel—and it seemed like revenge for the way Easterby left, when Kraft was at his lowest. Texans executives asked Easterby what exactly had happened in New England, and Easterby told them about Kraft's proposed dual-reporting structure and the big meeting between him and Belichick on one side and the owner on the other. He denied that he had tampered. He had worked with Caserio for six years. They were close friends. He knew Caserio wanted out. He didn't *need* to tamper. The Patriots eventually withdrew the charge. When Belichick was asked about it, he seemed to side with his former executive over his boss, telling reporters that the tampering situation "didn't have anything to do with Jack Easterby."

For most of two decades, Kraft, Belichick, and Brady had seemingly stood together, knowing that if they were unified, few could touch them.

But now, with internal disagreements playing out in public for the second time in two years, it was worth wondering if that was ever truly the case—if time and age had revealed the decay rather than caused it.

TOM BRADY WAS MISERABLE, even as the winning continued. New England was 8–0 heading into Baltimore to face the 5–2 Ravens on November 3. The defense was one of Belichick's best ever, with 2019 Defensive Player of the Year Stephon Gilmore leading perhaps the most talented and effective secondary the coach had ever overseen. The offense had scored at least 30 points in all of their wins except one. Still, the coaches knew that Brady wanted to be more involved in game plans. They would ask for his input, and he would give it—but, come kickoff, they did their own thing. It left Brady asking again why he put himself through all of this.

Brady's expectations of himself were always greater than those of anyone else, and what was unfolding on Sundays wasn't good enough for him. He always viewed each play through the prism of his limits and its possibilities, and it was that talent—for understanding his limits and finding a way to transcend them—that allowed him to seem limitless. But it was never easy, and the costs were significant. For years, Brady had gone to dark places after a game if he felt that he hadn't reached his potential over that particular 60-minute slice of football. That hardwiring was tough enough for Brady himself to live with, and he saw it passed down to Benny, his second son's patrimony. Benny wasn't as enamored with sports as Jack, who played fantasy football—and drafted quarterback Cam Newton of the Carolina Panthers over his own dad. Benny's passions in areas outside of sports first surprised Brady, and Gisele had to explain to him that some boys are different. Vivian was easygoing, and spoiled by her dad. Both of his children with Gisele spoke Portuguese, her native language, of which Brady himself had only rudimentary knowledge. *"Papai não sabe nada,"* Gisele often said around the house—*Daddy doesn't know anything*. But Benny was not only impacted by the cruel side of his dad's profession and success—in 2018, a kid told Benny that they were friends only because his father was

Tom Brady—but he was also hard on himself. Brady knew what was in store: rage, insomnia, stewing, and the inability to shake this *thing* that had enriched and complicated his own life.

"This is not the path you want to go down!" he told Benny. He told his son to breathe, a futile trick his old man had once tried with him. Brady could control himself at 42 no more than as a child—he just hid it better—and he knew it wasn't going to disappear when he retired. The real work of life awaited him. He had been an absent brother at times, an unresponsive friend, a distracted husband and father. Like Belichick, Brady had made a choice long ago. The highs and lows of football had become the rhythm of his life. How things would look after football was not clear; all he knew was that he planned to seek counseling, as he had at Michigan with Greg Harden. What began as a quest to become Tom Brady would end with the sense of loss that having been Tom Brady would bring.

Before the Ravens game, Brady told the NBC broadcasting crew that he was "the most unhappy 8–0 quarterback in football," a frank admission that stunned Al Michaels, accustomed as sports journalists are to stock answers from athletes. But, by game time, Brady had recentered himself. It was the kind of test Brady loved, a test of self and team against a fellow contender. In only two years, the Ravens had completely reinvented their offense, in a way that New England's coaches fantasized about, and not only because they had coveted the player at the center of it all when he was coming out of college. Joe Flacco, the staid pocket passer, was out, and replacing him was Lamar Jackson, 22 years old—two years older than Brady's career—a cutting-edge force on the ground and in the air who seemed poised to join Patrick Mahomes and Deshaun Watson of the Texans among the league's next crop of superstar quarterbacks.

The game ended with New England overmatched and missing its familiar magic. After Baltimore's 37–20 win, Brady hugged Jackson. "Great game, dude," Brady said. "You played great."

"Appreciate that," Jackson said.

"Congratulations."

"GOAT," Jackson said, looking Brady in the eye. "The GOAT!"

Brady's lips pursed into a stiff half-smile. He genuinely hated it when people called him the greatest ever. Not because it embarrassed him, or because he didn't want to be seen as arrogant, but because he simply didn't feel it, didn't think in those terms. He only saw ways to improve, new things to accomplish, and he was on a team that seemed ready to try to improve without him.

46

PLEASE STAY, TOMMY

AS NEW ENGLAND CONTINUED, IN THE FALL OF 2019, to beat inferior teams and fail against elite ones, Gisele Bündchen began the process of moving out. Both Tom and Gisele were careful when asked about the future, no matter who asked. Teammates, friends, parents, staff—anyone could leak, setting off days of chatter, and Brady didn't want his future to be a distraction for the Patriots. Brady's drive from Brookline to the stadium—exactly 30 minutes, out of their winding driveway behind the gates, away from the vast lawn, which Brady loved to watch the sun etch over in the morning quiet, where he had played catch with Gisele during his suspension in 2016, past the security booth, which was often vacant, and left onto Woodland Road, a quiet little street encased by large trees, so leafy in the summertime that it became a verdant tunnel, winding to I-95, easing off to Route 1, lined by empty lots back in 2000 and fully developed now, evidence that he had helped build not just a dynasty, but an entire local economy—afforded him the chance to listen to the radio, often to Howard Stern, whom he loved, and also a fleeting chance to chat with friends and reflect.

He had arrived young and single and invisible and now was a global celebrity married to a global celebrity who hosted his kids' birthday parties on his and his wife's immense lawn. The fans always yelled, "Tawmmeee," as if he was family, and even if he rarely acknowledged them, he heard them, felt them in the core of his being. How could he not?

Packing was going to be a challenge for Brady. He had accumulated a lot of stuff over the years. Long ago, Gisele had stored away some of his most prized possessions—the end-zone pylons he snagged from big games, the ball from his first Super Bowl, the cleats from his second one. Brady didn't know where she had put them. Still, he often reminded himself of his luck: he had never had to change cities, in 20 years of professional sports. How many athletes could say that? Brady had watched friends fall victim to Belichick's knife, in the locker room one year and gone the next—sometimes the next month—forced to relocate their families. Brady was the guy who always stayed—same number, same locker area. But the founding Belichickian ethos that had made the Patriots so hated and successful over the years—the emotionless pursuit of victory—finally touched the untouchable quarterback, lest he think otherwise.

SATURDAY JANUARY 4, 2020, was a bad night for tailgating in Foxborough. The air was thick and wet before the Patriots faced the Tennessee Titans in the wild-card round, so people found shelter in bars near the stadium, where it was warm and stuffy, the windows fogging up as pregame radio and television shows broadcast live. Fans seemed nervous. You could feel it. All year, whenever NBC Sports Boston's Tom Curran and ESPN's Jeff Darlington or Adam Schefter reported that this might be it for Brady in New England, there was the predictable backlash from a fan base wary of the press, with diehards calling into radio shows to decry the use of "anonymous sauces," dismissing all the journalists on the story as clickbait experts. But by now, even the most blinkered Patriots fans knew. Brady ran onto the field for warm-ups, streaking down the sideline from the north end zone to the south and toward a sign that read, PLEASE STAY TOMMY.

The game was unlike any Patriots playoff game during the dynastic run, not because they lost, but because Bill Belichick and Tom Brady looked like they had lost a measure of confidence in one another. Brady seemed unsurprised when Belichick's handpicked receivers struggled to separate from Titans defenders or ran the wrong routes, leaving him no margin for error. And Belichick—with the season on the line, New England down 14–13 with 3:17 left and facing a fourth and four from its 37—took the ball out of Brady's hands, electing to punt. The man who promised that he would never coach scared now believed more in his defense's ability to slow an offense that it struggled to stop all night than in Tom Brady to gain four yards. The result was chastening: the Titans ran the ball and ran down the clock—deploying Belichick's offensive penalty loophole against him—before punting and pinning the Patriots at their one-yard line with 15 seconds left.

Brady jogged onto the field, as he had so many times before, though now briefly shaking his head, the resignation apparent in his manner. Moments before, he had tried to manufacture hope. "I'm going to have to throw one up in the air, we're gonna have to go up and make a catch," he told his receivers. "So, if we get position, I'm going to give you a shot to go up and make the play, all right?" Now he needed a miracle. New England called a hook-and-lateral. Titans coach Mike Vrabel saw it coming from the sideline, alerting his players as they lined up. The play had no chance. Brady threw into coverage, and the ball was tipped into the air and landed in the arms of Logan Ryan, the former Patriot who earlier had dropped an easy interception. He danced into the end zone with Brady's final pass as a Patriot, providing the final points in a 20–13 Titans win.

After the game, Brady seemed strangely relieved, as if the interception didn't bother him. He insisted that it was "hopefully unlikely" that he would retire, but made no promises of a return, whether to the Patriots or to the sport. Tom Brady had been on his way out all year, but now was not the time for goodbyes. He carried his daughter through the empty stadium tunnels. At home, he was awake, staring at a screen as a wet Saturday night turned into a dry Sunday morning. The last pass— *his* last pass—gnawed at him. He sent Logan Ryan a private message on Instagram.

Why couldn't you drop both? Why did you have to catch one?

A FEW WEEKS LATER, Tom Brady and Bill Belichick were on the field before the Super Bowl, in matching crimson sports jackets. Right before kickoff—the Kansas City Chiefs against the San Francisco 49ers, Mahomes against Garoppolo—many of the living members of the NFL 100 all-time team were honored, all wearing the same special sports jackets, with the league shield as an emblem over the chest. Belichick was also wearing some of his rings—you knew it was a special night if he did that. The quarterbacks were introduced last. Brady stood alongside Joe Montana, Dan Marino, John Elway, Peyton Manning, Brett Favre, and Roger Staubach. This time, he wasn't booed.

Kickoff neared. The group ambled off the field, a procession of football royalty. Brady and Montana were among the last to leave, in private conversation on football's most public stage, stopping to talk into each other's ear so that the cameras couldn't hear. By now, Montana was more than Brady's idol; he was his friend, even though he had piled on during Deflategate, refusing to buy Brady's excuse. Montana thought Brady should stay in New England—the transition to a new team and playbook for an older quarterback was harder than anyone realized—but it seemed moot. He figured there was no way the Patriots would let Brady leave and retire elsewhere.

Listening to Brady at the Super Bowl, Montana could tell something was wrong that went beyond the matter of a new contract. Brady wanted to be treated like a valued and astute football mind. "They'd ask my advice," Brady told Montana. "I'd tell them, and they don't take it."

Montana was surprised. But then, he knew how these things end. Bill Walsh spent the second half of the 1980s eager to replace Montana with Steve Young, determined to move on from any player, even an icon—*especially* an icon—a year early rather than a year late. It infuriated Montana. When his family hosted Young for Christmas dinner, his daughter said, "Is this the guy we hate?" Montana found a higher level, playing the best football of his career and winning two more Super Bowls. But then he injured his elbow, and Young began what would be a Hall of Fame career, giving the team the opening it needed. Belichick had learned from Walsh, maybe too well. The legacies of the greatest quarterbacks, like the game itself, were often beyond their control.

47

THE COLLEGE KID

MIKE VRABEL WAS AT THE NFL COMBINE WHEN HE looked up from the monotony of workouts and saw Tom Brady and Julian Edelman on a television, sitting courtside at a Syracuse basketball game with Jimmy Fallon. Something about the entire scene struck Vrabel as odd. It wasn't that they were at a random college game at the Carrier Dome. It was their hair. Two pretty men looked slightly prettier.

Vrabel texted them: *Hey, did you guys get highlights for the basketball game?*

Rather than texting a response, Edelman FaceTimed Vrabel. Brady, of course, used to highlight his hair. But that was a long time ago, and now age had done its work around the temples. Edelman's hair, though—it was suspiciously golden, vaguely boy-bandish. Edelman clapped back at Vrabel, yelling with the crowd behind him. Cameras caught it all, and with Brady's free agency looming, it set off a round of social media babble. Was Vrabel recruiting Brady to join Tennessee?

A camera zoomed in on them. Edelman looked at the lens and said, "He's coming back!"

Brady forced a smile behind clenched teeth, shaking his head.

After the game, Brady and Edelman were ushered to a VIP room encased by black curtains and filled with 20 or so donors and famous alums. This was never really Brady's scene, but he was gracious if not enthusiastic, posing for pictures, glad-handing and small-talking. A Syracuse junior named Sean Dorcellus observed Brady, hoping to get a chance himself. When a donor wanted to talk about the Syracuse game, or the Dome, or just about anything else, Brady stared intently and chit-chatted. But the moment anything New England was raised, even the championships, Brady shut down, not even faking a smile, subtly steering his attention to the next lurking fan. As always, Brady's demeanor expressed what he refused to say.

Soon, it was Dorcellus's turn. He introduced himself, telling Brady how much he appreciated the quarterback's statement on Kobe Bryant, who a month earlier had died in a helicopter crash in the hills northwest of Los Angeles, along with his daughter Gianna and seven others.

That got Brady's attention, and he locked in on Dorcellus, tuning out the rest of the room. Bryant's death had deeply affected Brady, a peer gone so young, and he spent many nights in tears, missing the idea of Bryant as much as Bryant himself. He felt that they shared a mentality, an internal drive few could comprehend, much less understand, and Bryant's death reaffirmed Brady's desire to play football. He knew that day might come for him at any time, so why not do what he loved? The morning of Bryant's funeral, Brady posted a short essay titled "What's Really Important?" It was five paragraphs—long by Brady's standards, the king of the two-sentence email—and it was one of the first times Brady had something meaningful to say about something other than football. Dorcellus had been moved to learn that one icon drew inspiration from another, and he said that the third paragraph—on the effect Kobe had on those around him, how he could make people feel special through a mere interaction—hit him especially hard.

Now Brady was in a position to do that himself. He looked at the credential dangling from Dorcellus's neck and asked what he did. Dorcellus, still an undergraduate, explained that he was a part-time staffer in the Syracuse athletic department, trying to figure out what to do after graduation. He wanted to be in sports. Should he work for a team? An agency? A league? A big decision loomed.

Brady enjoyed talking about things that were real, and the idea of a new beginning energized him. For weeks, he had deflected all talk of his future—even when Ben Affleck and Matt Damon joint-texted him, asking about his plans, Brady responded with a shrug emoji—but over the next few minutes, he opened up to a college kid. He gave Dorcellus the classic advice of picking a career that he loved—but then told him something he'd learned over the course of two decades in professional football: it might not be enough to just love your job. You had to want to live in the world the job created. Working with people you like, a tribe with a common goal, would make your professional life far happier than any accolade, salary, or a company's prestige could. You need to do the work you love, at a place and with people you love.

You have to feel—Brady repeatedly returned to this word— "appreciated."

As free agency neared, Brady was alone in the house his family had mostly vacated, pondering his future. Don Yee was still his agent, but Brady was also acting on his own, quietly putting out feelers himself, leaving owners and executives to wonder if he had a free-agency plan. No matter how many hints those close to him dropped to reporters— Jeff Darlington said on air that he would be "stunned" if Brady returned to the Patriots—few around the league seemed to believe it. Many of the executives who did due diligence found that Brady was so driven by an animus toward Belichick that they couldn't tell whether he actually was seeking a fresh start or he just needed leverage to force Kraft to step in. But Kraft had told friends at the Super Bowl that New England wanted Brady—though maybe not until he was 45 years old. Tom Brady had been underestimated his entire life, and now two of the men who knew him best, knew what he was capable of, were treating him as so many had before. They should have known better.

Brady was going to play until 45. It was non-negotiable. As long as he could perform—"When I suck, I'll retire," he'd said—he was going to give it everything, as he always had.

Brady did not force confrontations, and neither did Belichick, but he also wasn't one to bluff. He and Belichick spoke on the phone, not about a new deal—Belichick acted as if Brady was still under contract, which was technically true until March 17—but about potential roster improvements. The call left Brady underwhelmed, and served as a reminder that nothing was going to change in New England. Bill was Bill: he looked for bargains, not splashy imports. Brady began the call wanting to leave, and felt no different after it.

Ever a list guy, Brady jotted down what he desired in a new situation, 20 or so things: Warm weather—he was sick of the cold, and so was his wife. Proximity to Jack, who lived with his mom in New York—or out west, near his parents. A two-year contract for a total of $50 million, not an outrageous demand, as it would make him only the eighth-highest-paid quarterback for 2020. A team that was already good, and whose coach valued collaboration. A good team. Not a great one—he was not necessarily chasing a seventh ring. That surprised those closest to him. Maybe when the season came around, his compulsion to win would take over. But right now, Brady simply needed something different for the final chapter, and in late February, he tried to assert control. He reached out to Wes Welker, who was now the 49ers' receivers coach, and let him know that if San Francisco was interested, it would be his choice—no free-agency tour, no bidding war, full stop; he would end his career where his love of football began, in scarlet and gold, allowing his parents to drive to games for the first time since the 1990s.

At first, the 49ers didn't buy that Brady was truly interested. Regardless, signing him would be complicated. Jimmy Garoppolo might have garnered a few Super Bowl MVP votes if San Francisco hadn't collapsed late against the Chiefs, giving up 21 points in the final six minutes. Still, with just over two minutes left, down 24–20, Garoppolo had a chance to pull off what he had watched Brady do twice on the biggest stage, a chance to separate himself forever with a Super Bowl–winning drive. It started off promisingly, with two completions. But then Garoppolo missed three straight passes and was sacked on fourth down, effectively ending the game.

Brady rarely failed in those moments. He knew it, and he knew that that the 49ers' coaches knew it.

It was a ruthless move, revealing more Belichick in Brady than he wanted to admit. The 49ers were tepid. Brady would be 43 when the season started, with an arm that scouts insisted had faded as 2019 went on. Brady was sensitive to that critique. Over the previous summer, while on vacation in Montana, he had told Guerrero that his goal was to be able to throw the ball 68 yards. He tossed it 71, so he upped the goal to 74. By the end of the trip, he had hit 74 yards. In the playoff loss to Tennessee, he threw an incomplete Hail Mary at the end of the first half that traveled 65-some yards.

The 49ers realized they had to listen. One of the greatest football players of all time, capable of elevating an entire building with his preparation and mentality alone, was offering his services. Kyle Shanahan instructed the offensive coaches to watch all of Brady's 2019 throws. He did so himself, turning his Cabo vacation into a film session. San Francisco executives quietly reached out to a few friends around the league, asking about the logistics of acquiring an aging future Hall of Famer— and what Garoppolo might fetch in a trade. A first- and a third-round pick? That seemed high, the 49ers learned.

The conversations didn't stay quiet for long. Reporters wondered if Garoppolo was on his way out. The 49ers' coaching staff had quiet doubts about Garoppolo, even before the Super Bowl, feeling that it took an inordinate amount of energy to get his head ready for game day and that he perhaps lacked Brady's extreme drive for excellence. In the playoffs, Shanahan had called plays like a coach with limited faith in his quarterback, leaning heavily on the running game. Some in the building felt that Shanahan was too hard on Garoppolo, causing him to play tentatively. The coaches liked Garoppolo personally—and so did his teammates, enough to elect him captain—but Shanahan was open to the idea of an upgrade. But then, almost as fast as the 49ers' interest in Brady rose, it died. The coaches liked Brady's film—but didn't love it. He was better than Garoppolo, they thought, but not that much better—not so much that it was worth trading away a locker-room leader, not to mention one who was nearly 15 years younger and coming off a Super Bowl appearance. A few days before free agency began, the 49ers decided to stick with their guy. This time, Garoppolo won.

He ended up playing in only six games in 2020 due to an ankle injury. The 49ers missed the playoffs, and in March of 2021, they traded two- first round picks and swapped first-round picks with the Dolphins to move up to the number three spot in the draft and pick Garoppolo's successor and someone Shanahan could personally groom: a precocious dual-threat quarterback out of North Dakota State named Trey Lance.

48

TOMPA BAY

I N EARLY MARCH, THE NATION STOPPED. A CONTAGIOUS new virus was spreading across the globe, overwhelming hospitals, taking people who thought they had the flu, producing images of goodbyes over FaceTime and, soon enough, of trucks lined up in New York City filled with body bags. Some states went into lockdown. The NBA, NHL, and Major League Baseball suspended their seasons. March Madness was canceled before it began. The NFL was lucky—there are no games in March, even though some owners and fans wouldn't be opposed to the idea—and moved forward as many companies and organizations did: over Zoom. Free agency was done virtually, which meant no tour for Brady—no fancy dinners, no reporters tracking his plane, no NFL version of the contest for LeBron James. He didn't mind. After 20 years, he had visited almost every stadium and had traded enough gossip to know each organization's dirt. A tour would be a ridiculous fuss, and if there was anything he hated, it was fusses.

With the chance to pick his destination for the first time since high school, Brady faced a set of narrowing options, just as he had in 1995. Tennessee signed the resurgent Ryan Tannehill to an extension worth a guaranteed $91 million, picking a journeyman over a living legend, a decision that would have been unthinkable a year earlier. The Raiders, now in Las Vegas, planned to put in a call, but even though Brady had spoken with Mark Davis ringside at a fight in January—even though UFC president Dana White, a Patriots fan, told the press that "if that dude isn't playing for Boston, he's playing here"—neither Brady nor the team seriously considered one another.

The market for the greatest quarterback ever, once rumored to include up to ten teams, ended up constituting the Chicago Bears, Los Angeles Chargers, and Tampa Bay Buccaneers. And, of course, the New England Patriots. Just past noon Eastern on March 16, two days before free agency, the league's legal tampering period began and Jason Licht, the Buccaneers' general manager, called Yee. Licht had worked in the Patriots' scouting department two separate times, and had been in the draft room in 2000. He believed Brady wouldn't leave New England, but it was worth a shot.

"You made a good decision to call," Yee said.

Licht hung up unexpectedly encouraged. From the outside, the Bucs were a strange fit: an un-iconic franchise for an icon, with an all-time winning percentage of .387—the worst across all American professional sports teams. But Tampa Bay checked a lot of Brady's boxes: sun and warmth, easy flight for Jack, major talent on both sides of the ball in need of a missing piece, an offensive-minded head coach in Bruce Arians, who had spent a career not only fostering a collaborative environment, not only fixing cocktails after games for staff and players, but nurturing and learning from some of the game's best quarterbacks—above all, Peyton Manning. For Brady, going to Tampa would be like converting from Catholicism to hedonism. He watched film of the Bucs, taking notes on Arians's offensive style and on their dynamic receivers.

By the end of the day, Brady had ruled out only one potential suitor. He had been mentally gone from New England for a long time, but there was one thing left to do.

EARLY IN THE EVENING of March 16, Tom Brady texted Robert Kraft and asked if he was up for a socially distanced visit. Kraft told Brady to come over. With Brady's contract due to void the following afternoon, Kraft assumed this was good news—that Brady wanted to quietly negotiate a new deal, just the two of them, like old times. Brady drove the four minutes to Kraft's house, and sat in his living room to deliver news that he had imagined delivering for a long time.

Brady told Kraft how much he loved him, how much he appreciated what they had accomplished, but . . .

"We're not going to continue together."

Kraft seemed surprised. Maybe it was the idealist in him. Maybe he didn't want to admit how badly things were broken. Both men started to cry. Kraft stared at Brady, thinking back to that skinny, confident kid carrying a pizza in 2000. Brady thanked Kraft for all that he had done for him and his family. They spent hours in conversation. By 9:30, it was time for Brady to go. There was no hug and kiss goodbye, not during a pandemic.

Brady hoped to visit Belichick to get out in front of his own news. But Belichick said he wasn't available—Brady told friends he thought that was telling—so they spoke by phone. It was a good call. Belichick told him he was the best player he'd ever coached—"best player the league had ever seen," Brady later recounted to a friend—and that it was a privilege to coach him. It was a good way to end their run together. Their relationship was permanently altered as they talked. They were no longer overlord and star employee, but two individuals who together had accomplished something unprecedented.

Later that night, Brady wrote two statements: one for the fans, one for the organization. He read them over FaceTime to Jim Gray, cruising through the fan statement. But when he read the one about Kraft, Belichick, and his teammates—"I couldn't be the man I am today without the relationships you have allowed me to build with you"—he teared up, unable to continue. A silent minute passed. He finished, and in a social media announcement at 8:44 the next morning, under the headline "Forever a Patriot," Brady informed the world that he would not be forever a Patriot after all.

BRADY HAD CYCLED TO an emotional place from which he insisted, both publicly and privately, that his departure wasn't rooted in acrimony. He wasn't angry with anyone, he told friends. He believed he was departing on good terms. That was important. He no longer wanted to be a robotic soldier, the embodiment of an oppressive culture he'd helped create and had now lost faith in. He was free to be himself, and he saw his true self as ready to find out if there was another way to win outside of Belichick's methods. But the morning of Brady's announcement, Kraft spoke with Patriots beat writers to explain the loss, leaving the NFL Network little doubt as to why Brady left. "Think about loving your wife, and for whatever reason, there's something—her father or mother—that makes life impossible for you, and you have to move on." A few days after Brady signed with his new team, he wrote an essay for the *Players' Tribune*, focused on endings and beginnings. He thanked Kraft by name. He didn't thank Bill Belichick.

TWO DAYS AFTER Brady's long talk with Kraft, at about 4 p.m. on March 18, he connected with Licht and Arians on a call. The Bucs had prepared a sales pitch, calling it Operation Shoeless Joe. "Build it, and he will come" was the running joke. They had studied Brady's film and listened to his performances when he had been wired for sound or caught venting on the sideline by cameras—clues into his mindset. Unlike New England, the Bucs had weapons: a long, Moss-like target in Mike Evans, an explosive threat in the emerging Chris Godwin, a lithe speedster in Scott Miller. There was also a rumor that Rob Gronkowski was considering stepping out of retirement to join Brady in Tampa.

Licht paced in Arians's kitchen as he spoke with Brady. Arians looked on. It was going well, from their perspective. Brady asked Licht if the wideouts were good guys, one ex-Patriot to another.

"No doubt," Licht said.

Brady seemed sold—and started to pitch himself to *them*. He had studied the roster, even the defense, and the entire NFC South division. Licht didn't know Brady well from their New England days, but at least one aspect of him hadn't changed, despite all of the wins and fame and glory and ego: he was earnestly grateful. Years earlier, an associate had emailed Brady a copy of a Michael Lewis speech called "Don't Eat Fortune's Cookie." It was a dissertation about luck, and how loath successful people are to admit its role in their lives. "Don't be deceived by life's outcomes," Lewis said. Brady had built his incomparable career by amassing control over an uncontrollable game, attempting to all but eliminate luck. I once asked him whether he ever paused to consider randomness in his career, the little breaks that went his way—the Tuck Rule—and his face tightened, as if insulted. But something about Lewis's speech resonated with him, cutting to his core. "Wow," he said after reading it. "Now that was awesome." He now felt fortunate that a team believed in him—and eager to reward it.

After about 45 minutes, Licht handed the phone to Arians. The coach stated his view that they had a Super Bowl team. They needed someone to help them believe. You come, Arians told Brady, and we will win the Super Bowl. Arians described his offense and how much he valued collaboration. "I always let my quarterbacks have a say in what we're doing," he said. "I've always given my quarterbacks leniency, and"—he emphasized, as if to make clear—"you're *Tom Brady*."

Arians was getting fired up, and when he gets fired up, he starts to cuss. Licht watched as his coach dropped f-bombs with startling frequency, even by NFL standards, like lemmings off a cliff, and hoped that Brady wasn't put off by them. Brady loved it all. Before the two-way pitch call with the Bucs ended after 90 or so minutes, Arians handed the phone back to Licht. The GM had one more issue to raise. "It's a small thing," Licht said, "but when you're here, it could be a big thing." It had to do with jersey numbers. Chris Godwin was Tampa's number 12.

"Yeah, I know that," Brady said. "I don't care what jersey I'm wearing. I just want to win a Super Bowl. I'm actually thinking about number 7. Is seven available?"

"I think so," Licht said. "Why seven?"

"Go after that seventh Super Bowl, that's pretty cool."

Godwin ended up handing over number 12, but Licht was excited: he knew where Brady's mind was. Licht and Arians adjourned to a local restaurant, sitting outside, six feet apart, and looking at each other in disbelief. Brady kept saying "we" during the call, which Arians took as a good sign.

Brady heard a pitch from the Chargers, but it only confirmed that Tampa was the right spot. On March 20, Brady sat in his kitchen, wearing a black hoodie, and signed a new contract. Jack snapped a picture from across the counter. Within weeks, Brady's people applied to trademark the phrase "Tompa Bay." Many football minds wondered how Brady would fit with Arians, not only in terms of coaching style, but of playing style. Would the high wear off if the losses piled up? Might

Brady *miss* the pain? Would Arians's offensive motto—"No risk it, no biscuit"—bother a quarterback whose genius was rooted in identifying and taking the highest-percentage play? That was for tomorrow. Today, Brady looked happy and relieved as he signed his name in black ink.

49

WARTIME
PROFITEER

AMERICA ONLY KNEW THEM TOGETHER, AND NOW that they were apart, Bill Belichick and Tom Brady further revealed themselves during a strange and dangerous time. The country was divided between those who believed in the virus's potency and those who did not, and while the friend of Brady and Belichick in the White House downplayed the virus and later suggested that people could inject disinfectant to protect themselves from it, the coach sat in his living room, in front of a bookshelf with a framed issue of *Life* from 1947, its cover bearing a shot of Nantucket's Sankaty Head Lighthouse, and stared into a camera for a public service announcement, to be released on the Patriots website, his words slow and precise, his tone grave, thanking medical professionals and speaking the language of his craft. "We are facing a difficult opponent. It will take teamwork, discipline, and commitment to do the right things all the time. . . . There are plenty of things we cannot do right now, but let's focus on what we can do. We can adapt, we can adjust, and we can make better decisions right now for the betterment of the future. As I tell our team, let's keep stringing good days together, and we will get through this." The video was posted on April 1 and went viral.

This was a different Belichick. He had always owned his darkness in a way that Brady did not, never caring how he came off, even explicitly unrepentant. But now, Belichick was clearly deeply concerned. Maybe it was because he saw where this thing was headed, and how American culture was uniquely unsuited to handle a crisis that seemed to require the type of obedience that he was an expert in fostering. Maybe it was because he was almost 68 years old and among those most vulnerable. A man who had defied what one person could control in his sport now spoke with the certainty that there were limits to what humans could control, and urged his country to remember that before it could win, it had to not lose.

Brady was one of many NFL stars to participate in a video asking people to stay home. But in the months after leaving New England—he seemed to relish his freedom, joining Howard Stern for more than an hour on air and reminding listeners of the untrue truth that nobody had wanted him out of high school—he also saw a business opportunity. In May, TB12 released a new product called Protect. Brady personally billed it as an "immunity blend supplement created to support a healthy immune system to help you stay strong." TB12 CEO John Burns told Yahoo!, "Now more than ever, it's important to have daily support for a healthy immune response." A 30-day supply of the vitamins cost $45. The campaign seemed different than promoting water as a sunburn preventative, or hawking $100 TB12 sleepwear, or even pitching anti-concussion water. During a pandemic, six-time Super Bowl champion Tom Brady was marketing immunity pills, an "unethical and misleading" product, medical experts told *Forbes*, and bordering "on wartime profiteering," the *Boston Globe* wrote.

Brady had already put a curious spin on the moment when he spoke virtually at the Adobe Summit in April, a conference for business leaders and other celebrities. At the end of his nine-minute talk, he said, "I think we're in the midst of a big recalibration right now. Maybe the world is telling us to slow down a little bit, you know?" He paused, then smiled. "Everyone needs to chill out and recalibrate some of their priorities. And I think this world is moving at a very fast pace, so we better find ways to recalibrate or else, you know? It's amazing how the world finds a way when it's needed to just do that."

Laura Wagner of Vice News reached out to the Bucs and asked if Brady was indeed referring to the pandemic—and if he indeed saw the virus as an order from on high to "chill out." The team punted to Brady's new publicist, Stephanie Jones, whose company represented other luminaries, including Dwayne "The Rock" Johnson, Venus Williams, and Justin Bieber. She accused Vice of publishing clickbait and offered no further comment. Brady seemed more disconnected than callous, reflecting the values of a portion of the globe-trotting elite for whom human longevity is human destiny, regardless of the cost. Yet his behavior surprised even his friends, as if pitching an immunity product his fans would "love" was inconsistent with the caring guy they knew. But it was entirely consistent. He could have so much faith in his own approaches and theologies that he saw *any* limitation, even off the field, as something to transcend. And Brady's actions and statements amid a pandemic that threatened older people and those with preexisting health problems first were also perhaps inevitable, and not just because he had a product to shill. His enemy had long ago ceased to be other teams, and had become the undefeated forces of age and time.

A FEW WEEKS LATER, Brady drove his sports car to a white house in South Tampa to visit Byron Leftwich, the Bucs' offensive coordinator. It was around 11 a.m. He parked and entered the house, dropping his bags on the floor in the entryway. He raised his head and saw an unfamiliar face sitting at the kitchen island and looking up from a computer.

"What's up, man?" Brady said.

"Man's" name was David Kramer. He normally locked his front door, but the house was for sale and people were regularly coming in and out, so it was unlocked. He had seen a tall shadow behind the glass in the door. He vaguely recognized the man in his entryway, under a baseball hat, but he was mostly wondering why he was in his house.

"I don't know, dude," the man replied, with a touch of sarcasm. "You tell me."

Brady's eyes changed, from warm to scared. "Am I at the wrong house?" he asked.

"I think you are, but you look familiar. Where are you supposed to be going?"

"I'm supposed to be at Byron's house."

Oh my God, Kramer thought, *it's Tom Brady!* He wanted to say something—hello, even cracking a Michigan joke, since he was an Ohio State fan—but he seized up.

"Byron's is next door," Kramer said.

"I'm so sorry, sir," Brady said. "I'm so sorry."

He grabbed his bags and was gone. Kramer ended up telling the story to TMZ, and it made national news. It was a small, fun anecdote, even a sign of Brady's new freedom, until stories appeared suggesting that Brady and Leftwich might have violated pandemic rules with the visit, forcing the league office to open an inquiry. Kramer started to get hate mail from Bucs fans. He freaked out. What would happen if Brady were to be suspended? Would he have to move, not only to a new place, but to a new city? But the league determined that there was no violation.

It had been quite the first month for Brady in Tampa. A few days earlier, he had been asked by a city employee to stop working out at a downtown park that was closed due to the pandemic. After TMZ broke the Kramer news, Brady tweeted, "Trespassing in parks, breaking and entering . . . Just making myself at home in Tompa Bay!"

HE WAS ALSO PREPARING for a football season that by midsummer was not certain to happen. An estimated $9 billion was on the line if the league had to cancel its season due to the pandemic. The NBA and NHL had restarted games in bubble cities across North America, a strategy the NFL had essentially ruled out. If it played games in empty or nearly empty stadiums, the league was facing a loss of up to $5.5 billion in revenue.

On July 17, the owners and league executives convened on a confidential video call to decide on the season.

"This is a volatile situation," Roger Goodell said.

The meeting featured many of the quirks of prior league conferences, with some owners not paying attention and concern over leaks outweighing concern over policy. Goodell believed the league could start on time, with testing and tracing protocols. He pleaded with owners to not jam governors to try to open stadiums to fans. Games without fans would not be ideal, but it was better than no games at all. "Don't force it," he said.

What about if a governor allowed full stadiums? Jim Irsay of the Colts asked. It seemed on track to happen in Indiana. "We're about to have the Indy 500," he said.

"I don't think that's going to happen," Goodell said, looking exasperated.

Robert Kraft repeatedly asked his fellow owners not to discuss details of the call once it was over. The league still hadn't finalized plans with the union, and owners would lose leverage if their expectations became public. It had been another busy year for Kraft and DeMaurice Smith, negotiating a new collective bargaining agreement. Owners had threatened to lock out the players if they didn't agree to expand the regular season for the first time since 1978, from 16 games to 17. Talks paused in the fall of 2019, and restarted only after a secret meeting between Kraft and Smith at Michael Rubin's Manhattan apartment. A new CBA was ratified over the same weekend in March that the World Health Organization declared a global health emergency.

Robert and Jonathan Kraft had been one of the few ownership groups across sports who not only immediately understood the gravity of the situation, but helped, both by lending resources and by reportedly refusing to cut staff as revenues dropped. In the spring, Massachusetts governor Charlie Baker was speaking with Jonathan, relieved that the state had secured almost two million N95 masks from China, but angry that he, the governor, had no way to ship them to Boston. "Do you think people who have airplanes would be willing to fly over?" Baker asked.

Jonathan volunteered the team plane. The logistics were a nightmare: The FAA needed to waive its regulatory requirements for international travel. The Krafts needed a law firm and embassies to help with the necessary permit and visas to land in China. A 12-person crew was assembled, including four pilots. The plane flew to China, stopping for an electronics upgrade in Ohio and to rest in Anchorage. Once in Shenzhen, the crew had only three hours to load the masks. It filled the plane with as many as possible in two hours and 57 minutes, then flew home. It landed with 1.2 million masks, then returned to China to pick up the remaining 500,000. The Krafts paid $2 million, about half of the cost of the endeavor, the other portion coming from the state.

Now Kraft was at the center of the owners call, pleading with colleagues not to leak. Jerry Jones, videoconferencing from off the coast of Washington State in his superyacht, backed him. Kraft tried to make a joke, reminding Jones that it was easier for his team to keep the call confidential because he was also the Cowboys general manager. Most of us have to tell other people, who will tell the media, Kraft said.

It was met with silence. Nobody got it. Kraft tried to explain that it was a compliment to Jones, that it was a good thing that Jones held both titles. Goodell moved on to the next topic.

Toward the end of the call, everyone seemed exhausted—from the stress of the pandemic, a long year of negotiating with the union, and never-ending videoconferences. But before adjourning, Vikings owner Zygi Wilf wanted to speak.

"So, we're opening?" he asked.

"We plan on opening," Goodell replied.

"Should we do another one of these calls when things are agreed to?" Wilf asked, referring to the union.

"Sure," Goodell said, preemptively tired.

Jones then unmuted himself and argued that the league should declare that the season was starting on time.

"Our body language needs to reflect confidence."

"Well said, Jerry," Goodell replied.

50

I HOPE I PLAY IN IT

THE NFL'S 101ST SEASON ARRIVED ON TIME, AMID the pandemic and staggering unemployment rates and protests over systemic racism and efforts by the highest official in the land to undermine the election. Gillette Stadium was unrecognizable on September 13, when the Patriots took the field in the season opener against the Miami Dolphins, with no fans and Cam Newton at quarterback. Robert and Jonathan Kraft stood on the field under the late-summer sun, faces shielded by masks, watching Newton warm up. He wore jersey number 1. He was a former league MVP with the Carolina Panthers who had signed with the Patriots in June, for only $550,000 guaranteed, with incentives potentially raising his pay to $6.45 million. He had suffered injuries the past few seasons, but when he was healthy, Newton had earned not only Jack Brady's respect as his preferred fantasy football quarterback over his father, but also Belichick's respect—attained the best way possible: by defeating him. Newton was 2–0 against New England, including a win in Foxborough. Many thought that when Newton joined New England, he would be a backup to second-year quarterback Jarrett Stidham, but Newton took over the team as though he'd been running it for years. He won the starting job and was elected as a team captain.

Shortly before kickoff, Robert and Jonathan retired to the owners' box. The season was about to begin, and the experience they'd known for most of their tenure as owners was about to officially end. Newton huddled with a few offensive players. "Rock 'n' roll on three!" he yelled. New England's first new quarterback since 2001 ran onto the field.

LATER THAT DAY, after New England beat Miami, Tom Brady's Tampa Bay Buccaneers played in New Orleans against the Saints and Drew Brees. Each day during training camp, Brady had gone to the "driving range," as Arians put it—20 or so minutes during practice to work on fundamentals. Arians marveled at Brady's mechanics, doubting that Brady's arm was ever sore due to such a clean release. Brady fell in love with Florida fast. He rented Derek Jeter's house on the water. If anything, the hardest thing about Bucs camp was the heat: Brady normally liked to throw with receivers after practice, but it was so hot that everyone was too tired and hit the showers early.

One day before the season, Brady sat with Rob Gronkowski, who had signed with Tampa a month after Tom did, and filmed a team-produced video called *The Friendship Test: Tommy and Gronky*. Brady was bronzed and relaxed, soaking his feet in a kiddy pool. "It's a little toasty out here today," he said.

The host asked them questions about each other, and they laughed and smiled. The last one was "Which is Tom's favorite ring?"

"I know this one," Gronk said. "I know it! Oh wow: Gisele loves this one, too."

Brady glared at him.

"Heh-heh, heh-heh," Gronk said.

Gronk wrote, "The next one!"

Both men were enjoying themselves, the subtext manifest throughout: this was different. Gronkowski hadn't gone through grinding issues with his former coach and team for a year, but he now felt liberated, too, just like his quarterback. Yet, against the Saints, it wasn't clear if greater happiness would translate into results on the field. Brady threw two interceptions, including one returned for a touchdown. Speaking to the press after the game, Arians put both interceptions on Brady. The first, he said, was an "overthrow." The second? "Bad decision." Arians seemed a little too eager to project a Belichickian front, holding no superstar above accountability. But if that was his intent, something was off. In Belichick's two decades of coaching Brady, did he ever blame him from the podium for a mistake? Belichick always spoke in terms of *we*—players needed to play better, coaches needed to coach better, the team needed to do everything better—and to publicly call out a player, when the coach knew well that many plays impact a game, ran counter to Belichick's entire leadership philosophy. Plus, at the postgame press conference, he had yet to analyze the film. He knew that whatever he said would be scrutinized and turned into headlines, and so he said little, protecting both himself and the team.

Sure enough, a day after the game, Arians walked it all back, issuing a self-correction. One of the interceptions wasn't on Brady, he said. The receiver ran the wrong route.

THE NIGHT AFTER the Patriots beat the Dolphins, Jeannette Belichick died of natural causes at age 98. She was buried next to her husband on a quiet hill overlooking the water on the Naval Academy's campus, with the tombstone of a rear admiral behind them and three rear admirals to the left. Bill Belichick received support from around the league, including from Pete Carroll and John Harbaugh. For as much as Bill learned the game from his dad, he had watched a lot of football with his mom. Steve was always away on scouting trips during the fall, Friday nights through Sunday mornings, and so it was just Jeannette and Billy, in their two-story house on Aberdeen Road in the south end of Annapolis, with a big yard and woods at the end of the street, a house Belichick refused to sell, even after his mom moved out, renting it to Navy coaches, wanting to keep it in the family. They listened to games on the radio and watched them on television, hundreds in all, and became close in a way that was harder for Belichick to do with his sons. As an adult, Belichick was the one always working late and away from home. Steve Belichick was now calling plays as the Patriots' outside linebackers coach; Brian was the safeties coach. A third generation not only coaching, not only coaching football, not only coaching defense, but, as Brian often said, "making up for lost time." They spent 12 to 16 hours a day for much of the year alongside their dad, learning the craft, but most of all, continuing something that was both bigger than all of them and small enough to feel like a family affair.

DURING THE EXACT TIME when Belichick lost his mother, Tom Brady nearly lost his father. Unlike their son, Tom and Galynn Brady regularly wore masks, two 76-year-olds who took the pandemic seri-ously. But in early September, both came down with a nagging cough. Tom Sr. took a test at an urgent care clinic and was diagnosed with COVID-19—so was Galynn—and with pneumonia. The next day, he couldn't breathe. He spent the following 18 days in a hospital, unable to lift his head, hold a conversation, or, for the first time ever, care about his son's games. Each day, the hospital told Galynn that her husband's condition was "stable," a word she learned to hate. It was unnerving. On the opposite side of the country, saddled with restrictions, Tom Brady was one of the millions of Americans who had no choice but to Face-Time sick loved ones daily and hope. The grandkids made Tom Sr. post-ers to keep his spirits up: *We love you, Papa.* Tom Sr. later characterized it as "life or death," but both of Brady's parents recovered. Then, when Tom Sr. returned home, he collapsed and tore up his knee, and was headed back to the hospital.

Tom and Galynn spoke to Tommy about his at-times-casual indiffer-ence to the virus. Brady believed in his vitamin regime, maybe believed his body was bulletproof. By now, it was the only way he knew.

WEEKS INTO THE SEASON, the Bucs were not a bad team, but had yet to find their identity. The predictions that Brady and Arians might not be a good fit seemed to be accurate, the quarterback, at his best, relying on a thousand cuts and the coach in love with the deep ball. Michael Lombardi noticed a sequence in a late-season *Monday Night Football* game against the Los Angeles Rams and wondered if Tampa owner-ship was going to have to choose between the two men at season's end. Brady had the ball at midfield with just over two minutes left in the first half, the score tied at 14. Belichick had taught Brady to think globally in two-minute situations: score points, but also run the clock, leaving the opponent little time to answer—complementary football at its fin-est. That wasn't Arians's style. On first down, the Bucs called a deep pass down the left sideline, a low-percentage throw that fell incomplete and stopped the clock. Two plays later, Brady threw incomplete again and the Bucs punted. The Rams marched down the field and hit a field goal. That three-point halftime difference ended up being the difference in the final score. It was the type of moment that galled Belichick—and, by extension, Brady.

Reports surfaced that Brady and Arians were frustrated with each other, but it seemed to be a reflection more of the team not playing to its potential than anything personal. Arians was impossible not to like. He and Brady had plans to play golf during the bye week; the league stopped it, citing coronavirus protocols. Brady told friends that even on his worst day in Tampa, he never regretted leaving New England. The day before games, Brady would sit on the $2 million yacht he had purchased, and after games ended, he'd race home to join his kids in the pool. His friends in Florida were mostly rich older men, such as real estate mogul Jeff Soffer. Brady bought property on Indian Creek Island outside of Miami, otherwise known as Billionaire Bunker, where his neighbors would be Jared Kushner and Ivanka Trump. He publicly swore he would never live in the Northeast again, which some of his old fan base took personally. Everyone was disconnected during the pandemic, but Brady seemed to disconnect himself from what he once was—or, maybe, now became what he might always have been.

Against the Chicago Bears on October 8, the Bucs had an offensive series so disastrous that they ended up in a fourth and 27. On the sideline, Brady ripped into his offensive line for the first time in his young career with his new team, or at least, the first time witnessed by the world. "You fucking guys!" he yelled. "Wake the fuck up!" But with 38 seconds to go, it was Brady who seemed to doze off. He threw incomplete on fourth down, then seemed confused. He had thought it was third down, not fourth down. He held up four fingers, thinking he had one more shot. He didn't. An image of him looking puzzled went viral, and even Brady had to laugh at himself. After LeBron James won his fourth NBA title, Brady posted that picture of himself, holding up four fingers, with James's head on the quarterback's body, and congratulated him.

With a month to go, Tampa had a 7–5 record. Finally, the coaches adjusted. Arians and offensive coordinator Byron Leftwich incorporated more short passes and more of a running game, helping to keep defenses off balance and allowing Brady more time when he did take the occasional shot downfield. And Brady recalibrated his standards. He was long accustomed to holding receivers to his own lofty expectations, but after weeks of not being on the same page, something needed to change. Brady coaxed his wideouts to define their goals, for self and team, and then held them to those expectations instead of his own. Before the Bucs played the Minnesota Vikings, Brady turned to Arians and said, "It'll be our best day."

"Should be," Arians said.

Of all of Brady's qualities, his steadfast optimism continued to be his most unwavering trait. He might struggle to manage his emotions after a loss, but he always rebounded. The Bucs won their final four regular-season games, finishing 11–5. They made the playoffs as a wild card, needing to win on the road—incredibly, a first for Brady, who had won the AFC East a total of 17 times in the 18 full seasons he played in New England. The Bucs beat Washington in the first round, New Orleans and Drew Brees in the divisional round, and held off Green Bay and Aaron Rodgers in the NFC Championship Game to send Tom Brady to his astounding tenth Super Bowl—twice more than Elway, the nearest competitor among starting quarterbacks—and Arians to his first. "The belief he gave to this organization that it could be done—it only took one man," Arians said.

After the Green Bay game ended, the first thing Brady did was run to the sideline, on the edge of the stands, and point.

"Can I say hi to my son?" he asked a security guard.

Jack ran down the Lambeau Field stairs, bundled in winter gear. Later in 2021, he would be 14, the same age his dad was when he first decided to give football a shot. He had been with his dad at many points along the strange journey of the past year, since he snapped the shot of Tom signing the contract. Brady opened his arms.

"Love you, kiddo," he said. "How about that? We're going to the Super Bowl."

Heading back to their new home—where, coincidentally, the Super Bowl would be played—Brady and Gronk walked on the tarmac to the team plane, reprising their video from 2019, after New England beat the Chiefs. Brady stared at the camera and shrugged while Gronk strutted behind him, showing off his NFC championship T-shirt. Gronk had been a role player for most of the season, and the fourth quarter against Green Bay had been one of the worst of Brady's career, with two interceptions—three in all that day—but the two of them had connected on a screen pass that went for 29 yards in the fourth quarter, setting up the decisive field goal. When Brady checked his phone, he saw that he had a congratulatory text from his former owner.

ROBERT KRAFT WANTED to be in the Pro Football Hall of Fame. That was no secret. What makes a transcendent owner is up for debate—especially among Hall of Fame voters—but if Jerry Jones and Pat Bowlen of the Denver Broncos and Eddie DeBartolo Jr. of the San Francisco 49ers had been deemed worthy over the prior few years, Kraft had a strong case. In quiet moments, Kraft sometimes asked the voters he knew well, What's the appeal of Jones? It seemed to be a way of asking, What has Jones done that I haven't? Kraft had engineered one of the greatest trades in NFL history, bringing Belichick to New England. He had stewarded unparalleled on-field continuity and excellence. He had served as the lead architect of CBA and broadcast deals, helping the league earn billions and reach unrivaled popularity. Jones was the face of the deals that saw the Rams relocate to Los Angeles and the Raiders to Las Vegas, but Kraft was a power broker behind the scenes. In the fall of 2020, a book about the Patriots' run called *The Dynasty* was published, written by the talented Jeff Benedict. Kraft had been generous in granting access to himself. Like many of Benedict's books, this was a bestseller. A former Patriots executive believed that its audience was not just the masses and the Patriots season-ticket holders who received a complimentary copy from the team, but the Hall of Fame's 48-person selection committee. Kraft had come up short the past two years. Some voters said privately that Orchids of Asia was still the problem. Others felt that owners are so seldom elected—only 14 are in Canton—that they didn't want to enshrine another so soon after DeBartolo in 2016, Jones in 2017, and Bowlen in 2019. In March of 2021, the NFL announced new broadcast deals worth about $110 billion over ten years. Goodell went out of his way to credit Kraft's hard work. At the videoconference on March 30 where Kraft spoke to fellow owners and credited others for help on the deal, his internet connection was spotty and kept cutting in and out. But the quiet concerns in ownership circles over Kraft's judgment turned out to be greatly misplaced. He had done his job, and done it well. Kraft entered the 2021 regular season at 80 years old, one of the most powerful people in American sports, with more rings than he could wear on one hand, and still, a dream on hold.

BILL BELICHICK HAD PROMISED everyone he wouldn't do this. He wasn't going to be Marv Levy, on the sidelines and wearing a headset in his 70s. But here he was, soon to turn 69 in April 2021, and not ready to leave, not like this, not after a 7–9 season. Cam Newton had been injured and slowed as well by COVID-19. He missed throws that he once hit in his sleep. Julian Edelman started only one game and would retire after the season as one of Belichick's favorite players and worthy of Hall of Fame consideration. What was more surprising than the Patriots' losing record, more surprising than some of the ugly football on display— after the Rams whipped New England 24–3, Belichick told Los Angeles head coach Sean McVay, "You killed us"—was that the man who never accepted excuses from others started to make them for the team and for himself. In the middle of the season, after New England had lost four consecutive games for the first time since 2002 and it became obvious that the team that had seemed immune to the laws of the NFL was finally relenting to them, Belichick was asked during a radio interview about the team's performance and salary cap situation.

"We sold out and won three Super Bowls, played in a fourth and in an AFC Championship Game."

Sold out. Belichick insisted that he wasn't blaming outside factors. It was, he argued, "just a fact" that the team lacked depth because of its salary cap situation and because key players, including Dont'a Hightower, had opted out due to the virus. Months before the season, in truth, Belichick had telegraphed that it would be different, saying that "over the last two decades, everything we did, every decision we made in terms of planning" was "to make things best for Tom Brady." But it was still startling to hear. Belichick was apparently being frank with the fans after two decades of working to conceal his true thoughts. Still, Belichick's comments could be read as a means of deflecting criticism. It wasn't just that Brady was gone and the team was old. It was old in part because of years of underperforming draft classes, overseen by Belichick, with the supposed next generation of Patriots greats and role players never arriving. Belichick seemed to know that he needed a year to recalibrate and reset, leaving no doubt that he was in it until the team had turned around.

More than ever, Belichick was going to have to rely on himself. For almost 20 years, he had deployed a system designed to adapt to change and the loss of key personnel, from players to his bloodline of young coaches and scouts. But his staff had been raided for years, leaving some of Belichick's friends to wonder if he was now stretched too thin, doing more than ever even as he approached the Marv Levy line. On January 7, 2021, Nick Caserio finally left for Houston, joining Jack Easterby, who was learning that life as a team executive was harder than being a behind-the-scenes therapist to the locker room. He had become a controversial figure in Houston after Bill O'Brien was fired a month into the 2020 season. A pair of *Sports Illustrated* investigations in a two-month span concluded that a man charged with improving team culture had helped destroy it. Belichick publicly defended Easterby, and so did owner Cal McNair, who repeatedly insisted that the blame directed at Easterby was unwarranted, but the damage was so extensive that Easterby and his family checked into a hotel due to death threats. It set off another round of stories about how Belichick charges struggled away from Foxborough.

That criticism wasn't quite fair anymore. Brian Flores had coached well in Miami, turning around a moribund and talentless team. Former special-teams coach Joe Judge showed promise with the Giants. The Titans, led by former Patriots scout Jon Robinson and Mike Vrabel, reached the playoffs again. As for the one who should have got away: for three straight years, Josh McDaniels had lost out on head-coaching jobs, all to candidates with a fraction of the experience and success and organizational insight. Nobody doubted that McDaniels was a brilliant assistant coach for Bill Belichick, but what that meant outside of Foxborough remained unclear. It seemed that the market had reached a conclusion: there was no Patriot Way. There was only Bill Belichick and Tom Brady. Nothing about them was replicable; now that the Patriots were returning from orbit, what stood out as much as their brilliance was their singularity.

And, of course, Tom Brady was the most singular of them all. The day after Brady and the Bucs beat Green Bay to send themselves to the Super Bowl, the *Boston Globe*'s Dan Shaughnessy published a column titled "Final Score: Tom Brady 1, Patriots 0." "All precincts have reported and it's official: Brady has beaten Bill Belichick and Bob Kraft in a landslide," he wrote. "Ten months after leaving New England because the Patriots were done with him, Brady showed the world he's still got the goods. The Patriots, who had no real plan to replace their quarterback, finished 7–9 and out of the playoffs. Meanwhile, Brady is going to his 10th Super Bowl; with the clown car Tampa Bay Buccaneers, no less."

Belichick would enter the 2021 season in the same place he had been in 20 years earlier: charged with cleaning up the roster and in need of luck at the most vital position. He was always disciplined and expert at bringing in key players at discounted rates, using Brady's salary as leverage in negotiations. But what did that mean without Brady? Before the Super Bowl, Tom Brady Sr. tweaked Belichick to the *Boston Herald* by saying, "I'm guessing he's a little bit on the hot seat." Robert Kraft was blunt about his coach's performance when he later said that "I don't feel we've done the greatest job the last few years" in the draft. Of all of New England's disappointments of 2020, one of the most glaring was that Jarrett Stidham, a quarterback entering his second year whom Belichick had drafted in the fourth round out of Auburn in 2019, wasn't deemed good enough or trustworthy enough to start a single game, even when Newton was out with COVID. Belichick had won the lottery with Brady and had developed a Super Bowl–caliber replacement in Jimmy Garoppolo, and now he was left with the stark reminder that, after all of the decades he had spent thinking about football, after all of the ways his greatness enriched and subtracted from his life, his profession is and always will be a quarterback's game. Belichick was in the beginning stages of searching for the latest of Tom Brady's potential successors, with film playing on his monitor and the clicker in his hand and no shortcuts, the rhythms and motions of his entire adult life, well into his years as a senior citizen, searching for something nobody knew how to find.

On April 29, the night of the NFL Draft, Belichick sat in the Patriots war room with Robert and Jonathan and a few personnel executives. All of them wore masks, one of the few teams to do so. Their pick—fifteenth in the first round—arrived. The Patriots had been more aggressive in free agency than ever before in Belichick's tenure, spending about $162.5 million in guaranteed money for 19 players. And they had re-signed Cam Newton and penciled him in as the starter. Still, the long-term hole at the game's most important position hovered over them. In the days leading up to the draft, rumors swirled around the league that the Patriots would trade for Garoppolo, sending Belichick's original planned replacement for Brady—his prized replacement, his "seamless" replacement—back to him. San Francisco seemed to have backed itself into an impossible corner, moving up to draft a quarterback while trying to hold onto an expensive temporary starter who had a no-trade clause in his contract, giving him power over his future. There was an informal call between a high-level representative of the Patriots and a high-level 49ers official. What was Garoppolo's price? New England wondered if a second-rounder would suffice—calling it even from 2017. But the 49ers wouldn't take less than a first. For the moment, at least, San Francisco was counting on Garoppolo to be the quarterback for 2021. The Patriots reached the same conclusion as San Francisco—they liked the potential of the available first-round quarterbacks more than Garoppolo—and moved on.

Now Mac Jones, a star quarterback out of the University of Alabama, was still on the board. Although Belichick had insisted that he never drafted by position or group, never drafted to fill predetermined team deficiencies—he tried to collect good football players and then figured out how best to deploy them—this time, a glaring need met opportunity. Belichick rose from a chair, with his mask nestled below his nose, and fondled his tie as he collected his brain trust.

"We're all good with this?" Belichick said. Yes, they replied.

"Bill, you want me to get him?" Berj Najarian asked.

"Yep, I'm good with it."

Najarian called Jones, like he had called Tom Brady more than two decades before. It was the first time in Belichick's entire career as a head coach that he picked a quarterback in the first round. Jones was accurate and tough and carried a discernible and requisite cockiness. In 2019, he posted on social media a shirtless photo of his skinny and unimposing self alongside Tom Brady's iconic photo from 2000—Brady would joke that the draft was the annual Post Tom's Shirtless Combine Photo on Twitter Day—and after the Crimson Tide won the national championship in 2021, Jones posed shirtless and with a cigar. Belichick had relied heavily not only on Jones' 2020 performance—the quarterback completed 77.4 percent of his passes, with 41 touchdowns and only four interceptions—but on the word of Nick Saban, a "great resource," Belichick later said, who knows more about football than anyone on "any level."

Najarian dialed Jones, and then soon Belichick was speaking with him. "Hey, Mac, it's Bill Belichick. Congratulations. . . . Look forward to working with you. A lot of Tides up here. You'll fit right in." It had been a longer night than expected for Jones. Some teams believed he might be drafted as high as third overall. But when Jones greeted Roger Goodell for the ceremonial hug on stage, he whispered in the commissioner's ear that this team—New England—"This is what I wanted."

Jones represented more than a landmark pick for Belichick. He was another chance—the latest new chance—for the coach to hold together something inherently fleeting and fragile: success in the NFL, and his own unmatched coaching career. Both Belichick and Brady are creatures of habit and of discipline, and possess a relentless focus, but most of all, they are creatures of hope, architects of finding and exploiting the next opportunity. It's all Bill Belichick has ever asked for—and for four decades running, all he's ever needed.

Brady was doing it again, too: he was moving the goalposts. He was asked during Super Bowl week if, assuming he continued to perform at a high level, he would play past 45. "Oh, definitely," Brady said. While one can only imagine Gisele Bündchen's reaction, it was a predictable answer. Brady lived by and through his quarterbacking. He was sometimes more than a quarterback, but he was never less. When people suggested to him that he was like Michael Jordan, driven by a raging compulsion to be the best, Brady tepidly agreed, but shifted toward something more basic, simple enough to be overlooked or dis-regarded: love. Belichick had once commissioned an internal study to examine the traits of great athletes. He wanted to know why they turned into legends, and if there was an element from past examples that the Patriots could use as a predictor. Michael Jordan, Kobe Bryant, Tiger Woods, and others—including Brady—were interviewed, asked about their upbringings, belief systems, the validation they felt after a win, and the lonely devastation after a loss. The study found that most immortal athletes circled around a common theme, rage and anger and the need to dominate serving as primary motivators. Jordan measured his self-worth in winning, a byproduct of a genuine belief that his father had loved his brother more than him. Bryant possessed a deep and dark desire to humiliate his opponent. Woods was ruthless, cutting off every iteration of his entire inner circle until none remained, and so impossi-bly difficult to know that he lacked true friends.

Brady, though, was different. He had a phenomenal focus that made others want to please him and not let him down. He was pitiless on the field, but to be effective, he didn't need to manufacture conflict. Not always, at least. He believed he was at the peak of his powers not when he was measuring the size of the chip on his shoulder, but when he was in a loving and supportive environment.

A study commissioned by Belichick to reveal traits of superior com-petitors ended up revealing his own blind spot. He had based an entire, brilliant system on adaptability. But the sports world, at least, had changed, with athletes—especially NBA players and quarterbacks—wanting to be more than faceless cogs in a machine, wanting more power and say. Tom Brady had been curious if there was another way of winning, and while nobody was arguing that Bruce Arians was a bet-ter coach than Bill Belichick, or even close, the seamlessness of Brady's proficiency and performance was making his former coach's methodol-ogies look antiquated, even silly.

It was *better* to be feared—but was it necessary?

No wonder Brady loved Tampa and Arians. If he missed practice in New England, it was as if he had broken a moral code. "No days off" was one of Belichick's many rallying cries. In Tampa, Arians didn't care if

Brady took a day off. He needed him on Sunday, not Wednesday. Arians could do more than admit that Brady was the missing piece for his team, which he did publicly many times in the lead-up to the Super Bowl. He could allow both himself and Brady to feel joy and optimism.

Brady was at home alone in the 12 days before the Super Bowl, isolating himself from the world, except for a visit from Tom House, taking every precaution regarding the virus, giving him more time to study. Each night at 11 p.m. before the Super Bowl, Brady texted each of his team-mates on the Bucs with a simple message: *We WILL win.* On Super Bowl Sunday, against Patrick Mahomes and the defending-champion Kansas City Chiefs, Brady did what he's always done: he ground his opponent down, one unremarkable throw at a time. He threw three touchdown passes, all in the first half, bringing his combined 2020 regular-season and playoff total to 50. Up 21–6 at halftime, he walked the locker room, saying, "We got a half to go. Don't let up." But the game was never really in doubt. Tampa's defensive line annihilated Kansas City's depleted offensive line, turning Mahomes into a scrambler who scrambled almost exclusively around his own backfield. With Peyton Manning looking on from a suite—he had just been elected to the Hall of Fame, while Tom Brady had assembled a Hall of Fame career in the five years *since* Manning had retired—Tampa won, 31–9, the largest margin of Brady's seven Super Bowl wins. *Seven*, a sum that exceeded any NFL franchise.

"You're a legend, man," Mahomes said to Brady after the game.

Brady's family found him as the stage was assembled. Jack hugged him first, then Vivian, then Benny, then Bündchen, a moment that felt both new and familiar, as it always did, newness its own kind of familiarity. "What more do you have to prove?" she asked him. Brady tried to change the subject, hoping to avoid answering. "You guys happy?" Brady asked. "I'm happy." In the locker room a few moments later, Jason Licht hugged Brady, overcome with an emotion that he had experienced before but was different now, running the team rather than serving in the scouting department. "This is unbelievable," Licht said, smiling.

"Hey, you did good, J," Brady replied. "You did good."

The end of the game seemed like the end of an argument. But, as always, Brady saw it not as the end of anything, but as the continuation of something. He didn't even seem tired after the Super Bowl, nor did he the morning after, running on two hours of sleep, which he took in his daughter's bed after he handed over his bedroom to visiting family. He was less in awe of what he had just done than excited about it as a launching point for whatever was next—what was still out there to accomplish, what notions and preconceptions he could redefine, having already redefined them many times.

ALMOST 20 YEARS EARLIER, on an early-November evening, Tom Brady had stood outside a small stadium as a larger one was under construction next door. It was cold and dark. We had first met less than an hour earlier. He was 24 years old, a lanky sixth-round pick with his backpack full of beer, and nobody knew if he would finish the season as New England's starter. We made small talk, surrounded by unknowns. Who the New England Patriots were as a team after their franchise player had nearly lost his life, who Tom Brady was or would become, this young man with the ball in his hands, trying to hold on to his moment and author his story. He glanced at the unfinished building and said, "I hope I play in it."

He was on the cusp in so many ways, straddling his own present and future as well as the team's and the region's—and yet, in that barren lot, as distant light etched his face, he had a glimmer of something palpable and rare: certainty. What exactly that meant, nobody knew, not even him. And that was the point, and was the point all along. Football was so deeply personal to him, going so far beyond throwing touchdown passes and winning games. What could he become? What could he prove—to us, sure, but mostly to himself? Behind him was the skeleton of what would be Gillette Stadium. Tom Brady looked at its frozen navy steel and saw something out there for the taking.

ACKNOWLEDGMENTS

F INISHING A PROJECT LIKE THIS—IN A GLOBAL PAN-
demic, amid travel restrictions and virtual schools and the dull
fear all of us felt—required the help, kindness, and patience of
more people than I could ever thank. But I'll try.

Thank you:

To my parents, Kirk and Beth, who supported me from the moment
that I decided—no, that I *needed*—to become a journalist.

To my immediate and extended family members: Cody, Lauren,
Brielle, and Aria Rice; Mary Sullivan Wickersham; Jim Dunn; Marcia
Goldstein; Bill Overholt; the Haaheim family; and Christine, Chantal,
Matthew, and David Dunn.

To dear friends and neighbors who helped navigate life, work, the
aftermath of a hurricane that knocked out power for a week, and who
cared for my children as if they were their own: Matt Moscardi, Courtney Rowe, Sen, Nina, and Dylan; Brian and Kat Pencz; Kerri-Lynn
O'Neill; Ari Barrenechea; Courtney Nicastro; Michelle DePalma; Patty
DeMorro; Tania Taft; and Cory and Gail Shane.

To my ski crew: Phil Levis and Mary Bruce; Kevin Stange and Megan
Tompkins-Stange; Justin and Maggie Harth; Travis Harth; and Colin
Harbke.

To David Black, for your bulletproof friendship and steadfast belief
in me.

To Dan Gerstle, who supported, reassured, answered calls at all
hours, and who, in carefully considering each line and each chapter, not

only made this book the best it could be, but helped find a book's most essential quality: its voice.

To all at Liveright and W. W. Norton who contributed to this project, including Peter Miller, Cordelia Calvert, Nick Curley, Zeba Arora, Rebecca Munro, Lloyd Davis, Rebecca Homiski, Anna Oler, Steve Attardo, and Steven Pace. Also, to Chip Namias, for the publicity wizardry.

To Tricia Huerta, for the transcriptions.

To all of the players, coaches, general managers, executives, owners, lawyers, agents, and others around the NFL who have helped me with this project and others over the years.

To my current and former colleagues at ESPN, where I've been a writer almost longer than I haven't: Eric Adelson, Ben Arledge, Stephania Bell, Gary Belsky, Scott Burton, Heather Burns, Taffy Brodesser-Akner, John Clayton, David Cummings, Luke Cyphers, Cristina Daglas, John Dahl, Jeff Darlington, Scott Eden, Bruce Feldman, Neil Fine, Mike Fish, David Fleming, Charlotte Gibson, Ian Gordon, Dan Hajducky, John Hassan, Jemele Hill, Ryan Hockensmith, Gary Hoenig, Becky Hudson, Baxter Holmes, Kevin Jackson, Jena Janovy, Mike Johns, Tim Keown, Raina Kelley, Mina Kimes, Paul Kix, David Kraft, John Kosner, Chris and Leah LaPlaca, Dan Le Batard, Joon Lee, Bob Ley, Jackie MacMullan, Seth Markman, John Mastroberardino, Elizabeth Merrill, Gueorgui Milkov, Chris Mortensen, Jay Jay Nesheim, Mike Ogle, John Papanek, Mike Philbrick, John Pluym, Stacey Pressman, Nate Ravitz and family, Jason Reid, Lauren Reynolds, Ryen Russillo, Dianna Russini, Emily Schaible and family, Jason Schwartz, Ramona Shelburne, Bill Simmons, John Skipper, Michael Smith, Sarah Spain, Chris Sprow, Ryan Spoon, Pablo Torre, Rachel Ullrich, Scott Van Pelt, John A. Walsh, Chin Wang, and Steve Young. To anyone I missed, I apologize.

To journalists whose friendship I treasure and whose work I admire: Kent Babb, Greg Bedard, Greg Bishop, Albert Breer, Jason Cole, Peter King, Rick Maese, Charles Robinson, Michael Rosenberg, and Michael Silver.

To Tim Rasmussen, for the photo shoot.

To Anthony Olivieri, who helped research and fact-check the book while navigating a full-time job, raising a young family along with his wife, Sylvia, and mourning the loss of his grandfather, Papa Mario, due to this horrible virus.

To Jimmy Pitaro, who gave me his "full support" to pursue this book—and meant it.

To Kevin Merida, who saw this project's potential from the start and encouraged me to chase it.

To Rob King, who counseled and lead-blocked.

To Connor Schell, who always checked in to see how the book was coming, both as a colleague and as a friend.

To Ian O'Connor, who provided confidence throughout.

To Don Van Natta, an inspiration, great journalist and friend, and reportorial force who helped with this project.

To Kevin Van Valkenburg, who always answers the phone and listens.

To Tom Junod, the greatest of all time—as a writer, pal, mentor, and Shelter Island host.

To Chad Millman, Chris Buckle, Eric Neel, and Mike Drago, whose advice, friendship, wisdom, brilliance, and methodologies for delivering story feedback—Chad with casual indifference, Chris with trademark bluntness, Eric with unrelenting love, Mike with various combinations of all three—have redefined what it means to be an editor.

To Rick Telander and the late Ken Denlinger, for long believing that I had a book in me.

To my Mizzou crew: Justin Heckert, Tony Rehagen, and Steve Walentik, all of whom provided a perfect mix of laughs and banter—about Missouri sports, the St. Louis Blues, politics and life—when I needed it most.

To Wright Thompson, the best friend anyone could ask for, since college. I couldn't have done this without you—and by *this*, I mean not only this book, but also my career. There are not enough ways to thank you, but a down payment will begin at P. J. Clarke's.

And finally, to my family. Maddie smiled, hugged, occasionally brought breakfast to my office, and, as the most talented writer in the family—most talented everything, really—showed me how it's done, finishing two sci-fi books in the past year. Grant giggled, sprinted, opened the office door to check on me, out of curiosity and maybe out of concern, and grew to reach the switch and turn off the light without standing on his tiptoes, as a way to tell me that it was time to close the laptop. Alison loved, listened, advised, forgave, understood, and endlessly encouraged. I'm forever grateful, and I love you all.

NOTES ON SOURCES

THE VAST MAJORITY OF THE MATERIAL IN THESE PAGES IS DERIVED
from hundreds of interviews lasting hundreds of hours during my two-decade
career as a writer at ESPN or in the past year for this book. Tom Brady, Bill
Belichick, and Robert Kraft declined to be interviewed specifically for this project. Most of the interviews were on the record. Some, especially when it came
to sensitive information, were on background, meaning that I agreed not to
identify the subjects by name, but would use a general title—coach or player
or executive or friend or associate—or on deep background, meaning that I
agreed to not identify them at all. Where dialogue appears within quotation
marks, it comes from the speaker, a firsthand witness, or notes or recordings
from that moment. Where dialogue is paraphrased, it reflects only a lack of
certainty about precise wording. Where specific thoughts or feelings are noted,
they come from the person identified—either directly to me or from the bevy
of press conferences, books, newspaper and magazine articles, and films the
person has participated in over the years—or someone to whom she or he has
expressed those thoughts or feelings directly.

I also relied on hundreds of books, newspaper articles, magazine pieces,
films, and online stories from the past 20 years. I'm indebted to those who have
covered this team and era so well on various ESPN platforms, especially but
not limited to ESPN.com, *ESPN The Magazine*, ESPNBoston.com, ESPN Radio,
espnW, *The Undefeated, Grantland, SportsCenter, E60, Outside the Lines,* The
ESPN Daily podcast, 30 for 30, *NFL Live,* and *NFL Sunday Countdown.*

The work of NFL Films, and director Ken Rodgers, was invaluable.

Thank you to the staffs of the *Boston Globe, Boston Herald, Providence Jour-
nal, Boston Sports Journal, Wall Street Journal,* the *Athletic,* and the *Ringer;*
WEEI and 98.5 the Sports Hub; Pro Football Talk, NBC Sports, especially Peter
King and Mike Florio; and *Sports Illustrated,* especially Michael Silver, Greg
Bishop, Jenny Vrentas, and Tim Layden.

Below are additional chapter-by-chapter notes.

Prologue

The information in this chapter comes primarily from events that I witnessed and interviews with Walt Anderson and with firsthand sources. Also:

Tom Brady's Instagram account.

Gisele Bündchen's Instagram account.

Seth Wickersham, "The Story Behind the Split of Tom Brady, Bill Belichick and the Patriots," ESPN.com, March 22, 2020.

Tom E. Curran, "The Surreal Dawn of a New Era in Foxboro," NBC Sports Boston, August 18, 2020.

1. One of a Kind

The information in this chapter comes primarily from interviews with Tom Brady, Tom Brady Sr. and Galynn Brady, Mike Riley, Mike Johnson, Charlie Weis, Tom MacKenzie, John Kirby, and other sources. Also:

Year of the Quarterback, "The Brady 6: Journey of the Legend No One Wanted," NFL Films, aired April 12, 2011, ESPN.

Charles P. Pierce, *Moving the Chains: Tom Brady and the Pursuit of Everything* (New York: Farrar, Straus and Giroux, 2007).

Tom Brady, *The TB12 Method: How to Achieve a Lifetime of Sustained Peak Performance* (New York: Simon & Schuster, 2017).

Jason Cole, *Elway: A Relentless Life* (New York: Hachette, 2020).

Seth Wickersham, "The Brady Hunch," *ESPN The Magazine*, December 24, 2001.

Dirk Chatelain, "Tom Brady Was Always the Big One That Got Away from Mike Riley," *Omaha World-Herald*, March 9, 2015.

Dax Shepard, host, "Tom Brady," *Armchair Expert* (podcast), September 10, 2020, https://armchairexpertpod.com/pods/tom-brady.

Tom Brady, Commencement Address, Forman School, May 30, 2020.

2. You Want to Leave? Go 'Head!

The information in this chapter comes primarily from interviews with Tom Brady, Tom Brady Sr. and Galynn Brady, Mike Riley, Mike Johnson, Mike DeBord, Stan Parrish, Greg Harden, and other sources. Also:

Year of the Quarterback, "The Brady 6: Journey of the Legend No One Wanted," NFL Films, aired April 12, 2011, ESPN.

Charles P. Pierce, *Moving the Chains: Tom Brady and the Pursuit of Everything* (New York: Farrar, Straus and Giroux, 2007).

Tom Brady, *The TB12 Method: How to Achieve a Lifetime of Sustained Peak Performance* (New York: Simon & Schuster, 2017).

Seth Wickersham, "The Brady Hunch," *ESPN The Magazine*, December 24, 2001.

Tom Brady, "The Only Way Is Through," *Players' Tribune*, April 6, 2020.

Eric Adelson, "Tom Brady's Guru," *The PostGame*, January 11, 2011, http://www.thepostgame.com/features/201101/tom-bradys-guru.

Dirk Chatelain, "Tom Brady Was Always the Big One That Got Away From Mike Riley," *Omaha World-Herald*, March 9, 2015.

Leigh Montville, "Golden Boy," *Sports Illustrated*, August 3, 1998.

Michael Rosenberg, "Tom Brady as You Forgot Him," *Sports Illustrated*, January 9, 2012.

Mark Leibovich, "Tom Brady Cannot Stop," *New York Times Magazine*, February 1, 2015.

Dax Shepard, host, "Tom Brady," *Armchair Expert* (podcast), September 10, 2020, https://armchairexpertpod.com/pods/tom-brady.

Tom Brady, keynote speech at Serra High, February 27, 2012.

Tom Brady, speech to the University of Michigan football program, August 22, 2013.

60 Minutes, Tom Brady interview with Steve Kroft, aired November 4, 2005, CBS.

3. DREW'S OUT, YOU'RE IN

The information in this chapter comes primarily from interviews with Tom Brady, Tom Brady Sr. and Galynn Brady, David Nugent, Brad Seely, Eric Mangini, Charlie Weis, Damon Huard, and other sources.

Tom Brady, "The Only Way Is Through," *Players' Tribune*, April 6, 2020.

America's Game: The Super Bowl Champions, "The Story of the 2001 New England Patriots," NFL Films, aired February 8, 2007, NFL Network.

Peter King, "What Price Mediocrity," *Sports Illustrated*, October 2, 2000.

Alan Greenberg, "Bledsoe's Record Deal: 10 years, $103 Million," *Hartford Courant*, March 8, 2001.

E:60, "Drew Bledsoe: Better with Age," produced by Max Brodsky, aired January 26, 2020, ESPN.

Ian O'Connor, *Belichick: The Making of the Greatest Football Coach of All Time* (Boston: Houghton Mifflin Harcourt, 2018).

Dirk Chatelain, "Tom Brady Was Always the Big One That Got Away from Mike Riley," *Omaha World-Herald*, March 9, 2015.

Sally Jenkins, "Tom Brady and Bill Belichick's Secret? It's Not Personal; It's Just Business," *Washington Post*, January 27, 2017.

Seth Wickersham, "Brothers in Arms," *ESPN The Magazine*, November 26, 2001.

David Halberstam, *The Education of a Coach* (New York: Hyperion, 2005).

60 Minutes, Tom Brady interview with Steve Kroft, aired November 4, 2005, CBS.

Seth Wickersham, "The Brady Hunch," *ESPN The Magazine*, December 24, 2001.

4. I WON'T SCREW UP AGAIN

The information in this chapter comes primarily from a visit to the Belichick Collection at the United States Naval Academy and interviews with Tom Brady, Brad Seely, Eric Mangini, Charlie Weis, Dante Scarnecchia, Romeo Crennel, Mike Martz, and other sources. Also:

Michael Holley, *Patriot Reign: Bill Belichick, the Coaches, and the Players Who Built a Champion* (New York: William Morrow, 2004).

Ian O'Connor: *Belichick: The Making of the Greatest Football Coach of All Time* (Boston: Houghton Mifflin Harcourt, 2018).

Ron Jaworski with Greg Cosell and David Plaut, *The Games that Changed the Game: The Evolution of the NFL in Seven Sundays* (New York: ESPN Books, 2010).

Michael Lombardi, *Gridiron Genius: A Master Class in Winning Championships and Building Dynasties in the NFL* (New York: Crown Archetype, 2018).

30 for 30, "The Four Falls of Buffalo," produced by Michelle Girardi Zumwalt, aired December 12, 2015, ESPN.

30 for 30, "The Two Bills," directed by Ken Rodgers, produced by NFL Films, aired February 1, 2018, ESPN.

Sarah Spain, host, "Development: Scott Pioli," *That's What She Said with Sarah Spain* (podcast), January 14, 2020, https://www.espn.com/radio/play/_/id/28481449.

America's Game: The Super Bowl Champions, "The Story of the 2001 New England Patriots," NFL Films, aired February 8, 2007, NFL Network.

Tim Keown, "Special Ops," *ESPN The Magazine*, December 10, 2001.

5. HANG TIGHT

The information in this chapter comes primarily from interviews with Robert Edwards, Paul Tagliabue, and other firsthand sources. Also:

Michael Holley, *Patriot Reign: Bill Belichick, the Coaches, and the Players Who Built a Champion* (New York: William Morrow, 2004).

Ian O'Connor, *Belichick: The Making of the Greatest Football Coach of All Time* (Boston: Houghton Mifflin Harcourt, 2018).

Jeff Benedict, *The Dynasty* (New York: Avid Reader Press, 2020).

Bill Parcells and Nunyo Demasio, *Parcells: A Football Life* (New York: Crown Archetype, 2014).

30 for 30, "The Two Bills," directed by Ken Rodgers, produced by NFL Films, aired February 1, 2018, ESPN.

Bill Belichick, press conference, January 4, 2000.

David Halberstam, *The Education of a Coach* (New York: Hyperion, 2005).

America's Game: The Super Bowl Champions, "The Story of the 2001 New England Patriots," NFL Films, aired February 8, 2007, NFL Network.

6. How Do You Like That?

The information in this chapter comes primarily from events I witnessed firsthand and from interviews with Tom Brady, Charlie Weis, Brad Seely, Mike Pereira, David Nugent, and other firsthand sources. Also:

America's Game: The Super Bowl Champions, "The Story of the 2001 New England Patriots," NFL Films, aired February 8, 2007, NFL Network.

Amy Trask with Michael Freeman, *You Negotiate Like a Girl: Reflections on a Career in the National Football League* (Chicago: Triumph, 2016).

Seth Wickersham, "Brady's Big Grin," ESPN.com, January 21, 2002.

7. Turkey Zero

The information in this chapter comes primarily from interviews with Charlie Weis, Romeo Crennel, Eric Mangini, Brad Seely, Damon Huard, Mike Martz, David Nugent, Tom Brady Sr., and other firsthand sources. Also:

America's Game: The Super Bowl Champions, "The Story of the 2001 New England Patriots," NFL Films, aired February 8, 2007, NFL Network.

E:60, "Drew Bledsoe: Better with Age," produced by Max Brodsky, aired January 26, 2020, ESPN.

Michael Silver, "Patriots Missiles," *Sports Illustrated*, February 4, 2002.

Michael Holley, *Patriot Reign: Bill Belichick, the Coaches, and the Players Who Built a Champion* (New York: William Morrow, 2004).

Ian O'Connor, *Belichick: The Making of the Greatest Football Coach of All Time* (Boston: Houghton Mifflin Harcourt, 2018).

David Halberstam, *The Education of a Coach* (New York: Hyperion, 2005).

Ron Jaworski with Greg Cosell and David Plaut, *The Games that Changed the Game: The Evolution of the NFL in Seven Sundays* (New York: ESPN Books, 2010).

Michael Silver, "Pat Answer," *Sports Illustrated*, February 11, 2002.

Steve Wyche and Jim Trotter, hosts, "Michael Holley and Michael Smith: Brotherhood, Ball, and Belichick," *Huddle and Flow* (podcast), December 17, 2020.

Arlen Specter Senatorial Papers, University of Pittsburgh.

"Up Front," *People Weekly*, February 18, 2002.

8. NO BRIDGES HIGH ENOUGH TO JUMP OFF

The information in this chapter comes primarily from events I witnessed first-hand and from interviews with Tom Brady, Tom Brady Sr., Charlie Weis, Brad Seely, Mike Shanahan, and other firsthand sources. Also:

Michael Holley, *Patriot Reign: Bill Belichick, the Coaches, and the Players Who Built a Champion* (New York: William Morrow, 2004).

Bill Belichick, "O.K., Champ, Now Comes the Hard Part," *New York Times*, January 26, 2003.

Wright Thompson, "The Mastermind," *ESPN The Magazine*, September 20, 2016.

America's Game: The Super Bowl Champions, "The Story of the 2003 Patriots," produced by NFL Films, aired April 30, 2007, NFL Network.

Cam Wolf, "Tom Brady's Watches Have a Lot to Say," GQ.com, July 9, 2020, https://www.gq.com/story/tom-brady-iwc-watch-collection-interview.

Michael Silver, "Snow Doubt About It," *Sports Illustrated*, December 15, 2003.

Jeff Howe, "Fifteen Years Later, the Shock of the Patriots' Intentional Safety Still Echoes," *Athletic*, November 1, 2018.

Seth Wickersham, "Brady Talks About Being Clutch," ESPN.com, January 19, 2007.

NFL 100 All-Time Team, produced by NFL Network, aired 2019–20.

9. CAN YOU IMAGINE?

The information in this chapter comes primarily from events I witnessed first-hand and from interviews with Tom Brady, Tom Brady Sr., John Huet, Bill Belichick, Charlie Weis, Damon Huard, Charles Woodson, David Nugent, Rosevelt Colvin, Greg Harden, and other firsthand sources. Also:

"Pat Hand," *ESPN The Magazine*, January 19, 2004.

Michael Smith, "Patriots Beat Texas in OT Despite Critical Errors," *Boston Globe*, November 24, 2003.

"Inside Track," *Boston Herald*, February 27, 2002.

Charles P. Pierce, *Moving the Chains: Tom Brady and the Pursuit of Everything* (New York: Farrar, Straus and Giroux, 2007).

"Up Front," *People Weekly*, February 18, 2002.

Tom Brady interview, *The Howard Stern Show*, aired April 8, 2020, SiriusXM.

Stan Grossfeld, "Here's What Tom Brady Sr. Said While Reminiscing About His Famous Son," *Boston Globe*, December 23, 2019.

"Inside Track," *Boston Herald*, November 6, 2001.

"Inside Track," *Boston Herald*, November 26, 2001.

"Inside Track," *Boston Herald*, June 3, 2002.

"Inside Track," *Boston Herald*, April 2, 2002.

"Inside Track," *Boston Herald*, April 4, 2002.

America's Game: The Super Bowl Champions, "The Story of the 2003 Patriots," produced by NFL Films, aired April 30, 2007, NFL Network.

Michael Silver, "Snow Doubt About It," *Sports Illustrated*, December 15, 2003.

10. THANK YOU, PEYTON

The information in this chapter comes primarily from events I witnessed firsthand and from interviews with Peyton Manning, Archie Manning, Tony Dungy, David Cutcliffe, Tedy Bruschi, Romeo Crennel, Eric Mangini, Brad Seely, Damon Huard, Marty Meehan, Tom Brady Sr. and other firsthand sources. Also:

SEC Storied, "The Book of Manning," directed by Rory Karpf, aired September 24, 2013, ESPN.

America's Game: The Super Bowl Champions, "The Story of the 2003 Patriots," produced by NFL Films, aired April 30, 2007, NFL Network.

John Ed Bradley, "Like Father, Like Son," *Sports Illustrated*, November 19, 1993.

Mark Ribowsky, *In the Name of the Father: Family, Football, and the Manning Dynasty* (New York: Liveright, 2018).

Tim Layden, "Thank You, Peyton," *Sports Illustrated*, March 17, 1997.

John Kryk, "Brady, Manning First Appeared on Same Football Field in 1993—and Got Tutored by Bill Walsh," *Toronto Sun*, January 17, 2014.

Seth Wickersham, "Trust Me on This," *ESPN The Magazine*, December 20, 2004.

Peter King, "Manning at His Best," *Sports Illustrated*, November 16, 2009.

Peyton Manning, retirement speech, March 7, 2016.

David Halberstam, *The Education of a Coach* (New York: Hyperion, 2005).

Michael Lombardi, *Gridiron Genius: A Master Class in Winning Championships and Building Dynasties in the NFL* (New York: Crown Archetype, 2018).

Ian O'Connor, *Belichick: The Making of the Greatest Football Coach of All Time* (Boston: Houghton Mifflin Harcourt, 2018).

Gary Myers, *Brady vs. Manning: The Untold Story of the Rivalry that Transformed the NFL* (New York: Crown Archetype, 2015).

Troy Brown and Mike Reiss, *Patriot Pride: My Life in the New England Dynasty* (Chicago: Triumph, 2015).

Seth Wickersham, "Smith Steps Up for Patriots," ESPN.com, January 18, 2004.

11. THE TROPHY IS COMING BACK HOME

The information in this chapter comes primarily from events I witnessed first-hand and from interviews with Brad Seely, Brian Kinchen, Eric Mangini, Jason Licht, Charlie Weis, and other firsthand sources. Also:

> *America's Game: The Super Bowl Champions*, "The Story of the 2003 Patriots," produced by NFL Films, aired April 30, 2007, NFL Network.

> Ian O'Connor, *Belichick: The Making of the Greatest Football Coach of All Time* (Boston: Houghton Mifflin Harcourt, 2018).

> "Fight to the Finish," *Sports Illustrated*, February 9, 2004.

> David Halberstam, *The Education of a Coach* (New York: Hyperion, 2005).

> Ron Kroichick, "Brady Living in a Dream World," *San Francisco Chronicle*, February 4, 2004.

12. EVERY DAY BUT GAME DAY

The information in this chapter comes primarily from events I witnessed first-hand and from interviews with Bill Belichick, Eric Mangini, Brad Seely, Dante Scarnecchia, Romeo Crennel, Charlie Weis, scouting reports and game plans I obtained, the Belichick Collection at Navy, and other firsthand sources. Also:

> Michael Silver, "Three Ring Circus," *Sports Illustrated*, February 14, 2005.

> *America's Game: The Super Bowl Champions*, "The Story of the 2004 Patriots," produced by NFL Films, aired January 28, 2007, NFL Network.

> John Powers, *Fridays with Bill: Inside the Football Mind of Bill Belichick* (Chicago: Triumph, 2018).

> *30 for 30*, "The Two Bills," directed by Ken Rodgers, produced by NFL Films, aired February 1, 2018, ESPN.

> David Fleming, "Away Games," *ESPN The Magazine*, June 4, 2007.

> Bill Belichick, interview with WEEI radio, November 10, 2020.

> David Halberstam, *The Education of a Coach* (New York: Hyperion, 2005).

> Ian O'Connor, *Belichick: The Making of the Greatest Football Coach of All Time* (Boston: Houghton Mifflin Harcourt, 2018).

> Michael Lombardi, *Gridiron Genius: A Master Class in Winning Championships and Building Dynasties in the NFL* (New York: Crown Archetype, 2018).

> Dan Wetzel, "Bill Belichick's Stiff-Arm of Camouflage Campaign an Unlikely Coincidence," Yahoo! Sports, November 18, 2015.

> Kevin Duffy, "Before He Became Bill Belichick's Right-Hand Man, the Mysterious Ernie Adams Worked on Wall Street," *Boston Globe*, July 17, 2002.

> Wright Thompson, "Who Is This Guy?" ESPN.com, 2008.

> *A Football Life*, "Bill Belichick," produced by NFL Films, aired September 15 and September 22, 2011, NFL Network.

13. 20/20S

The information in this chapter comes primarily from interviews with Bill Belichick, Eric Mangini, Romeo Crennel, Charlie Weis, Brad Seely, Dante Scarnecchia, and other firsthand sources. Also:

Seth Wickersham, "It Takes a Genius," *ESPN The Magazine*, September 7, 2009.

A Football Life, "Cleveland '95," produced by NFL Films, aired October 3, 2012, NFL Network.

David Halberstam, *The Education of a Coach* (New York: Hyperion, 2005).

Ian O'Connor, *Belichick: The Making of the Greatest Football Coach of All Time* (Boston: Houghton Mifflin Harcourt, 2018).

John Powers, *Fridays with Bill: Inside the Football Mind of Bill Belichick* (Chicago: Triumph, 2018).

Michael Smith, "Law Out to End Days as a Patriot," *Boston Globe*, March 13, 2004.

Tom Brady, press conference, October 19, 2016.

Kevin Duffy, "So You Want to Work for Bill Belichick? Former Patriots Assistants Recall Intense Interview Process," *MassLive*, December 12, 2016.

Michael Holley, *Patriot Reign: Bill Belichick, the Coaches, and the Players Who Built a Champion* (New York: William Morrow, 2004).

14. THE SLEEPER

The information in this chapter comes primarily from events I witnessed firsthand and from interviews with Tom Brady, Brad Seely, Eric Mangini, Romeo Crennel, and other firsthand sources. Also:

America's Game: The Super Bowl Champions, "The Story of the 2004 Patriots," produced by NFL Films, aired January 28, 2007, NFL Network.

Troy Brown and Mike Reiss, *Patriot Pride: My Life in the New England Dynasty* (Chicago: Triumph, 2015).

Peter King, "Gripping Story," *Sports Illustrated*, September 11, 2006.

Gary Myers, *Brady vs. Manning: The Untold Story of the Rivalry that Transformed the NFL* (New York: Crown Archetype), 2015.

Brett Martin, "The 50 Best Jobs in America," *Men's Journal*, November 2004.

15. SOMETHING VERY SPECIAL

The information in this chapter comes primarily from events I witnessed firsthand and from interviews with Tom Brady Sr., Brad Seely, Charlie Weis, Joe Banner, Deion Branch, Romeo Crennel, and other firsthand sources. Also:

Seth Wickersham, "The Next Great NFL Coach Is . . . ," *ESPN The Magazine*, January 11, 2010.

Lee Jenkins, "In '98, McNabb and Syracuse Beat Brady and Michigan," *New York Times*, February 2, 2005.

America's Game: The Super Bowl Champions, "The Story of the 2004 Patriots," produced by NFL Films, aired January 28, 2007, NFL Network.

Anthony Gargano and Bob Cooney, WPEN radio, January 29, 2018.

Ron Borges, "Patriots Turned to Screens to Bypass Aggressive Eagles," *Boston Globe*, February 7, 2005.

David Halberstam, *The Education of a Coach* (New York: Hyperion, 2005).

Ian O'Connor, *Belichick: The Making of the Greatest Football Coach of All Time* (Boston: Houghton Mifflin Harcourt, 2018).

Michael Silver, "Three Ring Circus," *Sports Illustrated*, February 14, 2005.

60 Minutes, Tom Brady interview with Steve Kroft, aired November 4, 2005, CBS.

16. ALL YOU HAVE IS YOUR NAME AND REPUTATION

The information in this chapter comes primarily from events I witnessed firsthand and from interviews with Dwight Freeney, Eric Mangini, Mike Shanahan, Jeff Triplette, and other firsthand sources. Also:

David Halberstam, interview with WEEI radio, November 2, 2005.

David Halberstam, *The Education of a Coach* (New York: Hyperion, 2005).

Jeff Benedict, *The Dynasty* (New York: Avid Reader Press, 2020).

Seth Wickersham, "Enough's Enough," *ESPN The Magazine*, September 12, 2005.

Michael Silver, "Sandbox Boys," Yahoo! Sports, September 14, 2007.

Seth Wickersham, "Belichick in the Spotlight," ESPN.com, April 12, 2006.

17. PROTECT THE SHIELD

The information in this chapter comes primarily from interviews with Paul Tagliabue, other firsthand sources, and a copy of Roger Goodell's speech I obtained. Also:

Judy Battista, "Goodell Gets Enough Votes to Lead NFL," *New York Times*, August 9, 2006.

18. WHO DOES THAT?

The information in this chapter comes primarily from events I witnessed firsthand and from interviews with Tom Brady, Tom Brady Sr. and Galynn Brady, Rodney Harrison, Ellis Hobbs, Donté Stallworth, and other firsthand sources.

NFL 100 All-Time Team, produced by NFL Network, aired 2019–20.

Ian O'Connor, *Belichick: The Making of the Greatest Football Coach of All Time* (Boston: Houghton Mifflin Harcourt, 2018).

Jeff Benedict, *The Dynasty* (New York: Avid Reader Press, 2020).

Seth Wickersham, "2007 Patriots Still Wonder What Might Have Been," ESPN.com, June 28, 2013.

Ron Borges, "Brady Goes Out on a Limb for Branch," *Boston Globe*, August 2, 2006.

Albert Breer, "Safety in Numbers: Meriweather Fills the Void at Corner," *Boston Herald*, August 4, 2007.

John Tomase, "Belichick Happy to Get Last Laugh," *Boston Herald*, October 21, 2007.

19. Remain Inconspicuous

The information in this chapter comes primarily from interviews with Mike Westhoff, Mike Shanahan, Rodney Harrison, Danny Fisher, and other first-hand sources. Also:

Ian O'Connor, *Belichick: The Making of the Greatest Football Coach of All Time* (Boston: Houghton Mifflin Harcourt, 2018).

Don Van Natta Jr. and Seth Wickersham, "From Spygate to Deflategate: Inside What Split the NFL and Patriots Apart," *ESPN The Magazine*, September 28, 2015.

Jeff Benedict, *The Dynasty* (New York: Avid Reader Press, 2020).

Arlen Specter Senatorial Papers, University of Pittsburgh.

Knute Rockne, *Coaching: The Complete Notre Dame System of Football* (New York: Devin-Adair, 1931).

Mike Fish, "Former Patriots Video Assistant Hints at Team's Spying History," ESPN.com, February 1, 2008.

Drew Magary, "Jay Glazer: The NFL's Biggest Bomb Thrower," *GQ*, January 2014.

20. 18–0*

The information in this chapter comes primarily from events I witnessed firsthand and from interviews with Tom Brady, Tom Brady Sr. and Galynn Brady, Ellis Hobbs, Donté Stallworth, Larry Izzo, Heath Evans, Rosevelt Colvin, Asante Samuel, Brad Seely, and other firsthand sources. Also:

Ian O'Connor, *Belichick: The Making of the Greatest Football Coach of All Time* (Boston: Houghton Mifflin Harcourt, 2018).

Seth Wickersham, "2007 Patriots Still Wonder What Might Have Been," ESPN.com, June 28, 2013.

Seth Wickersham, "What More Could Tom Brady Want?," *ESPN The Magazine*, May 13, 2013.

Ron Jaworski with Greg Cosell and David Plaut, *The Games that Changed the Game: The Evolution of the NFL in Seven Sundays* (New York: ESPN Books, 2010).

John Powers, *Fridays with Bill: Inside the Football Mind of Bill Belichick* (Chicago: Triumph, 2018).

21. Girlie Man Limps Home

The information in this chapter comes primarily from events I witnessed firsthand and from interviews with Tom Brady, Tom Brady Sr. and Galynn Brady, Ben Watson, Donté Stallworth, Brad Seely, and other firsthand sources. Also:

Seth Wickersham, "What More Could Tom Brady Want?," *ESPN The Magazine*, May 13, 2013.

Michael Rosenberg, "Tom Brady as You Forgot Him," *Sports Illustrated*, January 9, 2012.

Gisele Bündchen interview, *The Tonight Show Starring Jimmy Fallon*, aired October 5, 2018, NBC.

Gisele Bündchen, *Lessons: My Path to a Meaningful Life* (New York: Avery, 2018).

Tom Brady interview, *The Howard Stern Show*, aired April 8, 2020, SiriusXM.

Dax Shepard, host, "Tom Brady," *Armchair Expert* (podcast), September 10, 2020, https://armchairexpertpod.com/pods/tom-brady.

Tom Chiarella, "Just Throw the Damn Ball, Tom Brady," *Esquire*, August 2008.

22. Burn That Game

The information in this chapter comes primarily from events I witnessed firsthand and from interviews with Tom Brady, Tom Brady Sr. and Galynn Brady, Donté Stallworth, Heath Evans, Brad Seely, Kyle Brady, Tedy Bruschi, Eli Manning, Asante Samuel, Shaun O'Hara, Marty Meehan, other firsthand sources, and from Senator Arlen Specter's papers. Also:

Seth Wickersham, "What More Could Tom Brady Want?," *ESPN The Magazine*, May 13, 2013.

America's Game: The Super Bowl Champions, "The Story of the 2007 Giants," produced by NFL Films, aired September 3, 2008, NFL Network.

Peyton's Places, ESPN.

Ian O'Connor, *Belichick: The Making of the Greatest Football Coach of All Time* (Boston: Houghton Mifflin Harcourt, 2018).

Seth Wickersham, "2007 Patriots Still Wonder What Might Have Been," ESPN.com, June 28, 2013.

John Tomase, "Source: Patriots Employee Filmed Rams," *Boston Herald*, February 2, 2008.

Trey Wingo, host, *Trey Wingo Presents: Half-Forgotten History* (podcast).

Greg Bishop and Pete Thamel, "Senator Wants NFL Spying Case Explained," *New York Times*, February 1, 2008.

Mike Fish, "Former Patriots Video Assistant Hints at Team's Spying History," ESPN.com, February 1, 2008.

23. Cover-Up

The information in this chapter comes primarily from interviews with Danny Fisher, Mike Martz, other firsthand sources, and from Senator Arlen Specter's papers. Also:

Don Van Natta Jr. and Seth Wickersham, "From Spygate to Deflategate: Inside What Split the NFL and Patriots Apart," *ESPN The Magazine*, September 28, 2015.

Jeff Benedict, *The Dynasty* (New York: Avid Reader Press, 2020).

John M. R. Bull, "Trump Schmoozes to Show Support for Specter," *Morning Call*, September 2, 2004.

Don Van Natta Jr. and Seth Wickersham, "Son, Ghostwriter of Late Senator Say Trump Intervened to Stop Probe of Patriots' Spygate Scandal," ESPN .com, May 26, 2021.

"Exclusive: Belichick Talks on Spygate," CBS News, May 16, 2008, https:// www.cbsnews.com/news/exclusive-belichick-talks-on-spy-gate/.

Maggie Haberman and Katie Rogers, "Still Standing, Jared Kushner and Ivanka Trump Step Back in the Spotlight," *New York Times*, July 28, 2018.

Ian O'Connor, *Belichick: The Making of the Greatest Football Coach of All Time* (Boston: Houghton Mifflin Harcourt, 2018).

24. One Thing I'm Not Is Scared

The information in this chapter comes primarily from interviews with Bernard Pollard and Bill Belichick. Also:

Tom Brady, *The TB12 Method: How to Achieve a Lifetime of Sustained Peak Performance* (New York: Simon & Schuster, 2017).

David Fleming, "No More Questions," *ESPN The Magazine*, October 4, 2016.

A Football Life, "Bill Belichick," produced by NFL Films, aired September 15 and September 22, 2011, NFL Network.

Peter King, "Tom Brady Is Back," *Sports Illustrated*, June 1, 2009.

The Sopranos, season 6, episode 20, "The Blue Comet," directed by Alan Taylor, written by David Chase and Matthew Weiner, aired June 3, 2007, HBO.

Ian O'Connor, *Belichick: The Making of the Greatest Football Coach of All Time* (Boston: Houghton Mifflin Harcourt, 2018).

Jason Cole, "Bill Belichick Q&A," Yahoo! Sports, November 6, 2009.

David Halberstam, *The Education of a Coach* (New York: Hyperion, 2005).

Zak Keefer, "The Best Peyton Manning Stories You've Never Heard," *Indianapolis Star*, October 4, 2017.

NFL 100 All-Time Team, produced by NFL Network, aired 2019–20.

25. I'M NOT BILL BELICHICK

The information in this chapter comes primarily from events I witnessed firsthand and from interviews with Eric Mangini, Ken Shipp, Bill Belichick, Josh McDaniels, Tom Brady, Mike Holmgren, and other firsthand sources. Also:

Seth Wickersham, "It Takes a Genius," *ESPN The Magazine*, September 7, 2009.

Seth Wickersham, "Five Days in the Life of Eric Mangini," *ESPN The Magazine*, August 24, 2010.

Seth Wickersham, "Shipp Shaped Belichick's Thinking," ESPN.com, September 4, 2009.

Seth Wickersham, "Why 10 Super Bowl Appearances Isn't Enough for Tom Brady," ESPN.com, February 3, 2021.

Ian O'Connor, *Belichick: The Making of the Greatest Football Coach of All Time* (Boston: Houghton Mifflin Harcourt, 2018).

"Broncos, McDaniels Fined $50k Each," ESPN.com, November 27, 2010.

Andrew Das, "Eric Mangini's Revenge," *New York Times*, November 8, 2010.

26. THAT'S A LOT OF F—K YOUS!

The information in this chapter comes primarily from events I witnessed firsthand and from interviews with DeMaurice Smith, Domonique Foxworth, Jeff Saturday, and other firsthand sources. Also:

Don Van Natta Jr. and Seth Wickersham "Inside the Dual Legacies of NFL Players' Union Boss DeMaurice Smith," ESPN.com, February 23, 2021.

America's Game: The Super Bowl Champions, "The Story of the 2011 Giants," produced by NFL Films, aired September 4, 2012, NFL Network.

Victor Cruz with Peter Schrager, *Out of the Blue* (New York: Celebra, 2012).

Dan Wetzel, "Tom Brady in a Postgame Daze of Disappointment After Another Super Bowl Loss to the Giants," Yahoo! Sports, February 6, 2012.

Greg A. Bedard, "Bill O'Brien: 'That Wasn't a Drop,'" *Boston Globe*, March 2, 2012.

27. ALEJANDRO!

The information in this chapter comes primarily from events I witnessed firsthand and from interviews with Tom Brady, Tom Brady Sr. and Galynn Brady, Tom House, and other firsthand sources. Also:

Seth Wickersham, "What More Could Tom Brady Want?," *ESPN The Magazine*, May 13, 2013.

Bruce Feldman, *The QB: The Making of Modern Quarterbacks* (New York: Crown Archetype, 2014).

Seth Wickersham, "Out Route," *ESPN The Magazine*, February 12, 2014.

Tom Brady, *The TB12 Method: How to Achieve a Lifetime of Sustained Peak Performance* (New York: Simon & Schuster, 2017).

Chris Sweeney, "Tom Brady's Personal Guru Is a Glorified Snake-Oil Salesman," *Boston Magazine*, October 9, 2015.

28. Love in the Time of Belichick

The information in this chapter comes primarily from events I witnessed firsthand and from interviews with Tom Brady, Matthew Slater, Devin McCourty, and other firsthand sources. Also:

Seth Wickersham, "Patriots Love in the Time of Deflategate," *ESPN The Magazine*, February 16, 2015.

Ian O'Connor, *Belichick: The Making of the Greatest Football Coach of All Time* (Boston: Houghton Mifflin Harcourt, 2018).

Seth Wickersham, "The Ugly Truth About Peyton Manning," *ESPN The Magazine*, November 26, 2013.

Michael Lombardi, *Gridiron Genius: A Master Class in Winning Championships and Building Dynasties in the NFL* (New York: Crown Archetype, 2018).

Joon Lee, "Jimmy Garoppolo Is Superman in Disguise," *Bleacher Report*, July 23, 2018.

Jeff Benedict, *The Dynasty* (New York: Avid Reader Press, 2020).

Seth Wickersham, "What More Could Tom Brady Want?," *ESPN The Magazine*, May 13, 2013.

Master Tesfatsion, "Untold Stories," *Bleacher Report*, September 16, 2020.

Seth Wickersham and Tom Junod, "Tom Brady's Most Dangerous Game," *ESPN The Magazine*, November 1, 2017.

29. Fight Song

The information in this chapter comes primarily from events I witnessed firsthand and from interviews with Tom Brady, Tom Brady Sr., Lane Kiffin, and other firsthand sources. Also:

Seth Wickersham and Tom Junod, "Tom Brady's Most Dangerous Game," *ESPN The Magazine*, November 1, 2017.

Ted Wells et al., *Investigative Report Concerning Footballs Used During the AFC Championship Game on January 18, 2015* (New York: Paul, Weiss, Rifkind, Wharton & Garrison LLP, 2015).

Do Your Job: Bill Belichick and the 2014 Patriots, produced by NFL Films, aired September 9, 2015, NFL Network.

Greg Bishop, "Tom Brady Looks Better than Ever for the Patriots," *Sports Illustrated*, December 14, 2014.

Kevin Van Valkenburg, "Julian Edelman Enjoys His Moment," *ESPN The Magazine*, February 19, 2015.

100%: Julian Edelman, directed by Kyler Schelling, written by Assaf Swissa, Kyler Schelling, and Chris Pape, aired June 28, 2019, Showtime.

Seth Wickersham, "Brady Proves More Nimble," ESPN.com, November 3, 2014.

Michael Lombardi, *Gridiron Genius: A Master Class in Winning Championships and Building Dynasties in the NFL* (New York: Crown Archetype, 2018).

30. THE MAKEUP CALL

The information in this chapter comes primarily from events I witnessed firsthand and from interviews with Greg Harden and other firsthand sources. Also:

Ted Wells et al., *Investigative Report Concerning Footballs Used During the AFC Championship Game on January 18, 2015* (New York: Paul, Weiss, Rifkind, Wharton & Garrison LLP, 2015).

Tom Brady, transcript of testimony at NFL appeal hearing, June 23, 2015.

Do Your Job: Bill Belichick and the 2014 Patriots, produced by NFL Films, aired September 9, 2015, NFL Network.

Ian O'Connor, *Belichick: The Making of the Greatest Football Coach of All Time* (Boston: Houghton Mifflin Harcourt, 2018).

Tom Brady interview, *Dennis and Callahan Show*, WEEI-FM, January 19, 2015.

Greg A. Bedard, "Pats Sources: Strong Statements by NFL Officials Left Out of Wells Report," *Sports Illustrated*, May 11, 2015.

Bill Pennington, "Eli Manning's Footballs Are Months in the Making," *New York Times*, November 23, 2013.

Rob Demovsky, "Aaron Rodgers: Fully Inflate Footballs," ESPN.com, January 20, 2015.

Paul Kuharsky, "Jeff Blake: Every Team Deflates Footballs," ESPN.com, January 28, 2015.

Mike Florio, "Leinart Says 'Every' Quarterback Tampers with the Ball, Except One," Pro Football Talk, January 21, 2015.

Greg A. Bedard, "The Accidental Coach of the Cleveland Browns," *Sports Illustrated*, June 19, 2014.

Seth Wickersham, "Patriots Love in the Time of Deflategate," *ESPN The Magazine*, February 16, 2015.

"From Spygate to Deflategate: Inside What Split the NFL and Patriots Apart," *ESPN The Magazine*, September 28, 2015.

Don Van Natta Jr., and Kevin Van Valkenburg, "Rice Case: Purposeful Misdirection by Team, Scant Investigation by the NFL," ESPN.com, September, 19, 2014.

Tom Brady's emails turned over as part of Deflategate inquiry.

Dan Wetzel, "Why Tom Brady's Fourth Super Bowl Title May Mean the Most to Him," Yahoo! Sports, February 2, 2015.

31. MALCOLM, GO!

The information in this chapter comes primarily from events I witnessed firsthand and from interviews with Tom Brady, Tom Brady Sr., scouting reports I obtained, and other firsthand sources. Also:

Do Your Job: Bill Belichick and the 2014 Patriots, produced by NFL Films, aired September 9, 2015, NFL Network.

America's Game: The Super Bowl Champions, "The Story of the 2014 Patriots," produced by NFL Films, aired September 8, 2015, NFL Network.

Peter King, "The Super Bowl Story, According to Tom Brady," SI.com, February 9, 2015.

Tom Junod, "Theater of Pain," *Esquire,* February 2013.

Michael Lombardi, *Gridiron Genius: A Master Class in Winning Championships and Building Dynasties in the NFL* (New York: Crown Archetype, 2018).

Ted Wells et al., *Investigative Report Concerning Footballs Used During the AFC Championship Game on January 18, 2015* (New York: Paul, Weiss, Rifkind, Wharton & Garrison LLP, 2015).

Seth Wickersham, "Jubilant Relief for Tom Brady," ESPN.com, February 2, 2015.

Tom Brady's emails turned over as part of Deflategate inquiry.

Terry Blount, "Russell Wilson: 'No Doubt' in Play Call," ESPN.com, February 3, 2015.

NFL 100 All-Time Team, produced by NFL Network, aired 2019–20.

32. I HAD TO DO IT FOR THE FANS

The information in this chapter comes primarily from events I witnessed firsthand and from interviews with David Nugent and other firsthand sources. Also:

Wright Thompson, "Michael Jordan Has Not Left the Building," *ESPN The Magazine,* February 14, 2013.

Ted Wells et al., *Investigative Report Concerning Footballs Used During the AFC Championship Game on January 18, 2015* (New York: Paul, Weiss, Rifkind, Wharton & Garrison LLP, 2015).

Casey Sherman and Dave Wedge, *12: The Inside Story of Tom Brady's Fight for Redemption* (New York: Little, Brown, 2018).

Jackson Wald, "How Keegan Bradley Had to Face Michael Jordan and Tom Brady in an Epic Pick-Up Basketball Game," Golf.com, July 14, 2020, https://golf.com/news/keegan-bradley-pickup-basketball-game/.

Bill Belichick, interview on *The Late Show with David Letterman*, aired February 11, 2015, CBS.

Don Van Natta Jr. and Seth Wickersham, "From Spygate to Deflategate: Inside What Split the NFL and Patriots Apart," *ESPN The Magazine*, September 28, 2015.

Tom Brady, transcript of testimony at NFL appeal hearing, June 23, 2015.

America's Game: The Super Bowl Champions, "The Story of the 2014 Patriots," produced by NFL Films, aired September 8, 2015, NFL Network.

Mark Leibovich, "The Uncomfortable Love Affair Between Donald Trump and the New England Patriots," *New York Times Magazine*, February 1, 2017.

33. HOW DID YOU GET BLOOD ON THERE?

The information in this chapter comes primarily from events I witnessed and from interviews with firsthand sources. Also:

Don Van Natta Jr. and Seth Wickersham, "From Spygate to Deflategate: Inside What Split the NFL and Patriots Apart," *ESPN The Magazine*, September 28, 2015.

Do Your Job: Bill Belichick and the 2014 Patriots, produced by NFL Films, aired September 9, 2015, NFL Network.

Greg Bishop, Michael Rosenberg, and Thayer Evans, "Bill Belichick, Patriots Past Cheating Stokes Suspicion," *Sports Illustrated*, September 8. 2015.

Tom Brady's emails turned over as part of Deflategate inquiry.

Chuck Klosterman, "Tom Brady Talks to Chuck Klosterman About Deflategate (Sort Of . . .)," *GQ*, November 18, 2015.

Kevin Van Valkenburg, "Tom Brady's Big Reveal," *ESPN The Magazine*, January 21, 2016.

Seth Wickersham, "The Drive That Never Ends," *ESPN The Magazine*, September 7, 2016.

NFL 100 All-Time Team, produced by NFL Network, aired 2019–20.

Casey Sherman and Dave Wedge, *12: The Inside Story of Tom Brady's Fight for Redemption* (New York: Little, Brown, 2018).

Phil Perry and Tom E. Curran, hosts, *Quick Slants* (podcast), February 2, 2017, https://www.nbcsports.com/boston/new-england-patriots/quick-slants-podcast-super-bowl-51-edition.

34. Definitely Human

The information in this chapter comes primarily from interviews with Todd Anson, Romeo Crennel, and other firsthand sources. Also:

Seth Wickersham and Tom Junod, "Tom Brady's Most Dangerous Game," *ESPN The Magazine*, November 1, 2017.

Joon Lee, "Jimmy Garoppolo Is Superman in Disguise," *Bleacher Report*, July 23, 2018.

Seth Wickersham, "For Kraft, Brady, and Belichick, Is This the Beginning of the End?," ESPN.com, January 5, 2018.

Kevin Van Valkenburg, "Tom Brady Felt the Michigan Love, Maybe for the First Time," ESPN.com, September 21, 2016.

Casey Sherman and Dave Wedge, *12: The Inside Story of Tom Brady's Fight for Redemption* (New York: Little, Brown, 2018).

Donald Trump, speech in Manchester, New Hampshire, November 7, 2016.

Kellyanne Conway, interview with Fox News, January 24, 2017.

Seth Wickersham, "The Disappearance of the Hoodie," ESPN.com, February 1, 2017.

David Maraniss, *When Pride Still Mattered: A Life of Vince Lombardi* (New York: Simon & Schuster, 1999).

Tom Brady Sr., interview with KGO radio, September 8, 2015.

Kevin Van Valkenburg, "Brady's Revenge," *ESPN The Magazine*, February 6, 2017.

35. For Your Mom, Bro

The information in this chapter comes primarily from events I witnessed firsthand and from interviews with John Elway and other firsthand sources. Also:

Do Your Job, Part 2: Bill Belichick and the 2016 Patriots, produced by NFL Films, aired September 3, 2017, NBC.

America's Game: The Super Bowl Champions, "The Story of the 2016 Patriots," produced by NFL Films, aired September 6, 2017, NFL Network.

Julian Edelman with Tom E. Curran, *Relentless: A Memoir* (New York: Hachette, 2017).

Peter King, "Tom Brady Tells the Story of the Super Bowl 51 Comeback," *Sports Illustrated*, February 13, 2017.

Pete Prisco, "Matt Ryan Explains Exactly What Happened in the Falcons' Super Bowl Collapse," CBS Sports, July 19, 2017.

Seth Wickersham, "How a Brady–Goodell Connection Lingered over the Super Bowl," ESPN.com, February 6, 2017.

36. THE PLIABILITY MOVEMENT

The information in this chapter comes primarily from events I witnessed first-hand and from interviews with Tom Brady, Pete Carroll, and other firsthand sources. Also:

Seth Wickersham, "Why Richard Sherman Can't Let Go of Seattle's Super Bowl Loss," *ESPN The Magazine*, June 12, 2017.

Elizabeth Merrill, "A Falcons Locker Room That Refuses to Wallow in Super Bowl Disaster," *ESPN The Magazine*, September 4, 2017.

Tom Brady, *The TB12 Method: How to Achieve a Lifetime of Sustained Peak Performance* (New York: Simon & Schuster, 2017).

Gretchen Reynolds, "Tom Brady's 'The TB12 Method' Is Hefty but Short on Science," *New York Times*, September 20, 2017.

Tom vs. Time, directed by Gotham Chopra, streamed January 25–March 12, 2018, Facebook Watch.

Mark Leibovich, "Tom Brady Gave a Filmmaker Unusual Access to His Private Life," *New York Times*, January 9, 2018.

Seth Wickersham and Tom Junod, "Tom Brady's Most Dangerous Game," *ESPN The Magazine*, November 1, 2017.

Seth Wickersham, "For Kraft, Brady and Belichick, Is This the Beginning of the End?," ESPN.com, January 5, 2018.

Greg A. Bedard, "How Much of a Concern Is This Alex Guerrero/Bill Belichick Rift for the Patriots?" *Boston Sports Journal*, December 20, 2017.

Bob Hohler, "Bill Belichick Curbs Privileges of Tom Brady's Associate Alex Guerrero," *Boston Globe*, December 19, 2017.

37. YOU THINK BOB KRAFT CAME AFTER YOU HARD

The information in this chapter comes primarily from events I witnessed first-hand and from interviews with firsthand sources. Also:

Don Van Natta Jr. and Seth Wickersham, "NFL Owners Struggled to Retain Control After Trump's Attacks, Rise of Player Protests," ESPN.com, October 1, 2017.

Don Van Natta Jr. and Seth Wickersham, "Standing Down," *ESPN The Magazine*, October 27, 2017.

Mark Leibovich, *Big Game: The NFL in Dangerous Times* (New York: Penguin, 2018).

Ken Belson and Mark Leibovich, "Inside the Confidential NFL Meeting to Discuss National Anthem Protests," *New York Times*, April 25, 2018.

Don Van Natta Jr. and Seth Wickersham, "Roger Goodell Has a Jerry Jones Problem, and Nobody Knows How It Will End," *ESPN The Magazine*, December 4, 2017.

38. I Don't Want to Play for Bill Anymore

The information in this chapter comes primarily from interviews with first-hand sources. Also:

Mark Leibovich, *Big Game: The NFL in Dangerous Times* (New York: Penguin, 2018).

Casey Sherman and Dave Wedge, *12: The Inside Story of Tom Brady's Fight for Redemption* (New York: Little, Brown, 2018).

Nicki Jhabvala, "Kyle Smith Leaves Washington Football Team for Same Player Personnel Role with Atlanta Falcons," *Washington Post*, January 29, 2021.

Michael Lombardi, *Gridiron Genius: A Master Class in Winning Championships and Building Dynasties in the NFL* (New York: Crown Archetype, 2018).

Seth Wickersham, "For Kraft, Brady and Belichick, Is This the Beginning of the End?," ESPN.com, January 5, 2018.

Joon Lee, "Jimmy Garoppolo Is Superman in Disguise," *Bleacher Report*, July 23, 2018.

Tom vs. Time, directed by Gotham Chopra, streamed January 25–March 12, 2018, Facebook Watch.

Ian O'Connor, *Belichick: The Making of the Greatest Football Coach of All Time* (Boston: Houghton Mifflin Harcourt, 2018).

Mike Reiss, "Bill Belichick Played Small but Notable Role in Jaguars' Turn-around Season" ESPN.com, January 21, 2018.

Aaron Wilson, "Texans in Turmoil: Relationship Between Coach Bill O'Brien, GM Rick Smith Called 'Toxic,'" *Houston Chronicle*, December 30, 2017.

Bob Hohler, "Bill Belichick Curbs Privileges of Tom Brady's Associate Alex Guerrero," *Boston Globe*, December 19, 2017.

Seth Wickersham and Tom Junod, "Tom Brady's Most Dangerous Game," *ESPN The Magazine*, November 1, 2017.

Tom E. Curran, "Patriots Run Feels Like It's Winding Down," NBC Sports Boston, December 29, 2017.

Rich Cimini, "Robert Kraft: To Keep a Good Thing Going, Egos Must Stay in Check," ESPN.com, January 21, 2018.

39. It's Not Brain Surgery

The information in this chapter comes primarily from interviews with first-hand sources. Also:

Tom vs. Time, directed by Gotham Chopra, streamed January 25–March 12, 2018, Facebook Watch.

Jeff Benedict, *The Dynasty* (New York: Avid Reader Press, 2020).

Dan Pompei, "The Redemption of Josh McDaniels," *Bleacher Report*, September 29, 2016.

40. LIGHTS OUT

The information in this chapter comes primarily from events I witnessed firsthand and from interviews with Chad Morris and other firsthand sources. Also:

America's Game: The Super Bowl Champions, "The Story of the 2017 Eagles," produced by NFL Films, aired September 5, 2018, NFL Network.

Jeff Benedict, *The Dynasty* (New York: Avid Reader Press, 2020).

Greg Bishop and Ben Baskin, "A Play Call for the Ages and a (Backup) QB That Amazes: How the Eagles Won Super Bowl LII," *Sports Illustrated*, February 6, 2018.

Ben Court, "Why Tom Brady Will Never Quit," *Men's Health*, August 6, 2019.

Belichick & Saban: The Art of Coaching, directed by Ken Rodgers, aired December 10, 2019, HBO.

Zach Berman, *Underdogs: The Philadelphia Eagles' Emotional Road to Super Bowl Victory* (New York: Running Press, 2018).

41. PLEADING THE FIFTH

The information in this chapter comes primarily from interviews with firsthand sources. Also:

Tom Brady interview, *The Howard Stern Show*, aired April 8, 2020, SiriusXM.

Tom vs. Time, directed by Gotham Chopra, streamed January 25–March 12, 2018, Facebook Watch.

Jeff Benedict, *The Dynasty* (New York: Avid Reader Press, 2020).

Belichick & Saban: The Art of Coaching, directed by Ken Rodgers, aired December 10, 2019, HBO.

Josh Berhow, "Phil Mickelson's US Open Prep? A Round of Golf with Tom Brady," Golf.com, June 12, 2018.

42. ONCE YOU STOP, YOU'RE DONE

The information in this chapter comes primarily from interviews with Michael Rubin, Brian Decker and other firsthand sources. Also:

Seth Wickersham, "Formal Vote Before Passing NFL's Anthem Policy Not Taken, League Says," ESPN.com, May 24, 2018.

Tom vs. Time, directed by Gotham Chopra, streamed January 25–March 12, 2018, Facebook Watch.

Angelique Fiske, "Krafts, McCourty, Harmon Speak on Criminal Justice Reform," Patriots.com, April 27, 2018.

Ian O'Connor, *Belichick: The Making of the Greatest Football Coach of All Time* (Boston: Houghton Mifflin Harcourt, 2018).

ESPN staff, "Josh Gordon's Tenure in Cleveland Ends with Trade to Patriots," ESPN.com, September 17, 2018.

Belichick & Saban: The Art of Coaching, directed by Ken Rodgers, aired December 10, 2019, HBO.

Seth Wickersham, "Man on a Mission," ESPN.com, August 10, 2016.

Greg A. Bedard, "With Gronkowski's Usage vs. Chiefs, Patriots Braintrust Leaves No Doubt Who Is NFL's Top TE," *Boston Sports Journal,* October 15, 2018.

43. RIGHT, T?

The information in this chapter comes primarily from interviews with first-hand sources and from police reports. Also:

Greg Bishop and Ben Baskin, "How the Patriots Built Football's Greatest Dynasty," *Sports Illustrated,* February 4, 2019.

May Jeong, "'You Won't Believe What Happened': The Wild, Disturbing Saga of Robert Kraft's Visit to a Strip Mall Sex Spa," *Vanity Fair,* November 2019.

44. WE'RE CHAMPS, MAN!

The information in this chapter comes primarily from interviews with first-hand sources and from police reports. Also:

Elizabeth Merrill, "Patriots RB Jonas Gray's Brush with Fantasy vs. Reality, Five Years Ago," ESPN.com, November 13, 2019.

Do Your Job Part III: Bill Belichick and the 2018 Patriots, produced by NFL Films, aired September 4, 2019, NFL Network.

Belichick & Saban: The Art of Coaching, directed by Ken Rodgers, aired December 10, 2019, HBO.

45. TALK TO MR. KRAFT

The information in this chapter comes primarily from events I witnessed first-hand and from interviews with firsthand sources. Also:

Ben Volin and Nora Princiotti, "'Character Coach' Jack Easterby Is Leaving the Patriots," *Boston Globe,* February 28, 2019.

Andrew Beaton, "Robert Kraft Apologizes as Defense Attorneys Say Investigation Was Illegally Conducted," *Wall Street Journal,* March 23, 2019.

Michael S. Schmidt, *Donald Trump v. the United States: Inside the Struggle to Stop a President* (New York: Random House, 2020).

Dom Cosentino, "Robert Kraft Is the Silent Center of the NFL Meetings," *Deadspin,* March 26, 2019.

NFL 100 All-Time Team, produced by NFL Network, aired 2019–20.

"For Sale: Tom Brady Puts Brookline Home on the Market," NBC Sports Boston, August 6, 2019.

Tom Brady interview, *The Howard Stern Show*, aired April 8, 2020, SiriusXM.

Tom Brady interview, *Good Morning America*, aired April 7, 2021, ABC.

Tom Brady interview with Oprah Winfrey, Oprah Winfrey Network, aired June 17, 2018.

Dax Shepard, host, "Tom Brady," *Armchair Expert* (podcast), September 10, 2020, https://armchairexpertpod.com/pods/tom-brady.

Robert Klemko, "There's More to Antonio Brown's History," *Sports Illustrated*, September 16, 2019.

Robert Klemko, "Antonio Brown Accuser Says He Sent Her 'Intimidating' Text Messages After SI's Story," SI.com, September 19, 2019.

Tom E. Curran, "Patriots Fallout: Taking Stock of the Damage Left by Antonio Brown," NBC Sports Boston, September 26, 2019.

Seth Wickersham, "The Story Behind the Split of Tom Brady, Bill Belichick and the Patriots," ESPN.com, March 22, 2020.

46. PLEASE STAY, TOMMY

The information in this chapter comes primarily from events I witnessed firsthand and from interviews with firsthand sources. Also:

Tom vs. Time, directed by Gotham Chopra, streamed January 25–March 12, 2018, Facebook Watch.

Mark Leibovich, "Tom Brady Cannot Stop," *New York Times Magazine*, February 1, 2015.

Tom Brady, "The Only Way Is Through," *Players' Tribune*, April 6, 2020.

Seth Wickersham, "The Story Behind the Split of Tom Brady, Bill Belichick and the Patriots," ESPN.com, March 22, 2020.

Good Morning Football, aired May 15, 2020, NFL Network.

Joe Montana interview, *The Jake Asman Show*, KFNC radio, August 12, 2020.

Steve Young with Jeff Benedict, *QB: My Life Behind the Spiral* (Boston: Houghton Mifflin Harcourt, 2016).

47. THE COLLEGE KID

The information in this chapter comes primarily from interviews with Sean Dorcellus and other firsthand sources. Also:

Seth Wickersham, "The Story Behind the Split of Tom Brady, Bill Belichick and the Patriots," ESPN.com, March 22, 2020.

The Camera Guys, NBC Sports Boston, June 8, 2020.

48. TOMPA BAY

The information in this chapter comes primarily from interviews with Jason Licht and firsthand sources. Also:

Tom Brady interview, *The Howard Stern Show*, aired April 8, 2020, SiriusXM.

Jeff Benedict, *The Dynasty* (New York: Avid Reader Press, 2020).

Seth Wickersham, "The Story Behind the Split of Tom Brady, Bill Belichick and the Patriots," ESPN.com, March 22, 2020.

Jim Gray with Greg Bishop, *Talking to GOATS: The Moments You Remember and the Stories You Never Heard* (New York: William Morrow, 2020).

Tom Brady, "The Only Way Is Through," *Players' Tribune*, April 6, 2020.

Michael Lewis, "Don't Eat Fortune's Cookie," commencement address at Princeton University, June 3, 2012.

Jason Licht interview, *The Peter King Podcast*, January 27, 2021.

49. WARTIME PROFITEER

The information in this chapter comes primarily from interviews with Jason Licht, David Kramer, and other firsthand sources. Also:

Angelique Fiske, "We'll Get Through This Together," Patriots.com, April 1, 2020.

Vinciane Ngomsi, "Boost Your Immune System After Each Workout with Protect, a New Plant-Based Supplement from Tom Brady's TB12," Yahoo! Sports, May 18, 2020.

Alex Reimer, "Tom Brady's 'Immunity' Vitamins Are Unethical and Misleading, Medical Experts Say," *Forbes*, May 20, 2020.

Dan Shaughnessy, "Thoughts on Tone-Deaf Tom Brady," *Boston Globe*, May 22, 2020.

Laura Wagner, "Does Tom Brady Think COVID-19 Was Sent to Make Us All 'Chill Out'?," *Vice*, April 2, 2020.

Don Van Natta Jr. and Seth Wickersham, "Inside the Dual Legacies of NFL Players' Union Boss DeMaurice Smith," ESPN.com, February 23, 2021.

Andrew Beaton, "How the New England Patriots' Plane Flew a Million N95 Masks Out of China," *Wall Street Journal*, April 2, 2020.

50. I HOPE I PLAY IN IT

The information in this chapter comes primarily from interviews with Jason Licht, Harold Goodwin, and other firsthand sources. Also:

"The Friendship Test: Tommy and Gronky," Buccaneers.com, September 10, 2020, https://www.buccaneers.com/video/tom-brady-rob-gronkowski -tampa-bay-friendship-test-tommy-gronky.

Deyscha Smith, "Bill Belichick Paid Tribute to His Mother, Jeannette, Who Passed Away Monday," *Boston Globe*, September 17, 2020.

Tom Brady Sr. and Galynn Brady, interview with Andrea Kremer, *NFL GameDay*, aired February 7, 2021, NFL Network.

"Tom Brady's Parents Both Battled COVID-19 Last Year; Tampa Bay Buccaneers QB Was 'Stressed Out,'" ESPN.com, January 25, 2021.

Greg Bishop and Jenny Vrentas, "Magnificent Seventh: How Tom Brady's Bucs Became Super Bowl Champions," *Sports Illustrated*, February 8, 2021.

Michael Lombardi, "Neither Tom Brady Nor Bruce Arians Is Wrong, but They're Wrong for Each Other," *Athletic*, December 1, 2020.

Peter King, "Ten for Tom: Brady Heading Back to Another Super Bowl, Bringing Buccaneers to Meet Chiefs in Tampa," *Football Morning in America*, NBCSports.com, January 25, 2021.

Karen Guregian, "Tom Brady Sr. on Son's Split with Patriots: 'Guys Move,'" *Boston Herald*, January 26, 2021.

Charlie Weis, SiriusXM NFL Radio, October 31, 2020.

Ordway, Merloni & Fauria, WEEI radio, November 2, 2020.

Jenny Vrentas and Greg Bishop, "Jack Easterby's Rise to Power and the Chaos that Followed," *Sports Illustrated*, December 10, 2020.

Jenny Vrentas and Greg Bishop, "How Jack Easterby Held On, and Why Deshaun Watson Might Slip Away from the Texans," *Sports Illustrated*, January 16, 2021.

Dan Shaughnessy, "Final Score: Tom Brady 1, Patriots 0," *Boston Globe*, January 24, 2021.

"Inside the Patriots Draft Room: Round 1," Patriots.com, April 30, 2021, https://www.patriots.com/video/inside-the-patriots-draft-room-round-1.

Michael Irvin, host, *Michael Irvin Podcast* (podcast), February 12, 2021.

Tom Brady interview, *The Late, Late Show with James Corden*, aired March 2, 2021, CBS.

Seth Wickersham, "The Story Behind the Split of Tom Brady, Bill Belichick and the Patriots," ESPN.com, March 22, 2020.

Seth Wickersham, "Brothers in Arms," ESPN The Magazine, November 26, 2001.

INDEX